1 MONTH OF
FREE
READING

at

www.ForgottenBooks.com

By purchasing this book you are eligible for one month membership to ForgottenBooks.com, giving you unlimited access to our entire collection of over 700,000 titles via our web site and mobile apps.

To claim your free month visit:

www.forgottenbooks.com/free122709

ISBN 978-0-483-70451-0
PIBN 10122709

HEARINGS

BEFORE THE

SUBCOMMITTEE ON
CIVIL AND CONSTITUTIONAL RIGHTS

OF THE

COMMITTEE ON THE JUDICIARY
HOUSE OF REPRESENTATIVES

ONE HUNDRED THIRD CONGRESS

FIRST AND SECOND SESSIONS

OCTOBER 14, 1993, MAY 11 AND 25, 1994

Serial No. 74

inted for the use of the Committee on the Judiciary

U.S. GOVERNMENT PRINTING OFFICE

WASHINGTON : 1994

For sale by the U.S. Government Printing Office
tendent of Documents, Congressional Sales Office, Washington, DC 20402
ISBN 0-16-046396-3

HEARINGS

BEFORE THE

SUBCOMMITTEE ON
CIVIL AND CONSTITUTIONAL RIGHTS

OF THE

COMMITTEE ON THE JUDICIARY
HOUSE OF REPRESENTATIVES

ONE HUNDRED THIRD CONGRESS

FIRST AND SECOND SESSIONS

OCTOBER 14, 1993, MAY 11 AND 25, 1994

Serial No. 74

inted for the use of the Committee on the Judiciary

U.S. GOVERNMENT PRINTING OFFICE

WASHINGTON : 1994

For sale by the U.S. Government Printing Office
tendent of Documents, Congressional Sales Office, Washington, DC 20402
ISBN 0-16-046396-3

COMMITTEE ON THE JUDICIARY

JACK BROOKS, Texas, *Chairman*

DON EDWARDS, California
JOHN CONYERS, JR., Michigan
ROMANO L. MAZZOLI, Kentucky
WILLIAM J. HUGHES, New Jersey
MIKE SYNAR, Oklahoma
PATRICIA SCHROEDER, Colorado
DAN GLICKMAN, Kansas
BARNEY FRANK, Mas~ ' ··
CHARLES E. SCHU
HOWARD L. BER/
RICK BOUCHER,
JOHN BRYANT, :
GEORGE E. SAN(
CRAIG A. WASHI
JACK REED, Rho
JERROLD NADLE
ROBERT C. SCOT
DAVID MANN, O!
MELVIN L. WATT
XAVIER BECERR

HAMILTON FISH, JR., New York
CARLOS J. MOORHEAD, California
HENRY J. HYDE, Illinois
F. JAMES SENSENBRENNER, JR.,
 Wisconsin
BILL McCOLLUM, Florida
GEORGE W. GEKAS, Pennsylvania
HOWARD COBLE, North Carolina

S1

PATRICIA SCHR(
BARNEY FRANK,
CRAIG A. WASHI
JERROLD NADLE

CONTENTS

HEARINGS DATES

OPENING STATEMENT

WITNESSES

Page

LETTERS, STATEMENTS, ETC., SUBMITTED FOR THE HEARINGS

APPENDIX

VOTING RIGHTS

THURSDAY, OCTOBER 14, 1993

House of Representatives,
Subcommittee on Civil and Constitutional Rights,
Committee on the Judiciary,
Washington, DC.

The subcommittee met, pursuant to notice, at 10:09 a.m., in room 2226, Rayburn House Office Building, Hon. Don Edwards (chairman of the subcommittee) presiding.

Present: Representatives Don Edwards, Jerrold Nadler, Henry J. Hyde, Howard Coble, and Charles T. Canady.

Also present: Representative Melvin L. Watt.

Staff present: Catherine LeRoy, counsel; Melody Barnes, assistant counsel; and Kathryn Hazeem, minority counsel.

OPENING STATEMENT OF CHAIRMAN EDWARDS

Mr. EDWARDS. The subcommittee will come to order.

I believe I am one of the few Members left who was here when we passed the greatest civil rights law in our history. I think the Voting Rights Act of 1965 compares favorably with the omnibus bill of 1964. And it completely turned around our country in terms of voting rights for African-Americans. It has been remarkably successful and there has been no dissension throughout the land on how very successful it was.

In 1982, was it Mr. Hyde, that we amended it and made it stronger. Mr. Hyde and I traveled throughout the country and held hearings in all different parts of the country, and we found serious deficiencies at that time in the Voting Rights Act as it was being administered, and we came back and passed amendments in 1982 that brought the Voting Rights Act back to full strength. And it has been something in American history that has made us very proud throughout the world.

The problem this morning is that—and we are going to start a series of hearings—in June of this year there was what some of us consider a rather bizarre decision by the U.S. Supreme Court. Certainly it was an unfriendly decision to voting rights. And the name of the case was *Shaw* v. *Reno*. And it has become the topic of great discussion in the country, and we have to look at it and see the implications and what is down the way.

Beginning today, this subcommittee is going to conduct a series of hearings to discuss the Voting Rights Act and the issues that have been brought up by the Supreme Court in the *Shaw* case.

These hearings are going to give us the opportunity to talk with activists, attorneys, scholars, and others. And we are honored to have several distinguished witnesses here this morning. And we hope that the testimony will give us greater insight into this very important issue.

Mr. Hyde.

Mr. HYDE. Thank you, Mr. Chairman.

In this hearing, we will briefly explore the issue of race and the distribution of electoral power.

From the Declaration of Independence to the fourteenth amendment to the 1964 Civil Rights Act, our founding documents and our laws have consistently recognized the principle of individual equality. For years, this Nation has taken steps towards racial equality based upon the fundamental premise that the law should treat all individuals equally, that men and women should be judged by the content of their character, in the words of Martin Luther King, Jr., rather than the color of their skin. Equal protection of the law.

We recognize that ours is not yet a color-blind society. Some of our witnesses today, however, seem to question whether a color blind society is achievable or even desirable. I only know that Americans of all races reject the idea of racial preferences, and most Americans are, at best, uncomfortable about drawing gerrymandered political districts based on the race of the inhabitants. Such districts create the implicit assumption that perhaps we are not equal after all, if people of one race can only be represented by someone of the same race.

And one might say of the same gender. The Voting Rights Act started out as an effort, an incredibly successful effort, to tear down artificial barriers to voter participation of southern blacks. It has since been transformed into an effort to maximize the strength of minority votes. And there are some, such as law professor Lani Guinier, who argue that the Voting Rights Act requires more than proportionate representation.

Properly interpreted, she argues that the Voting Rights Act requires that minorities obtain a proportionate share of legislative successes. I believe that view was repudiated and shown to be out of the mainstream when President Clinton withdrew her nomination to head the Civil Rights Division of the Department of Justice.

Access to the ballot, without respect to race, is not a complex public policy question. Gerrymandering to maximize minority office holding is. We need to be careful that the cure doesn't turn out to be more fatal to the patient than the disease.

I want to thank the chairman for holding a hearing on this very important issue, and I look forward to the testimony of the witnesses.

[The opening statement of Mr. Hyde follows:]

OPENING STATEMENT

OF

CONGRESSMAN HENRY J. HYDE

Thank you, Mr. Chairman.

In this hearing we will briefly explore the issue of race and the distribution of electoral power.

From the Declaration of Independence to the Fourteenth Amendment to the 1964 Civil Rights Act, our founding documents and our laws have consistently recognized the principle of individual equality. For years this nation has taken steps toward racial equality based on the fundamental premise that the law should treat all individuals equally -- that men and women should be judged by the "content of their character" rather than the color of their skin.

We recognize that ours is not yet a color-blind society. Some of our witnesses today, however, seem to question whether a color-blind society is achievable or even desirable. I only know that Americans of all races, reject the idea of racial preferences and most Americans are, at best, uncomfortable about drawing gerrymandered political districts based on the race of the inhabitants. Such districts create the implicit assumption that perhaps we are not equal after all, if people of one race can only be represented by someone of the same race.

The Voting Rights Act started out as an effort -- a incredibly successful effort -- to tear down artificial barriers to voter participation of Southern blacks. It has since been transformed into an effort to "maximize" the strength of minority votes. And there are some, such as law professor Lani Guinier, who argue that the Voting Rights Act requires more than proportionate representation. Properly interpreted, she argues, the Voting Rights Act requires that minorities obtain a proportionate share of legislative successes. I believe that view was repudiated and shown to be out of the mainstream when President Clinton withdrew the nominiation of Ms. Guinier to head the Civil Rights Division of the Department of Justice.

Access to the ballot without respect to race is not a complex public policy question: gerrymandering to maximize minority officeholding is. We need to be careful that the cure does not turn out to be more fatal to the patient than the disease -- that packing minorities into racially gerrymandered districts does not make government <u>less</u> responsive to their needs.

I want to thank the Chairman for holding a hearing on this very important issue and look forward to hearing the testimony of the witnesses.

Mr. EDWARDS. Thank you very much, Mr. Hyde. In a future hearing, in the near future, we intend to have Professor Guinier here to explain her point of view, which is very interesting and challenging.

Mr. Coble.

Mr. COBLE. No opening statement.

Mr. EDWARDS. Mr. Canady.

Mr. CANADY. No opening statement.

Mr. EDWARDS. I believe all of the members of the panel should come up and sit down at the witness table. We welcome all of you. I am going to ask Mr. Hyde to introduce our first witness, Professor Norrell.

Mr. HYDE. Thank you, Mr. Chairman.

Our first witness, Robert J. Norrell, is the director for the Center of Southern History and Culture and an associate professor of history at the University of Alabama in Tuscaloosa.

His work focuses on the history of the South and of American race relations. Mr. Norrell's first book, which discussed the civil rights movement in Tuskegee, won the 1986 Robert F. Kennedy Book Award. His lectures on democracy and race in 20th century America are the basis of a forthcoming book from Oxford University Press.

Our second witness——

Mr. EDWARDS. Why don't we introduce them as they speak.

You are all asked to keep your statements relatively short because we are always short of time around here. But without objection, all of your statements, both your statements, will be made a part of the permanent record.

And, Professor Norrell, you may proceed.

STATEMENT OF ROBERT J. NORRELL, DIRECTOR, CENTER FOR SOUTHERN HISTORY AND CULTURE, AND ASSOCIATE PROFESSOR OF HISTORY, UNIVERSITY OF ALABAMA, TUSCALOOSA, AL

Mr. NORRELL. Thank you, Mr. Chairman. I would like to focus my remarks on the significance of electoral forms and governing processes to politics in this country.

Mr. EDWARDS. I believe the mike should be a little closer to you. Thank you. Bring it right up close.

Mr. NORRELL. Thank you.

My written testimony goes on into some explanation how, after generations of having the vote denied to African-Americans, the Voting Rights Act of 1965 finally opened access to the ballot and led to the enfranchisement of blacks and other minorities near the level of other Americans. And the recently enacted National Voter Registration Act should enhance, further, the goal of opening access to the franchise among Americans.

The full enjoyment of democratic rights, however, have always depended on more than access to the ballot. Like men through the ages have contemplated the nature of government power, the southerners, Thomas Jefferson, James Madison, and James C. Calhoun, understood that electoral forms and governing processes affected the influence of the ballot, the forms, and processes often making the vote much more or much less potent in achieving desired ends.

The separation of power and responsibility of the U.S. Congress is perhaps Mr. Madison's and other Founders' clearest acknowledgment of the importance of governmental forms and processes of the creation of just and lasting democracy.

Mr. Calhoun's penetrating arguments for the minority rights of southerners, many made within this great institution, also testified to the importance of the forms and processes of government for ensuring the consent of the governed.

As inheritors of the political wisdom of Jefferson, Madison, and Calhoun, white southerners in the post-Civil War South knew well the relationship between the right to vote and the exercise of real political power. But in the aftermath of war and in the midst of several million freed African-Americans, these white southerners created antidemocratic electoral forms and processes to cancel out the Democratic rights of the freed people.

Allow me to offer a few examples of antidemocratic devices from my own State, Alabama, to suggest the pattern that held throughout the South.

In Mobile, municipal elections were changed from single member districts to at-large arrangements after white-supremacist Democrats regained power from black-supported Republicans.

In Montgomery, the city changed its size to remove black voters from the city in order to remove black voters from this municipal decisionmaking processes.

Judges, commissioners, and voter registrars in some counties were changed from elective positions to appointed positions by the governor in order to remove those offices from the control of black majority electorates. Some counties set bonds for office holders higher than African-Americans could provide, and thus they were not allowed to occupy offices to which they had been duly elected.

Congressional districts were gerrymandered to consecrate black voters in a single district in order to minimize black representation in Congress. And during the mid and late 1870's and after the direct primary was instituted in Alabama expressly to regain white political supremacy, the direct primary helped democratic candidates earn legitimacy as the choice of the majority of whites. None of these forms were inherently racist. Often they were meant to subvert the will of a black majority. But at others they meant to enhance the authority of a white majority. But in every case, they were put to a white supremacist purpose.

In the 1940's in Alabama and throughout the South, whites took renewed interest in applying antidemocratic forms and procedures. African-Americans having been largely disfranchised in the South, it became apparent in the 1940's that African-Americans were mounting a challenge to disfranchisement. Inspired by the intense national discussion of democratic values as the United States challenged fascism and racism in Asia and Europe in World War II, southern blacks began to protest against the denial of their right to vote by filing suits against disfranchisement. In 1944 blacks in Texas succeeded in getting the U.S. Supreme Court in the case of *Smith* v. *Allwright* to declare the white primary as method of disfranchisement.

In response to this challenge, rising challenge of African-Americans in the 1940's and 1950's, southern whites began to adjust their electoral forms in order to minimize black voters influence. The main thrust of this was to create electoral forms that gave maximum influence to majorities.

The clear and correct assumption on the part of white southerners in the 1940's and 1950's was that white majorities would be able to ensure white control over elective office. Whites in black belt areas in the 1940's and 1950's were genuinely fearful of living under black rule.

As you noted, I wrote a book about one such place, Tuskegee, AL, which sits in a county which has historically been more than 80 percent black. And in 1957 the city officials attempted a drastic change to protect themselves from a black majority. They gerrymandered the town's boundaries to remove all but 12 of its 400 black voters.

In the case of *Gomillion* v. *Lightfoot* in 1960, black citizens of Tuskegee argued that the gerrymander had the effect of disfranchising them. Mr. Justice Frankfurter wrote that the inescapable human affect of this essay in geometry and geography was to deny colored citizens and only colored citizens from their voting rights, allowing the gerrymander to stand, Frankfurter wrote, "would sanction the achievement by a State of any impairment of voting rights whatsoever so long as it was cloaked in the garb of realignment of political subdivisions."

With the *Gomillion* decision, the Federal judiciary entered what Justice Frankfurter had earlier called the political thicket of electoral forms and processes in order to guarantee the democratic rights of black Americans.

The passage of the Voting Rights Act of 1965 signaled, again, to some southern whites that it was time to rearrange electoral forms and process in order to minimize or dilute the impact of millions of new black votes. And what sometimes appeared to be a rerun of post-reconstruction Southern history, State legislatures in the South instituted electoral devices that enhanced the influence of white majorities: at-large elections, numbered-post provisions, and multimember districts. Once again, offices were changed from elected to appointed positions.

But history didn't repeat itself. Using the powers of the Voting Rights Act to ensure that black votes were meaningful, black voters appealed these decisions to the Federal judiciary, and the courts have acted generally to assure that the black votes have the same impact that the white's did.

The U.S. Justice Department used its authority to assess the impact of electoral changes prior to their implementation in Southern States, a power that has not only overturned some actions, but it has also forestalled the creation of forms and procedures that dilute black political strength.

In recent months, the stream of progress that began to flow in 1965 toward a just democracy for African-Americans and other minorities seems to have been diverted. In the case of *Presley* v. *Etowah County Commission,* the U.S. Supreme Court allowed a change in the governing processes of a county commission in Alabama that effectively stripped a black commissioner of his main authority. The Court chose to make a distinction between voting and governance which the court ruled was beyond the reach of the Voting Rights Act unless intentional discrimination was proved.

The history of my State and region teaches clearly that electoral forms and governing processes must be held strictly accountable to standards of racial equality as we hold voting registration if we intend to create a just democracy. The *Presley* decision makes it harder to achieve that end.

So too, I think to some of the positions taken during the national discussion of voting rights that accompanied the nomination of Professor Guinier to head the Justice Department's Civil Rights Division. Professor Guinier's advocacy of electoral forms that promoted minority representation and empowerment, limited voting and cumulative voting, super majorities, were portrayed as radical and even un-American. The treatment of Guinier's views was ahistorical. The highest political value in this republic, as conceived by James Madison and the Founders and explained most clearly in the Federalist Papers, was not ruled by the majority but consent of the governed.

To be sure, consent often was given by a majority vote; but the Founders also sought to earn the consent of minorities by creating a form of minority government that assigned some power to a minority interest. The opponents of Guinier exalted majority rule at the expense of the more fundamental principle of the consent of the governed.

In the recent decision of *Shaw* v. *Reno* the court objected to congressional redistricting plan in North Carolina on the basis of its apparently exclusively racial person. The court naturally looked to the decision in *Gomillion* v. *Lightfoot* for compelling precedent against political gerrymanders based on race.

The context of the *Gomillion* decision was different from *Shaw* v. *Reno*. First, the Tuskegee gerrymander disfranchised blacks; no whites are disfranchised by the North Carolina gerrymander.

Second, the Tuskegee gerrymander was conceived in secret by whites and executed without any black consent. North Carolinians, white and black, generally know the purpose of the new districting arrangement and have consented through their legislative deliberations.

Third, the Tuskegee gerrymander was created in a climate of bitter white supremacist feeling. The North Carolina plan emerged from the context of the need for black empowerment and a just American democracy.

The court warns that North Carolina's redistricting plan threatened to divert Americans from the goal of a color blind democracy. The history of this Nation suggests to me that the idea of a color blind democracy, however noble, is at present an unattainable ideal. Democracy cannot be color blind because the people are not color blind. We remain a society in which blacks and whites are deeply alienated. The very high levels of racially polarized voting in Southern States today testify to the continued race consciousness of the people of my region. The centuries of white supremacy still weigh too heavy on us to expect our people, black or white, to be blind to color.

Let's embrace ideals that are more realistic. The recent history of the South shows that what can be attained is the empowerment of African-Americans and other minorities. Minority office holding vests people who were disfranchised for generations with the sense that American democracy has a place for them. It elicits from African-Americans a consent to being governed that otherwise has not been achieved.

Indeed, minority office holding has gained legitimacy among whites who a generation ago may have feared it. The history of the South reveals that blacks and most whites understand the need to have racial representatives in politics because we in the South understand the legitimacy of a racial point of view. Because Americans from other regions are more likely to reject racial thinking ideologically, they are also more likely to denounce the need to have representatives who identified by race. Southerners, both black and white, are steeped in generations of racial alienation and are more likely to understand the efficacy of black people representing black people.

In conclusion, let me say that the *Shaw* and the *Presley* decisions threaten to reverse the course of progress toward empowerment of historically disfranchised Americans that began with the Voting Rights Act of 1965 and continued through a quarter century of implementation of that act and its renewals.

I believe that this divergence of late is based in part on the misunderstanding of the history of disfranchisement in the United States and on a misreading of what are the most fundamental political values of our Nation.

I encourage the Congress to think through our history as a people who have believed in political freedom but denied it to many among us and to take the next steps necessary for ensuring a just democracy for all Americans.

Mr. Chairman, if I might, I would like to add just at the end that we are honored today to have the plaintiff in *Gomillion* v. *Lightfoot*, Dr. Charles Gomillion, who lives in Washington, now in his 94th year.

Dr. Gomillion, would you stand?

Mr. EDWARDS. We welcome him, too. Thank you for coming.

[The prepared statement of Mr. Norrell follows:]

TESTIMONY

before the House Judiciary Committee's
Subcommittee on Civil and Constitutional Rights

Robert J. Norrell

Director, Center for Southern History and Culture and
Associate Professor of History, University of Alabama

October 14, 1993

My name is Robert J. Norrell, and I am a historian at the University of Alabama in Tuscaloosa. I am a native of Alabama, and except for my time in college and graduate school in Virginia and two years visiting in England, I have always lived in Alabama. I have devoted most of my professional life--about 15 years--to studying the history of the South and of black-white relations in the United States.

I have been asked to testify about the history of voting rights problems in our country, with special emphasis on the nature of those problems in recent decades. Allow me to talk first about access to the ballot and then about electoral forms and governing processes.

The Right to Vote, Lost and Retrieved

In the years just after the Civil War, the Fourteenth and Fifteenth Amendments opened the ballot box to recently- freed African-Americans. For a few years blacks in the South, under the protection of the United States government, enjoyed the rights and privileges of democracy in approximately the same ways that whites did.

But after the U.S. government withdrew its protection from blacks in the South in the 1870s, whites moved to limit and finally to abolish the democratic rights of African-Americans. Starting in the 1870s and continuing through the first decade of this century, southern whites deployed a variety of tactics--violence, ballot-box fraud, poll taxes, "good character" requirements, literacy tests, and the white primary--to disfranchise blacks. The vast majority of southern blacks were denied the right to vote during the two-thirds of this century.

The Voting Rights Act of 1965 finally opened access to the ballot and led to the enfranchisement of blacks and other minorities near the level of other Americans. The recently-enacted National Voter Registration Act should advance even further the goal of open access to the franchise among Americans.

The Significance of Electoral Forms and Processes

Full enjoyment of democratic rights have, however, always depended on more than access to the ballot. Like men through the ages who had contemplated the nature of government power, the southerners Thomas Jefferson, James Madison, and John C. Calhoun understood that electoral forms and governing processes affected the influence of the ballot--the forms and processes often making the vote much more or much less potent in achieving desired ends. The separation of power and responsibility in the United States Congress is perhaps Mr. Madison's and the other Founders' clearest acknowledgment of the importance of governmental forms and processes to the creation of a just and lasting democracy. Mr. Calhoun's penetrating arguments for the minority rights of southerners--many made within this great institution--also testified to the importance of the forms and processes of government for ensuring the consent of the governed.

As inheritors of the political wisdom of Jefferson, Madison, and Calhoun, white southerners in the post-Civil War South knew well the complex relationship between the right to vote and the exercise of real political power. But in the aftermath of war and in the midst of several million freed African-Americans, these white southerners created anti-democratic electoral forms and processes to cancel out the democratic rights of the freed people.

Allow me to offer examples of these anti-democratic devices from my home state to suggest the pattern that held generally throughout the South. In Alabama in the 1870s and 1880s, municipal elections in Mobile were changed from single-member districts to an at-large arrangement after white-supremacist Democrats regained power from black-supported Republicans. In Montgomery, whites shrank the city's size in order to remove black voters from municipal decision-making.

Judges, commissioners, and voter registrars in some counties were changed from elective offices to positions appointed by the governor in order to remove those offices from control of black-majority electorates. Some counties set bonds for officeholders higher than blacks could provide, and thus African-Americans were not allowed to occupy offices to which they had been duly elected. In Alabama and several southern states, congressional districts were gerrymandered to concentrate black votes in a single district in order to minimize black representation in Congress.

During the mid- and late 1870s, the direct primary was instituted expressly to regain white political supremacy, because the direct primary helped Democratic candidates earn legitimacy as the choice of a majority of whites. The origins of primary elections in Alabama thus lay partly in white supremacist intent.

The history of Alabama and the South in the immediate post-Civil War decades suggests that democratic forms of election and processes of government--including the direct primary, the bonding of officeholders, and the setting of district lines--were used extensively and creatively to undermine the democratic rights of blacks. None of these forms or procedures was inherently racist. Often the forms and procedures were meant to subvert the will of a black majority; at other times they were intended to enhance the authority of a white majority. But in every case, they were put to a white supremacist purpose.

In the 1940s in Alabama and throughout the South, whites took renewed interest in applying anti-democratic forms and procedures when it became apparent that African-Americans were mounting a real challenge to disfranchisement. Inspired by the intense national discussion of democratic values as the United States challenged fascism and racism in Europe and Asia during World War II, southern blacks began to protest against the denial of their right to vote by "standing-in" at boards of registrars and suing in court. In 1944 blacks in Texas succeeded in getting the United States Supreme Court in *Smith v. Allwright* finally to declare the white primary in violation of the Fourteenth and Fifteenth Amendments. Subsequent efforts to create new barriers to voter registration in the South were knocked out by federal courts.

Southern whites, recognizing that disfranchisement could not withstand the black challenges if African-Americans were supported by a federal judiciary upholding the Fifteenth Amendment, moved to adjust electoral forms in order to minimize black voters' influence. The main thrust of these efforts was to fashion electoral arrangements that gave maximum influence to majorities. The clear and correct assumption was that white majorities would be able to ensure white control over elective offices.

Starting at about the time of the Texas white primary decision, many county commissions in Alabama were changed from single-member-district to at-large arrangements. In 1951 single-shot voting (voting fewer times than there were places open in multi-member districts) was outlawed in Alabama municipal elections in order to enhance the authority of the majority. The same purpose was achieved in all state-wide elections in Alabama in 1961 with a numbered-post requirement. The Alabama pattern of enhancing majority-vote requirements was part of a region-wide effort to shore up white political supremacy in the 1940s, 1950s, and early 1960s.

Whites in Black Belt areas were genuinely fearful of living under black rule. I wrote a book about one such place, Tuskegee, Alabama, which sits in a county that historically has been more than 80 percent black. In 1957 the white officials of that town attempted a drastic change in electoral form to protect themselves from a possible black majority. They gerrymandered the town's boundaries to remove all but 12 of its 400 black voters.

In the case *Gomillion v. Lightfoot* (1960), black citizens of Tuskegee argued that the gerrymander had the effect of disfranchising them. Speaking for a unanimous court overturning the Tuskegee gerrymander, Mr. Justice Frankfurter wrote that the "inescapable human effect of this essay in geometry and geography" was to deny "colored citizens, and colored citizens only" their voting rights. Allowing the gerrymander to stand, Frankfurter wrote, "would sanction the achievement by a State of any impairment of voting rights whatever so as it was cloaked in the garb of the realignment of political subdivisions." With the *Gomillion* decision, the federal judiciary entered what Justice Frankfurter had earlier called "the political thicket" of electoral forms and processes in order to guarantee the democratic rights of black Americans.

Democracy after the Voting Rights Act

The passage of the Voting Rights Act of 1965 led many Americans black and white to believe that African-Americans' political rights were now secure. That was an understandable but naive faith. The Voting Rights Act signalled to some southern whites that it was time to rearrange electoral forms and processes in order to minimize, or dilute, the impact of millions of new black votes. In what sometimes appeared to be a re-run of post-Reconstruction southern history, state legislatures in the South instituted electoral devices that enhanced the influence of white majorities--at-large elections, numbered-post provisions, and multi-member districts. Once again, offices were changed from elected to appointed positions.

History did not, however, repeat itself. Using the powers of the Voting Rights Act to ensure that black votes were in fact meaningful, black plaintiffs appealed these forms and procedures to the federal judiciary, and the courts generally have acted to ensure that blacks' votes had about the same impact as whites'. The United States Justice Department used its authority to assess the impact of electoral changes prior to their implementation in southern states, a power that has not only overturned some actions but has also forestalled the creation of forms and procedures that dilute black political strength.

In recent months, however, the stream of progress that began to flow in 1965 toward a just democracy for African-Americans and other minorities seems to have been diverted. In the case of *Presley v. Etowah County Commission* (1992), the U.S. Supreme Court allowed a change in the governing processes of a county commission in Alabama that effectively stripped a black commissioner of his main authority. The Court chose to make a distinction between voting and governance, which the Court ruled was beyond the reach of the Voting Rights Act unless intentional racial discrimination was proved.

The history of my state and region teaches clearly that electoral forms and governing processes must be held as strictly accountable to standards of racial equality as we hold voter registration if we intend to create a just democracy. The *Presley* decision makes it harder to achieve that end.

So too do some of the positions taken during the national discussion of voting rights that accompanied the nomination of Professor Lani Guinier to head the

Justice Department's Civil Rights Division. Professor Guinier's advocacy of electoral forms that promoted minority representation and empowerment--limited voting, cumulative voting, and super-majorities--were portrayed as radical and even un-American. The treatment of Guinier's views was ahistorical: The highest political value in this republic, as conceived by James Madison and the Founders and explained most clearly in the *Federalist Papers*, was not rule by the majority but consent of the governed. To be sure, consent often was given by a majority vote, but the Founders also sought to earn the consent of minorities by creating a form of republican government that assigned some power to minority interests. The opponents of Guinier exalted majority rule at the expense of the more fundamental principle of the consent of the governed.

In the recent decision *Shaw v. Reno*, the Court objected to a congressional redistricting plan in North Carolina on the basis of its apparent exclusively racial purpose. The Court naturally looked to the decision in *Gomillion v. Lightfoot* for a compelling precedent against political gerrymanders based on race.

The context of *Gomillion* was very different from that of *Shaw v. Reno*. First, the Tuskegee gerrymander disfranchised blacks; no whites are disfranchised by the North Carolina gerrymander. Second, the Tuskegee gerrymander was conceived in secret by whites and executed without any black consent; North Carolinians, white and black, generally know the purpose of the new districting arrangement and have consented to it through their legislative deliberations. Third, the Tuskegee gerrymander was created in a climate of bitter, white supremacist feeling; the North Carolina district plan emerged from a context of the need for black empowerment in a just American democracy.

The Court warned that North Carolina's redistricting plan threatened to divert Americans from the goal of a color-blind democracy. The history of this nation suggests to me that the ideal of a color-blind democracy, however noble, is at present an unattainable ideal. Democracy cannot now be color-blind because the people are not color-blind. Despite profound changes in the last few decades, we remain a society in which blacks and whites are deeply alienated. The very high levels of racially-polarized voting in southern states today testify to the continuing race consciousness of the people of my region. The centuries of white supremacy still weigh too heavy on us to expect our people, black or white, to be blind to color.

Let us strive for ideals that are more realistic. The recent history of the South clearly shows that what can be attained is the empowerment of African-Americans and other minorities. Minority office-holding vests people who were disfranchised for generations with a sense that American democracy has a place for them. It elicits from African-Americans a consent to being governed that otherwise has not been achieved.

Indeed, minority office-holding has gained legitimacy among whites who a generation ago may have feared it. The recent history of the South reveals that blacks and most whites understand the need to have racial representatives in politics because we assume the legitimacy of a racial point of view. Because Americans from other regions are more likely to reject racial thinking ideologically, they are also more likely to denounce the need to have racial representatives. Southerners, both black and white, are steeped in generations of racial alienation and thus are more likely to understand the desire for, and efficacy of, black people representing black people.

Conclusion

The *Shaw* and *Presley* decisions, as well as the negative response to Professor Guinier's views on electoral forms, threaten to reverse the course of progress toward empowerment of historically-disfranchised Americans that began with the passage of the Voting Rights Act of 1965 and continued through a quarter-century of implementation of that act and its renewals. I believe that this divergence is based in part on misunderstanding of the history of disfranchisement in the United States and on a misreading of what are the most fundamental political values of our nation. I encourage the Congress to think through our history as a people who have believed in political freedom but denied it to many among us and to take the next steps necessary for ensuring a just democracy for all Americans.

Mr. HYDE. Our second witness, Christopher James Geis, received his undergraduate degree in history from Western Carolina University in 1988.

As the director of media and research for the North Carolina Democratic Party, he was the party spokesman, press secretary, and research coordinator. While in that position, he worked on President Clinton's campaign as well as that of U.S. Senator Terry Sanford and Gov. Jim Hunt. Mr. Geis also has extensive experience as a reporter. At the Winston-Salem Journal, he covered local and State governments. He is a freelance journalist and copy editor on the news desk of the journal.

STATEMENT OF CHRISTOPHER GEIS, COPY EDITOR, WINSTON-SALEM JOURNAL, AND FORMER DIRECTOR OF MEDIA RESEARCH, NORTH CAROLINA DEMOCRATIC PARTY

Mr. GEIS. Thank you, Mr. Hyde. Thank you, Mr. Chairman.

Mr. Chairman and members of the subcommittee, let me thank you for the opportunity to speak before you today.

I come before you today not as a political or legal scholar, but as an observer of politics in North Carolina for the last several years first as a reporter for the Winston-Salem Journal, one of the largest daily newspapers in North Carolina; then as press secretary for the North Carolina Democratic Party; and finally as a copy editor on the news desk of the journal, where I am currently employed.

As a reporter, I covered a number of political races, including the 1990 U.S. Senate race between Senator Jesse Helms and challenger Harvey Gantt. Mr. Gantt was the first black person to be nominated for major statewide office in North Carolina since Reconstruction. Later, as the Democratic Party's press secretary, I worked on a number of political campaigns, including that of Ralph Campbell, whose election last year as State auditor marked the first time that a black person has been elected to a major statewide office.

I have long been fascinated by politics in our State and across the South because of the racial dynamics that have surrounded those politics.

I should say up front, that I come to the whole issue of race with a strong bias. I am deeply concerned about improving relations among the races, and about seeing that black people and other minorities share equally in the American dream.

It is my belief that the Voting Rights Act of 1965 is one of the most important and moral pieces of legislation in our Nation's history, and it was a courageous Congress and President who made it law. It has had some positive effects on North Carolina. In the last 11 years, the number of blacks elected at the local and State levels has risen dramatically. As an example, the number of blacks now in the legislature has risen from four to 25 so that blacks now make up 15 percent of the legislature.

Having more black legislators has been a good thing for North Carolina, I believe, because the legislature of today which also includes more women and more Republicans presents a truer mirror of North Carolina than the legislatures of the past.

But despite what I say to you, I come to you today to warn that we are entering an important and delicate period in our State's political history and that the Voting Rights Act, as interpreted by a growing number of people, could now become an enemy of the progress we have made in race relations in North Carolina and elsewhere.

I am not proposing that we go back and undo the changes of the last 10 years that have resulted from the voting Rights Act as amended in 1982.

I also believe that the Congressman elected to represent the 12th District, Melvin Watt, is an excellent representative of both the black and white voters of the district. I believe Mr. Watt is of such stature that he could win in districts that are not majority black.

And, in defense of the North Carolina Legislature, which did not want to draw a second black district, if the law requires a second black district in North Carolina, the I–85 district makes the most possible sense because it is the State's only predominantly urban district. The State's minority population is too scattered otherwise to draw a compact second district.

But I believe that we are now at a point where to carve up minority districts and segregate voters by race even more will only do harm to the progress that we have already made. That is why I was concerned when President Clinton nominated Lani Guinier earlier this year to head the Justice Department's civil rights section. Ms. Guinier's views were deeply troubling to me.

Ms. Guinier said in a series of law review articles that whites are a "hostile, permanent majority"; that "mainstream democrats do not accept black democrats"; that whites elected with black votes still ignore black voters; and that some black leaders are not "authentic" but rather are "tokens."

I disagree with her pessimistic and cynical views and with those of other like-minded people, and I believe that the evidence shows that the conclusions, at least as they apply to North Carolina, are false.

Many good people of both races and both parties share this opinion. They are concerned that, if the Voting Rights Act is construed to require even more majority-minority districts, we will, in essence, have two political worlds: a white world where white office holders, elected by all white electorates, go about their business, ignoring their black colleagues; and a black world, where black office holders, elected from all black districts, are nevertheless still in a minority in a legislature and so can safely be ignored because their constituents have no power to influence white majority politicians. This is something that I do not want to see happen.

In North Carolina, many citizens prodded by their own consciences and not by any quota crazy Federal Government have worked very hard over the years to build a biracial political cooperation that I believe is the envy of many other states. This has been particularly true in the Democratic Party. Let me cite some examples:

In 1990, Harvey Gantt, a black man, was nominated for the U.S. Senate seat held by Senator Jesse Helms. Mr. Gantt, after having finished first over three major white opponents in the first primary election, won, with ease, a runoff primary over a white opponent who was strong enough in his own right to be elected attorney general of North Carolina last year in a landslide. Mr. Gantt then earned 47.4 percent of the vote of the people of North Carolina in the general election against Mr. Helms, who, having been elected four times, is arguably one of the most successful politicians in the State's history. Mr. Gantt's showing was better than two other white opponents who had run against Senator Helms in previous years and virtually equalled that of Mr. Helm's strongest challenger ever. Mr. Gantt is considered a strong candidate for a future Senate race.

Also in 1990, Daniel Blue, a black State representative from Raleigh, was elected the speaker of the North Carolina House of Representatives by a biracial, Democratic coalition of legislators, most of them white. He became the first black to hold that position in North Carolina and one of only two black speakers in the entire country.

Last year, Mr. Blue was unanimously reelected by the Democratic majority in the legislature, which includes twice as many white legislators as it does black legislators. He is considered a strong candidate for statewide office. He became speaker by doing his job well and by earning the trust and respect of his white and black colleagues.

It is worth noting also that last year the white majority democratic coalition in the House of Representatives named a black Representative, Milton "Toby" Fitch, to the party's No. 2 leadership position: majority leader.

Also last fall, Ralph Campbell was elected the State auditor of North Carolina. He is the first black to win statewide executive office. He was elected with 53 percent of the vote of the citizens of North Carolina, outpolling some veteran white democratic incumbents who were reelected to their State posts and equaling the numbers of Governor Jim Hunt, who last year won a third turn.

North Carolina has also elected blacks to the North Carolina Supreme Court and the North Carolina Court of Appeals in recent years. And blacks have been elected mayor in three of the State's largest cities: Charlotte, Raleigh, and Durham—all of which have white majorities.

This is the progress that North Carolina has been making in recent years. This success only two decades removed from the ending of segregation, refutes the claims by people such as Ms. Guinier who say that whites are a permanently hostile majority in the political arena, that white Democrats don't accept their black counterparts, and that black leaders who are elected are "tokens," perhaps the most degrading comment of all. All of the men I have mentioned have strong and deep ties to the black community.

There has been other progress in North Carolina. Last year the Republican Party fielded strong black candidates in its primaries for State labor commissioner and State superintendent of public instruction. The latter candidate lost a close runoff in a race where virtually all voters were conservative whites.

I know North Carolina is not alone. In Mississippi, perhaps the State with the most violent racial history in the country, one of your former colleagues, Mike Espy, won reelection by carrying 70 percent of the white vote in 1990. "The Almanac of American Politics 1992" said that Espy "is now so popular that he could win in a white majority district." The report added, "Espy broke the back of the old segregationist politics, and proved that it is possible for a black candidate to win anywhere in the country."

It is true that Mr. Espy first won election as a result of having a majority black district carved up because of the Voting Rights Act, and I accept the need for some action; but once given the chance to represent white voters, Mr. Espy earned their respect and support. If we continue to insist on dividing our electorate by racial quotas even more, how can we ever break the back of the old segregationist politics in other places?

The idea of creating districts that are safe for minorities is rooted in a good cause, the cause of correcting past injustice. But instead of empowering minorities, these districts merely put them on the margins, safely herded away into black sections that can be easily forgotten by whites.

It is an "other-side-of-the-tracks" mentality, and it is dangerous for a society that should be bringing people together.

Let me return to the North Carolina congressional example. Last year, the Justice Department forced the State to draw a second minority district, and that district elected Mr. Watt of Charlotte. That city is now represented by a white Congressman, Alex McMilan, who has mostly white constituents, and by Watt, who is black and has a majority of black constituents.

It is my contention that Mr. Watt could have won an election from the old, majority white Ninth District. As evidence, I cite the fact that Watt's close friend, Harvey Gantt, carried this half urban, half rural district with 54 percent of the vote in the 1990 Senate race.

What, other than good conscience, would make a Congressman from a district that has only white voters care about the needs of black voters? Senator John Breaux, a Democrat from Louisiana, said that when districts are packed with mostly minorities and other districts become mostly white, minorities' "interests get pushed to the margins." But he said, "When you start out with 25 percent minorities in your district, there isn't any question you have to weigh the interests of all those folks."

I can easily envision a legislator from a white district saying: "Who cares what the blacks think? They're not in my district, and they're not my problem."

What if we ignore the progress I have cited and let ourselves believe what such thinkers as Ms. Guinier say? What if we continue to insist that blacks be represented by blacks, and whites by whites, by carving up districts that increase racial separatism and political polarization?

Last week, I spoke with Lacy Thornburg, who was North Carolina's attorney general from 1984 to 1992 and who argued the 1986 Supreme Court case *Thornburg* v. *Gingles*. What should I tell the committee? I asked Mr. Thornburg.

"We don't want to resegregate the races," he told me. "We've come too far. The question now is, how far do you go until you start doing what you were trying to remedy? The cure is worse than the disease. You start a new disease."

North Carolina and the rest of the country do not need a new disease that poisons the political arena with racial separatism.

Many black leaders in North Carolina share my concerns. During the redistricting process in 1991 and 1992, they expressed them.

State Representative Mickey Michaux, a veteran legislator, told those who wanted to pack minorities into two black congressional districts, "What you are actually doing is taking all of the minorities and putting them in two districts and saying, you all have got what you want, now go about your business and leave us alone." Earlier, he warned that it is wrong to assume that all blacks are all alike. "We consider ourselves part of the total electorate. We are not monolithic."

Representative Fitch, whom I have mentioned, likened many black districts to political reservations, where blacks' influence in surrounding districts and in other elections would be minimal.

Another black representative, James Green, responded to some who sought to draw more minority districts for their own partisan benefit: "We don't hope that you're asinine enough to believe that this is going to benefit African-Americans."

Finally, it was Speaker Blue, the first black speaker in North Carolina, who protested the Federal Government's insistence on having a second black district by saying that North Carolina, not the Federal Government, knows what is best for North Carolina. In a newspaper column, he wrote: "I still believe that the Voting Rights Act was designed to prevent the fracturing or packing of the black vote, not to require stringing black voters together to create a district and in the meantime help Republicans get elected."

Let me conclude my remarks by, once again, stressing that we must be vigilant in coming years not to allow our country to be resegregated along racial lines.

I realize that politics is only part of the whole arena of relations between the races, but it is an important one. If we say to our black citizens that they can be represented only by people of their race and we allow white citizens to be represented only by whites politicians, I say we are doing our Nation a disservices.

Let us fight discrimination where it exists and promote racial harmony. But let us not guarantee that on election day blacks and whites will forever be separate, because if they are separate they will also remain forever unequal.

Thank you.

Mr. HYDE. Thank you, Mr. Geis.

[The prepared statement of Mr. Geis follows:]

REMARKS BY CHRISTOPHER J. GEIS

Mr. Chairman and Members of this Subcommittee, let me thank you for the opportunity to speak before you today.

I come before you today not as a political or legal scholar, but as an observer of politics in North Carolina for the last several years -- first as a reporter for the Winston-Salem Journal, one of the largest daily newspapers in North Carolina; then as press secretary for the North Carolina Democratic Party; and finally as a copy editor on the news desk of the Journal, where I am currently employed.

As a reporter, I covered a number of political races, including the 1990 U.S. Senate race between Senator Jesse Helms and challenger Harvey Gantt. Mr. Gantt was the first black person to be nominated for major statewide office in North Carolina since Reconstruction. Later, as the Democratic Party's press secretary, I worked on a number of political campaigns, including that of Ralph Campbell, whose election last year as State Auditor marked the first time that a black person has been elected to a major statewide office.

I HAVE LONG BEEN fascinated by politics in our state and across the South because of the racial dynamics that have surrounded those politics.

I should say up front, however, that I come to the whole issue of race with a strong bias. I am deeply concerned about improving relations among the races, and about seeing that minorities share equally in the American dream.

It is my belief that the Voting Rights Act of 1965 is one of the most important and moral pieces of legislation in our nation's history, and it was a courageous Congress and President who made it law. It has had some positive effects on North Carolina. In the last 11 years, the number of blacks elected at the local and state levels has risen dramatically. As an example, the number of blacks now in the North Carolina General Assembly has risen from four to 25 so that blacks now make up 15 percent of the legislature.

Having more black legislators has been a good thing for North Carolina, I believe, because the legislature of today -- which also includes more women and more Republicans -- presents a truer mirror of North Carolina than the legislatures of the past.

BUT DESPITE WHAT I say to you, I come to you today to warn that we are entering an important and delicate period in our state's political history, and that the Voting Rights Act, as interpreted by a growing number of people, could now become an enemy of the progress we have made in race relations in North Carolina.

Many of you are familiar with North Carolina's recent experience with congressional redistricting. The North

Carolina legislature's plan for dividing the state into 12
congressional districts was rejected by the U.S. Justice
Department, which said that having one district with a
majority of black residents was not good enough. The
Justice Department, using its interpretation of the amended
Voting Rights Act, required the legislature to draw a quota
of two black-majority districts. That effort resulted in
the infamous Interstate 85 district that snakes 160 miles
along an expressway, stringing together pockets of inner-
city black voters from one end of the state to another.

In June of this year, the Supreme Court, in a ruling
that could strike down the redistricting plan, said in
''Shaw v. Reno'' that the district ''bears an uncomfortable
resemblance to political apartheid,'' and added: ''It is
unsettling how closely the North Carolina plan resembles
the most egregious racial gerrymanders of the past.''
(''Shaw v. Reno,'' Supreme Court opinion, No. 92-357, June
28, 1993.)

Apartheid and segregation are antithetical to the idea
of a free and democratic nation. But, Mr. Chairman, that is
where we are headed if we continue to divide our citizens
by race and herd them onto political reservations that
perpetuate a tribe-like politics more familiar in some
Third World countries or Soviet Republics. And I fear that,
in North Carolina, some of the progress that has been made
could be threatened by a political resegregation of the
races.

I am not proposing that we go back and undo the
changes of the last 10 years that have resulted from the
Voting Rights Act as amended in 1982.

I also believe that the congressman elected to
represent the 12th District, Melvin Watt, is an excellent
representative of both the black and white voters of the
district. I believe Mr. Watt is of such stature that he
could win in districts that are not majority-black.

And, in defense of the North Carolina legislature,
which did not want to draw a second black district, if the
law requires a second black district in North Carolina, the
I-85 district makes the most possible sense because it is
the state's only predominantly urban district. The state's
minority population is too scattered otherwise to draw a
compact second district.

But I believe that we are now at a point where to
carve up minority districts and segregate voters by race
even more will only do harm to the progress that we have
already made. That is why I was concerned when President
Clinton nominated Lani Guinier earlier this year to head
the Justice Department's civil-rights section. Ms.
Guinier's views were deeply troubling.

Ms. Guinier said in a series of law-review articles
that whites are a ''hostile, permanent majority''; that
''mainstream Democrats do not accept black Democrats'';
that whites elected with black votes still ignore black
voters; and that some black leaders are not ''authentic''
but rather are ''tokens.'' (''Guinier Miss,'' The New
Republic, June 14, 1993.)

I disagree with her pessimistic and cynical views, and
with those of other like-minded people, and I believe that
the evidence shows that the conclusions, at least as they
apply to North Carolina, are false.

Many good people of both races and both parties share
this opinion. They are concerned that, if the Voting Rights
Act is construed to require even more majority-minority
districts, we will, in essence, have two political worlds:
a white world where white office-holders, elected by all-
white electorates, go about their business, ignoring their
black colleagues; and a black world, where black officeholders, elected from all-black districts, are nevertheless
still in a minority in legislatures and so can safely be
ignored because their constituents have no power to
influence white-majority politicians.

IN NORTH CAROLINA, MANY citizens -- prodded by their
own consciences and not by any quota-crazy federal
government -- have worked very hard over the years to build
a biracial political cooperation that I believe is the envy
of many other states. This has been particularly true in
the Democratic Party.

Let me cite some examples:

-- In 1990, the Democrats nominated a black man,
Harvey Gantt, for the U.S. Senate seat held by Senator
Jesse Helms. Mr. Gantt, after having finished first over
three major white opponents in the first primary election,
won with ease a runoff primary over a white opponent who
was strong enough in his own right to be elected Attorney
General of North Carolina last year in a landslide. Mr.
Gantt then earned 47.4 percent of the vote in the general
election against Mr. Helms, who, having been elected four
times, is arguably one of the most successful politicians
in the state's history. Mr. Gantt's showing was better than

two other white opponents who had run against Senator Helms in previous years, and virtually equalled that of Mr. Helm's strongest challenger ever. Mr. Gantt is considered a strong candidate for a future Senate race.

-- That same fall, Daniel Blue, a black state representative from Raleigh, was elected the Speaker of the North Carolina House of Representatives by a biracial Democratic coalition of legislators, most of them white. He became the first black to hold that position in North Carolina -- and one of only two black Speakers in the country. Last year, Mr. Blue was unanimously re-elected by the Democratic majority in the legislature, which includes twice as many white legislators as it does black legislators. He is considered a strong candidate for statewide office. He became speaker by doing his job well and by earning the trust and respect of his white and black colleagues. (News articles, Winston-Salem Journal, Dec. 8, 1992, and Nov. 23, 1990.)

-- It is worth noting also that last year the white-majority Democratic coalition in the legislature named a black representative, Milton ''Toby'' Fitch, to the party's No. 2 leadership position: majority leader.

-- Also last fall, Ralph Campbell was elected the State Auditor of North Carolina, becoming the first black to win statewide executive office. He was elected with 53 percent of the vote -- outpolling some veteran white Democratic incumbents who were reelected to their state posts and equaling the numbers of Governor Jim Hunt, who last year won a third term. (News article, Winston-Salem Journal, Nov. 5, 1992.)

-- North Carolina has also elected blacks to the North
Carolina Supreme Court and the North Carolina Court of
Appeals, and blacks have been elected mayor in three of the
state's largest cities: Charlotte, Raleigh and Durham, all
of which have white majorities.

THIS IS THE PROGRESS THAT North Carolina has been
making in recent years. This success, only two decades
removed from the ending of segregation, refutes the claims
by people such as Ms. Guinier who say that whites are a
permanently hostile majority in the political arena, that
white Democrats don't accept their black counterparts, and
that black leaders who are elected are ''tokens'' --
perhaps the most degrading comment of all. All of the men I
have mentioned have strong and deep ties to the black
community.

There has been other progress in North Carolina as
well. Last year the Republican Party fielded strong black
candidates in its primaries for state Labor Commissioner
and state Superintendent of Public Instruction; the latter
candidate lost a close runoff in a race where virtually all
voters were conservative whites.

I know North Carolina is not alone. For example, in
Mississippi, perhaps the state with the most violent racial
history in the country, one of your former colleagues, Mike
Espy, won re-election by carrying 70 percent of the white
vote in 1990. ''The Almanac of American Politics 1992''
said that Espy ''is now so popular that he could win in a
white-majority district.'' The report added: ''Espy broke
the back of the old segregationist politics, and proved

that it is possible for a black candidate to win anywhere in the country.'' (''The Almanac of American Politics 1992,'' Mississippi section.)

It is true that Mr. Espy first won election as a result of having a majority-black district carved up because of the Voting Rights Act, and I accept the need for some action; but once given the chance to represent white voters, Mr. Espy earned their respect and support. If we continue to insist on dividing our electorate by racial quotas even more, how can we ever break the back of the old segregationist politics in other places?

Let me also cite the mayor of Cleveland, Michael R. White, who was featured earlier this week on the front page of The Wall Street Journal. Mr. White, who is black, won his race by combining white votes with black votes and offering a message that appealed to both races. ''We're trying to practice the art of addition, the politics of inclusion,'' he told the newspaper. ''There's a forest fire of division right now. The city won't survive with a black strategy or a white strategy.'' (News article, The Wall Street Journal, Oct. 11, 1993.)

This is the kind of thinking we need from our white leaders and our black leaders. Our nation will not survive with a white strategy or a black strategy.

THE IDEA OF CREATING districts that are safe for minorities is rooted in a good cause, the cause of correcting past injustice. But instead of empowering minorities, these districts merely put them on the margins -- safely herded away into black sections that can be easily forgotten by whites.

It is an "other-side-of-the-tracks" mentality, and it is dangerous for a society that should be bringing people together.

Let me return to the North Carolina congressional example. Last year, the Justice Department forced the state to draw a second minority district, and that district elected Melvin Watt of Charlotte. That city is now represented by a white congressman who has mostly white constituents and by Watt who is black and has a majority of black constituents.

It is my contention that Mr. Watt could have won an election from the old, majority-white 9th District. As evidence, I cite the fact that Watt's close friend, Harvey Gantt, carried this half-urban, half-rural district with 54 percent of the vote in the 1990 Senate race.

We could have had two black representatives last year without having created the infamous I-85 district. Would that not be better than having taken the tortured path we took?

The new congressional districts packed almost half of the state's black voters into two of our 12 districts. I don't believe that North Carolinians want to resegregate their state in this fashion.

What, other than good conscience, would make a congressman from a district that has only white voters care about the needs of black voters? Senator John Breaux, a Democrat from Louisiana, said that when districts are packed with mostly minorities, and other districts become mostly white, minorities' "interests get pushed to the margins." But he said, "When you start out with 25 percent minorities in your district, there isn't any question you have to weigh the interests of all those folks." (Supreme Court Preview, 1993-1994, College of William & Mary, July 4, 1993, article from the Chicago Tribune.)

I can easily envision a legislator from a white district saying: "Who cares what the blacks think? They're

o

not in my district, and they're not my problem.''

WHAT IF WE IGNORE the progress I have cited and let ourselves believe what such thinkers as Ms. Guinier say? What if we continue to insist that blacks be represented by blacks, and whites by whites, by carving up districts that increase racial separatism and political polarization?

Last week, I spoke with Lacy Thornburg, who was North Carolina's Attorney General from 1984 to 1992 and who argued the 1986 Supreme Court case ''Thornburg v. Gingles.'' What should I tell the committee? I asked.

''We don't want to resegregate the races,'' he told me. ''We've come too far. The question now is how far do you go until you start doing what you were trying to remedy. The cure is worse than the disease. You start a new disease.''

North Carolina and the rest of the country do not need a new disease that poisons the political arena with racial separatism.

MANY BLACK LEADERS IN North Carolina share my concerns. During the redistricting process in 1991 and 1992, they expressed them.

State Representative Mickey Michaux, a veteran legislator, told those who wanted to pack minorities into two black congressional districts: ''What you are actually doing is taking all of the minorities and putting them in two districts and saying you all have got what you want, now go about your business and leave us alone.'' (News article, Winston-Salem Journal, Jan. 17, 1992.) Earlier, he warned that it is wrong to assume that all blacks are all alike. ''We consider ourselves part of the total electorate. We are not monolithic,'' he said. (News article, Winston-Salem Journal, Jan. 11, 1990.)

Representative Milton ''Toby'' Fitch, whom I have mentioned, likened many black districts to ''political reservations,'' where blacks' influence in surrounding districts and in other elections would be minimal. (Editorial column, Winston-Salem Journal, Jan. 12, 1992.)

Another black Representative, James Green, responded to some who sought to draw more minority districts for their own partisan benefit: ''We don't hope that you're asinine enough to believe that this is going to benefit African-Americans.'' (News article, Winston-Salem Journal, Jan. 9, 1992)

Finally, it was Speaker Blue, the first black Speaker in North Carolina, who protested the federal government's insistence on having a second black district by saying that North Carolina, not the federal government, knows what is best for North Carolina. In a newspaper column, he wrote: ''I still believe that the Voting Rights Act was designed to prevent the fracturing or packing of the black vote, not to require stringing black voters together to create a district and in the meantime help Republicans get elected.'' (Editorial guest column, Winston-Salem Journal, Feb. 22, 1992.)

As an aside, I would like to say that, if the Republicans made a stronger effort to make black voters feel welcome in their party, they might be pleasantly surprised with their success. I believe that the

Republicans are missing an opportunity to attract many
black voters. Not all blacks, after all, share the views of
the Democrats who represent them. I believe that if the two
parties courted the black vote more equally, it would be
better for black voters, and it would go along way to
reducing the racial polarization we see in our politics.

LET ME CONCLUDE MY remarks by once again stressing
that we must be vigilant in coming years not to allow our
country to be resegregated along racial lines.

I realize that politics is only part of the whole
arena of relations between the races, but it is an
important one. If we say to our black citizens that they
can be represented only by people of their race, and we
allow white citizens to be represented only by white
politicians, I say we are doing our nation a disservice.

Let us fight discrimination where it exists and
promote racial harmony. But let us not guarantee that on
election day blacks and whites will forever be separate,
because if they are separate they will also remain forever
unequal.

Thank you.

Mr. HYDE. Kenneth Spaulding is an alumnus of Howard University and the University of North Carolina School of Law. Before entering private practice, Mr. Spaulding served as a member of the North Carolina House of Representatives for three terms. While in that position, he was instrumental in the redistricting efforts and helped to increase minority participation from 4 in 1981 to 12 in 1983.

In 1984, he was a candidate for the U.S. Congress. Mr. Spaulding is now a senior partner at Spaulding & Williams in Durham, NC.

STATEMENT OF KENNETH SPAULDING, ESQ., SPAULDING & WILLIAMS, 1984 NORTH CAROLINA CONGRESSIONAL CANDIDATE, DURHAM, NC

Mr. SPAULDING. Mr. Chairman, Mr. Hyde, and members of the subcommittee, I am Kenneth Spaulding, a former candidate for the U.S. House of Representatives.

As a candidate for the U.S. House of Representatives from the State of North Carolina and prior to the most recent redistricting, it was politically necessary and mandatory that I review the voting patterns in the Second Congressional District. This historical review inevitably required the forthright addressing of both the political party voting patterns and the district's racial voting patterns.

The Second Congressional District, for almost 100 years, tended to be strongly democratic. Its representatives, since Reconstruction, were always white males. I clearly satisfied the first historical category. I am a Democrat.

I did not, however, satisfy the second historical category in that I am a nonwhite male. With this in mind, I reviewed briefly the efforts of other African-Americans who had previously run for this same. Howard Lee, a former mayor of Chapel Hill, ran and was defeated. Eva Clayton, long-time community and civic leader, well-educated and extremely articulate, ran and was defeated. H.M. "Mickey" Michaux, former State representative, former U.S. attorney and very gifted political leader, ran and was defeated.

In short, it was quite obvious that each and every African-American citizen, regardless of their high degree of education, community involvement, previous record of service, capabilities, and abilities had been unsuccessful in their attempts to represent the Second Congressional District.

The historical record was also very clear in that the entire North Carolina delegation to the U.S. Congress was all white and all male.

It was my firm desire to face all of these odds and to again offer our State and the Second Congressional District an opportunity for diversity as well as to help end our State's unenviable position of sending a racially segregated delegate to the U.S. Congress.

The voting patterns in the district clearly proved that said patterns were not color blind. The district was approximately 64 percent white and 35 percent African-American. The Democratic voters were approximately 60 percent white and 40 percent African-Americans. This district, therefore, was an integrated and diverse district.

It was my personal and political desire that I garner white votes as well as black votes. It was also my firm conviction that a black-elected officeholder could represent both white and black citizens alike.

The biggest obstacle that I saw was not my political philosophy which was fiscally conservative, firm on issues of crime and a moderate approach to congressional issues, but was a glass wall that existed because of race consciousness in voting patterns.

With this in mind, from the beginning of my campaign for Congress to the end, I worked just as hard to cultivate white votes as I did to cultivate black votes. Efforts were made personally on the radio, to the press media, and through direct mailing to attract white voters to my candidacy.

These efforts were successful in my home county of Durham which had 6 years of intimate knowledge of my character, voting record, and leadership skills. Outside of Durham, the efforts were more difficult because the voters had to become knowledgeable of me as a candidate. This was even more complicated due to the fact that many of the new potential white voters had historically and consistently showed an unwillingness to vote for nonwhite candidates.

Therefore advertising, campaigning, and person-to-person efforts were directed in an integrated and biracial manner. It was my campaign's strategy to find every white vote that I could and convert it, while continuing to become known in the new black voter's communities across this 10-county district. USA Today did a feature story on my efforts to win over white voters as I had previously done in Durham.

As I campaigned across the district, it became clearer and clearer that no one person could eradicate the race consciousness that existed in the very fabric of people's daily lives. In the closing weeks, I felt within that the race consciousness obstacle was too ingrained in people's work lives, school lives, even church lives, and social lives, and in particular, in potential voters's political lives.

This recognition caused me to work even harder, personally, to follow through on my commitment to a color blind campaign. I felt that change could only come by example and hard work, even if victory for the primary was lost. There were too many white supporters who had faith in my candidacy and too many black voters who shared hope in my efforts.

It was ironic and unfortunate that white and black supporters who had unified in a manner unparalleled in the Second Congressional District would run into the same glass wall of race consciousness voting which, in effect, was created in legislature after legislature by redistricting efforts to discourage black participation and representation.

Even though there was not an electoral victory, I feel that both white and black supporters felt a sense of accomplishment in coming so close, 48 percent of the primary vote, to success when race conscious voting was so prevalent.

Also, the voting pattern of Durham in May 1984 clearly showed that once many white voters became familiar with black elected officeholders, race conscious voting became less prohibitive.

Parenthetically, the aforementioned was shown not only in this congressional race when Durham was strongly supportive of my candidacy but also in my three successful legislative races. Illustratively, my State house races began with my receiving a strong black vote plus a respectable number of white votes in 1978, to finish third in a 6-person field, 3-seat primary.

In each ensuing race, I maintained a strong black vote and increased my white vote to very significant and large numbers. The congressional primary confirmed this color blind trend in Durham County. The lesson that I have learned from this experience, I feel, confirms the need for Voting Rights Act remedies and court approval of remedial efforts to eradicate historically embedded race conscious voting.

The Voting Rights Act serves as a remedial tool which helps to shatter the glass wall of race conscious voting which is ingrained in too many voters even in 1993. I want to make it very clear that there are many white voters who refuse to let race make their political decisions and choices.

However, there are still too many systemic effects of society and politics which defeat the individual efforts of black candidates. Often race conscious voting choices are subconscious. I equate this subconscious emotional response to recent studies that neighborhoods are perceived as turning black or going black when as little as one quarter of the neighboring residents are, in fact, black.

Psychologically, race consciousness is an emotion, not a logical rational response. It is often not felt with malice, but its effect can be just as detrimental.

Arguably, a case in point is our U.S. Supreme Court's divided opinion in *Shaw* v. *Reno*. We have a U.S. Supreme Court whose composition does not adequately reflect the diversity of our America in many ways. Nondiversity of background may lead to nonmalicious intellectual postulations which reflect a perspective that is consistent with the issue that needs remedying. I would argue that this most recent issue on its face shows a paucity of understanding of some Members themselves to the real issue of race consciousness which the Court has been asked to address.

The subconscious emotional response which exists, yet which is rarely articulated, has now arguably shown up in the reasoning of the majority's opinion. This rarely articulated response may be presented in the form of a question: When is black too much black?

When is black too much black? This question and emotion is pervasive in American life, yet rarely openly acknowledged or addressed. One could argue that it is a part of our psychic that is rarely consciously addressed, yet often unconsciously acted upon.

The U.S. Supreme Court's recent opinion of *Shaw* v. *Reno*, in my opinion, has now finally placed this question before the American people, our American courts. And our American value system.

When is black too much black? It would seem that the court feels, as many others sometimes subconsciously feel, that a majority-minority district is a black district.

Unfortunately, some see a majority black district as being an all-black district or a segregated district. American Heritage Dictionary defines "to segregate" as, "one to separate or isolate others from a main body, to impose the separation of a race or class from the rest of society." The truth of the matter is that majority-minority districts are not all-black districts, regardless of one's psychological subconscious emotion relating thereto.

These two North Carolina congressional districts are, in fact, integrated districts. The 12th Congressional District has approximately 47 percent white voting age population and approximately 42 percent total white population. The First Congressional District has approximately 47 percent white voting age population and approximately 42 percent total white population. These are integrated districts.

However, in *Shaw* v. *Reno*, the Supreme Court, through its divided opinion, states that

Today we hold only that appellants have stated a claim under the equal protection clause by alleging that the North Carolina General Assembly adopted a reapportionment scheme so irrational on its face that it can be understood only as an effort to segregate voters into separate voting districts because of their race and that separation lacks sufficient justification.

The Court's majority seems to go further in an arguably incorrect subconscious race conscious manner when it again appears to see these two districts has all-black or too-black districts. The Court's majority says, a reapportionment plan that includes in one district individuals who belong to the same race but who are otherwise widely separated by geographical and political boundaries and who may have little in common with one another but the color of their skin bears uncomfortable resemblances to political apartheid.

"Apartheid" is defined from the same aforementioned source as an official policy of racial segregation promulgated in the republic of South Africa. Apartheid is clearly a separation of people totally and exclusively by race.

Again, one could argue that some members of the Court have failed to consciously understand that these districts are not all black districts, are not segregated districts, are not separated by race. These are very racially integrated districts. These districts are no more segregated than District No. 11, which is 91 percent white and 7 percent black, or District No. 10, which is 93 percent white and 5 percent black, or Districts 2, 3, and 4, which are approximately 76 percent white and 21 percent black.

The issue again retreats to the rarely articulated question even for the Court's own introspective analysis: When is black too much black?

In short, one must wonder if race consciousness in voting patterns and its subconscious motivations do not sometimes interfere with and cloud our intellectual reasoning.

It should be made very clear that not all whites and not all Supreme Court justices fall prey to the oftentimes comfortable subconscious emotion of race consciousness in their decisionmaking affairs. Justice White's dissenting opinion shows a historical awareness of North Carolina and a sensitization for constructive court action to help remedy the psychological and destructive vestiges of a previously negative chapter of American history.

In regard to North Carolina's plan, Justice White states:

Nonetheless, the notion that North Carolina's plan under which whites remain a voting majority in a disproportionate number of congressional districts and pursuant to which the State has sent its first black representatives since Reconstruction to the U.S. Congress, might have violated appellant's constitutional right is both a fiction and a departure from the settled equal protection principles. Seeing no good reason to engage in either, I dissent.

Mr. Chairman and members of this committee, if the U.S. Supreme Court re-reviews the North Carolina redistricting plan, hopefully the Court's majority will see how this plan has finally integrated the North Carolina's congressional delegation. This plan has ended almost a 100-year history of segregated representation by North Carolina in the U.S. Congress, and has not been in violation of the equal protection clause of our U.S. Constitution.

Mr. Chairman and members of this committee, I feel that these hearings are of significant importance to the open and frank refinement and discussion of the Voting Rights Act. I have offered these comments in an effort to be as open and candid as possible so that the exchange of ideas and opinions would be of some useful value to your deliberations.

This type of intellectual and pragmatic exchange in my opinion is more valuable than rhetoric or responses based on crises. Your hearings are not only important to the U.S. Congress but they are of crucial importance to continuing and everlasting efforts of Americans seeking the democratic principles of freedom and equal opportunity.

Thank you.

[The prepared statement of Mr. Spaulding follows:]

STATEMENT BY KENNETH B. SPAULDING TO THE
HOUSE SUBCOMMITTEE ON CIVIL AND CONSTITUTIONAL RIGHTS
OCTOBER 12, 1993

As a candidate for the U. S. House of Representatives from the State of North Carolina and prior to the most recent redistricting, it was politically necessary and mandatory that I review the voting patterns in the Second Congressional District. This historical review inevitably required the forthright addressing of both the political party voting patterns and the district's racial voting patterns.

The Second Congressional District, for almost 100 years, tended to be strongly Democrat. It's Representatives, since Reconstruction, were always white males. I clearly satisfied the first historical category. I was and am a Democrat. I did not, however, satisfy the second historical category in that I was a non-white male. With this in mind, I reviewed briefly the efforts of other African Americans who had previously run from this same Congressional District. Howard Lee, former Mayor of Chapel Hill, ran and was defeated. Eva Clayton, longtime community and civic leader, well-educated and extremely articulate, ran and was defeated. H. M. "Mickey" Michaux, former State Representative, former U. S. Attorney and very gifted political leader, ran and was defeated. In short, it was quite obvious that each and every African American citizen, regardless of their high degree of education, community involvement, previous record of service, capabilities and abilities, had been unsuccessful in their attempts to represent the Second Congressional District. The historical record was also very clear in that the entire North Carolina Delegation to the United States Congress was all white and all male.

It was my firm desire to face all of these odds and to again offer our State and the Second Congressional District an opportunity for diversity, as well as, to help end our State's unenviable position of sending a racially segregated delegation to the U. S. Congress.

The voting patterns in this District clearly proved that said patterns were not "color blind". The District was approximately 65% white and 35% African American. The Democratic voters were approximately 60% white and 40% African American. This district, therefore, was an integrated and diverse district.

It was my personal and political desire that I garner white votes as well as black votes. It was also my firm conviction that a Black elected officeholder could represent both white and black citizens, alike.

The biggest obstacle that I saw was not my political philosophy which was fiscally conservative, firm on issues of crime and a moderate approach to Congressional issues, but was a "glass wall" that existed because of "race consciousness" in voting patterns. With this in mind, from the beginning of my campaign for Congress to the end, I worked just as hard to cultivate white votes as I did to cultivate black votes. Efforts were made personally, on the radio media, the press media and direct mailing to attract white voters to my candidacy.

These efforts were successful in my home county of Durham which had six years of intimate knowledge of my character, voting record and leadership skills. Outside of Durham, the efforts were more difficult because the voters had to become knowledgeable of me as a candidate. This was even more complicated due to the fact that many of the new potential white voters had historically and consistently shown an unwillingness to vote for non-white candidates.

Therefore, advertising, campaigning and person-to-person efforts were directed in an integrated and bi-racial manner. It was my campaign's strategy to find every white vote that I could and convert it, while continuing to become known in the new black voters' communities across the ten county district. USA Today did a feature story on my efforts to win over white voters as I had previously done in Durham.

As I campaigned across the district, it became clearer and clearer that no one person could eradicate the "race consciousness" that existed in the very fabric of people's daily lives. In the closing weeks, I felt within that the "race consciousness" obstacle was too ingrained in people's work lives, school lives, church lives, social lives and in particular in potential voters' political lives.

This recognition caused me to work even harder, personally, to follow through on my commitment to a "color blind" campaign. I felt that change could only come by example and hard work, even if victory for the primary was lost. There were too many white supporters who had faith in my candidacy and too many black voters who shared "hope" in my efforts.

It was ironic and unfortunate that white and black supporters who had unified in a manner unparalleled in the Second Congressional District would run into the same "glass wall" of "race consciousness" voting which in effect was created in legislature after legislature by redistricting efforts to discourage black participation and representation.

Eventhough, there was not an electoral victory, I feel that both white and black supporters felt a sense of accomplishment in coming so close (48% of the Primary vote) to success when "race conscious" voting was so prevalent. Also, the voting pattern of Durham in May of 1984 clearly showed that once many white voters became familiar with black elected officeholders, "race conscious" voting became less prohibitive. (Parenthetically, the aforementioned was shown not only in this Congressional race, when Durham was strongly supportive of my candidacy, but also in my three successful legislative races. Illustratively, my State House races began with my receiving a strong black vote plus a respectable number of white votes in 1978, to finish 3rd in a six person field-three seat primary. In each ensuing race, I maintained a strong black vote and increased my white vote to very significant and large numbers. The Congressional Primary confirmed this "color blind" trend in Durham County).

The lesson that I have learned from this experience, I feel, confirms the need for Voting Rights Act remedies and Court approval of remedial efforts to eradicate historically embedded "race conscious" voting.

The Voting Rights Act serves as a remedial tool which helps to shatter the "glass wall" of "race conscious" voting which is ingrained in too many voters even in 1993. I want to make it very clear that there are many white voters who refuse to let "race" make their political decisions and choices. However, there are still too many systemic effects of society and politics which defeat the individual efforts of black candidates. Often, "race conscious" voting choices are subconscious. I equate this subconscious emotional response to the recent studies which show that neighborhoods are perceived by some whites as "turning black" or "going black" when as little as one-quarter of the neighboring residents are, in fact, black. Psychologically, unfortunately, "race consciousness" is an emotion, and not a logical, rational response. It is often not felt with malice, but its effect can be just as detrimental. Arguably, a case in point is our U. S. Supreme Court's divided opinion in Shaw v. Reno. We have a United States Supreme Court whose composition does not adequately reflect the diversity of our America in many ways. Non-diversity of background may lead to non-malicious intellectual postulations which reflect a perspective which is consistent with the issue which needs remedying. I would argue that this most recent opinion on its face shows a paucity of sensitization by some members, themselves, to the real issue of "race consciousness" which the Court has been asked to address. The subconscious emotional response which exists, yet which is rarely articulated, has now, arguably, shown up in the reasoning of the majority's opinion. This rarely articulated response may be presented in the form of a question - "**When is black, too much black?**"

When is black, too much black? This question and emotion is pervasive in American life, yet rarely openly acknowledged or addressed. One could argue that it is a part of our psychic that is rarely consciously addressed, yet often unconsciously acted upon.

The U. S. Supreme Court's most recent opinion of <u>Shaw v. Reno</u>, in my opinion, has now finally placed this question before the American people, our American Courts and our American value system.

<u>**When is black, too much black?**</u> It would seem that the Court feels, as many others sometimes subconsciously feel, that a majority-minority district is a black district. Unfortunately, some see a majority black district as being an <u>all</u> black district or a segregated district. The **American Heritage Dictionary** defines "to segregate" as: 1)"to separate or isolate from others or from a main body"; 2)"to impose the separation of (a race or class) from the rest of society". The truth of the matter is that majority-minority districts are not <u>all black districts</u> regardless of one's psychological subconscious emotion relating thereto. These two North Carolina Congressional Districts are in fact **INTEGRATED** districts. The 12th Congressional District has approximately 47% white voting age population and approximately 42% total white population. The 1st Congressional District has approximately 47% white voting age population and approximately 42% total white population. These are **INTEGRATED DISTRICTS.**

However, in <u>Shaw v. Reno</u>, the Supreme Court, through its divided opinion, states that "..today we hold only that appellants have stated a claim under the Equal Protection Clause by alleging that the N. C. General Assembly adopted a reapportionment scheme so irrational on its face that it can be understood only as an effort to <u>segregate</u> voters into <u>separate</u> voting districts because of their race, and that separation lacks sufficient justification". The Court's majority seem to go further in an arguably incorrect subconscious "race conscious" manner when it again appears to see these two districts as <u>all black</u> or <u>too</u> black districts. The Court's majority says, "A reapportionment plan that includes in <u>one</u> district individuals who belong to the <u>same</u> race, but who are otherwise widely separated by geographical and political boundaries and who may have little in common with one another but the color of their skin, bears uncomfortable resemblances to political <u>apartheid</u>".

<u>Apartheid</u> is defined from the same aforementioned source as "an official policy of <u>racial segregation</u> promulgated in the Republic of South Africa." Apartheid is clearly a separation of people totally and exclusively by race. Again, one could argue that some members of the Court have failed to <u>consciously</u> understand that these districts are not all black, are not segregated, and are not separated by race. These are very racially <u>integrated</u> districts. These districts are no more segregated than District #11 which is 91% white and 7% black, or District #10 which is 93% white and 5% black, or Districts 2, 3, and 4 which are approximately 76% white and 21% black. The issue again retreats to the rarely articulated question even for the Court's own introspective analysis, <u>**When is black, too much black?**</u>

In short, one must wonder if "race consciousness" in voting patterns and its subconscious motivations do not sometimes interfere with and cloud our intellectual reasoning.

It should be made very clear that not all whites and not all Supreme Court Justices fall prey to the oftentimes comfortable subconscious emotion of "race consciousness" in their decision making affairs. Justice White's dissenting opinion shows an historical awareness of North Carolina and a sensitization for constructive Court action to help remedy the psychological and destructive vestiges of a previously negative chapter of American history. In regard to North Carolina's plan, Justice White states, "Nonetheless, the notion that North Carolina's plan, under which whites remain a voting majority in a disproportionate number of congressional districts, and pursuant to which the State has sent its first black representatives since Reconstruction to the United States Congress, might have violated appellants' constitutional rights is both a fiction and a departure from settled equal protection principles. Seeing no good reason to engage in either, I dissent."

In conclusion, if the United States Supreme Court re-reviews the North Carolina redistricting plan, hopefully, the Court's majority will see how this plan has finally integrated North Carolina's Congressional delegation. This plan has ended almost 100 years of segregated representation by North Carolina in the United States Congress, and has not been in violation of the "Equal Protection Clause" of our U. S. Constitution.

Mr. Chairman and members of this Committee, I feel that these hearings are of significant importance to the open and frank refinement and discussion of the Voting Rights Act. I have offered these comments in an effort to be as open and candid as possible, so that the exchange of ideas and opinions would be of some useful value to your deliberations. This type of intellectual and pragmatic exchange, in my opinion, is more valuable than rhetoric or responses based on crises. Your hearings are not only important to the United States Congress, but they are of crucial importance to the continuing and everlasting efforts of Americans seeking the democratic principles of freedom and equal opportunity.

Mr. HYDE. Mr. Chairman, we are honored to have Randall Kennedy with us this morning. He has taught at Harvard Law School since 1984. He is a Rhodes scholar and a 1982 graduate of Yale Law School.

After law school, Mr. Kennedy clerked for Judge K. Skelly Wright of the U.S. Court of Appeals in the District of Columbia, and for the late Justice Thurgood Marshall of the Supreme Court.

Mr. Kennedy has written on the greatness of Justice Marshall, competing conceptions of racial discrimination, and racial critiques of legal education.

Professor Kennedy.

STATEMENT OF RANDALL KENNEDY, PROFESSOR, HARVARD UNIVERSITY LAW SCHOOL, CAMBRIDGE

Mr. KENNEDY. Thank you, Mr. Chairman. It is a great pleasure to have the opportunity to testify before the subcommittee. Controversies over the basic ground rules governing the distribution of political representation have emerged as a subject of widespread notice in the aftermath of three events.

One is the uproar that surrounded the nomination and then the withdrawal of Prof. Lani Guinier to head the Civil Rights Division of the Department of Justice.

The second is a striking augmentation of black political power, a change in American life that has, among other things, noticeably affected the racial composition of the House of Representatives. Never in the history of the Nation have there been more black Members in the House.

A third event is the Supreme Court's recent ruling in *Shaw* v. *Reno* that, in some circumstances, the Constitutional rights of nonblacks are violated when States purposefully seek to create congressional jurisdictions in which blacks comprise the voting majority.

These three events are interrelated. *Shaw* put a question mark next to the process by which many blacks have recently been elected; of the 16 blacks elected to Congress in 1992, 13 represent districts purposefully designed to contain a majority of black voters.

Professor Guinier put a question mark next to this process as well, finding it inadequate to the task of fully and effectively integrating blacks into all aspects of governance.

Finally, a wide array of observers put a question mark next to Professor Guinier, or at least the prospect of her becoming an assistant attorney general, because they found the measures she favors disturbingly radical.

In the brief time that I have with you, I cannot possibly hope to untangle the skein of issues implicated by these events. I can, however, suggest avoiding certain habits of mind that cripple productive thinking on how to improve our current situation.

First and most importantly, we need to recognize and counteract the strong impulse abroad in our political culture to ignore or deny the extent to which racial minorities are unfairly disadvantaged by rules and customs that, because of their strong majoritarian bias, unduly favor whites in electoral competition.

In *Shaw*, the 5 to 4 majority of the Justices appeared captivated by the idea that purposefully creating black majority districts may balkanize us into competing racial factions, as if before affirmative, race-conscious districting North Carolina's political arena was free of racial divisions.

It was left to the dissenting justices to note that North Carolina had traditionally been balkanized with a white majority faction completely monopolizing all the congressional seats; that it was only after the 1990 redistricting that, for the first time since the turn of the century, blacks were able to join the State's congressional delegation; and that even after the creation of the two black majority districts, whites remain a voting majority in 10 of North Carolina's 12 congressional districts.

A second lamentable habit is laziness compounded by parochialism, traits that become disturbingly evident during the controversy over Professor Guinier's nomination. While there are certainly respectable grounds on which to disagree with Professor Guinier and the ideas she advances, some influential persons who participated in the episode showed themselves to be ignorant not only of the complexities of her work but ignorant too of the various strands of democratic thought in the United States and around the world.

If you will let me digress for a moment to indicate that, over and over again, Professor Guinier has been criticized as a person who is in favor of safe districting. This is rather ironic since she has very trenchantly criticized race-conscious, single-member districting.

She has criticized it on a variety of grounds. First, she notes that it offers an incentive to residential racial separatism and for minorities penalized dispersion which seems especially to hurt Hispanics.

Second, Professor Guinier observes that race-conscious, single-member districts cannot adequately address the multiracial character of many districts.

Third, it is done by self-interested political professionals who frequently put the preservation of their own power above all competing concerns.

Fourth, Professor Guinier objects to the way that single-member districting buttresses the hegemony of the two-party system marginalizing third-party challengers and encouraging a religiously centrist, lowest-common-denominator style of politics hostile to any ideas outside of the mainstream.

Fifth, she complains that it impedes the construction of trans-racial political coalitions.

Professor Guinier believes that race-conscious districting is constitutional; but as a policy matter, she has criticized it rather trenchantly. Yet over and over and over again, one hears her characterized as a person who has mindlessly embraced race-conscious districts. She is really asking, how can we improve the current situation? And she is really proposing voting schemes alternative to those which are currently in place.

Some who have criticized Professor Guinier as antidemocratic and un-American act as if they had never read James Madison and the Federalist Papers or considered the obstacles to majoritarianism built into the Bill of Rights, bicameral legislatures, and quotas dictating that all States must be represented by two Senators, regardless of differences in populations; or customs like the Senate filibuster by which minorities compel majorities to take their interests into account.

Some of Professor Guinier's critics speak as if there was only one truly democratic way. Pressed to justify withdrawing her nomination, our President remarked that in her writings she had seemed to advocate proportional representation, which, indeed, she does. And President Clinton suggested that these sorts of proposals were antidemocratic and difficult to defend.

But as an unsigned editorial in the New Yorker caustically noted, President Clinton's view "will come as news to the good people of Germany, Spain, the Netherlands, and Sweden. Indeed, most of the electorates of continental Europe including those of the liberated East, elect their legislatures under some form of proportional representation."

A third habit, related to the second, is a tendency to avoid the effort of staying alert to the requirements of our specific conditions by following unquestioningly overused slogans. Color blindness has become such a slogan. Some devotees of it fail to recognize that, as my recently deceased senior colleague at Harvard, Paul Freund, observed, Justice Harlan's reference to color blindness is not a reference to constitutional text but it is a constitutional metaphor. There is nothing in the text of the constitution that should prevent legislatures from purposefully assuring racial minorities of meaningful integration into all aspects of democratic governance.

The idea of color blindness retains much of its allure in part because of its estimable lineage as a slogan of liberation. In the 1940's, 1950's, and 1960's, against the backdrop of laws that used racial distinctions to exclude blacks from opportunities available to whites, it seemed that racial subordination could be overcome simply by mandating the application of race-blind law.

That was an error. This error should not prevent us, however, from benefitting from the experience of the past quarter century, experience that shows that colorblind procedures may be sufficient to attain racial justice in some circumstances but not in others.

It would be tragic if color blindness, a metaphor used by Justice John Marshall Harlan in an unsuccessful effort to prevent de jure racial barriers in the 19th century, was used successfully to limit our thinking about possible ways of uprooting de facto racial barriers in the late 20th century.

Thank you very much.

Mr. HYDE. Thank you, Professor Kennedy.

[The prepared statement of Mr. Kennedy follows:]

HARVARD LAW SCHOOL

CAMBRIDGE · MASSACHUSETTS · 02138

Testimony from Randall Kennedy, Professor, Harvard Law
School, to be given to the Congress of the United States,
House Judiciary Committee, Subcommittee on Civil and Con-
stitutional Rights, October 15, 1992.

➤ ➤ ➤

It is a great pleasure to have the opportunity to
testify before the House Judiciary Committee's Subcommittee
on Civil and Constitutional Rights. I have been informed
that what prompts this occasion for discussion is a desire
to explore certain features of ongoing debates over race relations policies, particularly those that regulate the allocation of electoral power.

Controversies over the basic groundrules governing
the distribution of political representation have emerged as
a subject of widespread notice in the aftermath of three
events. One is the uproar that surrounded the nomination,
and then the withdrawal, of Professor Lani Guinier to head
the Civil Rights Division of the Department of Justice. The
second is a striking augmentation of black political power,
a change in American life that has, among other things,
noticeably affected the racial composition of the House of

Representatives. Never in the history of the nation have there been more black Members in the House. A third event is the Supreme Court's recent ruling in <u>Shaw v. Reno</u> that in some circumstances the constitutional rights of non-blacks are violated when states purposefully seek to create Congressional jurisdictions in which blacks comprise the voting majority.

These three events are inter-related. <u>Shaw</u> put a question mark next to the process by which many blacks have recently been elected; of the 16 blacks elected to Congress in 1992, 13 represent districts purposefully designed to contain a majority of black voters. Professor Guinier put a question mark next to this process as well, finding it inadequate to the task of fully and effectively integrating blacks into all aspects of governance. Finally, a wide array of observers put a question mark next to Professor Guinier, or at least the prospect of her becoming an Assistant Attorney General, because they found the measures she favors disturbingly radical.

In the brief time that I have with you, I cannot possible hope to untangle the skein of issues implicated by these events. I can, however, suggest avoiding certain habits of mind that cripple productive thinking on how to improve our current situation.

First and most importantly, we need to recognize and counteract the strong impulse abroad in our political cul-

ture to ignore or deny the extent to which racial minorities
are unfairly disadvantaged by rules and customs that, because of their strong majoritarian bias, unduly favor whites
in electoral competition. In Shaw, the 5-4 majority of the
Justices appeared captivated by the idea that purposefully
creating black majority districts "may balkanize us into
competing racial factions" -- as if before affirmative,
race-conscious districting North Carolina's political arena
was free of racial divisions. It was left to the dissenting
Justices to note that North Carolina had traditionally been
balkanized, with a white majority faction completely monopolizing all the Congressional seats; that it was only after
the 1990 redistricting that, for the first time since the
turn of the century, blacks were able to join the state's
Congressional delegation, and that even after the creation
of the two black majority districts, whites remain a voting
majority in ten of North Carolina's twelve congressional
districts.

A second lamentable habit is laziness compounded by
parochialism, traits that became disturbingly evident during
the controversy over Professor Guinier's nomination. While
there are respectable grounds on which to disagree with
Professor Guinier and the ideas she advances, some influential persons who participated in that episode showed themselves to be ignorant not only of the complexities of her
work, but ignorant, too, of various strands of democratic

thought and practice within the United States and around the world. Some condemned Guinier as if they had never read James Madison and The Federalist Papers or considered the obstacles to majoritarianism built into the constitutional structure -- including the Bill of Rights, bicameral legislatures, and quotas dictating that all states must be represented by two Senators regardless of differences in populations -- or reflected in customs -- like the Senate filibuster -- by which minorities compel majorities to take their interests into account.

Some of Professor Guinier's critics spoke as if there was only one truly democratic way. Pressed to justify withdrawing her nomination, President Clinton remarked that in her writings she had seemed to advocate proportional representation, which he termed "antidemocratic and difficult to defend." But as an unsigned editorial in the New Yorker caustically noted, Clinton's view "will come as news to the good people of Germany, Spain, the Netherlands, and Sweden. . . . Indeed, most of the electorates of continental Europe, including those of the liberated East, elect their legislatures under some form of proportional representation."

A third habit, related to the second, is a tendency to avoid the effort of staying alert to the requirements of our specific conditions by following unquestioningly overused and over-broad slogans. "Color-blindness" has become such a slogan. Some devotees of it fail to recognize that,

as my recently-deceased senior colleague Paul Freund observed, Justice Harlan's reference to color blindness is not
a reference to constitutional text but to constitutional
metaphor. There is nothing in the Constitution that should
prevent legislatures from purposefully assuring racial
minorities of meaningful integration into all aspects of
democratic governance.

The idea of color-blindness retains much of its allure
in part because of its estimable lineage as a slogan of
liberation. In the forties, fifties, and sixties, against
the backdrop of laws that used racial distinctions to exclude blacks from opportunities available to whites, it
seemed that racial subordination could be overcome simply by
mandating the application of race-blind law. This error
should not prevent us from benefiting from the experience of
the past quarter century, experience that shows that colorblind procedures may be sufficient to attain racial justice
in some circumstances but not in others.

It would be tragic if "color blindness," a metaphor
used by Justice John Marshall Harlan in the an unsuccessful
effort to prevent de jure racial barriers in the nineteenth
century, was used successfully to limit our thinking about
possible ways of uprooting de facto racial barriers in the
late twentieth century.

Mr. HYDE. Lastly, we will hear from Joseph Broadus who is an assistant professor at George Mason School of Law.

He was a law clerk for Judge Joseph Hatchet of the fifth circuit and has worked as a legislative analyst for the Florida House of Representatives.

He teaches a variety of subjects at George Mason including constitution law.

We are delighted to have you here, Professor.

STATEMENT OF JOSEPH E. BROADUS, ASSISTANT PROFESSOR, GEORGE MASON SCHOOL OF LAW, FAIRFAX, VA

Mr. BROADUS. Thank you. And I am happy to be here.

I take this opportunity to appear before the subcommittee to provide background and analysis on two cases by the U.S. Supreme Court that proved greatly troubling. And those cases are *Presley* v. *Etowah* and *Shaw* v. *Reno.*

In the *Presley* case, which addressed the reach of section 5 of the Voting Rights Act, it found that revisions that changed or limited the powers or duties of office did not violate the section 5 provision.

And in *Shaw* v. *Reno*, we know that we discovered that section 5 was not a shield from claims by majority group members that precleared redistricting had violated the rights of the majority by racial gerrymandering.

These holdings have sparked the debate on the continuing effectiveness of the Voting Rights Act and, for a considerable period, critics as diverse as Abigail Thernstrom from Boston College and Pennsylvania's Lani Guinier had questioned the theoretical assumption and practical consequences of the Voting Rights Act. But these cases have transformed that discussion from an academic one to one of front page importance and one at the center stage of the political process. One cannot overestimate the significance of this enterprise in reviewing the Voting Rights Act.

The Voting Rights Act lies at the heart of an historic effort to achieve interracial democracy. And if its prescriptions are either flawed or hampered in their operation, a shadow is cast on the prospects of building a colorblind society.

The section 5 preclearance procedures are expansive. They regulate all rules governing voting. They include both qualifications or prerequisites for voting and any standard practice or procedure with respect to voting. However small, if a change procedural or substantive effected voting it will be covered by the act. And the court has decided over a long series of cases to read these provisions expansively and to cover a wide range of procedures.

But the *Presley* case presented what the Court majority felt was something different. In these two Alabama counties, the county commissioners are responsible for repair and maintenance of the roads. And what had occurred was that, as a result of earlier Federal litigation, in two separate cases, requirements were made to expand the size of these commissions and to provide for election of new members. And in both cases, in both of these counties, reforms were made in the organization and operation of these county road commissions.

In one case, four of the holdover commissioners voted to maintain their present control over expenditures in their assigned districts while assigning to the newly elected members, which included a minority member, the duties of being responsible for the maintenance of the courthouse and the supervision of county's garbage house.

And they voted to change the character of the office greatly, and they voted that expenditures would be no longer regulated by the commissioners in the districts but they would be regulated by a vote of the commission majority. This resulted in a claim backed by the Justice Department that this amounted to diluting the vote of the minority voters because if they could acquire office, it wasn't as powerful, it wasn't as useful to them in achieving their objectives as it was prior to the change.

But the Supreme Court refused to recognize a claim on this basis under section 5, making the claim that it couldn't determine how to, on a principled basis, draw a distinction between any change in office or procedure as compared to any other change.

And an example that it gave was, what if this change had been, for example, a change in the tax rate or a change in the amount of budgeting, could that have been said to have diluted the power of representatives?

The court said that it would have, since a well-funded county was more powerful than one, a lower tax base or lower funding rate, it said that what hadn't been presented was any formula that would permit it to distinguish between this case and any other case involving a change in procedure, and that change in powers of office did not constitute a violation of the preclearance procedures.

This case, for many, is deeply troubling. It is deeply troubling because, after years of struggle and much litigation, people acquire an office, only to discover that the powers and consequences of holding that office have been greatly diminished. But also disturbing is the point raised by the court. How is the court to make a principle determination of which characteristics of office holding and procedures cannot be changed without invoking a problem under the Voting Rights Act?

If Congress is concerned with the problem presented by the *Presley* case, then it must address two questions. One is the question of whether or not it is consistent with its goals and objectives to prohibit the activity involved in that case. And the other one is: How can it craft language or a method for achieving that without leaving the Court, without direction as to the extent to which it is free to interpret changes in structures and procedure so that they are clearly under the Voting Rights Act and the Court doesn't end up arbitrating almost every dispute inside of local governments.

I know it may seen extreme to suggest that the court might end up being drawn into a wide range of disputes when the Voting Rights Act principles appear so clear. But one should consider the recent Colorado case of *Evans* v. *Romer,* which applying logic from *Hunter* v. *Erickson* determined that any time any significantly identifiable group of voters were disinfranchised in their ability to have the same impact that they had previously had to process, that there would be a constitutional equal protection violation. Notice that the group doesn't have to be a protected class or a suspect class. It said "any group."

Now this case may prove to be an anomaly; but if you compare it to the trend in cases like *Shaw* v. *Reno,* you see that there is this growing problem between the two sides of this problem. And one is whether or not what we are seeking is equal protection.

In terms of equal procedures just having the same rules apply to everyone or whether we are seeking to achieve something that might be called a historic mission. That is dismantling the old system that existed in much of the South and assign power, a role of power to the white majority.

If this task is merely one of guaranteeing neutral procedures, it may be an easier one. But the complaint that is raised against neutral procedures is that they may be independent if there is, in fact, no historic change from the prior prevailing pattern.

Precisely what the debate is about between critics as diverse as Guinier and Thernstrom is the consequence of taking on that task of trying to remold that historic shape of society. And precisely what the debate is about in *Shaw* v. *Reno,* between the majority and the minority, is whether or not the consequences of permitting race-based remedies are more detrimental in the long run to the process of self-government and to the position of the minority than the occasional consequences of the functioning of the political system which results are adverse consequences.

It is a question which may, to some, appear to be overly theoretical. After all, the suit in *Shaw* v. *Reno* was not brought by minority group members living in the district who sought to—who felt they had been discriminated against because they will be classified on the basis of race. It was brought by majority group members.

And while their formal motivation is that they were concerned about an equal protection violation, perhaps, as in many things political, their motivation was a concern for their influence in the shape of that district. And that is an all together legitimate concern for any voter to be concerned about, their influence inside their district.

But what we are going to have to face is that this question, which occurs in employment discrimination law, occurring in voter law, is a question of values and a question of objectives, whether those objectives are merely to be there formally or whether there is some outcome that is preferred and whether that outcome is to use the power of the Government to help to transfer power to those who have been without it for so long.

Thank you.

[The prepared statement of Mr. Broadus follows:]

Testimony

of

Professor Joseph E. Broadus

George Mason University School of Law

before a

Subcommittee of the Judiciary Committee

of the

United States House of Representatives

Considering Changes to the

Voting Rights Act of 1965

October 14, 1993

Thank you, Mr. Chairman, for the opportunity to appear before
the Subcommittee today. My intent is to provide background and
analysis of two recent and for many greatly troubling U.S. Supreme
Court cases addressing the reach of Section 5 of the Voting Rights
Act of 1965. Section 5 requires either administrative or judicial
preclearance of either substantive or procedural voting requirements
in jurisdictions covered by the provision. The goal of Section 5
is to provide a filter or block to protect minority voting rights
by subjecting proposed changes to impartial review prior to their
implementation. Presley v. Etowah, 112 S.Ct. 820 (1992) addressed
the reach of section 5, in limiting changes in the powers or duties
of an elective office. The more recent Shaw v. Reno, 61 LW 4818 (1993)
determined that Section 5 not only protected minority voters but
permitted members of the racial majority to challenge precleared
redistricting plans on grounds of racial gerrymandering. These
holdings have sparked a debate both over the continued effectiveness
of the Voting Rights Act; and a reinvigorated discussion of the
underlying premises and procedures of the Voting Rights Act.
For a considerable period critics as diverse as Harvard's Abigail
M. Thernstrom; and Pennsylvania's Lani Guinier have questioned
the theoretical assumptions and practical consequences of the
Voting Rights Act. But, these cases have transformed the discussion
from an academic one to front page news and occasion a thoughtful
evaluation of both policy and practice in this sensitive area.

One can not overestimate the significance of this enterprise.
One can not overestimate the significance of this enterprise.
The Voting Rights Act lies at the heart of an historic effort
to achieve interracial democracy and if its prescriptions are

either flawed are hampered in their operation a shadow is cast
on the prospects of building a colorblind society.

The Section 5, preclearance procedures are expansive. They
regulate all rules governing voting. This includes both
"qualification or prerequisite" for voting, and "any standard,
practice or procedure with respect to voting." See: 42 U.S.C.A.
1973c. However small, if a change procedural or substantive
, effected voting it was covered by the Act. The Act effected
a sweeping change in the nature of state federal relations.

IN **South Carolina v. Katzenbach**, 383 U.S. 301 (1968), the Court
acknowledged that the preclearance procedures were extraordinary
but an appropriate Congressional response to the "unremitting
response of some state and local officials to frustrate their
citizens' equal enjoyment of the right to vote."

In **Allen v. State Board of Elections**, the Court rejected
a narrow reading of Section 5 which would have limited cases
to review of rules regulating who may register to vote. Instead,
the Court applied the Section to rules involving qualification
of candidates, and state decisions on which offices should be
elective. The Court reasoned that the aim of the Act was to
target both subtle and obvious attempts to deny citizens their
right to vote.

The sweep of Section 5 was found to include the procedures
for write in voting; the change from single member to at large
voting; the change from elective to appointed office; rules
requiring officers to take unpaid leave while campaigning; and
changes in the number of office holders.

Under Section 5 procedures 1964 was a benchmark year. Proposed
changes would be compared with procedures in the year prior to
the enactment of the Voter Rights Act to determine if the shift
resulted in a discriminatory effect.

Presley concerned proposed changes in the duties of county
commissioners in two Alabama Counties. County Commissioner in
Alabama have principle duties related to roads. They supervise
and control road maintenance, repair, and construction.

In the baseline year of 1964, Etowah county had five
commissioners. Four were residency commissioners, and the
Fifth was the chairman. Each of the four residency commisioners
while elected at large represented a district and had control
of expenditures in his districts. The chairman was concerned
with budget and central management. Following federal litigation
in Dillard v. Crenshaw, under the terms of a consent decree the
commission was to be expanded to six members with each member
representing a district. But, the newly constituted commission
quickly voted 4-2, with the holder overs in the majority to
internally reorganize themselves. For purposes of administrative
the four prior elective districts would remain administrative
areas supervised by the commissioner who had represented them
in the past. The new commissioners would assume duties related
to the courthouse, and supervising the county engineer.

By a second vote, again 4-2, the commission voted to
end tradition and submit control of expenditures to majority
rule.

A similar development was taking place in Russell County. In the baseline year the county had 3 elected commissioners. Again following litigation the commission was expanded first to 5 members than to 7 members elected in districts. Again the three rural commissioner continued direct control of road expenditures in their districts. This practice was changed to give project and expenditure control to the county engineer in 1979 following a scandal involving one of the rural commissioners.

The two disputes were heard by a three judge panel which refused to find a Voting Rights violation. It rejected the governments claim that changes in duties were in effect a change in the power of voters to elect officials requiring preclearance. The panel applied a two part test. Did the change effect 1/ a significant change in the power exercised by government officials 2/ elected by, or responsible to, substantially different constitutencies of voters.

The Supreme Court affirmed the holding but adopted new logic. The Court held that to accept the governments position was to work an "unconstrained expansion of Section 5 coverage. The court reasoned that almost every time a local or state government changes an internal procedure it would implicate the Voting Rights Act. The federal court would be called upon in endless cases over matters far removed from the concerns of Congress in enacting the Voting Rights Act.

An example of how expansive that logic could become was demostrated by the Colorado Supreme Court in Evans v. Romer, where the state supreme court struck down a popularly

enacted state Constitutional amendment with reliance on the
U.S. Supreme Court holding in **Hunter v. Erickson**. In **Evans**, the
the court held that the constitutional right to vote was violated
anytime an identifiable group whether suspect class or not was
adversely effected by a change in governmental structure or
procedure.

While **Evans**, and **Erickson** are constitutional law rather
than statutory voter rights cases the definition of voting
within the meaning of the act, and for the purposes of equal
protection analysis should be assumed to permit evaluation.

The sweep of **Romer** is disturbing and a vindication of the
Courts expressed concern in **Presley** that to equate the powers
or procedures of office with voting was to invite general
judicial supervision of almost every aspect of government.

Presley remains disturbing. For the minority citizens of
the Alabama jurisdictions years of effort and struggle have
resulted in an empty victory, They have office but not the
power traditionally associated with it. They have single member
district but not the traditional capacity to represent. The
power is still at large.

But, the Court has properly identified a problem of
equal seriousness. How can the goals of the Act be achieved
without vesting the courts with what amounts to an unrestricted
license to intrude in ever aspect of government. In the long
run it will matter little if free self government for the
minority is lost to its traditional opponents or elites on
the bench.

The task than for Congress if it seeks to reverse **Presley**
is not merely to vindicate the expectations of the people of
Russell and Etovah counties and others covered by the act but
to take up the Courts challenge and provide a review standard
that appropriately limits judicial involvement. What is needed
is language which focuses like a laser beam on the problem that
was targeted by the Voting Rights Act the problem of expanding
free government and participation to the excluded. At the same
time Congress must be aware that involvement will mean little
if the governmental processes are broadly and generally submitted
to constant judicial supervision.

The sad part is that this problem need not be before the
Court at all. If only those elected to public office would
understand the meaning of fair play, and the golden rule.
If only they would treat others as they would wish to be
treated if they were the minority. But, Jefferson sumed it
up best: Power seldom dies and never resigns. We can expect
this struggle to continue. Congress will legislative and local
governments will evade. All will spend years in litigation.
And much ink will be spilled over the meaning of various
technical requirements to the Voting Rights Act.

The Courts concern in **Presley** is sincere and it is vital.
No doubt local officials hope that their tactics will wear
down the opposition. This is not likely. The best they can
hope for is to win the day. But, that will not be enough.
For they may win a battle only to forfeit a war. In the long
run the response of Congress and the Courts may be to craft
increasingly intrusive provisions.

And they will be resisted. The pattern of the 19th Century repeats itself in the 20th. The liberal inclusionist ethic of the North battles the provincialism of the South. Where once the issue was salvery the issue now is full and meaningful participation. While less immediately dramatic the long term consequences for self government may be as significant.

Just as a century ago the refusal to accept the norm about slavery led to war physical invasion, the 20th century refusal to accept the norm about full participation may led greater national legislative and judicial invasion. In the end leaders of the South were ironically willing to free and arm slaves to save their independence. But, it was too late. Perhaps, that will be our story to that too late the old guard will recognize the true cost of its ambitions.

Lastly, the matter of **Shaw v. Reno**, a case both larger and smaller than its apparent dimensions. The odd shaped district case. It is the **Bakke** and **Webber** of voting rights. The case the disrupts established expectations by extending the remedial legislation to the white majority as well as the historic minority groups. Each of these cases has occassioned shock and forced a re-evaluation of prevailing assumptions. Each has in the long run has less impact then then predicted for the worst case; and more impact than the best.

In the long run the same will be true of **Shaw**. Both because of congress's continuing supervision in this area and the court's utimate reluctance to overturn social progress.

Mr. EDWARDS. Well, we thank all of the witnesses. I am going to make a couple of observations and then yield, under the 5-minute rule, to Mr. Nadler, and also, Mr. Watt. Mr. Watt, we hope that you will participate in the questions.

This is a very perplexing problem for this subcommittee. It is especially since the *Shaw* decision was based on constitutional grounds and not on just a violation of the Voting Rights Act. We have been remarkably successful since 1965 by changing the structure, preventing gerrymandering, preventing all of the devices, especially in some States, of mechanically drawing districts, having single-party districts, and making it very difficult, especially for black Americans, to register to vote.

In Mr. Hyde's and my travels, we would go to jurisdictions where the registration office would be open Saturdays from 12 to 1; and if it was 1 o'clock, it would close. And certain lower income people would have to travel 100 miles to get there and find it closed and have to wait until the next week. Little devices like that were prevalent in 1981 and 1980, and we think that the 1982 amendments made quite a lot of difference.

I don't think that we should pull our punches about what has happened in the last few years. In many regards, the Supreme Court has been very hostile to the Voting Rights Act. *Presley* is an example of it where we feel that they went out of the way to say that this is not a voting rights issue. When a black person gets elected and goes to exercise the powers of his office and the majority whites take away his responsibilities, if that is not a voting rights violation, it is sure something.

And a year ago we crafted a reversal of that Supreme Court decision and reported it favorably from this subcommittee and unfortunately a lot of opposition developed and we have never been able to take it to the full House of Representatives.

This issue, *Shaw* v. *Reno,* is a tough one. We all thank you for delving into it. It is probably the most important and trickiest voting rights problem that we have faced since 1965. And we are going to have to examine it in great depth.

The gentleman from New York, Mr. Nadler, do have you any questions?

Mr. NADLER. Yes. Thank you.

I am not sure where to start or who to address the question to. Obviously the *Presley* decision, in my point of view, was an obnoxious decision in sabotaging the Voting Rights Act and sabotaging voters' rights. The *Shaw* decision is a much more difficult question for me.

Professor Norrell, let me ask you a number of questions.

What should the standard be in targeting racial districting? In a case argued recently before the Supreme Court, there was a situation in which I think it was a Hispanic district in the city of Miami or the county of Dade, I forget which, in which the population was about 50 percent; they created about 50 percent, exactly half, districts; and someone brings suit on the ground that if they had made more egregiously gerrymandered lines, they could have gotten an extra Hispanic district and they could have maximized it and made it more than 50 percent.

What is the proper standard to aim for in racially conscious districting?

Mr. NORRELL. Well, I think it is a standard that doesn't diverge far from what is the percentage of the groups's representation in that population.

Proportional representation, of course, is roundly denounced in this country. But for a democratic government to be legitimate in the eyes of people who identify themselves as a group from their historical experience, I think those people expect and, in my view fairly expect, to have about that kind of representation in democratic bodies.

And I think that it is less important to be precise than to establish a pattern of overall fairness in the minds of the people at large.

Mr. NADLER. By overall fairness, you mean overall proportionality?

Mr. NORRELL. Yes. That this history that we have of white majorities denying black minorities and, I suppose, Hispanic minorities, any representation is a tremendous burden to overcome; and it will only be overcome by careful attention.

Mr. NADLER. Do you think that, as a matter of law, the Voting Rights Act or the Constitution—two questions: Do you think, as a matter of law, the Voting Rights Act or the Constitution requires proportional representation? And, number two, if it doesn't, do you think it ought to?

Mr. NORRELL. No, on the first account. And I don't think it has to. But I am not against it. In very limited circumstances for peoples who have this long history of discrimination against them.

Mr. NADLER. One further question. We had a situation in a New York election last year that raised a lot of disturbing questions, and I would like you and maybe some others to comment on it.

The State legislature created a congressional districting process under a lot of pressure from both Federal and State courts. And different plans were proposed by Federal and State courts in the rest of the court house.

One district was sort of like the 12th District of North Carolina, extended through three different boroughs, went down highways and so forth and was a Hispanic majority district.

An incumbent Member of Congress ran in that district and eventually lost to a Hispanic candidate. The incumbent was told in no uncertain terms that he had no right to run, and that the people in the district were being told by the media that they ought not to vote for that person simply because he was the wrong race.

Now, how would you assess this kind of result of that kind of districting in terms of racial relations, in terms of promoting integration?

And how do you prevent it, or should you prevent it?

Mr. NORRELL. As I said in my statement, I think we are a society that is racially alienated. If Mr. Solarz, is that who we are talking about? He is an experienced politician, public servant, and he has every right to run in the district in which he lives and overcome whatever demographic obstacles might be presented.

I don't know the circumstances in New York, but I think it is unfair of the media or whomever it was that said that to him, that he couldn't seek that. That doesn't seem in the spirit of an open society to me.

Mr. NADLER. Anyone else want to comment on the general question?

Mr. SPAULDING. I would say that I agree with the answer presented. Certainly in this democracy, anyone can run for office if they are qualified to do so based on the laws of this country.

And, you know, you have, within these so-called black districts, but they are majority-minority districts, blacks who want to run. And maybe people like that particular person shouldn't run.

Mr. NADLER. Yes. Thank you.

Mr. SPAULDING. However, I think that is just a matter of politics of people who want someone to run and someone not to run. But as far as what democracy is all about, obviously anyone who wants to run can run.

Mr. NADLER. One further question on that if I may, of you, sir. Do you think that race-conscious gerrymandering, Mr. Geis talked about and Mr. Norrell both talked about the South. And I don't know if Mr. Norrell was limiting his comments to the South, but Mr. Geis gave an optimistic presentation of what was happening in one of the Carolinas, North Carolina electing black officeholders in white majority areas statewide. And he seems to believe that that is a natural progression which racially conscious districting has a potential to stop, if I gathered the import of what you are saying sir?

Mr. GEIS. Yes, sir.

Mr. NADLER. Would you comment on the validity of what he was saying, first of all? And second, if we continue down the path and have more race-conscious districting and districts become known as white districts or black districts or Hispanic districts—and I have seen the redistricting reports from New York that went into detail about how this district has this percentage of a racial group and the likelihood of electing them—if districts are done that way, what happens to the rights of the minority group within that district, the black and the Hispanic district, the Hispanic in the black district and so forth?

Mr. SPAULDING. First, let me say that I don't agree with all of the presentation that was presented by Mr. Geis.

In regard to progress in the legislature, I was there in the previous redistricting. When I went to the North Carolina House of Representatives, out of the 120 members of the State house there were 3 blacks. Out of 50 members of the State senate, there was 1 black. So there were four of us. We really didn't need to have a caucus.

Mr. NADLER. Have a lunch.

Mr. SPAULDING. Then what we did in the redistricting, we did look at race-conscious remedies to try to reverse what had occurred. And we were able to increase those numbers to approximately 12 in the house and 2 or so in the senate; still, not necessarily proportionate representation.

As to whether that is a goal or not, that is debatable by the scholars and others. But that increase was based on the fact of Voting Rights Act execution.

In regard to Harvey Gantt, very candidly with you, in North Carolina, we have a whole slew of races in which we are able to say, well, someone almost won who was black. And you know what we are striving for is a situation where we don't have to come before this committee or anywhere else and talk about, well, he did so well, he got 48 percent or 47 percent of the vote. That is fine.

But we have a slew of those candidates who are very well qualified and very good candidates, but they almost won.

In regard to Dan Blue, Dan Blue was elected from his legislative district; and he is the speaker of the house. He was not elected in a statewide electoral election. He was elected on the basis of campaigning within the general assembly, among the political figures there, officeholders. So that was not a statewide—even though it has statewide implications, it was not a statewide race.

I think the quote was made only two decades away from segregation was made as to the progress. I was a product of segregation and a product of integration. And I will tell you, as far as from a black or African-American perspective or whatever they call us now, the situation was such that I would certainly—and I feel many others would like to see a lot more progress as far as not only race relations but racial progress in electoral politics. So to tell us how well we have done in the decades since segregation, I really don't think, if you would ask most African-Americans, they would feel there has not been much progress in regard to that particular issue. There has been progress in a lot of other ways.

Mr. EDWARDS. There is a vote in the Chamber of the House. We are going to have to recess for a short time. And we will reconvene immediately after the vote, at which time, Mr. Hyde——

Mr. HYDE. No. I have to go to a luncheon, so I won't be back. And I regret it because I had a lot of questions to ask. But we have discrimination here too. It isn't racial. It is if you are a Democrat and you are the last one to come to the meeting; if you go first and you take all the time. So we all have our problems. Thank you.

[Recess.]

Mr. EDWARDS. The subcommittee will come to order.

The gentleman from Florida, Mr. Canady, is recognized.

Mr. CANADY. Thank you, Mr. Chairman.

I would like to start by addressing a question to Professor Kennedy. I just wanted to ask you how you deal with the concern raised by Mr. Geis in his testimony that racially gerrymandered districts will result in insulating white office holders from any influence from members of minority communities. I think that is a concern that has a lot of merit.

And I can see, just as a matter of practical politics, that that is how things might work out. And I look at the Florida delegation, for instance, the number of minority members we have in Florida, and the fact that much of the minority population of the State is crammed into those minority districts. That is going to have an impact, I would think, on the way the white officials and surrounding areas view their responsibilities.

That doesn't effect me, because my district has a significant minority population in it. But I think it does affect a good part of the State. And I think over the long term, the consequences of that could be bad for the minority populations.

What do you say about that, Mr. Kennedy?

Mr. KENNEDY. I think that it is a very real concern. And that, under certain circumstances, it might be such a concern that it would be counterproductive for minority communities.

I mean, what you are talking about is a practice of packing. And, indeed, already under the law, if it can be clearly shown that minority constituents are being packed together in order to essentially diminish their power, that is already against the law.

It gets to be a tough political guess, however, what actually benefits minority communities. Is it more of a benefit to have minority communities sort of with minority influence spread out? Or is it better to have minority political power concentrated into—for the sake of creating so-called safe seats? That is a very difficult political calculation.

The one thing I would say to you, it may very well be like you suggest, that under certain circumstances, isolation will be created essentially by taking pressure off of white representatives to look after the interests of their minority black constituents.

One question that one always has to ask, though, is: Compared to what? It is well enough to theorize and say that over the long run some of the reforms that have been created might, in some circumstances, be counterproductive. But the fact of the matter is, as I indicated, 13 of the 16 blacks elected to the U.S. Congress in 1992 came from purposefully created minority districts.

What does that mean? That means integration. That means black people having some say so. By the way, a say so to elect whom they want. Earlier this morning people kept talking about, does this mean that blacks only have to represent blacks? I don't know very many people who are in favor of the various sorts of reforms that make the claim that blacks can only represent blacks or only Hispanics can represent Hispanics. What I understand the claim to be is that we have to create voting schemes which allow minority communities effective political expression.

And sometimes that may come across best through the creation of minority-majority districts. There may be other forms in which that can best be expressed. What I am concerned about is a straitjacket being imposed so that reforms that allow minority communities to express themselves are stifled.

Mr. CANADY. OK. Thank you.

Let me turn to Professor Norrell. There were some comments in your testimony I wanted to refer to, if you will bear with me for a moment here.

In your written testimony—I think you said this in your spoken statement also—you state the recent history of this South revealed that blacks and most whites understand the need to have racial representatives in politics because we assume the legitimacy of a racial point of view.

Then you go on to distinguish that southern perspective from the rest of the country, which tends to reject racial thinking on an ideological basis.

In connection with that statement, I want to follow up on a question that Congressman Nadler asked. And I don't think it was directly responded to and as we were leaving in the confusion of going to the vote, I am not sure it was responded to.

And that is, what about the individuals in minority districts who are of a race other than that particular minority? What does this type of scheme do for them? What do you say to them, particularly in light of your comment?

Mr. NORRELL. I say to them, historically, that black people have not, for centuries, had representatives who were of their racial group to speak for them directly in governmental bodies. And it is only fair that African-Americans or Hispanic-Americans have a turn to represent themselves in those governmental bodies.

I would simply——

Mr. CANADY. Let me ask you this: In connection with that, do you think it would be fair to actually reject the principle that would prohibit packing so, as I understand the way this works now, you are supposed to put as many members of a particular minority group in a district as are necessary to ensure the election of someone from that minority but no more.

If you go beyond what is necessary to ensure the election of a person from that minority, you are engaged in packing the district and that is viewed as diluting the voting power of the minority.

But in light of your comment, would you suggest that we move to a system where we do just put people in districts where they are going to be with people of the same race, since you recognize the legitimacy of a racial point of view?

Mr. NORRELL. Well, it is very difficult to imagine that, given our particular forms of republican governance that you could do that. If we were willing to change the whole thing and go to some kind of proportional representation, that would be possible. But I don't think we are willing to do that.

My remarks really are to suggest that the creation of electoral forms that do put black people into governmental bodies is something that has, after centuries of racial discrimination in the South—and that is mostly what we are talking about—that has been accepted.

And the decision in *Shaw* suggests that it is legitimate for Americans because we have this value of color blind democracy. I am simply saying that the way things have worked out in the last quarter century in the South, that there is generally a consensus, I believe, among blacks and whites that blacks ought to have some representation in governmental bodies and that it doesn't violate the essential principles of most Southerners for that to occur.

Mr. CANADY. Let me go back to Professor Kennedy. In a quotation in your statement from the New Yorker, I believe, you cite an unsigned editorial in the New Yorker caustically noted

That the President's view concerning certain statements of Professor Guinier will come as news to the good people of Germany, Spain, the Netherlands, and Sweden * * *. Indeed, most of the electorates of continental Europe including those of the liberated East, elect their legislatures under some form of proportional representation.

Do you know if any of those systems in Europe have proportional representation based on race?

Mr. KENNEDY. I don't.

Mr. CANADY. Are you aware of any system anywhere else in the world that has a proposal system based on race? I don't know the answer.

Mr. KENNEDY. The answer to that is, yes. The answer to that is that there are many plural societies that are deeply divided along lines of ethnicity and along lines of race which have created models of consensual democracy with a political system that gives voice to groups and in there has to be some degree of consensus attained before policy matters are allowed to proceed to a final determination.

Mr. CANADY. Could you give some examples of some of those nations where that is occurring? Democracies where that occurs?

Mr. KENNEDY. No, I can't. I can cite the scholar that would be able to help you out with that, Aaron Lipschark, and actually the person who can be very helpful would be Lani Guinier.

Mr. CANADY. I understand from the chairman that we may have the opportunity to ask her directly.

Mr. KENNEDY. She would be a person who would be far more informed than I on this.

Mr. EDWARDS. Mr. Coble.

Mr. COBLE. Thank you, Mr. Chairman.

Mr. Chairman, I want to thank the panel. And I especially want to extend a cordial welcome to my two fellow Tarheels, Ken Spaulding to the east of my district, and Christopher Geis to the west.

And, Mr. Geis, I have constituents who read your journal. Although you are not in my district, and I might say that the journal is well represented on Capitol Hill. I don't see your correspondent in the room, but if he is not here, he is scurrying around somewhere in the shadows.

Folks in this body, we always hear about problems plaguing us. Oh, we have got to have the war on drugs—which of course is important—the war on poverty; got to enhance the quality of education; we depend on our children. Rarely do I hear race relations mentioned. And, folks, I am getting doggone tired of seeing blacks beating up on whites and whites beating up on blacks inflicting pain and permanent injury, killing one another.

I think this business of race relations, Mr. Chairman, has the potential of destroying us as a nation, polarizing it. And I am sure there are blacks and whites alike who thrive upon it. Oh, they love to fan the fires of discontent.

And if we can do anything to assuage this problem, Mr. Chairman, through the Voting Rights Act, I am the first guy to sign up.

I will never forget, Mr. Chairman, in 1986, the day after the election, a black man rushed up to me on the streets of Greensboro, he said, "Mr. Coble, I voted for you yesterday." And I said I was surprised because most of the black voters in my district traditionally vote Democrat. And I said, "I thank you for that." And he then went on to say, he said, "I was told I had better not vote for a Republican Congressman. He said, folks don't tell me how to vote in 1986." I will never forget it.

I regret that I didn't ask him if he would have voted for me, if he hadn't been told he couldn't. I don't know how he would have answered that. This man was fiercely independent, and he wasn't going to be told how to vote.

Now if we can use this forum on the Voting Rights Act to improve our situation, I want to be the first to do it.

Ken, in your statement, I interpreted to mean—and if I am mis-interpreting it, tell me—that it is your belief some white voters, maybe many white voters, either consciously or unconsciously op-pose African-American candidates for elective offices based upon racial fears or animosities.

Do you think also that that same theory would apply to African-American voters?

Mr. SPAULDING. Howard, you didn't necessarily misquote me, but you did. We served in the legislature together and we're Howard and Ken. But Mr. Congressman, let me say this——

Mr. COBLE. Still is.

Mr. SPAULDING [continuing]. I don't feel that blacks, African-Americans—in any way—say again what you thought.

Mr. COBLE. Well, as I read your statement, it appeared—and I am not saying this critically—that it was your belief and maybe your fear that many white voters either consciously or subcon-sciously oppose African-American candidates for elective offices based upon an inherent racial fear or a racial animosity?

Mr. SPAULDING. That is the word I was trying to get, animosity, that you had indicated. I don't think—well, some people would dis-agree. I am not really talking about animosity, meaning down right hatred. Hatred.

There is a way of life that has been erected in the South that got us where we are today and why we are trying to correct it. And that way of life has always generally been both the economic, polit-ical, and social structure based in such a way that nonwhites were in a subordinate position and whites were in a superior position as far as the way the system was executed.

Now, what has—what I feel in this situation is that whites don't necessarily, as I said, hate blacks. But they have a problem in put-ting them in positions that they might feel that are superior to what they are in their own station of life. So you are dealing with psychological and emotional as well as racial responses. And, see, that is what I think too often we try to look at, the race relations problem and the problems that we have just on a very superficial approach. And that is black animosity, white animosity.

The second part of your question is that obviously blacks don't feel that way in that we have a history of primarily voting for white candidates. Because we haven't been given as many opportu-nities to vote for African-Americans or blacks as we have for white candidates. And so, we are obviously well-accustomed to supporting and voting for white candidates.

But I think the Voting Rights Act is helping to help whites to have that opportunity of being able to see that once blacks are elected and are officeholders that they can support them, that they do see that we, in fact, represent their interests as well as are sen-sitive toward minority interests.

And I think that you are well aware, in the legislature when we served together, my legislation dealt with issues that were sen-sitive to the black community, and you know how I addressed it on the redistricting. But at the same time, I recognized responsibility to each and every voter of my district, and I worked just as hard to represent white constituents.

And that is another thing, a mindset that I think we need to really address. And that is black officeholders can represent white constituents.

To answer your question that you had asked earlier, you know, if it is 60 percent black and 40 percent white, if a black is elected, he or she can, in fact, represent that 40 percent white, and that 40 percent white population and constituents do know how to influence those particular elected officials. Common sense tells you, from the pragmatic point of view, when you are running for office, you want to win.

If you are a black candidate and nothing but black candidates are running, a smart black candidate is going to run and try to get as much of a black vote that he can get and then use the same amount of time to try to get that white vote, that 40 percent of that vote that is there; and he is going to try to get that to get elected.

I think that is what Mel Watt did in his district. And I think the numbers would show that. Let's don't feel, oh, we have this black district, which is really an integrated district, and we have got a black representative. Oh, what is going to happen to the white constituents. Because what is going to happen is the same thing that is going to happen in any democratic society. The person that is holding that office is going to want to stay in that office, and he is going to represent a majority of that.

And all blacks do not think alike. We are not all monolithic, and we have various views on the whole gamut of issues in American life, and especially in the Federal congressional situation.

So I hope that answers——

You know how lawyers talk a lot.

Mr. COBLE. Thank you, Ken.

Mr. Geis, let me shift to you a minute and direct attention to Mr. Watt's district. I told Mel Watt the other day, I told him, you probably represent the best known geographic district in the country. Everybody talked about the infamous geographic district in North Carolina that extends what, 150 miles, meandering down through my district.

A fellow came up to me in church and said, I mowed my lawn yesterday and cut grass in my district and in Mel Watt's district. This was about a month ago.

As we know, the case is back in the courts, has been remanded as a result of the 5 to 4 decision. And I am just thinking aloud now. I guess that could go one of at least three ways: the Court may well redraw the district lines on its own motion; it could direct our general assembly on going back to the drawing boards and draw lines again that would be more acceptable to the Supreme Court; or, in the third alternative, it could do nothing and leave the lines intact.

I am going to ask you to break out your magic wand, Mr. Geis. What would be your recommendation, if you could convey it to the general assembly, in the event that the court does assign that duty to our general assembly with instructions to redraw the congressional boundaries? What would be your instructions, if you have any?

Mr. GEIS. Could you put me on the spot any more, Congressman?

Mr. COBLE. I realize that is hypothetical and difficult to answer; but if you have an idea, I will accept that.

Mr. GEIS. I am not a lawyer. I think Mr. Watt's district is an interesting district. I think he represents his people very well. I think the majority of the views of the whites and black citizens are being represented by his being in Congress.

So from that sense, I don't think the district is bad. But what I am concerned about is future districting.

Ken and I were out in the hallway talking to a reporter earlier, and I wanted to correct an impression that I was against what has happened with the Voting Rights Act. One of the first sentences I uttered was that I thought it was one of the most moral pieces of legislation that we have seen. I am not against what has happened. I am against what could happen.

With regard to the 12th and 1st Districts, which is also majority black, the State has a good rationale for wanting to protect its incumbents and also has a rationale for having a single urban district. It is the first time that we have ever had a single urban district in Congress.

So those things are in support of the 1st and 12th Districts. But my hope is that, in 10 years, when we redraw the district lines, Mel Watt has done such a great job of representing his white constituents, could he win in what would be the old Ninth District, the Charlotte district. And we don't have to divvy these up so that each race gets its district, and we will have an improved racial situation.

I think a lot of it also goes back to how politics have to be conducted in a manner that doesn't appeal to our worst instincts on racial issues. I have been concerned about some candidacies that have appealed to the worst instincts of people's racial fears. It is troubling to me. And I think both parties need to reach out to the black vote.

As Ken said, the black vote is not all monolithic. I think a lot of black voters are very conservative.

Mr. EDWARDS. The time of the gentleman has expired.

Mr. COBLE. Thank you.

Mr. EDWARDS. Mr. Watt.

Mr. WATT. Thank you, Mr. Chairman, particularly for allowing me to come and participate in this hearing, since I am not a member of this subcommittee.

Mr. EDWARDS. Mr. Watt is a very distinguished member of the full Judiciary Committee. However, we welcome him.

Mr. WATT. I thank you for your comments and welcome the opportunity to participate in this matter that I obviously have a great deal of interest in.

I came without any intention of asking questions but to serve two purposes. The first of those purposes I can only approach by going back to the day following my election to this office and recalling a question that I was asked by a news reporter who was attempting to get to the historical significance of my election as the first minority Member, or one of the first minority Members of Congress, from North Carolina, in more than 90 years.

And the question the reporter asked was: What was the first thing you thought about after you knew that this victory was assured? And he thought I was going to couch it in some historical terms. And I told him that my honest reaction was a feeling of sorrow, and that feeling of sorrow had to do with the hundreds and possibly thousands of people, black people, who would have been as qualified to fill this position as I, and could have been elected to this congressional office and would have ably served in Congress but for the fact that their skins happened to be black.

And so the first reason that I came over was to say that, because Ken Spaulding is one of those people who, but for the fact that he was black, would have been elected to Congress in my opinion. He has all of the credentials and qualifications, and I think he has demonstrated that in his testimony this morning. So, I want to thank him for coming and participating and, more importantly, for paving the way for me to be sitting here in this seat on this side of the microphone and asking questions, rather than possibly responding from the other side.

The second reason, in all honesty, that I came was that I had read Mr. Geis' prepared statement. I got a copy of it yesterday. And I thought I needed to be here to quite possibly explode some of the myths that were implicit in Mr. Geis' testimony. I am not sure I even need to do that any more, because Ken Spaulding has pretty well exploded all of the myths that were implicit in his statement. He certainly has exploded the myth that I represent a black district. The truth of the matter is that my congressional district is the most integrated congressional district North Carolina has ever had.

He exploded the myth that somehow or another we should be, consider ourselves fortunate when we come close to winning an election. We used to say in our community that the only things where close counts is horseshoes and adolescent sex. And it certainly doesn't count in politics.

I take no redemption in having managed Harvey Gantt's almost successful campaign for the U.S. Senate against Jesse Helms.

There is one myth that I am not sure anybody other than myself could explode and requires some degree of speculation. Maybe it has two parts to this myth. One thing that Mr. Geis said is that Harvey Gantt had carried a majority of votes in Charlotte. I will tell you, and not many people know this because we never really make a big issue of it, in the second election that Harvey Gantt was mayor of Charlotte, when he was riding the crest of all of the national and local support, when everybody nationally and locally agreed that Harvey Gantt was one of the best mayors in the United States, Harvey Gantt did not get 50 percent of the white vote in Charlotte. And Charlotte is the liberal portion of the whole Ninth Congressional District.

So if anybody is sitting here under the illusion that Harvey Gantt got more than 50 percent of the white vote in any of his mayor's races or in his race for the Senate in the Ninth Congressional District, I think they are just wrong.

And so I certainly want to correct that myth that Mr. Geis has and is spreading around here.

The second part is speculation, he seems to have this notion that I could have won had I run in the old Ninth Congressional District. We obviously won't ever know that for fact. But I had the history of strong racially polarized voting. And in response to Howard's question, both black and white racially polarized voting, I might add, that suggested to me that if Harvey Gantt couldn't get 50 percent of the white vote, there was no way in hell I was going to get 50 percent of the white vote. And while we will never know, because I will never have the opportunity to run in the old Ninth Congressional District, I would simply say to you that I don't believe I could have won in the old Ninth Congressional District, regardless of the qualifications, and we don't even need to talk about the relative qualifications of the candidates.

There is one thing, though, that I want to conclude by saying that I didn't come intending to say, which is in support of what Mr. Geis is saying and in support of what Justice O'Connor has said, and that is that we all do strive for a time that we don't have to take race into account. I don't think there is any black or white person that could honestly say as an American first that we don't aspire to that high goal.

My response, though, is that in the interim, until we get to that point, minority people, Hispanics, blacks, deserve to have representation in every process. And if at some point we can reach the goal where it is not necessary to draw minority districts or take race into an account to assure that people have representation in the process, then I think I will be the first to join Mr. Geis' theory. I don't think that is going to happen by the year 2000 when we do the next census. I would have to differ with them on that.

But I certainly believe—no, I won't say that. I certainly hope that it happens sometime during the lifetime of my children.

Thank you, Mr. Chairman, again, for the opportunity.

Mr. EDWARDS. Thank you for the observations, Mr. Watt. I think they are very salient. And I think all the witnesses ought to comment on Mr. Watt's observations.

You know, I found in my experience when somebody starts to talk about a colorblind election, I know they are not somebody that I would agree with. You have a totally colorblind election system in this country, and hopefully some day we can, but you can't now. You certainly can't in California. And the legislature doesn't even try.

That is one of the reasons that we have a very well-balanced delegation here in Congress from California, there are members of every large minority group in California, except I don't think we have a Filipino. I think it works very well.

But my personal concern is with this *Shaw* decision. What is the Supreme Court up to? What are the majority, the five Justices, up to?

I have learned the hard way to distrust them. I have not found them friendly, the majority, for 7 or 8 years. I find them unfriendly to the Voting Rights Act and to Federal employment laws, generally.

We had to reverse four or five employment decisions in 1991. And we have got some targets out there that we should look at, this Richmond case about set-asides. That stops minority contractors in their tracks all over the country. And maybe there is a formula which will allow them to participate in contracting and municipal construction and so forth, which I think is a very healthy thing.

But, in the voting context, you run into the word "gerrymandering," "racial gerrymandering." I know that when we wrote the original Voting Rights Act, the big argument for days—it took days to write the bill—was whether or not to include the requirement that districts be compact.

And we decided, no, they are not going to be compact, that would not be one of the qualifications. And certainly Mr. Watt's district is not compact.

Let me tell you, a lot of districts in California are just about as strange looking as Mr. Watt's. But it has never come before the court, right out of the blue, that the equal protection clause of the Constitution could be violated with these strange looking districts because white people were being discriminated against, were being cut out of the process.

Well, we never thought of that. The court never said that about some of the districts where whites were carefully protected by the legislatures. That went on in this country, especially in North Carolina and other Southern States, for a hundred years.

So would anybody like to make an observation on what Mr. Watt and I have been talking about?

Mr. COBLE. Mr. Chairman, can I make a brief statement if I may?

Mr. EDWARDS. Yes.

Mr. COBLE. Mr. Geis, I don't want to put you on the spot twice; but I would like you, Mr. Chairman, if you wanted to, to maybe respond.

Mel, Congressman Watt referred to your myths. Would you like to be heard in response?

Mr. GEIS. I respect what Congressman Watt said. I worked to get him elected last year. Reporters don't print that because I work for a newspaper now. And I respect what Mr. Spaulding says, and their viewpoints are very good.

One thing that I would like to clarify is that even white Democrats who are elected in North Carolina don't get 50 percent of the white vote. Governor Hunt last year was elected with 45 percent, maybe less of the vote. However, politics are simply too racially polarized.

Mr. SPAULDING. Mr. Chairman, in regard to the Supreme Court, I am not coming necessarily as a scholar, but, really, as a pragmatist.

When you look at the Supreme Court, to me, it is not reflective of the diversity of backgrounds within this country in and of itself, much less the political or so-called legal theories or philosophies.

And what I tried to impart in my statement was that just because they put on those black robes and they sit on the bench does not mean that they can totally get rid of any subconscious emotional response when it comes to race.

And that is why I spend an inordinate amount of time trying to point out how they addressed the 1st and 12th Districts in *Shaw* v. *Reno*—as if these are black districts. And that is why I also discussed the studies about neighborhoods going black, turning black, when you get 25 percent or better, people moving in.

Mr. WATT. Sometimes, when you get one person moving in.

Mr. SPAULDING. It is a subconscious type of process that goes on. And I think that it must be actually out front on the agenda—and I think this has now occurred in *Shaw* v. *Reno*—before they will even be able to really think within the most inner-portions or recesses of their mind, to have their own introspections, to see if their own race consciousness very well could be a factor in their decisionmaking process.

Mr. EDWARDS. Well, they are establishing some law by this decision, which generally means that, in every judicial district in the United States, the Federal district judges will comply with the ruling in *Shaw*.

Now, does that concern you?

Does that concern you, Professor Kennedy?

Mr. KENNEDY. It certainly does. As I indicated before, my great fear is that the Supreme Court will put a constitutional straitjacket on the efforts to move our society toward a more just society.

And *Shaw*, of course is a somewhat muddy opinion. It is not all that clear what the Supreme Court meant. We are going to have to wait a while to see—I mean, the law is still in creation.

But there were certain features of the case, particularly this rhetoric about apartheid, for instance, which seemed so inappropriate. After all, apartheid means the exclusion, the total exclusion, the radical exclusion of a people of color from any part of governance. That is what has historically gone on in South Africa.

What happened in North Carolina was the complete opposite, of course. There was an effort to integrate, integrate the congressional delegation. And one of the great ironies of what is going on is that efforts toward integration are being condemned as separatist.

What people have been attempting to do, what people of good will who recognize the history of racial subordination in the United States, people who recognize that history and who want to do something about that history, have been trying to do is address that history through creating mechanisms to bring people of color into all aspects of American life. And the irony is that in the face of those efforts, people are now claiming that that is separatism, that that is apartheid. It is just the opposite.

Having said that, I think it is also important to recognize that the issues we are dealing with are complicated. I mean, there are people of good will who see things in a different way, and for good reason. And one of the reasons it is so complicated has something to do with a point that you made early on, Mr. Chairman, you made at the very beginning of the hearing. You compared the law involving voting with the law involving racial discrimination in another area. And there is one very big difference. With respect to employment law, for instance, the Federal law specifically tells people, you cannot discriminate.

And so the actual individuals, their conduct, is regulated. Well, we don't do that with respect to voting. We allow people to express their preferences based on all sorts of things, based on race, based on who they think looks better, who they think sounds better and all sorts of things, and maybe we could not make an effort.

Maybe it would be impossible to regulate the individual preferences of voters. Well, that makes it very difficult to really create an apparatus that would be racially fair. And so, at the same time I share your feelings about the Supreme Court. I am very distrustful of it. I am very critical of it.

I think its rulings over the past 10 to 15 years have given a lot of nourishment to those who are skeptical of the Supreme Court.

Having said that, I think we do have to recognize that there are real difficulties here and that to some degree, we have reached a place where there are real issues as to how to best advance the interests of minority communities. And those sorts of questions, the real difficulties cannot and should not be obscured.

There is more than just a question of the people of good will versus the people of bad will. The people of good will differ on these issues. And I am so happy that you are having these hearings, because there is going to have to be a lot of discussion and debate in order to thrash out these issues which are very complicated and difficult indeed.

Mr. EDWARDS. Thank you.

Professor Broadus, do you recognize also that there also has been a change in the law and that there might be dozens of congressional districts and other districts going down into the State legislatures and so forth where the same challenge can be made if Justice O'Connor's ruling becomes widespread.

Mr. BROADUS. I think the thing we have to remember is that the question addressed in *Shaw* v. *Reno* is only the jurisdictional question. That is whether or not a claim can be stated on this appearance, on the facial question of what the district looks like.

That doesn't answer the question of whether or not the district itself is actually in violation of the equal protection clause. And I think we are a long way from seeing the court reach that decision.

There is a lot of language in here, for example, when the court tells us that districts that are otherwise normal, compactness, the requirement that you said Congress excluded, when they seem to reach some kind of traditional appearance, then we already have law that says those are not going to be challenged.

We now have a law that says those that are irregular in shape and have this hint or suggestion on their face of having been structured for racial reasons and racial reason alone can be subjected to challenge.

The question is whether or not the Court, over time, will come back and evolve into a philosophy in the voting rights area similar to, as it has, in the employment area that would take a *Webber* or a *Bakke* approach, and that is that race may be a factor that is included among other factors but may not be the dominant reason, you know. And that, you know, has been a very difficult thing.

But if the court proceeds along that kind of line, then the net result of the *Shaw* case may be that it doesn't change that much in terms of the practical outcome of the shape of these districts.

And there are hints in *Reno* that the Court is open to hearing arguments about reasons for the shape of this district other than race. And I think that we have already heard from people in North Carolina that there are substantial historical, economic reasons for the shape of this district, that that corridor is significant. That it does link the urban areas.

So as long as race is only a factor among other factors, I think there was something that the court was attempting to do. And it may appear overly esoteric. But I think the Court is concerned with preserving the validity of its language. And it has used this language, the language that may be somewhat misleading in the complexity of political life, about color blindness, about neutrality; and it has used that at the same time, while recognizing that there is some great project going on, to work out new structures that are going to be more representative.

And I think what *Shaw* v. *Reno* stands for is this principle that the court is going to maintain, in theory, this color blindness; but it is willing to permit a much more complex kind of structure to be used in decisionmaking.

But we can't know that for certain until this case comes back on remand. But I think informed speculation would seem to be that you would get the same kind of result in the voting area that you got in the employment area and in other areas, that is that it may be included somehow as a factor. But they will have to work out a formula for that factoring.

Mr. EDWARDS. Well, I personally, having been here more than 30 years. The Voting Rights Act was working rather well. And I was thunder struck to read in the morning paper of the *Shaw* decision. It seemed to me that it struck at the roots of the Voting Rights Act. It certainly could result in a lot of remands in the State of California.

Does any member of the panel think that Congress should address this problem as difficult as it might be, legislatively? Any noes or yeses?

Mr. BROADUS. I think one of the things that the court may be attempting in the Shaw case, as it did in some of the earlier title VII cases that Congress has reversed, is it may be reflecting some of the burden of making these very tough decisions back on to the political branches.

And this case may be something of a signaling device that says, look, as to this choice as to whether or not compact districts are best or whether or not, you know, this diversity in the district is best, to a certain extent, we have laid out some rules and we are going to see that they are abided by. But they may also be signaling that, look, this is a situation in which the political branches are going to have to reengage and have to be once again involved in that process. And in that sense, this is something that Congress should well be considering now and trying to devise new formulas for.

Mr. NORRELL. Congressman Edwards, I certainly think the Congress should address the *Presley* matter, the reality that black elected officials can have their authority stripped from them by the actions of a duly elected white majority.

And I think that since that apparently could be addressed statutorily, that it should be. And it is difficult for me to construct in my mind now the constitutional amendment that would address *Shaw* v. *Reno*. It would take that, would it not?

Mr. EDWARDS. It would take a constitutional amendment, would it not, since the decision is based on the Constitution not a statute. Is that correct?

Mr. NORRELL. I suppose. It is a shame that that is what it would take. It seems to me that these decisions, and others that you have referred, to show a kind of willfulness to ignore the context of racial policies or policies that have a racial aspect to them.

It is inconceivable for a historian or perhaps even for a citizen who lives in a place that is as racially alienated as Alabama is, to see how one can make decisions about the voting rights or the economic opportunities and rights of an African-American without understanding the four centuries of discrimination that has taken place in this society.

And that appears to be, with the appropriation of the use of words like segregate and apartheid in the *Shaw* decision, what is happening.

Mr. EDWARDS. Thank you.

Mr. Canady do you have anything further to add?

Mr. CANADY. Yes. I would like to thank each of the panelists for being here. It has been very constructive. We appreciate your time.

And I want to follow up on what Professor Broadus said about the *Shaw* case. I think we don't know how this is going to work out. I mean, the court, in that opinion, did not say that there can be no race-conscious decisionmaking with respect to legislative districts. Very clear that they did not say that.

What remains unclear is what can be a sufficiently compelling justification for a district like the district in North Carolina. And only time will tell.

I, for one, think that any type of legislative approach on this would be certainly premature until we see where the cases are going. And we will know. But at this point, it would not make sense to me to approach this legislatively. We don't know what we would need to know to address it.

Mr. EDWARDS. Well, I would agree. I don't think that we are anywhere near coming up with a legislative response. But we do have to watch it very carefully to see how serious it is going to be, if it is going to cause great difficulties in voting patterns of the country.

But I think this subject has gotten off to an excellent start with these splendid witnesses. And all of us are very grateful for all of you being here today and testifying in such an intelligent manner and helpful manner to us. And I think we do have to close it today. And sorry for the delays. But this is the process where we have to survive.

But again, speaking for all the members of the House Judiciary Committee, we thank you.

[Whereupon, at 1:13 p.m., the subcommittee adjourned.]

VOTING RIGHTS

WEDNESDAY, MAY 11, 1994

House of Representatives,
Subcommittee on Civil and Constitutional Rights,
Committee on the Judiciary,
Washington, DC.

The subcommittee met, pursuant to notice at 9:38 a.m., in room 2237, Rayburn House Office Building, Hon. Don Edwards (chairman of the subcommittee) presiding.

Present: Representatives Don Edwards, Patricia Schroeder, Barney Frank, Henry J. Hyde, and Howard Coble.

Also present: Representative Melvin L. Watt.

Staff present: Catherine A. LeRoy, counsel: Melody Barnes, assistant counsel; and Kathryn A. Hazeem, minority counsel.

Mr. EDWARDS. Good morning, everybody. Welcome to the House of Representatives and the hearing room of the House Judiciary Committee.

I am Don Edwards, chairman of the Judiciary Subcommittee on Civil and Constitutional Rights, and I have been here a long time. I was here in the House and on the Judiciary Committee when we enacted the 1965 Voting Rights Act, which was a revolutionary piece of legislation. Some people consider it the greatest civil rights law that has ever been passed.

A lot has transpired since then. In 1981 and 1982, Mr. Hyde, who will speak to you in a minute, and I held hearings throughout the United States, especially in the South, about bringing up to date the Voting Rights Act. We were frankly shocked as we went through Texas and to Alabama, I believe, and other States and realized that a lot had to be done, that there was a lot of discrimination going on despite the 1965 Voting Rights Act. We came back and wrote the 1982 amendments to the Voting Rights Act, and it passed the House and Senate and is today law.

But since then a lot of things have happened. Quite a number of Supreme Court decisions are troubling to some of us. *Presley* has been troubling to some of us. We don't think we had that result in mind when we wrote the 1965 or the 1982 bills, and some of us on my side of the aisle were very disturbed with *Shaw* v. *Reno*. We want to talk about that and voting rights generally today. I deeply appreciate the witnesses, that are friends and experts, who have come to talk to us, and I yield now to my good friend and ranking Republican on the House subcommittee, Henry Hyde.

Mr. HYDE. I thank you, Mr. Chairman, and I might say parenthetically that you are much too modest. I believe you were here when the first 10 amendments were ratified to the Constitution.

Mr. EDWARDS. No, only the first eight.

Mr. HYDE. The first eight. You never did like 9 and 10, did you?

In any event, I do want to say that this is Congressman Edwards' last term, and the cause of good government, not just the cause of civil rights—certainly the cause of civil rights, but the cause of good government is losing in Congress, but not losing to the world, a very staunch and effective and zealous advocate. He will be missed immeasurably by many people, including some of us on this side of the aisle who don't always philosophically agree but who respect integrity and ability.

The Voting Rights Act of 1964 is, I think, the most successful civil rights legislation enacted ever by this Congress. Within a few short years of its passage, African-American voter participation, especially in the South, increased dramatically. But as we all know, passage of a law doesn't guarantee the disappearance of racial discrimination.

The 1982 amendments changed the Voting Rights Act by substituting a results test for the intent test. Under the act as amended, a violation could be proved by showing that a voting practice had the effect of diminishing minority voting strength. Despite all the protestations that the result test did not signal the beginning of proportional representation, redistricters of electoral maps, urged on by the Civil Rights Division of the Bush Justice Department, were convinced that it did. All prior principles of redistricting—geographic compactness, commonality of interest, unity of political entities—were overlooked as maps were drawn at all costs to create the maximum number of black and Hispanic majority districts. Instead of learning to engage in multiracial coalitions, Americans are being urged to act like tribal clans. Instead of moving toward the goal of a colorblind society, we are further entrenching a very race-conscious one.

I am deeply troubled by these developments, and I am pleased to have the opportunity to discuss them with the distinguished group that we have here today.

Before we begin, I would like to comment about this process. This is not the traditional hearing format that is used by this subcommittee, and I want to thank Mr. Edwards for accommodating my concerns about the format and the Congressional Research Service for their assistance, and I surely look forward to a lively and invigorating discussion.

Thank you, Mr. Chairman.

Mr. EDWARDS. Well, thank you very much, Mr. Hyde. Thank you for your gracious personal remarks.

Mr. Hyde and I have worked very closely together, in a friendly way too, which is not always true in the Congress, and I deeply appreciate it.

I think I would like to just mention that Kathryn Hazeem is the staff lawyer that assists Mr. Hyde in the subcommittee. Melody Barnes is in charge of this. She has worked with Kathryn in setting this useful meeting up today. And of course Catherine LeRoy is chief counsel. Thanks to the staff. They have done a good job.

Now the format is going to be that I will introduce our two people from the Congressional Research Service—we are very grateful to them, as Mr. Hyde said—and then Mr. Hyde will introduce briefly those who are here, our participants. We appreciate your coming. Then those who want to make an opening statement, please limit it to 1 or 2 minutes, because we do want to move along with a lively discussion. But that will be operated and managed by our two moderators.

On my right is Thomas Durbin. He is a legislative attorney with the American Law Division of the Congressional Research Service specializing in election law. Mr. Durbin is a graduate of Saint Mary's University and the Catholic University's Columbus School of Law. L. Paige Whitaker is a legislative attorney with the American Law Division of the Congressional Research Service specializing in election law. Ms. Whitaker is a graduate of the University of Maryland and the Catholic University's Columbus School of Law.

Mr. Hyde, will you introduce our participants?

Mr. HYDE. Yes, if I may.

Benjamin H. Griffith is a partner in the Cleveland, MS, law firm of Griffith & Griffith. Mr. Griffith's practice emphasizes Federal and State civil litigation and local government representation, including section 5 proceedings before the U.S. Department of Justice, and section 2 litigation. He is currently litigating a case on the Eastern Shore of Maryland in which a judge has employed cumulative voting as a remedy for a violation of section 2 of the Voting Rights Act.

Nelson Lund is associate professor of law at the George Mason University School of Law and executive editor of the Supreme Court Economic Review. Professor Lund served as a law clerk for the Honorable Sandra Day O'Connor of the U.S. Supreme Court during its 1987 term and as associate counsel to the President from 1989 to 1992.

Steven Markman is a former U.S. attorney, who now practices with the firm of Miller, Canfield, Paddock & Stone in Detroit, MI. He served as the chief counsel for the Senate Subcommittee on the Constitution for the Senate Judiciary Committee during Senate consideration of the 1982 amendments to the Voting Rights Act. He currently represents the State of Michigan in ongoing voting rights litigation.

Richard A. Samp is chief counsel to the Washington Legal Foundation, a public interest law and policy center. WLF has litigated numerous cases involving racial preferences and voting issues and has filed amicus curiai briefs in key voting rights cases.

Stuart Taylor is senior writer for the American Lawyer Media which owns the American Lawyer. He writes a biweekly column for seven weekly and daily newspapers, including the Legal Times, focusing on legal and political issues of national importance. He has written numerous articles on current controversies surrounding the Voting Rights Act.

And, Mr. Chairman, shall I introduce the others on the list you gave me?

Mr. EDWARDS. Yes, please.

Mr. HYDE. All right.

Other invited participants: Arthur Baer is director of the Puerto Rican Legal Defense and Education Fund's Voting Rights Project. Elaine Jones is director/counsel of the NAACP Legal Defense and Education Fund. Pamela Karlan is a professor of law at the University of Virginia School of Law. Ms. Karlan was counsel to one of the amici in the *Presley* v. *Etowah County Commission* case and has written extensively in the voting rights area. Dr. Allan Lichtman is a professor of history at American University, consultant to Vice President Gore, and an expert witness in the *Shaw* v. *Reno, Shaw* v. *Hunt,* and *Hays* v. *Louisiana* cases. And Bernadine St. Cyr is a community activist from New Roads, LA, and has been involved in local voting rights issues for many years.

Thank you, Mr. Chairman.

Mr. EDWARDS. Thank you, Mr. Hyde.

Mr. Durbin.

STATEMENT OF THOMAS M. DURBIN, LEGISLATIVE ATTORNEY, AMERICAN LAW DIVISION, CONGRESSIONAL RESEARCH SERVICE

Mr. DURBIN. Thank you, Mr. Chairman, Mr. Ranking Minority Member, professors, scholars, jurists, ladies, and gentlemen.

Paige Whitaker and I have been invited here basically to moderate, but we have been asked to present to you opening statements just to set the stage for our discussion, and in accordance with the founding principles of the Congressional Research Service, whatever we say is nonpartisan, objective, and neutral, and we will attempt to present it that way.

But you have in front of you a chart that I have prepared for the sake of brevity that I want to just briefly explain to you the history and evolution of congressional redistricting which often parallels State legislative redistricting and how we are today at a crossroads under the Voting Rights Act.

[The chart follows:]

87

HISTORY AND EVOLUTION OF CONGRESSIONAL REAPPORTIONMENT   AND REDISTRICTING

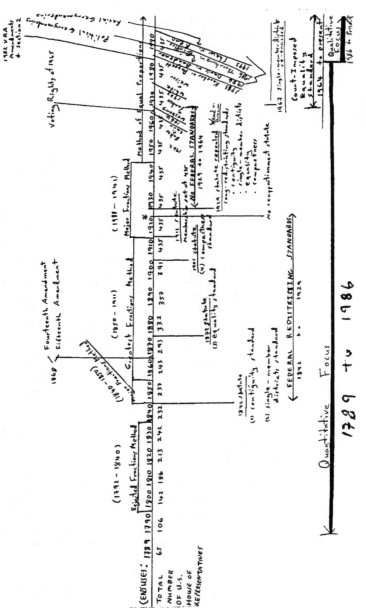

Thomas M. Durbin
Legislative Attorney
CRS/American Law Division
May 11, 1994

Mr. DURBIN. If you look at the horizontal line that goes through the center of the chart, you see decennial censuses every 10 years, and you see the total number of representatives, and you see how they have increased from 65 to the present 435 that was established in 1911.

In the early days of congressional redistricting, they were interested in obtaining more Members of the House of Representatives because the number of States were increasing and the population was increasing, so that there was not a concentration on other issues, it was a quantitative type of concentration.

However, what you see in this evolutionary process is that Congress decided to provide for the States some standards, some statutory standards. In 1942 they provided for two statutes, for contiguity and single member districts. In 1872 they provided for equality. In 1901 they provided for compactness.

However, as the twentieth century began, there were a lot of political problems with congressional redistricting. It became linked to partisanship probably in the same way that campaign financing is involved in partisanship today. So, in 1929 when Congress passed the reapportionment statute for the 1920 decennial census, they failed to mention redistricting standards of compactness, equality, and contiguity. The Court in a 1932 case, *Broom* v. *Wood,* asserted that since Congress didn't repeat them, they repealed them, so that after 1929, you had no Federal standards. In congressional redistricting, and even in State legislative redistricting to a certain extent, you had the law of the jungle, so that malapportionment was commonplace not only in Federal congressional redistricting but also in State legislative redistricting. The courts wouldn't touch it because of the political question doctrine, that it is better left to the State legislature to decide rather than the courts to decide.

Because of the malapportionment problem, because they were so gross, in the sixties the Supreme Court agreed to give this ability to redistricting, not only Federal but State. Actually, State first, in *Baker* v. *Carr* in 1962, and then *Reynolds* v. *Sims.* It was in 1964 that you had the Supreme Court addressing Federal redistricting, and the Court, because of a lack of a Federal statutory standard, imposed their own equality standard beginning with *Wesberry* v. *Sanders.* Then in the sixties, the seventies, and the eighties we saw a refinement of the equality standard so that you can see the focus of the Court was quantitative.

However, with the introduction of the Voting Rights Act of 1965 and the amendments of 1982, we begin to see a crossroads in congressional redistricting, a new focus, sort of a qualitative focus.

The reason why you use the dates 1986 at the bottom there, quantitative focus from 1789 to 1987 and a qualitative focus from 1986 to the present, is because of two U.S. Supreme Court decisions in 1986. One dealt with political gerrymandering, *Davis* v. *Bandemer,* and the other one dealt with racial gerrymandering on the State legislative redistricting. Its holdings in *Thornburg* v. *Gingles* have application to the congressional level.

At that time you see the focus of the Supreme Court changing. Not only is equality necessary—one person, one vote, equal representation for equal numbers of people—but now you have an emphasis that there is going to be recognized minority groups, and the Court is saying their interests have to be looked into. Now how you do it is a problem, and we are in that process right now. We are at a crossroads to see how we do that.

I am now going to turn this over to Paige Whitaker, who will now go into such aspects as essential provisions of the Voting Rights Act and essential Supreme Court cases.

STATEMENT OF L. PAIGE WHITAKER, LEGISLATIVE ATTORNEY, AMERICAN LAW DIVISION, CONGRESSIONAL RESEARCH SERVICE

Ms. WHITAKER. Good morning. It is my pleasure to be here. Thank you, Mr. Chairman, Mr. Ranking Minority Member. It is our pleasure to be here, and good morning and welcome to the distinguished scholar and guests.

Again, I would like to briefly make a statement bringing everyone up to speed on the Voting Rights Act and some of the key cases we will be discussing. Clearly, I am not doing this for the benefit of the panel—this is a distinguished panel that we have, quite expert in these areas—mostly for the purpose of the audience.

There are two key sections of the Voting Rights Act that invariably come up in a discussion of this type. Those are section 2 and section 5. I would like to go over them very briefly and then just a few of the key court cases that again invariably come up in a discussion on the Voting Rights Act.

Section 2, unlike section 5, applies nationwide. It created a right of action for private citizens or the Government to challenge discriminatory voting practices and procedures. Specifically—and keep this in mind throughout our discussion—section 2 provides that any voting qualification or prerequisite to voting or standard practice or procedure imposed by any State or political subdivision which results in the denial or the abridgement of the right of any citizen of the United States to vote based on race, color, or membership in a language minority—which was added in 1982—is prohibited. The relation to redistricting, therefore, is, if a congressional redistricting plan passed by a State is found to result in racial vote dilution, a claim could be made under section 2.

Section 5, in contrast, only applies to certain covered areas in the country. It sets forth a preclearance requirement requiring those areas of the country, whenever they want to make a change in any voting procedure, no matter how small, to preclear it, and they have to preclear it with either the Department of Justice or the U.S. District Court for the District of Columbia.

Now the key court cases that you will see coming up in today's discussion include the landmark 1986 Supreme Court case *Thornburg* v. *Gingles*. That case is critical because the Court found that for any court to decide whether there has been a violation of section 2 of the Voting Rights Act, it has to determine whether, as a result of the challenged practice, plaintiffs did not have an equal opportunity to participate in the political processes and to elect candidates of their choice.

The Court said, in making this kind of determination, an analysis of the totality of the circumstances must be done. Also the Court established a new tripartite test, a three-part test, and all prongs of the test must be proven in order to prevail, and they include: First, that the minority group is sufficiently large and geographically compact enough to constitute a majority in a single member district; second, that it is politically cohesive; and third, that the majority in those cases usually votes as a block in such a manner that it is usually able to defeat the minority group's preferred candidate.

And then note, as a result of *Thornburg,* many courts have construed the Voting Rights Act to mean, in a redistricting area, that a majority minority district must be created wherever possible.

So up until last June when *Shaw* v. *Reno* came down, the Voting Rights Act was seen to not only permit but to require policy makers in certain cases under certain circumstances to be race conscious when they draw district lines.

Then all of a sudden came *Shaw* v. *Reno,* and that was decided last June 1993. As many commentators have written, this appears to be a significant divergence from where the Court had been interpreting the Voting Rights Act prior.

The Court in this case found that if a redistricting scheme is so bizarre and so irrational on its face that it can be understood only to be a racial gerrymander, then it will only pass constitutional muster if a court finds that it was narrowly tailored to further a compelling governmental interest. So the underlying principle in *Shaw* is that racially gerrymandered redistricting plans are going to be subject to the same level of strict scrutiny that applies to other State legislation that classifies citizens according to race.

One other note. There has been a case that came down following *Shaw* where a lower court—it was a Federal district court—applied *Shaw,* and that was *Hays* v. *Louisiana,* and, basically using the *Shaw* case, the Court struck down a district on the principles that were set forth in *Shaw.*

So I hope that was a good brief overview, and I am sure we will be getting into these decisions in greater detail.

Now I would like to turn it over to Chairman Edwards who will be asking for brief opening statements from the participants.

Mr. EDWARDS. I believe for opening statements, if you care to make a brief one, we will just go around the room.

Mr. Baer.

STATEMENT OF ARTHUR A. BAER, DIRECTOR, VOTING RIGHTS PROJECT, PUERTO RICAN LEGAL DEFENSE AND EDUCATION FUND, INC.

Mr. BAER. I would like to thank the Subcommittee on Civil and Constitutional Rights on my behalf and on behalf of the Puerto Rican Legal Defense and Education Fund for this opportunity to enter a dialog concerning the application of the Voting Rights Act to legislative redistricting.

Over one hundred years ago, the Supreme Court in *Yick Wo* v. *Hopkins* stated that the right to vote is a fundamental political right because it is preservative of all rights. That statement is no less true today.

African-Americans, Latinos, Asians, Native Americans, and those protected under the Voting Rights Act often represent the poorest members of our society. More often than not, they are relegated to live in areas segregated by race and in communities of poverty. They also more often than not live in jurisdictions where whites vote as a bloc. Were it not for the protections of the Voting Rights Act, the preferred candidates of these protected classes would regularly be defeated and their voice excluded from the halls of government.

To deny them such a voice would deny those without the power of wealth, the power of government. It would relegate them to powerlessness, continued substandard education, segregation, and poverty. It would result in greater social alienation and tend to undermine the legitimacy of government. It would also deny them the remedy for which blood was spilled from Civil War battlefields to the streets of Philadelphia, MS, and for which Latinos as well as others have struggled—the right to participate as equals in our democracy.

It is through democratic equality that those who are poor can change public policies to ensure nondiscrimination and fair opportunities in education, employment, housing, and other areas. Just as our tripartite system of government and the Bill of Rights serves as checks and balances against the potential tyranny of unfettered democratic decisions, the Voting Rights Act serves as a check against self-perpetuating and exclusionary decisions by limited segments of our society. It ensures fairness and promotes legitimacy, a government for the people, by the people, and of the people.

Recent decisions of the Supreme Court, unfortunately, will entrench on that fairness and tend toward undermining the legitimacy of the Government. By its holding in *Rojas* v. *Victoria Independent School District* and *Presley* v. *Etowah County,* the Court has effectively held it is permissible to nullify the vote of Latino and African-American voters by taking away the legislative powers of their chosen representatives. By a decision in *Shaw* v. *Reno,* the Court has effectively elevated the value of districting aesthetics over the value of legislative inclusion. Both decisions are errant in their policy choices and, if possible, should be remedied by Congress.

I will leave you with this remark by Martin Luther King who wrote this some 30 years ago.

There are those who shudder at the idea of a political bloc, particularly a Negro bloc, which conjures up visions of racial exclusiveness. This concern, however, is unfounded. Not exclusiveness but effectiveness is the aim of bloc voting. By forming a bloc, a minority makes its voice heard. The Negro minority will unite for political action for the same reason that it will seek to function in alliance with other groups, because in this way it can compel the majority to listen.

It is well to remember that blocs are not unique in American life nor are they inherently evil. Their purposes determine their moral quality. In past years labor, farmers, businessmen, veterans, and various national minorities have voted as blocs on various issues, and many still do. If their objectives are good and each issue is decided on its own merits, a bloc is a wholesome force on the political scene. Negroes are, in fact, already voting spontaneously as a bloc. They voted overwhelmingly for President Kennedy and, before that, President Roosevelt. Development as a conscious bloc would give them more flexibility, more bargaining power, more clarity, and more responsibility in addressing candidates and programs. Moreover, a deeper involvement as a group in political life will bring them more independence. Consciously and creatively developed, political power may well in the days to come be the most effective new tool of Negroes' liberation.

Thank you, Mr. Chairman.
[The prepared statement of Mr. Baer follows:]

STATEMENT

OF

ARTHUR A. BAER

DIRECTOR, VOTING RIGHTS PROJECT

PUERTO RICAN LEGAL DEFENSE AND EDUCATION FUND INC.

BEFORE

THE

SUBCOMMITTEE ON CIVIL AND CONSTITUTIONAL RIGHTS

COMMITTEE ON THE JUDICIARY

UNITED STATES HOUSE OF REPRESENTATIVES

CONCERNING

THE VOTING RIGHTS ACT

MAY 11, 1994

INTRODUCTION

I would like to thank the Subcommittee On Civil And Constitutional Rights, on my behalf and on behalf of the Puerto Rican Legal Defense and Education Fund, for this opportunity to enter a dialogue concerning the application of the Voting Rights Act to legislative redistricting.

Over one hundred years ago the Supreme Court in _Yick Wo v. Hopkins_, 118 U.S. 356 (1886), stated that the right to vote is "a fundamental political right, because preservative of all rights." The statement is no less true today.

African-Americans, Latinos, Asians and Native Americans, those protected under the Voting Rights Act, often represent the poorest members of our society. More often than not they are relegated to live in areas segregated by race, and in communities of poverty. They also more often than not live in jurisdictions where whites vote as a bloc. Were it not for the protections of the Voting Rights Act, the preferred candidates of these protected classes would regularly be defeated, and their voice excluded from the halls of government. To deny them such a voice would be to deny those without the power of wealth, the power of government. It would relegate them to powerlessness, continued substandard education, segregation and poverty. It would result in greater social alienation and tend to undermine the legitimacy of government. See Appendix A.

It would also deny them the remedy for which blood was spilled from civil War battlefields to the streets of Philadelphia, Mississippi and for which Latinos, as well as others, have struggled - the right to participate as equals in our democracy.

It is through democratic equality that those who are poor, can change public policies to ensure non-discrimination and fair opportunities in education, employment, housing and other areas. Just as our tri-partite system of government and the Bill of Rights serve as checks and balances to the potential tyranny of unfettered democratic decisions, the Voting Rights Act serves as a check against self perpetuating and exclusionary decisions by limited segments of our society. It ensures fairness and promotes legitimacy - "a government for the people, by the people and of the people."

Recent decisions of the Supreme Court, unfortunately, will retrench on fairness and tend toward undermining the legitimacy of government. By its holdings in Rojas v. Victoria Independent School District, Civ. Act. No. V-87-16 (S.D. Texas, March 29, 1988), aff'd 490 U.S. 1001 (1989), and Presley v. Etowah County, 502 U.S. ___, 117 Ed. 2d 51 (1992), the Court has effectively held it is permissible to nullify the vote of Latino and African-American voters by taking away the legislative powers of their chosen representatives. By its decision in Shaw v. Reno, ___ U.S. ___, 61 U.S.L.W. 4818 (June 28, 1993), the Court has effectively elevated the value districting aesthetics over the value of legislative inclusion. See Appendix B. Both decisions are errant in their policy choices and, if possible, should be remedied by

Congress.

As Martin Luther King wrote some thirty years ago:

> There are those who shudder at the idea of a
> political bloc, particularly a Negro bloc,
> which conjures up visions of racial
> exclusiveness. This concern is, however,
> unfounded. Not exclusiveness but
> effectiveness is the aim of bloc voting; by
> forming a bloc a minority makes its voice
> heard. The Negro minority will unite for
> political action for the same reason that it
> will seek to function in alliance with other
> groups - because in this way it can compel the
> majority to listen.
> It is well to remember that blocs are not
> unique in American life, nor are they
> inherently evil. Their purposes determine
> their moral quality. In past years, labor,
> farmers, businessmen, veterans, and various
> national minorities have voted as blocs on
> various issues, and many still do. If the
> objectives are good, and each issue is decided
> on its own merits, a bloc is a wholesome force
> on the political scene. Negroes are, in
> fact, already voting spontaneously as a bloc.
> They voted overwhelmingly for President
> Kennedy, and before that for President
> Roosevelt. Development as a conscious bloc
> would give them more flexibility, more
> bargaining power, more clarity, and more
> responsibility in assessing candidates and
> programs. Moreover, a deeper involvement as a
> group in political life will bring them more
> independence. Consciously and creatively
> developed, political power may well, in the
> days to come, be the most effective new tool
> of the Negro's liberation.

Martin Luther King, Jr., Why We Can't Wait, p. 150-151 (1964).

SEGREGATION AND LACK OF POWER OF PROTECTED CLASSES

Only twenty-five years ago the Kerner Commission (the President's National Advisory Commission on Civil Disorder) stated:

"Our nation is moving toward two societies, one black, one white, separate and unequal."

Twenty years later in Quiet Riots (1988), a book edited by Fred Harris and Roger Wilkins, the authors revisited the issues raised by the Kerner Commission and concluded that:

> ... The Kerner report is coming true: America is again becoming two societies, one black (and, today, we can add to that, Hispanic), one white-separate and unequal.
>
> ... There is a large and growing urban underclass in America - principally made up of blacks and Hispanics in the central cities. They are more economically isolated, more socially alienated, than ever before.
>
> ... There are "quiet riots" in all of America's central cities: unemployment, poverty, social disorganization, segregation, family disintegration, housing and school deterioration, and crime are worse now. These "quiet riots" are not as alarming as the violent riots of twenty years ago, or as noticeable to outsiders. But they are even more destructive of human life.

[Id. at xii-xiii].

Over the past twenty-five years urban jurisdictions have become increasingly poor; increasingly non-white and unfortunately reflective of a geographically based class or caste system within the united states. Higher income and disproportionately white populations have left central cities to live in suburbs.

It may surprise many of you to realize that New York City, like the rest of urban America, is in a hidden or at least not openly discussed crisis - according to a 1992 study by the Community Service Society:

> - 1.8 Million people in New York City (or 25.2% of New York's population) live in poverty - more than the total population of Houston, Texas, our 4th largest city

- 76.6% of those in poverty in New York City are black or Latino

  - 43.1% of all Latinos live in poverty

  - 33.1% of all blacks live in poverty

  - 11.6% of all whites live in poverty

- Almost 800,000 children live in poverty in New York City, more than the total population of Indianapolis, Indiana

- The poverty rate for children in New York City is 39.3%

- 60.3% of all Latino children live in poverty

- 43.2% of all non-Hispanic black children live in poverty

- 17.1% of all non-Hispanic white children live in poverty[1]

There is a direct relationship between the degree of underrepresentation of different racial and ethnic groups in New York City and the percentage of that group that lives in poverty. The greater the underrepresentation of a group, the greater the poverty of that group.

Why is this important? Because there are essentially two avenues for obtaining and exercising Corporate power in America - one avenue is through private corporations - based on the decision of shareholders in selecting private boards of directors who will decide private investment, allocations of private goods and

---

[1] Terry J. Rosenberg, Poverty In New York City, 1991: A Research Bulletin (1992), at x, xi, xii, and 42.

services, and the creation or dimunition of private sector jobs - the other avenue is through public corporations based on the decision of voters in selecting representatives who will decide public investment, the allocation of public goods and services and the creation or dimunition of public sector jobs. See Appendix C.

Latinos and African Americans, as well as others, who disproportionately comprise the ranks of the poor, have disproportionately less capital, and are effectively disenfranchised from exercising power in the private corporate sector. Consequently, in order to begin to achieve social equality, it is critical for such groups to have an equal opportunity to elect representatives to public corporate bodies in order to create a cycle of empowerment and enfranchisement that is - to effect public policy to ensure better education, equal public and private sector job opportunities and inclusive economic development.

THE GOALS AND IMPACT OF THE VOTING RIGHTS ACT

The goal of the Voting Rights Act is to ensure that protected classes, i.e., those who congress has determined to have been traditionally, discriminatorily excluded from the electoral process - namely, African Americans, Latinos, Asians and Native Americans - are not denied an equal opportunity to elect representatives to public bodies. It does so by prohibiting discriminatory election practices, including discriminatory legislative districts. The act operates through, two major enforcement provisions: section 2 and section 5.

Section 2 applies to all jurisdictions. To sustain a redistricting challenge under section 2, a plaintiff generally has the burden of proving that there is (1) racial bloc voting, i.e., whites tend to vote for whites, blacks for blacks, latinos for latinos, etc., sufficient to prevent a protected class from electing a representative of their choice when submerged as a minority in a predominantly white district, (2) that the protected class is sufficiently large, geographically compact to be able to comprise a majority of a single member district, and (3) that the protected class is politically cohesive, (usually determined by whether they vote as a bloc). In addition, courts are required to assess the totality of the circumstances - including a history of discrimination in voting, employment and other areas, racial appeals in elections, exclusionary candidate stating processes and other similar factors, all or some of which may be proven - to determine whether equal political opportunity is denied in a jurisdiction.

Section 5 applies to certain jurisdictions, such as New York City, which had a prohibited electoral practice - in New York, an English only literacy test - and low voter turnout in certain benchmark years. If a jurisdiction is covered under section 5, the jurisdiction has the burden of demonstrating a change in voting has neither a discriminatory impact nor intent. More specifically, in redistricting, it must demonstrate that a change in districts does not have a retrogressive effect - i.e., does not reduce electoral opportunities of protected classes, does not intentionally dilute the vote of a protected class - and does not clearly violate section 2 of the act. It is a remedial statute requiring jurisdictions with a history of discrimination in voting to justify changes in voting before they are implemented.

Redistricting bodies are thus generally required to create minority districts to the extent there is racial bloc voting, and residential segregation in their jurisdiction. That is, were white bloc voting would cancel out minority voting strength if submerged in a predominantly white district, and where minority districts could otherwise be created because of patterns of residential segregation, they are normally required to be created. Under the general reasoning of the act, because of the existence of racial bloc voting and residential segregation, creating a district containing only a minority of a protected class causes that class to be unable to elect a representative of its choice and is prohibited.

There may be a proportionality defense, i.e., where minorities are elected in proportion to their population - no further districts need be created. Moreover, minority districts can choose to elect non-minority candidates. Conversely, if either there is no racial bloc voting or if there is no residential segregation, no minority districts are generally required to be created.

Some would argue, nevertheless, that even if there is racial bloc voting and residential segregation, minority voters should be denied equal political opportunity because the districts created "look strange," or are not elegant, or are not compact. Some also argue that creating minority districts results in racial division and the "balkanization" of communities by race.

In enacting the 1982 amendments to the Voting Rights Act, Congress rejected these argument. As congress stated: "to suggest that it is the results test [of section 2], carefully applied by the courts, which is responsible for ... instances of intensive racial politics, is like saying that it is the doctors thermometer which cause high fever."[2]

The Voting Rights Act does not cause segregative housing patterns or racial bloc voting; what it does, is require that where there are such circumstances, districts are not drawn to deny protected classes, equal electoral opportunity.

As to the creation of "strange looking districts," the districts created to comply with the Voting Rights Act may in infrequent instances look strange, but those instances are no more often than equally odd districts created for political purposes - after all, it has been suggested that the need to protect a white Democratic incumbent that was the basis of creating the controversial North Carolina highway district - a second African American, more compact district could have been created but a white Republican rather than a white Democrat may have won a congressional seat in the alternative configuration - which did not suit the goals of the democratically controlled North Carolina legislature.

---

[2] S. Rep. No. 97-417, 97th Cong., 2d Sess. 34, reprinted in, 1982 U.S.C.C.A.N. at 212.

Some argue, however, that creating geographically compact districts, even in the context of racial bloc voting and its consequential disenfranchisement of minority voters, is better, because such districts better reflect a community of interest than districts that aggregate less proximate African American or Latino neighborhoods. It is hard to believe that East Harlem has more in common with the silk stocking district than it does with the South Bronx. Indeed, Dean Macchiarola, former Chair of the New York City Districting Commission, recently wrote in a different context that some Manhattan neighborhoods "such as the Lower East Side, Harlem, and Washington Heights" have more in common with "outer borough New Yorkers" than with Manhattanites.[3]

With respect to those who argue that creating minority legislative districts causes balkanization, again, the Voting Rights Act does not create residential segregation; what it does is ensures segregated minority communities will not be denied political representation because of racially polarized voting.

Unfortunately, while I hear balkanization arguments made in the context of arguing against ensuring an effective franchise to minority voters, I rarely hear the same arguments with respect to the apparently acceptable "balkanization", caused by the suburban/urban split and the residential and political segregation, caused by that split. I do not hear anyone, for example, arguing for the Bronx/Westchester Unified School District or the

---

[3]   See, Frank J. Macchiarola, The Two New Yorks, 3 City Journal 57, 57-58 (1993).

Metropolitan New York School District - even though as University
of Chicago Professor Gary Orfield writes: "residential segregation
produces segregated schools and, as the current data... show,.
integrated schools are very likely to be much better on every index
measured."[4]

In terms of geographic equity, one must compare how many times
disproportionately poor, Latino and African American communities
have been divided, or raised, or used as sites for unwanted public
facilities such as, for example, incinerators, with how many times
similar occurrences have happened in disproportionately wealthier,
non-Latino and non-African American communities.   "In 1987 the
Commission For Racial Justice of the United Church of Christ
reported that three of every five black and Hispanic Americans live
in a community with uncontrolled toxic-waste sites."[5]   "In
communities with two or more [commercial hazardous waste]
facilities or one or more of the nation's five largest landfills,
the average minority percentage of the population was more than
three times that without facilities."[6]

---

[4]   Gary Orfield, Separate Societies: Have the Kerner
Warnings Come True? in Quiet Riots, supra at p. 111.

[5]   Regina Austin and Michael Schill, Black, Brown, Poor and
Poisoned: Minority Grassroots Environmentalism and the Quest For
Eco-Justice, 1 Kansas J. of Law and Public Policy 69, 69 (1991),
citing, United Church of Christ Commission For Racial Justice,
Toxic Wastes and Race: A National Report on the Racial and Socio-
Economic Characteristics of Communities with Hazardous Sites
(1987), at xiv.

[6]   Id., quoting, United Church of Christ Commission For
Racial Justice, Toxic Wastes and Race: A National Report on the
Racial and Socio-Economic Characteristics of Communities with
Hazardous Sites, (1987) at xiii.

Where there is fairer access to political representation -
there is fairer decisions with respect to the benefits and burdens
of society - including the placement of such community burdens as
an incinerator. Thus, a joint 1991 report by members of the New
York State Assembly's Committees on Environmental Conservation and
Health, and other members of the Assembly concluded: "the social,
economic and political position of minority and low-income
communities invites environmentally objectionable projects and
practices."[7]

CONCLUSION

The Voting Rights Act is not a panacea but a step in the right
direction. Hopefully, some time soon, residential segregation and
racially polarized voting will be past history, while equal
employment, economic, and educational opportunities will become
current history, leading to social equality and the elimination of
the dichotomy of predominately white, relatively wealthier suburbs
and predominately non-white relatively poor central cities, and
within our cities to the elimination of the dichotomy of
predominately white, relatively wealthier neighborhoods and
predominately non-white, relatively poor neighborhoods. Maybe then
the Voting Rights Act will be seen as a small and temporary step in
the transformation of our society to a more just society. Thank
you.[8]

---

[7]   Minorities And The Environment (1991) at p. 4.

[8]   Portions of this statement appeared as an op ed piece in
the July 27, 1993 edition of New York Newsday. Appendix D hereto.
Much of this statement was initially prepared for a presentation at
the Association of the Bar of the City of New York.

APPENDIX A

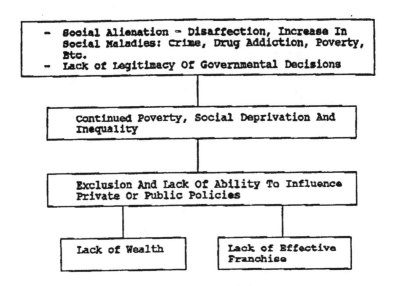

- Social Alienation - Disaffection, Increase In
  Social Maladies: Crime, Drug Addiction, Poverty,
  Etc.
- Lack of Legitimacy Of Governmental Decisions

Continued Poverty, Social Deprivation And Inequality

Exclusion And Lack Of Ability To Influence Private Or Public Policies

Lack of Wealth

Lack of Effective Franchise

EVA839.94

APPENDIX B

	VRA claims Clear	VRA Claim In Dispute	VRA Claims Clear Except For _Shaw v. Reno_	No VRA Claim _Presley v. Etovah Cnty. Comm'n._
VRA	Barriers To Franchise, Candidacies, Slating, etc.	Vote Dilution of Non-majority Constituency	Vote Dilution of Potential Majority Districts	Legislative Dilution, Barriers in Committee and Seniority Systems, Legislative Rules, etc.
	Little or no Political Discourse By Minority			Discourse Limited To That Allow By Legislative Elite
Nature of Discourse	Minor or Not Part Of Discourse	Democratic Discourse		Undemocratic Discourse
			Fair Legislative Mechanisms (Protect Minority Group Particip.)	Monolithic Control By Community Of Interest, Decision Making Discourse Unnecessary
	Minor or Not Part Of Discourse	Part of Discourse At (Local Level)	Part of Discourse @ Legislative Level	
Degree & Type Discourse	Community of Interest (Racial or Ethnic Fragmented) No Organized Influence Over Elections	Community of Interest (Not Fragmented) Have Influence Over Election Representative But Don't Control Outcome	Elect rep. (Community of Interest Sufficiently Large & Compact to Constitute Major of Single Member District)	Legislative Elite Control Decision Making Authority
Impact of Bs & VRA Response	Minor or no impact			No impact
	Minor or no influence on policy, services, etc.	Some minor Impact In Services, Legislative Policy Filtered Through Representative	Greater Impact On Legislative Policy, Budget, Direct Voice On Such Decisions	

4837.94

APPENDIX C

Decision on private corporate
policy, jobs training, marketing,
investment, disinvestment

Decision on public policy,
jobs, education, investment
or disinvestment (health-
care, etc.)

Limited by public laws,
public accountability and
fiduciary duties, etc.

Limited by Constitution,
and public accountability.

Private Corporate Boards
Corporate Bodies

Legislatures, etc.,
Public Corporate Bodies

Fairness maintained by quorum
rules, directors elected at
meetings, rules regarding time
and place of meetings, etc.

Fairness maintained by
14th-15th Amendments/
Voting Rights Act

Use of wealth to
purchase stock
and select
corporate board

Use of vote to
elect repre-
sentatives to
legislatures or
other repre-
sentative bodies

Individual
Capital based influence
over policy

Individual
Franchise based influence
over policy

SWA838.04

APPENDIX D

NEW YORK FORUM

ABOUT VOTING RIGHTS

Don't Confuse The Cure With The Cause

By Arthur A. Baer

Writing in these pages recently, Roland N. Castilyan urged that people seize the opportunity presented by the Supreme Court's ruling in the voting-rights case of Shaw vs. Reno and challenge New York City's current federal, state and city legislative district lines ("The Injustice of Gerrymanders," New York Forum, July 13). These lines, Castilyan warned, are contributing to "balkanization by racial classification, which the majority of the Supreme Court — and many New Yorkers — find offensive."

Got rast! It's not the creation of minority districts that balkanizes communities by race. The Voting Rights Act does not cause segregated housing patterns, nor does it cause racial bloc voting. What it does is require that where residential segregation exists and bloc voting by whites has kept candidates of color out of office, districts may not be drawn to deny minority voters equal electoral opportunity.

In enacting the 1982 amendments to the Voting Rights Act, Congress rejected arguments similar to Castilyan's. As Congress observed in the legislative history accompanying the amendments, holding (to not responsible for "instances of intensive racial politics, is like saying that it is the doctor's thermometer which causes high fever."

Unfortunately, while "balkanization" is a dirty word in arguments against ensuring an effective

Arthur A. Baer is director of the voting rights project for the Puerto Rican Legal Defense and Education Fund.

a Bronx/Westchester unified school district.

Over the past 25 years, American cities have become increasingly poor, increasingly non-white and increasingly reflective of a geographically based class or caste system. Higher-income and disproportionately white populations have fled the central cities to live in suburbs.

New York City, like the rest of urban America, is in crisis. According to a 1992 study by the Community Service Society:

• 1.8 million people in New York City (or 25.2 percent of its population) live in poverty — more than the total population of Houston, our fourth-largest city.

• More than 760,000 children in New York City

franchise to minority voters, one rarely hears objections to the "balkanization" caused by the residential and political segregation of the suburban/urban split. You don't hear anyone, for example, arguing for

—Continued on page 76

— Continued from page 38

(or 39.3 percent of our children) live in poverty — more than the total population of Indianapolis.

• 76.6 percent of New Yorkers living in poverty are black or Latino.

• 43.1 percent of Hispanic New Yorkers live in poverty.

• 33 percent of non-Hispanic black New Yorkers live in poverty.

• 11.6 percent of non-Hispanic white New Yorkers live in poverty.

There is a direct relationship between the extent of these different racial and ethnic groups' political representation and the percentage that lives in poverty. The less a group's representation, the greater its poverty.

Why is this important? Because there are essentially two avenues to power in America. One is through private corporations, and the other through the public corporation of government. Latinos and African Americans, as well as other minority groups who disproportionately fill the ranks of the poor, have little capital and are effectively disenfranchised from exercising power in the private sector. Consequently, if we are ever to begin to achieve social equality, it is critical for such groups to have an equal opportunity to elect representatives to public bodies.

The goal of the Voting Rights Act is to ensure that protected classes, i.e., those that Congress has determined to have been traditionally and discriminatorily excluded from the electoral process, are not denied that equal opportunity. That's why the Puerto Rican Legal Defense and Education Fund, on behalf of Latino plaintiffs, is suing the State of New York under the Voting Rights Act to create a third Congressional district in New York City with a Latino majority.

In his dissent from the Shaw vs. Reno decision, Supreme Court Justice John Paul Stevens reflected: "If it is permissible to draw boundaries to provide adequate representation for rural voters, for union members, for Hasidic Jews, for Polish Americans, or for Republicans, it necessarily follows that it is permissible to do the same thing for members of the very minority group whose history in the United States gave birth to the Equal Protection Clause. A contrary conclusion could only be described as perverse."

Challenging minority districts in New York is not color-blind — it's blind to the social context in which we all live.

Mr. EDWARDS. Thank you, Mr. Baer.
Let's just go right around the room.
Mr. Griffith.

STATEMENT OF BENJAMIN GRIFFITH, ESQ., GRIFFITH & GRIFFITH, CLEVELAND, MS

Mr. GRIFFITH. Yes, Chairman, Mr. Hyde.

My perspective is on two bases really. I am gathering it from my work with my own county in Boliver County, MS, and also from the standpoint of litigating these cases. The person seated to my right is probably one of the top experts in the country in the area of voting rights litigation, Professor Lichtman.

I am not here to advocate repeal, restriction, or abandonment of the fundamental goals of the Voting Rights Act. As this subcommittee and the Senate committee ably reported, there were abuses and there were needs that had to be addressed, and those were properly addressed in the Voting Rights Act amendments in 1982.

What has occurred, and I believe it is extremely unfortunate, is not a retrenchment but a return to racial separatism and the type of racial separatism that is found in deliberate racial gerrymandering of the type that was condemned in *Gomillion* v. *Lightfoot* three decades ago.

My concern is from the standpoint of what is going on in the actual cases where Federal judges are trying to implement these standards. What I see occurring is that, we have retreated from the original goals of the act, which were commendable. We in Boliver County, MS, would defend those goals to our dying breath; they bespeak the need for minority access, equality of opportunity to the political process.

In our county, which is 62 percent black, we have more black elected officials than any other county in the State of Mississippi. The State has more black elected officials than any other State in the Nation. This has been true for over 10 years, and it is not an accident. It is a process of biracial coalitions, of bridge building, that I am very fearful is going to be harmed and injured if this process continues toward what I believe is a definite tendency to disregard the racial polarization tendencies of present litigation.

Two problems have occurred. No. 1, is the Federal courts are in some instances disregarding the proportional representation disclaimer that was set forth in section 2. They are disregarding the clear mandate, that we call the Dole compromise, by creating not just liability standards but remedy standards that allow, and not just allow but sometimes mandate, proportionality based upon racial classifications or ethnic classifications.

No. 2, in a very recent decision that is on appeal to the fourth circuit—and I don't want this to be a forum for a particular case— a particular Federal court has ordered into effect a cumulative voting system remedy which, as Prof. Donald Horowitz's affidavit sets forth in great detail, can lead to exacerbation of racial polarization. It can lead to increased racial separatism. It is a very regrettable tendency, I believe, on the part of the Federal judiciary to allow these type of liability and remedy rulings and standards to actually promote racial separatism as opposed to coalition building which I think is the heart of and the beauty of section 2.

I believe that there is a need to return to the original standards. I have advocated in a statement to this subcommittee that perhaps in the Deep South where we have Federal judges who are African-Americans, where we have minority officials who are chairing county and municipal boards, we are in a position now to rethink and look back at the legislative history that essentially hung the noose around the southern States, and to allow, I believe, Federal courts in the South to decide section 5 issues rather than requiring jurisdictions to spend $200,000 a pop to litigate those issues in the D.C. district court as is going on now.

I believe that there is a lot of good in the Voting Rights Act. I would be the last person here to recommend that it be the subject of retrenchment or retreat. We do need to return to the original goals, though.

[The prepared statement of Mr. Griffith follows:]

WRITTEN STATEMENT SUBMITTED BY

Benjamin E. Griffith
GRIFFITH & GRIFFITH
Attorneys at Law
123 South Court Street
P. O. Drawer 1680
Cleveland, MS 38732
Phone No. (601) 843-6100
FAX No. (601) 843-8153

Subcommittee on Civil and Constitutional Rights
House Judiciary Committee
Room 2237, Rayburn House Office Building
Washington, D.C. 20515

May 11, 1994

BIOGRAPHICAL SKETCH OF BENJAMIN E. GRIFFITH

Ben Griffith is a partner in the Cleveland, Mississippi, firm of Griffith & Griffith. He is a 1975 graduate of the University of Mississippi Law Center, where he was a member of Phi Delta Phi, Omicron Delta Kappa, served on the Editorial Board of The Mississippi Law Journal and received the American Jurisprudence Award in federal jurisdiction. He has served as President of the National Association of County Civil Attorneys and Chairman of the Government Law Section of the Mississippi Bar. He is a member of the Governmental Liability Committee of the Defense Research Institute, and is an active member of the American Bar Association's sections of State, Urban and Local Government, Litigation, and Torts and Insurance Practice, and Recorder of the Litigation and Risk Management Section of the National Institute of Municipal Law Officers. He is past-President of the Mississippi Association of County Board Attorneys, and is serving a three-year term on the Professional Responsibility Committee of the Mississippi Bar. He is also a member of the Federal Bar Association, the Mississippi Trial Lawyers Association, American Trial Lawyers Association, Mississippi Defense Lawyers Association, and the Bar Association of the Fifth Federal Circuit. He is admitted to practice in the United States Supreme Court, the U. S. Court of Appeals for the Fourth Circuit, Fifth Circuit and Eleventh Circuit, and has been admitted to practice *pro hac vice* in the U. S. District Courts in Georgia, Louisiana, Tennessee, Maryland, Colorado, California and the District of Columbia.

He has served as the attorney for the Board of Supervisors of Bolivar County, Mississippi, since 1983.

Ben's practice emphasizes federal and state civil litigation and local government representation, including Section 5 proceedings before the United States Department of Justice and Section 2 litigation.

TABLE OF CONTENTS

TABLE OF CONTENTS (Continued)

Statement Presented to
Subcommittee on Civil and Constitutional Rights
House Judiciary Committee
Room 2237, Rayburn House Office Building
Washington, D.C. 20515

I appreciate the opportunity to participate in the Voting Rights Roundtable. Members of the Subcommittee and your predecessors have heard and will continue to hear diverse viewpoints regarding the effectiveness of the 1982 Amendments to the Voting Rights Act, particularly §2, the aim of which was "to enable minority voters to shape electoral systems so as to minimize the impact of racism in those exceptional communities in which it still held sway."[1] My remarks here today will focus upon the effectiveness of litigation under §2 and administrative proceedings under §5, from the perspective of Bolivar County, located in the heart of the Mississippi Delta. I will also touch on problems and concerns with respect to racial gerrymandering and proportional representation that have been experienced on the local government level by jurisdictions seeking to comply with the provisions of the Act, in Mississippi as well as other southern and border states. Finally, I intend to bring to the Subcommittee's attention recent federal court action involving cumulative voting system remedies for Voting Rights Act violations, plucked out of academia and utilized for the first time as a mandatory remedial alternative in §2 litigation.[2]

Bolivar County's Experience

Bolivar County is located in the Mississippi Delta and encompasses 923 square miles, with a length of 41 miles and width varying from 13 to 28 miles, making it the second largest county in the State of Mississippi. Its total population according to the 1990 census was 41,875, of which 62.87 percent was black.

---

[1] A. Thernstrom, Whose Votes Count? Affirmative Action and Minority Voting Rights 196 (Harvard Univ. Press, 1987).

[2] Cane v. Worcester County, Maryland, 840 F. Supp. 1081 (D. Md. 1994), further proceedings, ___ F. Supp. ___, 1994 W.L. 113660, 62 U.S.L.W. 2631 (D. Md. 1994), appeal pending, No. 94-1579, United States Court of Appeals for the Fourth Circuit.

Two of its fifteen incorporated municipalities are county seats, one located at Cleveland and the other at Rosedale, site of a slackwater port facility on the Mississippi River and one of the county's three industrial parks. Cleveland, named one of America's 100 Best Small Towns in 1993, is home to Delta State University, whose Lady Statesmen basketball team has won six national championships during the past two decades. Delta State University offers services to the general public in the field of education, and is of particular value to business and industry, through a cooperative agreement making laboratory and business research facilities available to industry, affording middle management personnel the opportunity to upgrade clerical and managerial skills, and providing the cultural advantages of a state-supported institution of higher learning. The Cleveland-Bolivar County Chamber of Commerce, the Rosedale-Bolivar County Port Commission, the Economic Development District of Bolivar County, and the Industrial Development Foundation through their coordinated efforts have achieved much success in bringing major industries to the county and furthering the economic development potential of Bolivar County. These coordinated efforts, as well as the county's efficient utilization of public and private funding, have led to national recognition on three occasions, including a 1982 Award for Industrial Development from the United States Department of Housing & Urban Development, a 1986 National Merit Award from the United States Department of Housing & Urban Development, and a 1987 National County Achievement Award from the National Association of Counties. In short, the county's overall policies, public and private investment programs, and industrial development efforts have secured job opportunities with major industrial and manufacturing employers, efforts which were based in part on action taken in 1973 by the Bolivar County Board of Supervisors in establishing a biracial committee to recommend ways of utilizing federal revenue sharing funds for the greatest benefit of the citizens, with emphasis on the need for more jobs for county residents. Bolivar County was the first county in the State of Mississippi to employ a County Administrator to assist in overall development efforts, and that individual, James B. Heidel, is now Director of the State Department of Community & Economic Development.

Redistricting After 1970 Census

Following the 1970 census, Bolivar County brought its five single-member district form of government into compliance with the one person-one vote standard of the United States Constitution, under a redistricting plan approved by the United States District Court for the Northern District of Mississippi.

Redistricting After 1980 Census

Following the 1980 census, the county again undertook to develop a new redistricting plan in order to bring the five supervisor districts into compliance with the one person-one vote standard, by virtue of population shifts during the preceding decade. During the course of §5 administrative proceedings, §2 of the Voting Rights Act was amended to incorporate the "results test" now embodied in 42 U.S.C. §1973. Following efforts to obtain §5 preclearance, on June 27, 1993, a class action was brought against the Bolivar County Board of Supervisors by eight black citizens seeking declaratory and injunctive relief against further use of the county's 1971 redistricting plan and against implementation of a revised redistricting plan based upon the 1980 census which was the subject of a §5 objection from the United States Department of Justice. Claims were asserted under §2 and §5 of the Voting Rights Act of 1965, as amended and extended, 42 U.S.C. §1973, et seq., 42 U.S.C. §1981 and §1983, and the Fourteenth and Fifteenth Amendments. Following disposition of the §5 claim, *Lucas v. Bolivar County*, 567 F. Supp. 453 (N.D. Miss. 1983), the county developed a redistricting plan embodying the one person-one vote principle and avoiding impermissible dilution of black voting strength, and at the conclusion of a five-day hearing which ended on October 11, 1983, the United States District Court for the Northern District of Mississippi concluded that the county's redistricting plan represented a good faith effort to afford blacks an equal opportunity to participate in elections and elect candidates of their choice, that the plan did not result in a denial or abridgement of the right of any citizen to vote on account of race, and that §2 was not violated. The Court also rejected the Plaintiffs' constitutional claims and approved the county's redistricting plan, directing the County Board of Supervisors to submit it to the Attorney General of the United States for §5 preclearance. *Lucas v. Bolivar County*, Civil Action No. DC83-136-WK-O (Memorandum of Decision February 14, 1984)(Keady, C.J.). The Attorney General precleared this redistricting plan in May 1984, and the Plaintiffs' appeal from the District Court's decision was dismissed by the United States Court of Appeals for the Fifth Circuit in 1985. *Lucas v. Bolivar County*, 756 F.2d 1230 (5th Cir. 1985).

Black Electoral Success: Reality, Not Theory

At the time of the trial of the §2 suit in 1983, Bolivar County had more black elected officials than any other county in the State of Mississippi, and the State of Mississippi had more black elected officials than any other state in the nation. The District Court's findings of fact reflected an intensely local appraisal of past and present political reality and a frank acknowledgment of the dissipation of any lingering effects of past official discrimination:

1. The Court finds as a fact that success at the polls for black candidates depends more upon one's competency and qualifications for the job and type of campaign conducted than upon the size of the BVAP, so long as it constitutes a majority of the total VAP (February 14, 1984, Memorandum of Decision, p.12).

2. The disparities between blacks and whites in education and income have been previously alluded to, and such disparities do, to some extent, hinder the ability of blacks to participate fully in the electoral process. This adverse impact has diminished greatly in recent years because of progress made in Bolivar County by blacks educationally, economically and politically. Although responsiveness of the county's Supervisors is not an issue in the case, the Defendants have made an impressive showing of the county's involvement in obtaining industries that afford job opportunities for black citizens, in developing affirmative action programs and in sponsoring job training programs (February 14, 1984, Memorandum of Decision, p.14).

3. [T]he Defendants' plan, when considered as a whole, insures the political viability of black candidates in four out of five districts and provides an opportunity for black voters commensurate with whites to participate effectively in the political processes and to elect candidates of their choice (February 14, 1984, Memorandum of Decision, p.20).

4. The credible evidence is that the success of candidates at the polls is generally determined by the factors of incumbency, experience, qualifications and vigorous community-wide campaigning, and not by race. Section 2 expressly disavows any right of proportional representation to the members of the protected class, and it should not be construed to guarantee the success of a candidate because of his race (February 14, 1984, Memorandum of Decision, p.26).

Redistricting After 1990 Census

Following release of the 1990 decennial census statistical data, the Bolivar County Board of Supervisors determined that population shifts during the preceding decade had resulted in a maximum relative deviation of over nineteen percent in the 1984 redistricting plan, and undertook to make necessary revisions for purposes of a §5 Submission, realizing that it had to act quickly in view of the approaching party primary elections scheduled for September 17, 1991. While the county was in the process of submitting a revised redistricting plan to the United States Department of Justice for §5 preclearance, two citizens brought a civil action against the county on August 21, 1991, seeking declaratory and injunctive relief, alleging that the present districts were unconstitutionally malapportioned, that any further elections under the existing or any unprecleared district should be enjoined and that the qualifying deadline and election schedule should be revised and delayed until a redistricting plan had been precleared by the U. S. Department of Justice or by the U. S. District Court for the District of Columbia pursuant to §5 of the Voting Rights Act. *Young v. Bolivar County, Mississippi*, Civil Action No. DC91-G133-B-O, United States District Court for the Northern District of Mississippi, Delta Division. On September 3, 1991, a Consent Decree was entered which allowed the party primary and general elections to go forward as scheduled under the present existing supervisor redistricting plan in effect since 1984. In the Consent Decree, the District Court specifically found that "a substantial justification exists for utilizing said redistricting plan for the aforesaid primary and general elections despite an apparent malapportionment reflected by a 19.68 percent maximum relative deviation."

Shortly before the commencement of the trial and entry of the Consent Decree which settled it, on August 26, 1991, Bolivar County, Mississippi, filed a civil action in the United States District Court for the District of Columbia against the United States of America for declaratory judgment under §5 of the Voting Rights Act of 1965, as amended. *Bolivar County v. USA*, Civil Action No. 91-2186 (MB), United States District Court for the District of Columbia. Extensive negotiations with attorneys representing the Voting Section of the Civil Rights Division of the U. S. Department of Justice have taken place during the pendency of this civil action, and it is anticipated that Bolivar County and the Justice Department may on or before June 20, 1994, file amended pleadings together with a proposed order or consent decree under which a redistricting plan based upon the 1990 census data will be judicially approved under §5 of the Voting Rights Act.

Financial Costs of Protracted Litigation: An Unfunded Mandate?

There is a growing realization—not just outside the Beltway—that federal mandates have grown out of control and that "no money, no mandate" legislation may be needed to protect vital state and local programs from the unlimited and growing number of burdensome federal mandates, not the least of which is found in the mandatory provisions of the Voting Rights Act. To put this in perspective, the total amount of litigation costs, including cost of defense, expert witness fees and court costs incident to the 1983 redistricting litigation up to and including dismissal in 1985 of the Plaintiffs' appeal by the United States Court of Appeals for the Fifth Circuit, exceeded $190,000. Plaintiffs in that litigation sought attorney's fees pursuant to 42 U.S.C. §1988, the Civil Rights Attorney's Fees Awards Act of 1976, which, significantly, were limited to approximately $10,000 by virtue of the fact that the county had filed a Rule 68 Offer of Judgment early in the proceedings, thereby limiting its liability for attorney's fees subsequent to the date of the Offer of Judgment, since the relief ultimately obtained by the Plaintiffs was not more favorable than that embodied in the Rule 68 Offer of Judgment. See *Marek v. Chesny*, 473 U.S. 1, 11, 87 L.Ed.2d 1, 10, 105 S.Ct. 3012 (1985)('civil rights plaintiffs--along with other plaintiffs--who reject an offer more favorable than what is thereafter recovered at trial will not recover attorney's fees for services performed after the offer is rejected.... To be sure, application of Rule 68 will require plaintiffs to ` think very hard' about whether continued litigation is worthwhile; that is precisely what Rule 68 contemplate').

Litigation costs, expert witness fees and court costs in the $5 declaratory judgment action filed in 1991 may exceed $200,000. Such costs incurred on the local government level are directly attributable to efforts to comply with the federal mandates of the Voting Rights Act. Congress will soon begin consideration of the Kempthorne/Condit Unfunded Mandates bills, H.R.140 and S.993, which enjoy bipartisan support from the majority of members in both Houses, 221 Representatives and 54 Senators as of April 29, 1994. Action on this mandate relief legislation has been scheduled for May 26, 1994.

Attainable Goals of the Voting Rights Act

It has been pointed out that Lyndon Johnson in 1965 called for and got the "Goddamnedest, toughest, voting rights bill" that his staff could devise.[3] The Act had as its goals racial fairness, equal access to the political and electoral process, and unimpeded opportunity on the part of minority citizens

---

[3] A. Thernstrom, Whose Votes Count? Affirmative Action and Minority Voting Rights 16 (Harvard Univ. Press, 1987), citing "In Southern Voting, It's Still ` White Only,' " *Atlanta Constitution*, — 7 December 1980, reprinted in Hearings before the Subcommittee on Civil and Constitutional Rights of the Committee on the Judiciary, U. S. House of Representatives, 97th Cong., 1st Session, on the Extension of the Voting Rights Act, May-July, 1981, p.280.

to participate in that process. Subsequent amendments in 1970, 1975 and 1982 purported to broaden the reach of the Act, while not intending to deviate from these goals.

The fundamental goals of the Voting Rights Act have been reached and will continue to be realized in Bolivar County, Mississippi. At this point in the history of Bolivar County, American politics and the fundamentally sound system of American democracy have evidently been working, and many African-American citizens have been elected to office and hold significant leadership positions in state and local government.[4]

---

[4] Illustrative of the extent of minority electoral achievement and empowerment are the following:

1. District 3 Supervisor Richard M. Coleman, who is now in his second term of office;
2. Bolivar County Election Commission Chairman and District 1 Commissioner David Washington;
3. District 3 Election Commissioner Monica Micou;
4. District 4 Election Commissioner Dr. Nathaniel Brown;
5. District 5 Election Commissioner Delilah Cherry;
6. Justice Court Judge Erma Inge, who is her fourth term of office;
7. Justice Court Judge Cardell Fletcher, who was formerly Chief Deputy Sheriff with the Bolivar County Sheriff's Department;
8. Circuit Clerk Rosie Simmons, who is serving her second term in this countywide office;
9. Bolivar County Judge Kenneth L. Thomas, formerly Municipal Court Judge for Rosedale, who is completing his first term of this countywide office and also running for the newly created position of Circuit Judge for the Eleventh Circuit Court District, Place Three;
10. Bolivar County Constable Robert L. Scott;
11. Bolivar County Constable Samuel Keith Tolliver;
12. Congressman Bennie Thompson, representing the Second Congressional District of the State of Mississippi, which includes all counties in the Mississippi Delta, his experience having included ten years as a member of the Hinds County Board of Supervisors and active participation in the National Association of Counties;
13. State Senator Willie Simmons, whose Senate district includes a substantial portion of Bolivar County, his electoral experience having included service as Cleveland School District (District IV) Trustee elected from a majority white district, and holding one of the top positions with the Mississippi Department of Corrections, equipping him with the necessary expertise to serve in a leadership role in the Senate's Corrections Committee;
14. State Senator Johnnie Walls, whose Senate district includes a portion of Bolivar County;
15. State Representative Linda Coleman, who has very ably served her constituents in the county during her first term in the Mississippi House of Representatives and is also running for the newly created position of Circuit Judge for the Eleventh Circuit Court District, Place Three;
16. City of Rosedale Mayor J. Y. Trice, who has played a significant role on the county and state level including service in leadership positions appointed by the Governor on the State Department of Education, and whose service to his fellow citizens have brought him the highest honors and recognition on the county level.
17. Mississippi Supreme Court Judge Reuben Anderson and Mississippi Supreme Court Judge Fred Banks, who defeated white opponents with significant support from white voters in 1986 and 1991, respectively. See *Magnolia Bar Association, Inc. v. Lee*, 994 F.2d 1143, 1148-49 (5th Cir. 1993).

This is the same fundamentally sound system of American democracy that has evidently been working elsewhere in the country, as in the Commonwealth of Virginia, a state with a black population of under 20 percent, which elected Douglas Wilder as Governor in 1989, and Illinois, which elected Carol Mosely-Braun to the United States Senate in 1992.

Access and Opportunity

The fundamental objective of the Voting Rights Act was to remove not only structural barriers but subtle and indirect barriers to minority access to the electoral process and participation in the political processes generally. While much remains to be done, we submit that the citizens of Bolivar County, particularly African-American citizens, are enjoying the open and equal access and abundant electoral opportunities consistent with the fundamental objectives of the Voting Rights Act, as amended and extended by the 1982 Voting Rights Act Amendments.

Concerns

We do have concerns over the present enforcement policy of the Voting Section of the Civil Rights Division, as well as certain strained judicial constructions of §2 of the Voting Rights Act which appear inconsistent with fundamental objectives of the Act. In voicing these concerns, we advocate returning the Voting Rights Act to its original goals of fair access and opportunity, and in so doing we are neither playing the role of messenger from the enemy camp nor advocates for moral laxity on Voting Rights.

First, it appears that the §2 disclaimer against proportional representation ["Nothing in this section establishes a right to have members of a protected class elected in numbers equal to their proportion in the population." 42 U.S.C. §1973(b) (1982)] is in some instances being given only lip service and in effect disregarded, and that proportional representation is actually being utilized both administratively and on occasion judicially as the ultimate standard for determining §2 liability as well as the legal adequacy of remedial alternatives for such violation. The "Dole compromise" embodied in the §2 disclaimer has been correctly recognized as "the ultimate back-stopping principle" of §2, but the chief enforcing agency as well

---

This list does not include the overwhelming majority of school board trustees on the six school boards in Bolivar County who are African-Americans, as well as the overwhelming majority of mayors and alderpersons who are the governing authorities in over 2/3 of the 15 municipalities in the county and are African-Americans.

-8-

as some courts have apparently lapsed into an inappropriate view of voter empowerment, confusing the right to have free and equal access to the ballot box and to have the vote that is cast count effectively, with the right of a voter to have his or her vote cast for the winner. This has resulted in a distortion of the core values of the Act, including the basic principle that

> the voter is enfranchised by having voted and by having his or her vote counted, without any diluting device, as any other voter in the final tally that determined the outcome. While a vote must have equal weight, it is not, even if cast by a member of the protected class, entitled to have a greater weight than any other vote.

Smith v. Brunswick County Board of Supervisors, 984 F.2d 1393, 1398 (4th Cir. 1993).

Second, the Department of Justice appears to have adopted the argument advanced by Professor Lani Guinier, which she refers to as the "authenticity assumption." This is in effect the argument made by the United States recently as *amicus curiae* in *Shaw v. Hunt, infra,* and "is based on the premise that black voters are better off with black Representatives in Congress. The logical extreme of this premise is obvious; it is ` Apartheid.'" (p.17, Plaintiffs' Reply Brief to the Post-Trial Brief of the United States as *Amicus Curiae,* April 22, 1994, *Shaw v. Hunt,* No. 92-202-CIV-5-BR, United States District Court for the Eastern District of North Carolina, Raleigh Division).

The logical converse to Professor Guinier's argument is that white voters are better off with white representatives, commissioners and supervisors, a position just as repugnant to American constitutional theory. *Id.* n. 18. It is counterproductive to improving race relations, and, ultimately, would discourage development of biracial coalitions and consensus between persons of different races. This point is developed more fully in the affidavit of Professor Stephan Thernstrom submitted in *Shaw v. Hunt, supra.*

Third, the Department of Justice appears to have developed a more restrictive definition of "racial gerrymander" since the United States Supreme Court's June 1993 decision in *Shaw v. Reno.* For example, in *Hays v. State of Louisiana,* 839 F. Supp. 1188 (W.D. La. 1993), appeal pending, No. 93-5152, United States Supreme Court, the Department of Justice has attacked the definition of a racial gerrymander in *Hays* as representing a "radical departure" from *Shaw v. Reno* that would "subject virtually all redistricting plans with majority-minority districts to strict scrutiny" (p.41, Post-Trial Brief for the United States, *Shaw v. Hunt,* April 12, 1994). This restrictive definition would permit a *Shaw*-type constitutional claim only with respect to geographically bizarre districts which are explainable only as an act of racial segregation. Even taking this most restrictive definition of "racial gerrymander" now utilized by the United States Department of Justice post-*Shaw*, there is no principled constitutional justification for a redistricting plan whose unusual shape is so linked to race that it equates to an explicit racial classification. Racial gerrymandering that results in a congressional district resembling a "bug splattered on a windshield" or a "Zorro" district that looks like Johnny Appleseed designed it, should certainly prompt strict scrutiny, "because it presumes a community of interest based on race, and in that way ` stereotypes' voters."

> It reinforces the perception that members of the same racial group--regardless of their age, education, economic status, or the community in which the[y] live--think alike, share the same political interests, and will prefer the same candidates at the polls.

Shaw v. Reno, infra, 113 S.Ct. at 2827.

Fourth, *Shaw v. Reno* is starting to have an impact upon §2 litigation. For example, when a court in a §2 case is presented by the Plaintiffs with an illustrative plan as a legally adequate demonstration that the *Gingles* precondition of "geographical compactness" could be met, it can ill afford to give only lip service to the "geographical compactness" requirement. If a jurisdiction's black population is simply too dispersed to permit creation of a geographically compact majority-black district, and if the proposed illustrative plan departs from traditional districting principles and is explainable only as an effort to segregate voters on the basis of explicit racial classifications, there can be no effective remedy and thus no §2 violation.[5]

---

[5]See *Clark v. Calhoun County, Mississippi*, 813 F. Supp. 1189 (N.D. Miss. 1993), wherein Chief Judge L. T. Senter found that the Plaintiffs failed to establish geographical compactness, stating at 1197-98:

> Although Plaintiffs have proved that the black population of Calhoun County is sufficiently large enough to constitute a majority in one district, they have failed to prove that this same minority group is geographically compact. Under Plaintiffs' proposed plan, blacks from three separate and distinct municipalities, each having diverse interests, were extracted to form District 1. This exercise results in extreme gerrymandering, Plaintiffs' proposed black district having been "drawn in an unusual or illogical manner to enhance the voting power of a particular...voting bloc at the expense of other individuals or groups who would be elected or help elect the candidates of their choice." ...If one assumes that all voting in Calhoun County will be based on race and not qualifications, then the District suggested by Plaintiffs may well accomplish the automatic election of a black Supervisor (citation omitted).

Accord, Houston v. Lafayette County, Mississippi, 841 F. Supp. 751, 765 (N.D. Miss. 1993)("By no means was the landmark legislation enacted to insure the success of black or other minority candidates by carving the political terrain into irregularly and artificially shaped designs and patterns that result in the deliberate

Fifth, a more recent development in §2 litigation has arisen in the context of jurisdictions wherein blacks or other minorities are geographically dispersed. As set forth more fully in the Affidavit of Duke University Professor Donald L. Horowitz, proponents of cumulative voting have offered it as a way for geographically dispersed minorities to secure representation. This alternative electoral system, which provides for a form of proportional representation, has been utilized at this point in American history for election of corporate boards of directors and in certain limited instances as the basis for settlement of voting rights litigation as approved by Consent Decrees. It was also used and ultimately abandoned in the State of Illinois as the basis for electing legislators. It has now been ordered by a federal court as a remedial alternative to be put into effect by an Eastern Shore county, marking the first instance in which a cumulative voting system remedy was ordered into effect by a court as a remedy for a judicially determined §2 violation. See *Cane v. Worcester County, infra*. As summarized by Professor Horowitz, the likely costs of cumulative voting have been ignored. It has rarely been used anywhere, and tends to promote "sweethearting" or tacit collusive agreements to limit competition, dramatically reducing interparty competition and leading to a decline in electoral accountability of representatives (Horowitz affidavit, pp. 4-7). Cumulative voting provides many incumbents with a free ride to re-election, and its principal effect may be to increase racial polarization and encourage exploitation of divisive racial issues, including an increase in the likelihood of white candidates engaging in racial appeals (Horowitz affidavit, pp.8,9). According to Horowitz, cumulative voting is a function of intense preferences, which in turn are fostered by racially polarized environments. "In the name of remedying racial polarization, cumulative voting would be likely to entrench it" (Horowitz Affidavit, p.10). The effect of this alternative electoral system is to create a positive incentive for racial appeals, and Horowitz concludes that cumulative voting may be conducive to and may lead to extremism and polarization within legislative bodies (Horowitz Affidavit, pp.11,13).

---

creation of ` safe' majority/minority districts reserved exclusively for minority candidates to represent.").

The Lani Guinier Nomination

In a series of articles challenging the claim that the presence of minority officeholders changes the dynamics of majority decisionmaking, a number of scholars including Lani Guinier, Professor at the University of Pennsylvania Law School, began "searching for ways to increase minority influence in systems that are fundamentally majoritarian in tone." B. Grofman, L. Handley and R. Niemi, **Minority Representation and the Quest for Voting Equality** 127 (Cambridge Univ. Press, 1992). Guinier and others argued:

> [i]n favor of formal mechanisms to give "proportionate influence," such as those found in some consociational democracies, in which, for example, groups may be allocated control of shares of certain government budgets.

Minority Representation, *supra* at 127-28.

According to Professor Guinier, the increase in the number of black elected officials "has not visibly altered the disadvantaged socioeconomic condition or social isolation of black voters" and "sustained black mobilization has not emerged despite some black electoral success."[4]

Guinier advocated a "proportional interest representation" theory, which was summarized in **Voting Rights and Democratic Theory: Where Do We Go From Here?**, *supra*, an approach which would restructure how legislatures pass laws, whereby they would function, not by majority rule, but by a consensus that required the backing of black and other minority representatives.

Guinier's writings were closely scrutinized on the occasion of her nomination for the office of Assistant Attorney General for the Civil Rights Division, a nomination which set the stage for a national debate on racial politics. Some commentators depicted Guinier as a racially paranoid social engineer whose

---

[4] **Minority Representation**, *supra* at 136. *See* L. Guinier, **The Triumph of Tokenism: The Voting Rights Act and the Theory of Black Electoral Success**, 90 Mich. L. Rev. 1077-1154 (1991); L. Guinier, **Keeping the Faith: Black Voters in the Post-Reagan Era**, 24 Harvard Civil Rights-Civil Liberties L. Rev. 393-435 (1989); L. Guinier, **Voting Rights and Democratic Theory: Where Do We Go From Here?**, In Bernard Grofman and Chandler Davidson, Eds., **Controversies in Minority Voting: A 25-Year Prospective on the Voting Rights Act of 1965** (Brookings Institution, Washington, D.C. 1992), Guinier called for "proportionate influence," which would be achieved by devices such as supermajority voting requirements and rotation of legislative presiding officers. L. Guinier, **Voting Rights and Democratic Theory**, *supra*. *See also* L. Guinier, **No Two Seats: The Elusive Quest for Political Equality**, 77 Va. L. Rev. 1413 (1991). *See* Lani Guinier, **Beyond Majoritarianism: A Theory of Representation of Minority Interests** (September 14, 1991)(unpublished manuscript)(on file with the Va. L. Rev. Assn.).

views about the Voting Rights Act are "startlingly extreme, unworkable, and as a matter of statutory interpretation, extraordinarily far-fetched." S. Taylor, "DOJ Nominee's 'Authentic' Black Views," in "Taking Issue," Legal Times, May 17, 1993, p. 23. Others, notably Duke Law Professor James E. Coleman, Jr., came to her defense:

> In a 1991 Michigan Law Review article, "Triumph of Tokenism: The Voting Rights Act and the Theory of Black Electoral Success," Guinier discusses the concept of "authentic representative" in the context of her detailed critique of the Theory of Black Electoral Success. That theory underlies the current race-conscious remedial approach, the aim of which is to elect black candidates. According to scholars who adhere to this view, an "authentic representative may be an individual who is community-based and culturally and physically similar to his or constituents." Guinier does *not* endorse this viewpoint in her Michigan article; she does *not* endorse it in any of her other writings; and she does *not* endorse it in fact. Indeed, she notes in the Michigan Law Review article that, if the concept were properly applied, an "authentic representative" need not be black as long as the source of their authority, legitimacy, and power base is the black community.

In a response, Stewart Taylor, Jr. stated in an article entitled "Who's Fooling Whom About Justice Nominee's Views," Legal Times, May 31, 1993, at 27:

> Guinier's supporters also, in my opinion, seem to believe they can sell her as a "mainstream" thinker only by disingenuously denying that she has ever said some things that she has, in fact, said rather clearly. They seek to divert attention from her attacks on majority rule as we know it, and her advocacy of a court-enforced system of "proportional power sharing" wherever black voters and legislators cannot win a "fair proportion" of their policy goals—such as "redistributing political power and economic wealth"-from a white majority.

On Thursday, June 3, 1993, President Bill Clinton announced that he was withdrawing his nomination of Lani Guinier to head the Justice Department's Civil Rights Division because he could not defend her views on voting rights.

> The President admitted that he had not read Guinier's legal writings before he nominated her and said he would not have made the nomination had he done so. He said his staff had not flagged him about the "intense controversy" her Law Review articles would spark and the "ordeal", as he phrased it, that Guinier would undergo as a result.

The Washington Post, June 4, 1993, p. 1.

The President's move ignited anger and sharp reactions from the civil rights community and the Congressional Black Caucus. Part of the aftermath of the Guinier nomination withdrawal included an editorial by Mary Ann Glendon, Professor at Harvard Law School, who stated:

> Why is it that the 43 year old legal educator had no inkling of how unrealistic were her prescriptions for one of America's gravest social issues? The fact is, by Professor Guinier's

student days in the 70's, the nation's elite law schools were increasingly exalting theory over practice, and judicial decisionmaking over ordinary politics. A growing disdain for the practical aspects of law, a zany passion for novelty, a confusion of advocacy with scholarship, and a mistrust of majoritarian institutions all contribute to a relatively homogenous political culture within the cloister. No wonder products of that hot-house environment wilt quickly in the open marketplace of ideas.

M. Glendon, "What's Wrong With the Elite Law Schools," Wall Street Journal, June 8, 1993, p. A-14.

Guinier herself characterized President Clinton's withdrawal of her nomination as "an unfortunate metaphor for the way race and racism are viewed in this society." Speaking at the Annual Convention of the NAACP in Indianapolis on July 13, 1993, Guinier stated:

> We are being defined, we are being characterized, we are being misrepresented by the people...who are not sympathetic to issues of quality and real democracy.... Unless we want to be known as race-obsessed radicals, we are no longer permitted to discuss racism in polite conversation or law articles.

Clarion-Ledger, July 14, 1993, p. 2.

Even before the Guinier nomination, much caustic and quite provocative commentary had been generated on the racial division, polarization and ghettoization which some see as inevitable consequences of the racial gerrymandering encouraged or facilitated by §2 of the Voting Rights Act.

Victimization Rhetoric

In a stinging editorial entitled "The High Cost of Playing Victim" published almost four years ago, John Leo made this trenchant analysis of the debate among blacks about victimization in an era of racial polarization:

> The rhetoric of victimization enforces the view that the poor and the demoralized are little more than observers in their own lives. It teaches the young that they cannot be expected to succeed, except perhaps as part of a complaining victim group. It mocks the connection between striving and success. It makes black-white alliances unlikely and it subtly depicts black success as a kind of commodity that whites control and refuse to dole out to blacks. This is a dead form of racial politics. Can't we get beyond it?

U. S. News & World Report, October 1, 1990, p. 23. (Emphasis added).

Black Empowerment, Not Racial Spoils System

Another commentator targeted the apparent racial polarization which, 28 years after the Civil Rights Act, continues to frustrate consensus on some of the most important issues facing our nation. Addressing what he labels "one of the most pernicious myths underlying racial division: that blacks and whites have fundamentally different views and aspirations," Clint Bolic, Litigation Director at the Institute

for Justice in Washington, wrote in 1992:

> This myth has fueled demagogues on both sides of the racial divide, especially in the aftermath of the Los Angeles riots. But poll results just released by the left-leaning Joint Center for Political Studies reveal that most blacks aspire like other Americans to safe streets, good schools and home ownership.
>
> Of equal import, the survey demonstrates that mainstream black Americans are far more conservative than most of the politicians and organizations that purport to speak for them. This philosophical gulf perhaps was most pronounced near the end of the Clarence Thomas confirmation hearings, when national groups like the NAACP stridently opposed the Supreme Court nominee while blacks in general approved by a 3 to 1 ratio (along with some local NAACP chapters).... Indeed, the remaining task of the civil rights struggle is not to redistribute opportunities through a divisive and counterproductive racial spoils system, but to empower those who have been denied opportunities.

C. Bolick, "Blacks and Whites on Common Ground," The Wall Street Journal, August 5, 1992. (Emphasis added)

Ghettoization

There are voices out there crying for a common ground that transcends racial class considerations, race-based allegiances, and race-based assignments of citizens to political groups. There are voices that rally against insidious efforts to define racial classes by identifying racially homogeneous precincts and electoral districts so as to herd people into racially segregated political groups. This sort of political "ghettoization," described by Professor Walter Berns of the American Enterprise Institute, in his testimony during the Senate hearings in 1982, S. Rep. No. 97-417, at 150, has unfortunately proved to be the path of least resistance in what we can only hope will be a handful of cases in which the federal courts have adopted a race-based mindset which cuts across the general forward direction of the developing body of §2 precedent.

Racial Gerrymandering and Majority/Minority Districts

The goals of §2 of the Voting Rights Act of 1965, as amended and extended, are to assure minority voters and equal opportunity to participate in the political process and equal access to that process. The ability to elect representatives of their choice is a key focus in §2 litigation.

Race should not become the basis for distributing voters in the redistricting process, nor should equal opportunity and access become synonymous with guaranteed electoral success. Unfortunately, racial gerrymandering has become a by-product of this redistricting process. It finds its roots in the same impermissible racial stereotypes that, over thirty years ago, excluded black voters from the city limits of Tuskegee, Alabama. See *Gomillion v. Lightfoot*, 364 U.S. 339, 340 (1960), describing the boundaries of the City of Tuskegee as "an uncouth 28-sided figure."

In the intensifying debate over the consequences of maximizing minority voting strength to assure proportional representation, diametrically opposed viewpoints have been expressed by Professor Abigail M. Thernstrom, author of Whose Votes Count? Affirmative Action and Minority Voting Rights (Harvard Univ. Press, 1987) and Frank R. Parker, Director of the Voting Rights Project of the Lawyers Committee for Civil Rights under Law, and author of Black Votes Count: Political Empowerment in Mississippi After 1965 (The Univ. of North Carolina Press 1990). In a scrupulously balanced and fascinating study of the evolution of the Voting Rights Act, Thernstrom exhibits sincere concern and sympathy for the struggles of African-Americans and the cause of racial justice, but makes a very strong argument for the proposition that a combination of an unrestrained federal judiciary and the exercise of exceedingly broad administrative discretion by the Civil Rights Division have resulted in a distortion of the original intent of the Voting Rights Act, turning it into a tool for affirmative action in the electoral arena and granting minority voters what is tantamount to an entitlement to proportionate racial representation. Whose Votes Count?, *supra* at 5. Highlighting the potential costs incident to maximizing minority office holding, Thernstrom concludes:

> The pressure for such interracial, interethnic coalitions lessens with the existence of single-member districts drawn to maximize minority office holding. Political necessity brings groups together. The majority-white county, city or district in which whites vote as a solid bloc against any minority candidate is now unusual. Especially in districts or localities with a substantial minority population, divisions among white voters send white candidates scurrying for those important black votes. The process not only enhances political integration but also may serve to heighten minority electoral influence.... Candidates who have joined hands in a victorious biracial coalition will tend to stick together on a governing body, since the next election is never far off. But when whites on a city council or other legislative body owe nothing to black support, blacks in the minority may find themselves consistently outvoted and thus isolated. *Id.* at 243-44.

Parker, on the other hand, disagrees with any notion that the Voting Rights Act has been reshaped into an unintended shield which provides African-American candidates with special protection from white competition. While evaluating these arguments in the context of electoral developments in Mississippi, Parker takes the position that prohibiting minority vote dilution will grant minority voters a remedy from discrimination but will not entitle them to proportional representation, contending that the arguments of such political scientists as Abigail Thernstrom "are part of an effort to roll back the advances that have been made. Full judicial protection against minority vote dilution has been critical to insuring representative government and the proper functioning of the democratic process." Black Votes Count, at 11-12.

Thernstrom counters by pointing out that

In every city with a significant minority population, at least one minority single-member district can be drawn, and, by Parker's reasoning, blacks have a right to such districts whenever it is possible to create them. That is, minority voters are entitled to control electoral outcomes--to elect whom they want--where methods of voting can be altered to permit such control. Precisely that commitment, however, had been ruled out by the Dole compromise; the statute had guaranteed no "fair share," only a "fair shake"--a chance to play the electoral game by fair rules. Yet Parker and others continue to push their view, and with overwhelming success.

Whose Votes Count?, at 229.

Wading into this debate is Lani Guinier, Professor of Law at the University of Pennsylvania, and the catalyst for a political firestorm which erupted when President Bill Clinton nominated her to the position of Assistant Attorney General for Civil Rights in April 1993 and thereafter withdrew the nomination after he "re-read" her law review articles. Guinier's recent book, The Tyranny of the Majority: Fundamental Fairness in Representative Democracy (The Free Press, 1994), a compilation of earlier articles, deals with the "authenticity assumption." Id. at 55. In discussing political authenticity, she writes:

Authentic leaders are those elected by black voters. In voting rights terminology, electoral ratification from majority-black, single-member districts establishes authenticity. These facts distinguish the authentic representatives from those officials who are handpicked by the "establishment," or who must appeal to white voters in order to get elected. Establishment-endorsed blacks are unlikely to be authentic where they are not elected as representatives of choice of the black community. In addition, these officials are not "of" ... the community if they are marginal community members whose only real connection with black constituents is skin color. Id. at 56.

In this regard, Professor Guinier responds to the critics of the authenticity assumption, including Abigail

Thernstrom:

> Some critics assert that the authenticity assumption is a meaningless cultural and descriptive concept. For example, Abigail Thernstrom, an outspoken critic of the conventional empowerment model, denies the empirical or theoretical validity of culturally similar representatives, because whites can represent black interests. Thernstrom attempts to revive the theory of virtual representation in which black interests are occasionally taken into account even if they are not actively promoted. Thernstrom argues that the single act of voting for any representative legitimates democratic self-government.
>
> Thernstrom's emphasis on color-blind virtual representation abstracts the black experience from its historical context. Virtual representation ignores the existence of group identity within the black community. Thernstrom's theory reduces electoral participation to the individual unit within the voting booth. At that level, the perception is most acute when one vote will have a negligible effect on the ultimate outcome. Moreover, in neglecting the role of blacks and whites as politically cohesive groups, Thernstrom's electoral self-legitimating focus fails to acknowledge the role that group identity plays in mobilizing political participation and in influencing legislative policy.

Guinier also takes issue with Thernstrom's view that current Voting Rights Act interpretations

and enforcement policies have deviated from the original legislative understanding of the right to vote.

The Tyranny of the Majority, *supra* at 211 n. 53 (apparently disagreeing with Thernstrom's viewpoint

that the 1965 Act was transformed unwittingly into a statutory mandate for black electoral success or "Job

Corps" for black elected officials).

The author of the Dole compromise had this to say about Ms. Guinier's "mind-bending cumulative-

voting schemes" and apparent emphasis upon proportional representation, guaranteed legislative outcomes,

and quotas:

> These are prescriptions not for equal opportunity, but for equal results and guaranteed legislative outcomes--the very principles rejected by the original drafters of the Voting Rights Act and by those, like myself, who fought hard for the Act's reauthorization.... I never thought I would see the day when a nominee for the top civil rights post at Justice would argue, not that quotas go too far, but rather that they do not go far enough.

(Statement of Senator Robert Dole on the nomination of Lani Guinier, May 20, 1993, Cong. Record-Senate,

S6171-72).

Even though we may never know the identity of the headline editor who attached the label "The

Quota Queen" to Clint Bolick's now famous editorial which was published in the April 30, 1993, issue of

The Wall Street Journal ("Clinton's Quota Queens," The Wall Street Journal, Friday, April 30, 1993),

Bolick, Litigation Director at the Institute for Justice in Washington, D.C., and author of <u>Grassroots</u> <u>Tyranny: The Limits of Federalism</u> (Cato Institute, 1993), brought to the forefront Ms. Guinier's views on the "simple-minded notions of majority rule," as well as her contention that the Voting Rights Act should require new procedures to insure "a fairer distribution of political power." As Bolick concluded:

> If these nominations are part of Mr. Clinton's payback to extreme left-wing elements of the Democratic Party, the price may prove too high... The reason is simple: white voters often view quotas as a barrier to opportunity, while few blacks or other minorities view them as beneficial in their individual circumstances.

> Mr. Clinton owes his election in no small part to the disappearance of the "Q" word from the political lexicon in 1992. If he persists in entrusting the civil rights law enforcement apparatus to the likes of Ms. Guinier..., the in-your-face civil rights agenda they no doubt will promote may ultimately be proved the most incendiary of political miscalculations.

The fundamental hostility which Professor Guinier's views display toward the American democratic system of government are not the subject of arguable interpretation of dense legal writings. Her words are clear and unambiguous:

> In my view, under the political equality and political empowerment norms of the Voting Rights Act, majority rule is fair voting procedure to the extent it provides each voter an equal opportunity to influence legislative decisionmaking, or a proportional stake in the legislative outcome.

L. Guinier "No Two Seats: The Elusive Quest for Political Equality," 77 Va. L.Rev. 1413, 1441-43 (1991).

Bearing in mind that proportional representation is not required by the Voting Rights Act, Professor Guinier goes much further:

> I argue that it is not merely a question of whether, on matters of substantive justice, minority rights trump majoritarian democracy. Instead, we ought to question the inherent legitimacy of winner-take-all majority rule. My claim is that disproportionate majority power is, in itself, so wrong that it delegitimates majority rule.... *Id.* at 1478.

As Professor Thernstrom has recently noted, such efforts to draw redistricting plans to separate blacks and whites into racially identifiable constituencies can be quite costly, a tendency which Professor Guinier appears to recognize. *See* <u>The Tyranny of the Majority</u>, *supra* at 71-118. These same concerns were expressed by Sandra Day O'Connor in *Shaw v. Reno, infra,* 125 L.Ed.2d at 535:

> Racial classifications with respect to voting carry particular dangers. Racial gerrymandering, even for remedial purposes, may balkanize us into competing racial factions....

Shaw v. Reno

In *Shaw v. Reno*, 508 U.S. ___, 113 S.Ct. 2816, 125 L.Ed.2d 511 (1993), the United States Supreme Court held that Appellants stated a valid claim under the Equal Protection Clause by alleging that the North Carolina General Assembly adopted a reapportionment scheme

> that is so extremely irregular on its face that it rationally can be viewed only as an effort to segregate the races for purposes of voting, without regard for traditional districting principles and without sufficiently compelling justification

113 S.Ct. at 2824.

To what extent are the minority protection purposes of the Voting Rights Act weakened by non-minority attacks based on the Constitution? The answer to this question may lie in a string of decisions emanating from U. S. District Courts, Three-Judge Courts and Courts of Appeals, as well as pending proceedings in North Carolina, Georgia and Texas. Post-*Shaw* jurisprudence is beginning to take shape.

These decisions are as follows:

1. *Hines v. Mayor and Town Council of Ashoskie*, 998 F.2d 1266, 1274 (4th Cir. 1993).

2. *Rural West Tennessee African-American Affairs Council, Inc. v. McWherter*, 836 F. Supp. 453 (W.D. Tenn. 1993).

3. *Hays v. State of Louisiana*, 839 F.Supp. 1188 (W.D. La. 1993), *appeal pending*, No. 93-5194, Supreme Court of the United States.

4. *Barnett v. Daley*, 835 F. Supp. 1063, 1070 (N.D. Ill. 1993).

5. *Cane v. Worcester County*, 840 F. Supp. 1081 (D. Md. 1994), *further proceedings*, ___ F. Supp. ___, 1994 W.L. 113660, 62 U.S.L.W. 2631 (D. Md. 1994), *appeal pending*, No. 94-1579, United States Court of Appeals for the Fourth Circuit.

6. *Marylanders for Fair Representation, Inc. v. Schaefer*, ____ F. Supp. ____ (Civil Action No. S92-510 and S92-1409, January 17, 1994).

7. *Houston v. Lafayette County, Mississippi*, 841 F. Supp. 751 (N.D. Miss. 1993).

The United States Department of Justice has also intervened in pending redistricting litigation in North Carolina and Georgia in *Shaw v. Hunt*, No. 92-202-CIV-5-BR, U. S. District Court, E.D. N.C., Raleigh Division, and *Johnson v. Miller*, C.A. No. CV194-008, U.S. District Court, S.D. Ga., Augusta

Division. According to Attorney General Janet Reno, the Justice Department is "committed to protecting minority rights that were achieved through redistricting after the 1990 census," (Justice Joins Redistricting Flap, A.P. February 23, 1994).

Hines v. Mayor and Town Council of Ahoskie

In *Ahoskie*, black voters brought a §2 challenge against the Town's at-large system for electing Town Council members and proposed an election plan which would have created three out of five single-member–minority-controlled districts. Holding that the District Court improperly reduced the Town Council from five members to four and erred in refusing to accept the Town's proposal in its entirety, the United States Court of Appeals for the Fourth Circuit also concluded that the District Court properly rejected the election plan proposed by the black voters, stating at 1274:

> Finally, a legislature may not devise a districting plan *solely* for the purpose of segregating citizens into separate voting districts on the basis of race without sufficient justification. *Shaw v. Reno.*

> In the present case, we believe that the plan proposed by Hines would violate these principles. Specifically, a plan giving a minority group a majority of the single-member districts would effectively "cancel out the voting strength" of the majority,...and provide the minority with a vote of greater weight than the majority. Nothing in the Act requires a remedy imposing over-proportional representation. Moreover, because Hines acknowledged that the *only* motivation for such a districting plan would be racial concerns, i.e., providing blacks with another representative on the Town Council, and there is apparently no sufficient justification for such a plan, we believe such a districting plan would violate the equal protection rights of white voters. *Shaw.*

Rural West Tennessee African-American Affairs Council, Inc. v. McWherter

On November 4, 1993, a three-judge district court held that Tennessee's Senate Reapportionment Plan violated §2 of the Voting Rights Act. One of the issues before the Court was the state policy underlying the redistricting plan. The Court noted that there were some practical problems with weighing state interests under the totality of the circumstances test under §2, namely, that the State's interests in an electoral scheme are only relevant to the extent that those interests are compromised by a possible §2 remedy. The Court stated at 465:

> When potential remedies do not impinge on the State's interests, those interests need not be considered. We have before us only two of the numerous possible remedies, both of which were presented by the Plaintiffs. The first plan was presented primarily to demonstrate that the first *Gingles* precondition can be met. The second plan was

-21-

submitted in response to concerns expressed by the Court and the State that Plaintiffs' plan ignored "traditional districting principles." *Shaw v. Reno*, 508 U.S. __, 113 S.Ct. 2816, 2824, 125 L.Ed.2d 511 (1993). Specifically, one of the proposed majority-black districts split six counties. Plaintiffs' second plan demonstrated that a second district could be created by splitting only Shelby and Madison Counties. Under the current plan, some counties are split in forming Senate districts, but no district splits more than one county.

The Court in *McWherter*, upon finding a §2 violation, ordered the State of Tennessee to submit

a new plan which complies with the Voting Rights Act and requested Plaintiffs to submit alternative plans,

suggesting that the State consider the views of the Plaintiffs and all other interested parties when drawing

a new plan. In this regard the Court made it clear that in fashioning a remedy the State would not be

required to draw districts to achieve maximum possible black representation in the Legislature, stating:

> The explicit rejection in the text of the statute of any right to *proportional* representation indicates that Congress did not intend to require *maximum* representation.... The evidence before us indicates that one more majority-black Senate district must be drawn in West Tennessee. A second majority black district would provide slightly more representation than the State's black voting age population require. It would create five black Senate districts in the state or more than fifteen percent of the districts when the black voting age population is 14.4 percent. The issue of creating a fifth black Senate district should be left to the political judgment of the legislature. It is not required by federal law. *Id.* at 467.

Hays v. State of Louisiana

In *Hays*, a three-judge court ruled in favor of the Plaintiffs who challenged the Louisiana

Congressional Redistricting Plan, concluding that the plan in general and Congressional District 4 in

particular were the products of racial gerrymandering and were not narrowly tailored to further any

compelling governmental interest, and that the Plaintiffs' right to equal protection was violated by the

plan. As posed by the three-judge court, the question before it was "does a state have the right to create

a racial majority-minority Congressional district by racial gerrymandering?" The Court answered its own

question:

> In simplest form, the answer–largely supplied by the United States Supreme Court's opinion in *Shaw v. Reno*, rendered during the pendency of this case–is "Yes, but only if the state does it right." *Id.* at 1191.

The Court found overwhelming evidence, both indirect and direct, that the redistricting plan was

the product of racial gerrymandering, stating:

We have already noted the narrow holding of *Shaw*: a plaintiff may state a claim under the Equal Protection Clause by alleging that the reapportionment scheme adopted by his state is so irrational on its face "that it can only be understood as an effort to segregate voters into separate voting districts because of their race...." *Shaw* primarily deals with the problem of proving racial gerrymandering indirectly or inferentially. Racial gerrymandering--says the Court in *Shaw*--can be inferred when districts are so bizarrely shaped that they presumptively bespeak an impermissible purpose.

But racial gerrymandering may--*a fortiori*--also be proved by direct evidence that a legislature enacted a districting plan with the specific intent of segregating citizens into voting districts based on their race. If everyone--or nearly everyone--involved in the design and passage of a redistricting plan asserts or concedes that design of the plan was driven by race, then racial gerrymandering may be found without resorting to the inferential approach approved by the Court in *Shaw*. The Court recognized in *Shaw* that "[n]o inquiry into legislative purpose is necessary when the racial classification appears on the face of the statute." The same is equally true when virtually unanimous, essentially uncontroverted direct trial evidence establishes racial classification, as it did here. *Id.* at 1195.

Physical Appearance

Shaw has generated somewhat colorful judicial prose with regard to the physical appearance of allegedly racially gerrymandered districts, and *Hays* provides yet another example, wherein the Court discussed the highly irregular appearance of Congressional District 4:

Like a fictional swordsman Zorro, when making his signature mark, District 4 slashes a giant but somewhat shaky "Z" across the state, as it cuts a swath through much of Louisiana. It begins north of Shreveport-in the northwestern corner of Louisiana, just east of the Texas border and flush against the Arkansas border--and sweeps east along that border, periodically extending pseudopods southward to engulf small pockets of black voters, all the way to the Mississippi River. The district then turns south and meanders down the west bank of the Mississippi River in a narrow band, gobbling up more and more black voters as it goes. As it nears Baton Rouge, the district juts abruptly east to swallow predominantly black portions of several more parishes. Simultaneously, it hooks in a northwesterly arc, appropriating still more black voters on its way to Alexandria, where it selectively includes only predominantly black residential neighborhoods. Finally, at its southern extremity, the district extends yet another projection--this one westward towards Lafayette--adding still more concentrations of black residents. On the basis of District 4's physiognomy alone, the Plan is thus highly irregular, suggesting strongly that the Legislature engaged in racial gerrymandering. *Id.* at 1199-1200.

Even **The Wall Street Journal** got into the act, describing the Fourth Congressional District as looking

as if it was designed by Johnny Appleseed. It begins life north of Shreveport on the Arkansas border, wanders east all the way to the Mississippi River, and then heads south, helter-skelter, toward the Gulf of Mexico.

(Wall Street Journal, July 14, 1993, Vol. CCXXI, No. 9, A1).

Traditional Redistricting Criteria

The Court in *Hays* also noted that the subject plan cavalierly disregarded traditional redistricting principles and criteria, including compactness, contiguity, respect for political subdivision, and commonality of interests.

Compactness

With regard to compactness, the Court in *Hays* noted that Congressional District 4 "snakes narrowly across Louisiana soil from end to end for more than 600 miles." *Id.* at 1200.

> A rectangle superimposed on the Z-shaped figure formed by District 4 would overlay two-thirds of the state. Additionally, as it winds along its erratic path, District 4 projects myriad diverticulae to encapsulate small sacs of otherwise widely dispersed black voters. No one could claim that District 4 is compact, at least not with a straight face. *Id.* at 1200.

Contiguity

The Court stated that Congressional District 4 only hypertechnically and thus cynically was confected to satisfy the traditional districting criterion of contiguity:

> When displayed on a map of the state, the district's boundaries seem several times to narrow to a single point. This impression reflects reality, for at some places along its attenuated path, District 4 is no more than 80 feet wide. Such tokenism mocks the traditional criterion of contiguity. *Id.*

Respect for Political Subdivisions

With regard to the criterion of respect for political subdivisions, the Court noted that of the 28 parishes touched by Congressional District 4, only four whole parishes were included, but the district annexed only "shards" of 24 other parishes, usually incorporating only the predominantly black fragments of those shattered regions and fragmenting all major municipalities except one into more than one Congressional district, "thereby destroying the common representation historically enjoyed by residents of the same municipality." *Id.* at 1201.

Commonality of Interest

With regard to the traditional redistricting criterion of commonality of interest, the Court found that Congressional District 4 with its irregular boundaries "subsumes bits of every religious, ethnic, economic, social and topographical type found in Louisiana." *Id.*

Non-Racial Factors

Finally, the Court disagreed with the Defendants' assertion that they could defeat a racial gerrymandering claim under *Shaw v. Reno* if any factor other than race played any cognizable role in the creation of the challenged redistricting plan, stating:

> The defendants evidently base their belief--that the presence of any non-racial motivating factor will excuse racial gerrymandering--on language found at the end of the *Shaw* opinion. There the Court indicates that the plaintiff states a claim under the Equal Protection Clause by alleging that a reapportionment plan is so irrational on its face "that it can be understood only as an effort to segregate voters...." This emphatically does not mean that if any other factor influenced the legislature, the Plaintiff is unable to establish a racial gerrymander. Rather, it means that if the contours and content of a redistricting plan can be wholly explained to be the product of one or more factors other than race, then the Defendants have created a competing inference. The Court must then weigh the competing inferences--as indeed it usually must--to decide whether the Plaintiff has proved his inference by a preponderance of the evidence. Thus, accurately stated, the question posed by *Shaw* is whether a redistricting plan can be reasonably conceived as the product of non-racial factors. In this case the plan cannot. *Id.* at 1202.

Direct Evidence of Racial Gerrymandering

In addition to indirect or inferential proof of racial gerrymandering, the Court in *Shaw* found that direct evidence clearly and forcefully demonstrated that the redistricting plan was the product of racial gerrymandering.

> Virtually every witness who testified at the trial (all without the benefit of a retrospective, self-serving view of *Shaw*) either affirmatively stated or accepted as gospel that the Plan was drawn with the specific intent of ensuring the creation of a second, safe, black majority congressional district: namely, District 4. The Defendants' witnesses either stated or conceded that the districts created by Act 42 were racially gerrymandered. Indeed, those witnesses, both lay and expert, spent most of their time at the trial discussing how large the percentage of registered black voters needed to be in the new majority black district to guarantee the efficacy of their racial gerrymander--an efficacy they view as the *sine qua non* of preclearance. *Id.* at 1204.

Strict Scrutiny and Compelling State Interests

The Court in *Hays* noted that the core principle underlying the *Shaw* decision was that racially gerrymandered redistricting plans were subject to the same strict scrutiny that applies to other state legislation classifying citizens on the basis of race, and in this case the Court rejected the four possible compelling state interests advanced by the Defendants to justify their racial gerrymandering, including

(1)   conformity with §2 of the Voting Rights Act;

(2)   conformity with §5 of the Voting Rights Act;

(3)   proportional representation of Louisiana blacks in Congress; and,

(4)   remedying the effects of past racial discrimination.

The Court concluded that uncontroverted evidence demonstrated that the plan was "not narrowly tailored to satisfy any of the supposedly compelling state interests advanced by the Defendants." *Id.* at 1207.

> We reach that conclusion first because the plan entails considerably more segregation than is necessary to satisfy the need for a second black majority district--even assuming arguendo that such a second district were itself justified--and second because the plan excessively burdens a variety of third party interests--dramatically so. *Id.*

The Court reasoned that voters have an equal protection right not to be segregated by their state legislatures or local governments into various voting districts on the basis of race, and that a plan will survive constitutional scrutiny only when it segregates "to no greater extent than is reasonably necessary to further a compelling governmental interest...." *Id.*

> The same can be said for a plan that supersaturates a majority-minority district, while concomitantly depleting adjacent majority-majority districts of minority voters. In this case, we find that the plan entails more constitutionally suspect segregation than necessary, and is therefore not narrowly tailored. Continuing to assume arguendo that some state interest has been identified which could justify the creation of a second black-majority district, this plan would have to be rejected as insufficiently narrowly tailored. It packs more black voters into District 4 than are reasonably necessary to give blacks a realistic chance to determine the outcome of elections there, provided that they exercise their right to vote. Also, the boundaries of the district violate traditional districting principles to a substantially greater extent than is reasonably necessary. *Id.*

Plan Not Narrowly Tailored

In concluding that the subject redistricting plan was not narrowly tailored, the Court identified a variety of factors germane to this analysis:

(1)   the necessity of the measure;

(2)   the efficacy of alternative race-neutral measures;

(3)   the availability of more narrowly tailored (less intrusive) measures;

(4)   the flexibility and duration of the measure; and,

(5)   the impact of the measure on the rights of third parties.

The Court also reasoned that a plan was not narrowly tailored if it adversely affected more interests, "if it generally wreaks more havoc, than it reasonably must to accomplish the articulated compelling state interest." *Id.* at 1208. In so concluding the Court noted that the plan embraced considerably more racial gerrymandering and thus more segregation than was needed to satisfy any advanced state interest, that it unnecessarily violated a host of historically important redistricting principles, thereby adversely affecting countless third party interests, and

> These several and varied interests--some constitutionally protected and others merely important--may not be callously sacrificed on the altar of political expediency, particularly when less broadly tailored plans are conceivable. *Id.* at 1209.

Barnett v. Daley

In *Barnett*, the U. S. District Court for the Northern District of Illinois dismissed separate challenges to the redistricting of Chicago's aldermanic wards following the 1990 census, holding that districts which provided blacks with a sufficient majority to select the candidate of their race in 19 out of 50 wards (38 percent), roughly corresponding to a 38.6 percent citywide black population, did not violate §2 of the Voting Rights Act or the Fourteenth or Fifteenth Amendments. Plaintiffs' central premise was that they were entitled to 22 African-American super-majority wards "simply because the creation of that number of wards is demographically feasible." *Id.* at 1068. The Court noted that one type of state voting practice that could give rise to a constitutional claim "is the new type recognized in *Shaw*." *Id.* at 1070.

> In *Shaw*, the Supreme Court held that appellants stated a valid claim under the Equal Protection Clause by alleging that the North Carolina General Assembly adopted a reapportionment scheme

>> that is so extremely irregular on its face that it rationally can be viewed only as an effort to segregate the races for purposes of voting, without regard for traditional districting principles and without sufficiently compelling justification. (Citation omitted.) The plaintiffs here make no such allegation of bizarre, irrational district configurations. Rather, they merely allege city-wide vote dilution. As a result, they do not have a claim under the Fourteenth or Fifteenth Amendments. Ironically, however, the plaintiffs' proposed remedy might provide white and Hispanic voters with a cause of action under *Shaw*. After all, by demanding maximum representation, the plaintiffs are requesting an intentional racial gerrymander in favor of African-Americans. *Id.* at 1070.

Cane v. Worcester County

In a January 7, 1994, Memorandum Opinion, the U. S. District Court for the District of Maryland upheld a §2 challenge to Worcester County's at-large system of electing Commissioners, finding in part that the *Gingles* geographical compactness requirement "is a relative concept which must be interpreted in light of Section 2's ` laudatory national mission' of opening the political process to minorities." *Cane v. Worcester County*, 840 F. Supp. 1081, 1086 (D. Md. 1994). Despite objections that a majority-minority district could be created only through blatant racial gerrymandering and by fracturing of three separate municipalities, and without regard to substantial evidence of the County's governmental justification for maintaining an at-large system of county government, and without regard to provisions of the Maryland Constitution clearly indicating a preference for maintaining political subdivision boundaries and in particular municipal boundary lines in the redistricting process, the Court concluded that the Plaintiffs had satisfied the geographical compactness requirement, stating:

> The plaintiffs' proposed Plan 1 is not unreasonably irregular in shape, considering the population dispersal within the county. The plan merely affirms the existing racial divisions in the county. While the plan does entail running the newly created districts across other voting district lines and through towns, this is unavoidable because of the heavily white population and the need to achieve a majority African-American population in one of the districts. The districts may not be symmetrical, but they are compact. They do not rely on districts that run through several "tentacle-like corridors" nor are the district's boundary lines so unreasonably irregular, bizarre or uncouth as to approach obvious gerrymandering. They are in line with the configurations of electoral districts that have been approved in other cases. *Id.* at 1086-87.

The District Court found §2 liability and rendered judgment for the Plaintiffs, directing Defendants to submit a remedial plan within sixty days. Defendants thereupon submitted as a legally acceptable remedial alternative for use during the 1994 election cycle, the electoral system and form of government established under Bill 93-6, which had become effective in May 1993 and under which no elections have been held. Plaintiffs also submitted three remedial plans, two of which were racially gerrymandered single-member district plans under which a majority/minority district bisected two and three municipalities, respectively, disregarded local and state government policy requiring respect for municipal and other political subdivision boundaries, and linked pockets of black concentrations together to form an elongated single-member district running the length of Worcester County, in disregard of traditional districting principles and political policy choices reflected in the legislative history of Bill 93-6. The third plan submitted by Plaintiffs was a cumulative voting system which up until this point in American jurisprudence had been utilized in the context of corporate law and in a limited number of jurisdictions through Consent

Decrees settling Voting Rights Act litigation. Under the cumulative voting system proposed by Plaintiffs, any group constituting more than 16.7 percent of the voters could elect a candidate if they cumulated their votes for that candidate, so that in an election for five positions on a county Board of Commissioners, each minority voter could aggregate his or her five votes and cast those for a single candidate.

The District Court in *Cane v. Worcester County* by Order dated April 4, 1994, 1994 W.L. 113660 62 U.S.L.W. 2631 (D. Md. 1994), rejected the Defendants' proffered Bill 93-6 plan as violative of §2 and ordered Defendants to change the electoral system of Worcester County to a cumulative voting system to be implemented within sixty days. The Court in so doing rejected Defendants' argument that Plaintiffs were required to introduce competent evidence demonstrating that Bill 93-6 was unacceptable and that it was improper to compare it to the old electoral system, stating:

> Such a review is impossible because there have been no elections under Bill 93-6. (Slip Op. at 6, Order dated April 4, 1994).

Defendants moved for a stay of the District Court's January 7, 1994, and April 4, 1994, Orders, based in part upon compliance with the traditional stay factors recognized by Fourth Circuit precedent, and argued that court-mandated implementation of a cumulative voting system violated constitutional principles of one person-one vote, federalism and separation of powers, and that Defendants were unable to bypass or ignore state law requirements which effectively precluded their compliance with the implementation order within sixty days. The District Court denied this Motion for Stay by Order dated May 2, 1994, whereupon Defendants-Appellants filed the Motion for Stay with the Fourth Circuit Court of Appeals on May 9, 1994, pursuant to Rule 8 of the Federal Rules of Appellate Procedure.

In their appeal to the Fourth Circuit, Defendants-Appellants in *Worcester County, Maryland v. Cane*, No. 94-1579, are challenging the District Court's finding regarding the *Gingles* preconditions of geographical compactness, minority political cohesion and white racial bloc voting as clearly erroneous, and are challenging the District Court's remedial order directing the County to implement a cumulative voting system as a §2 remedy. The challenge to the District Court's remedial order is predicated in part on *McGhee v. Granville County, North Carolina*, 860 F.2d 110 (4th Cir. 1988), in which the Fourth Circuit held that the District Court erred in rejecting Granville County's proposed single-member district plan as

150

a remedy for a stipulated §2 violation and in ordering into effect the Plaintiffs' proposal based on limited

voting in at-large elections. The Fourth Circuit in *McGhee* described the limited voting system as a "semi-

proportional" representational system, stating:

> The disclaimer in amended §2 of any "right" of racial minorities to proportional
> representation prevents a court from using proportional representation as the ultimate
> standard for assessing the legal adequacy of a remedial legislative redistricting plan. *Id.*
> at 118.

This viewpoint echoed that of Alexander Hamilton in the Federalist #35, who observed that a

proportional representation standard is not recognized in our Constitution and "would endanger our basic

political liberty."

In conjunction with their FRAP 8 Motion for Stay in the Fourth Circuit, the Defendants-Appellants

have submitted the affidavit of Duke University Professor Donald L. Horowitz, a copy of which is attached

to this statement. As Horowitz points out, the cumulative voting system remedy ordered into effect for

Worcester County by the District Court's April 4, 1994, Order and Memorandum Opinion is not just an

exotic electoral system, but has rarely been used anywhere except in relatively small local government

entities predicated on voluntary imposition of cumulative voting in the settlement of voting rights litigation,

approved by Consent Decrees. Illinois experimented with cumulative voting until it was repealed in a 1980

referendum, amidst a storm of public protest caused by the fact that cumulative voting produced safe

seats, which facilitated the legislature's approval of a salary increase for itself. See Affidavit of Donald L.

Horowitz, pp.4-8).[7]

---

[7]   As pointed out earlier in this statement, the negative consequences of cumulative voting are legion.
Empirical data has shown that cumulative voting tends to limit competition through "sweethearting"
(Affidavit of Donald L. Horowitz, p.7). It has produced dramatically reduced interparty competition and
a corresponding decline in the electoral accountability of representatives through the increase of safe seats
and long tenure in office (Affidavit of Donald L. Horowitz, pp.7-8). One of the principal effects of
cumulative voting is its tendency to increase and entrench racial polarization (Affidavit of Donald L.
Horowitz, pp.8,10). Cumulative voting is not only conducive to racial polarization, but increases the risk
of polarization and conflicts within the legislative body itself, making the aggregation of interests more
difficult by virtue of a system which rewards the expression of intense preferences and leads to strong
representation of intense preferences and special interests that might otherwise be confined to lobbying
activity (Affidavit of Donald L. Horowitz, pp.13-14). As applied to Worcester County, trial testimony made
it clear that this county is a heterogeneous and complex area, with separate and distinct population centers
consisting of Pocomoke City, a cosmopolitan, industrial and progressive town closely tied to adjacent
military and urban areas of Virginia; Snow Hill, the county seat, located in a rural area, inward looking,
agrarian and conservative; Berlin, oriented toward its history and tourism; Ocean City, a retirement area

Marylanders for Fair Representation v. Schaefer

Using an approach similar to that of the District Court in *Cane v. Worcester County*, the three-judge court in *Schaefer* rejected a racial gerrymandering challenge leveled against District 54-9, despite objections that the proposed district was bizarrely shaped, lacked geographical compactness and violated traditional districting principles. In the words of dissenting Judge Smalkin, this oddly-shaped creation "is a ` geographically challenged' creation, not a geographically compact one." (Smalkin, dissenting, Slip Op. at 6).

According to the majority in *Schaefer*:

Compactness is neither mentioned in the text of the Voting Rights Act nor required by the federal Constitution. See *Shaw*, 113 S.Ct. 2827.... The majority opinion in *Gingles*, from which the compactness requirement flows, unfortunately provides little guidance. Justice Brennan's opinion for the court explained that the compactness requirement was designed to bar §2 suits where no majority-minority district can be drawn because the plaintiff minority group members are "substantially integrated" or "spread evenly" throughout the challenged district. See 478 U.S. 50 and n. 17. Thus, as originally described by Justice Brennan, *Gingles'* compactness requirement simply precluded a finding of liability under §2 where no remedy was possible. In more recent cases, however, the Supreme Court has clearly indicated that the concept of compactness is not a hollow one. In *Growe v. Emison*, Justice Scalia referred to a State Senate District that "stretch[ed] from South Minneapolis, around the downtown area, and then into the northern part of the city in order to link minority populations" as an "oddly shaped creation" of "dubious" geographic compactness. *Growe*, 113 S.Ct. 1083, 1085 (Dicta). And, although its holding was granted in the Equal Protection Clause rather than the Voting Rights Act, the court in *Shaw v. Reno* certainly focused its attention on the non-compactness of North Carolina's 12th Congressional District. See *Shaw*, 113 S.Ct. 2822-31. But see *Id.* at 2831. (Expressly reserving the question whether the district at issue was "geographically compact" within the meaning of *Gingles*).

From these recent cases we discerned two guiding principles. First, courts should be reluctant to order the creation of voting rights districts of "bizarre" or "dramatically irregular" shape. *Id.* at 2820, 2825, 2831. Second, although a state can - and at times must - place great weight on race when redistricting, it may not do so to the exclusion of all traditional, non-racial redistricting principles, leaving a district that rationally can be

---

experiencing an influx of retirees from the Washington, D.C. area. These separate and distinct communities of interest reflect and embody a significant north-south regional division within the county, and it was the need to bridge these regional divisions that justified the county's utilization of at-large elections. On the contrary, court-mandated cumulative voting would likely foster the same polarization and conflicts which the county sought to bridge through at-large elections. Under the 93-6 electoral system, candidates would be required to receive support from all over the county, but not under a cumulative voting system, by which candidates would be rewarded through the voters' expression of intense preferences, leading to elected officials strongly representing special interests (Affidavit of Donald L. Horowitz, pp.13-14).

understood only as "an effort to classify and separate voters by race." *Id.* at 2828.... [P]ut differently, the case law suggests that we must pay attention to both geometric and substantive criteria when testing for compactness under *Gingles*....we are not, however, completely lacking in objective measurements that can serve at least as a proxy for the more sophisticated methods. The essence of defendants' argument is that the NAACP's proposed district takes two distinct pockets of dense black population - one in Salisbury, the other in Cambridge - and strings them together with a narrow rural corridor. The argument, however, cannot withstand scrutiny. District 54-9 is only 32 miles long at its greatest span. Under the state's plan, however, 14 delegates and 9 senators from around the state will be forced to serve constituents who are spread over a greater distance than District 54-9's 32 miles. *Cf. Jeffers v. Clinton*, 730 F. Supp. 196, 207 (E.D. Ark. 1989) (three-judge court) ("[plaintiffs'] alternative districts are not materially stranger in shape than at least some of the districts contained in the present apportionment plan", aff'd mem., 498 U.S. 1019 (1991); Legislative Redistricting Cases, 31 Md. at 591-92, 629 A.2d 654-55 (noting that a challenged district's "shape, while unusual, is no more odd than the rest of the districts. . . in the whole state"). The Defendants also complained that the NAACP's proposed districts use attenuated "corridors" - sometimes only two miles across - to link non-contiguous pockets of denser population. However, voting rights case law indicates that there is nothing extraordinary about this technique. See, e.g., *Neal v. Coleburn*, 689 F. Supp. 1426, 1435 (E.D. Va. 1988) (holding that plaintiffs satisfied *Gingles'* geographic compactness criterion even where "a number of fairly small pockets [of black population had to] be connected to create two election districts"). Indeed, the state apparently used a similar technique when drawing its own plan, as seven of its districts contained corridors less than half a mile wide. One passageway in the state plan's District 18 is less than <u>200 yards</u> across.

In short, if District 54-9 is not sufficiently compact, then the same can be said of many districts in the state's new legislative redistricting plan. That plan, however, has already withstood a challenge brought specifically on the ground of non-compactness. Only a few months ago, the Maryland Court of Appeals heard - and rejected - a claim that the state's plan violated Maryland's constitutional requirement that legislative districts "be compact in form." Md. Const. Art. III, §4; see <u>Legislative Redistricting Cases</u>, 331 Md. 580, 590-92, 629 A.2d 648, 654-55. We see no reason to reach a different result. Therefore, we conclude that plaintiffs have met the burden of proving that proposed District 54-9's shape and appearance are unobjectionable under *Gingles*. Next, we turn to the question of whether District 54-9's shape rationally can be understood only as "an effort to classify and separate voters by race." *Shaw*, 113 S.Ct. 2828. As an initial matter, we note that the NAACP drew many illustrative single-member districts on the Shore that had a significantly greater black population than District 54-9. The NAACP drew one district that contained 25% more voting-age blacks than District 54-9. Thus District 54-9 could not have been merely the result of an effort to maximize the number of black voters and to minimize the number of white voters in the proposed district. Other considerations must have come into play.

Indeed, upon closer inspection, District 54-9 evidences considerable regard for traditional, non-racial redistricting criteria. See *Shaw*, 113 S.Ct. 2822-32 (repeatedly invoking "traditional districting principles").

...[T]he district "consist[s] of adjoining territory." Md. Const. Art. III, §4. And unlike the North Carolina district challenged in *Shaw*, discrete pieces of District 54-9 are never merely "point contiguous," i.e., touching only at a common corner. See *Shaw*, 113 S.Ct. ──── 2821.

Third, District 54-9 gives "[d]ue regard...to natural boundaries." Md. Const. Art. III, §4. In interpreting this constitutional provision, the Maryland Court of Appeals has stated that it is preferable to avoid water crossings where there is no bridge or ferry. See *In Re: Legislative Districting*, 299 Md. 682, 475 A.2d 440. District 54-9 straddles the Wicomico River through much of Wicomico County, but the river presents no travel difficulties, as the district encompasses both the Upper Ferry crossing to the west of Salisbury and the Route 50 crossing in Salisbury itself. District 54-9 also crosses the Nanticoke River, as it must, since that river constitutes the entire border between Dorchester and Wicomico Counties, and the district was drafted to incorporate the Route 50 bridge that crosses the Nanticoke at Vienna.

Functional Test of Compactness

In footnote 45 at page 70 of its opinion, the three-judge court in *Schaefer* stated:

> In any event, since plaintiffs have proved their submergence claim, it is the responsibility of defendants to redraw the district lines in a manner that best accommodates the State's interests while remedying the Voting Rights Act violation. We also note that if the State decides to create a single-member district that is the same (or similar to) proposed District 54-9 and to leave the remainder of District 37 as an at-large, two-member district, the constituents in the remainder will be represented substantially as they would have been under the State's plan. As a practical matter, delegates can travel across District 54-9 to meet with constituents in District 37 just as they did before. The critical <u>functional</u> test of compactness clearly can be met. See *Dillard v. Baldwin County Board of Education*, 686 F. Supp. 1459, 1466 (M.D. Ala. 1988).

In his dissenting opinion, Judge Smalkin made the point that the fact that delegate District 20, located in Montgomery County outside the D.C. city line, had a "shape, while unusual, [that] is no more odd than the rest of the districts...in the whole state," "does not excuse the irregular shape of District 54-9, located in the rural counties on the Eastern Shore. *Id.* at 4 (Smalkin, Dissenting Opinion). Judge Smalkin also differed with the majority's interpretation of *Neal v. Coleburn, supra*, stating:

> Although it is true that the *Neal* opinion states that there is nothing impermissible about connecting small pockets of black population to create a majority-minority single-member district, that district must, based on its shape and appearance, still satisfy the *Gingles* compactness requirement. There are a substantial number of decisions that have found that attempts to connect pockets of black population with attenuated corridors did not satisfy the *Gingles'* compactness requirement. See, e.g., *Clark v. Calhoun County*, 813 F. Supp. 1189, 1197-98 (N.D. Miss. 1993) (extraction of blacks from three separate distinct municipalities, each having diverse interests, did not satisfy compactness requirement); *Burton v. Sheheen*, 793 F. Supp. 1366 (rejecting districts that slice and splice towns and counties or run "a thin snaking line back and forth across the county" as not geographically compact); *Clark v. Roemer*, 777 F. Supp. 445, 455 (M.D. La. 1990) (districts spread over three parishes not geographically compact).

With regard to traditional districting principles, Judge Smalkin also cited *Clark v. Calhoun County* and *Clark v. Roemer* for the proposition that many lower federal courts have expressly considered adherence to traditional districting principles to determine whether a particular district is geographically compact, stating:

> I do not believe that the district can be said to respect the boundaries of political subdivisions when it divides the three largest cities it touches - Salisbury, Cambridge and Fruitland.... Thus, far from respecting or adhering to the boundaries of political subdivisions, District 54-9 simply ignores those boundaries in order to carve out the predominantly black communities and connect them through narrow rural corridors to other, distinct and distant such communities. *Id.* at 7-8.

With regard to the factor of effective political representation, Judge Smalkin relied upon *Shaw*, 113 S.Ct. 2827, for the proposition that a court should also consider whether individuals who live in the district share sufficient interests-cultural, economic and political - that they can be effectively represented by a single delegate, noting that the Supreme Court in *Shaw* had expressed discomfort with a district comprised of individuals with nothing in common but their race, noting that because of the district's strange and irregular shape,

> it might be difficult for that delegate (in proposed District 54-9), in making his or her rounds, to know which Eastern Shore residents are his or her constituents, without employing a sophisticated navigational system such as GPS, or, at least on clear nights, celestial navigation. *Id.* at 9-10.

Smalkin concluded at page 11:

> It will be extremely difficult for a single delegate to represent effectively the diverse populations that are combined in District 54-9. The district combines the black populations of two distinct and distant municipalities.

Houston v. Lafayette County

In a Superseding Memorandum Opinion dated November 5, 1993, reported at 841 F. Supp. 751 (N.D. Miss. 1993), the U. S. District Court for the Northern District of Mississippi rejected a §2 challenge brought by minority plaintiffs who alleged that the existing single-member district plan operative in Lafayette County, Mississippi, resulted in minority vote dilution. In a county with a 26.4 percent black population, the minority plaintiffs contended that the present district scheme prohibited blacks residing within the county from electing a black candidate of their choice to hold the office of County Supervisor in any of the five single-member supervisory districts, and advocated creation of a majority black minority voting age population district for the county to enhance their chances of electing a black supervisor. Citing the fundamental purpose of the Voting Rights Act to eradicate impediments designed to deny blacks and other protected groups the right to vote and participate in the political process, the Court stated:

> By no means was the landmark legislation enacted to ensure the success of black or other minority candidates by carving the political terrain into irregularly and artificially shaped designs and patterns that result in the deliberate creation of "safe" majority-minority districts reserved exclusively for minority candidates to represent. The Supreme Court recently rejected this practice in the case of *Shaw v. Reno*,.... Through a majority opinion offered by Justice Day O'Connor, the Court expressed its extreme distaste for racial gerrymandering, stating, "Racial gerrymandering exacerbates the very patterns of racial bloc voting that a majority-minority district is sometimes said to counteract.... The practice bears an uncomfortable resemblance to political apartheid." *Shaw*, 113 S.Ct. at 2827. When race supersedes such relevant and natural factors as political and geographical boundaries and becomes the driving force behind the creation of legislative districts, the result is an "impermissible racial stereotype" that "members of the same racial group—regardless of their age, education, economic status, or the community in which they live—think alike, share the same political interests and will prefer the same candidates at the polls. *Shaw*, 113 S.Ct. 2827, *Houston v. Lafayette County, Mississippi*, *supra* at 765.

The Court in *Lafayette County* also took note of the criticisms of Professor Lani Guinier wherein she scrutinized the worthiness of electoral districts custom-designed for minorities, stating:

> Prior to the recent Supreme Court decision in *Shaw*, voting rights legal scholars already had begun to scrutinize the worthiness of electoral districts custom-designed for minorities. One of the most vocal critics has been University of Pennsylvania Law School Professor Lani Guinier. Professor Guinier, who has written extensively about the subject of voting rights, has raised questions concerning the inherent value of deliberately drawing districts exclusively for blacks and other minority groups. By desultorily separating blacks from white voters under their perceived auspices of the Voting Rights Act, the process of subdistricting becomes detrimental to blacks as well as whites by severely limiting their voting choices. When blacks are funneled into a majority-minority district, they effectively become segregated from white voters. Thus, they are deprived of any opportunities for formulating voting coalitions with moderate white voters who, in turn, have similarly been "submerged" into a racially homogenous white district on the assumption that white voters too are an indistinguishable "mass" of humanity. Such "districting strategies often promote non-competitive election contests, which further reduce voter participation and interest.... [S]afe, minority seats discourage political competition and thus further diminish [voter] turnout." Lani Guinier, <u>No Two Seats: The Elusive Quest for Political Equality</u>, 77 Va. L. Rev. 1413, 1455 (1991), *Houston v. Lafayette County, Mississippi*, *supra* at 766.

The Court in *Lafayette County* noted that Professor Guinier's criticisms should come as no surprise:

> Minority districts often foster complacent attitudes in the minority representative elected to hold the seat. Once elected to a safe seat, a minority representative can easily ignore constituents' needs. Perceived as heirs apparent by themselves and their constituencies, minorities elected to racially gerrymandered districts enjoy the security and comfort of knowing they hold relatively secure seats and are largely immune from attack. Indeed, "incumbents enjoy extraordinary leverage in self-perpetuation through gerrymandering."

Guinier, 1supra,at 1454. A seated minority representative in a legislative district purposely tilted with an abundant minority population holds a strong advantage that is often insurmountable, even to a minority challenger. Politicians elected to office from so-called "safe" minority districts ironically possess an unfair advantage over their constituents. The degree of accountability to voters is substantially diminished, and minority voters become casualties of the notion that "members of the same racial group...think alike, share the same political [views], and prefer the same candidates...." *Shaw*, 113 S.Ct. at 2818. Relegating blacks to majority-minority districts ultimately isolates them from the overall political process, and insulates the minority representative from voter dissatisfaction. *Houston v. Lafayette County, Mississippi, supra* at 766.

Shaw v. Hunt

On June 28, 1993, the United States Supreme Court in *Shaw v. Reno*, 113 S.Ct. 2816, 125 L.Ed.2d 611 (1993), held that the complaint stated a cause of action under the Fourteenth Amendment against the state defendants and remanded the case. On September 7, 1993, the three-judge court granted Defendant-Intervenor status to Ralph Gingles and other black North Carolina residents. Following the close of discovery, the Plaintiff-Intervenors moved for a preliminary injunction seeking to enjoin the use of the North Carolina Congressional Redistricting Plan for the 1994 elections and sought a temporary restraining order to extend the candidate filing period. The TRO application was denied on February 7 by the three-judge court.

The trial commenced on March 28, 1994, and the primary elections were held as scheduled on May 3, 1994, there being no opinion from the three-judge court as of that date.

By way of background, on February 22, 1994, the United States filed a Motion for Leave to Participate as *Amicus Curiae* in opposition to the Plaintiff-Intervenors' Motion for a Preliminary Injunction, arguing in its supporting memorandum that the balance of the hardships did not favor Plaintiff-Intervenors and that it was in the public interest to allow the election schedule to proceed until a ruling after the trial. In Brief for the United States in Opposition to the Plaintiff-Intervenor's Motion for a Preliminary Injunction, the United States recognized that the Supreme Court in *Shaw* had defined an "analytically distinct" Fourteenth Amendment claim for challenging racial gerrymanders, limited to exceptional cases where a redistricting plan is "so extremely irregular on its face that it rationally can be viewed only as an effort to segregate the races for purposes of voting, without regard for traditional districting principles and without sufficiently compelling justification" (Brief for the United States, p. 16, citing *Shaw*, 113 S.Ct. at 2826, 2832).

The United States in its brief also noted that the Plaintiff-Intervenors will be relying upon *Hays v. State of Louisiana*, *supra*, to prove their *Shaw* racial gerrymandering claim, based on evidence that the legislature intended to create majority-minority districts. It argued that the *Hays* decision "is a substantial expansion of *Shaw* and would subject virtually all redistricting plans with majority-minority districts to strict scrutiny" (Brief for the United States, *supra* at 16-17), and said that such an approach eliminates the *sine qua non* of *Shaw*, namely, districts that are geographically bizarre and explainable only as an act of racial segregation, and urged the three-judge court not to follow it, and that some consideration of race in redistricting is permissible. It is thus for the Court to determine whether race was such an overriding consideration "that race, and not the other factors, produced a plan that departs significantly from ' traditional districting criteria' and thus constitutes the functional equivalent of an explicit racial classification" (Brief for the United States, *supra* at 22).

The United States argued that proof of an intent to take race into account to draw a majority black district is not all that is necessary to subject a redistricting plan to strict scrutiny, and that a *Shaw*-type racial gerrymandering claim must be limited to plans in which the districts' bizarre shapes are so linked to race that they are the equivalent to an explicit racial classification (Brief for the United States, *supra* at 17-18).

The United States took the position that the North Carolina Congressional Districts could be rationally viewed in ways other than as an effort to segregate the races for purposes of voting, an argument apparently supported by evidence that the districts have distinct socio-economic and demographic characteristics and reflect communities of interest which mirror the demographic differences among the districts.

The United States also pointed to three possible justifications for drawing two majority-minority districts in North Carolina:

(1)   considerations of race justified by §5 preclearance requirements;

(2)   considerations of race justified by §2; and,

158

(3)　　considerations of race justified as a remedial measure to eradicate effects of past discrimination (Brief for the United States, *supra* at 22-23).

Johnson v. Miller

On January 13, 1994, Plaintiffs filed a Complaint challenging the 1992 redistricting of the Georgia delegation to the United States House of Representatives as violative of the Equal Protection Clause of the Fourteenth Amendment to the United States Constitution, alleging that the Eleventh Congressional District "is so irrational on its face that it can only be understood as an effort to segregate voters into separate voting districts because of their race." The Complaint also alleged that the Eleventh Congressional District "was created without regard to other considerations customarily considered in redistricting, such as compactness, contiguity, geographical boundaries, economic interests and respect for political subdivisions."

The Congressional District at issue in *Johnson* was configured in large part in response to objections by the United States Department of Justice based on §5 of the Voting Rights Act, to two earlier reapportionment plans that had created two as opposed to three majority black Congressional districts (Fulton County Daily, February 24, 1994, pp. 5-6). Plaintiffs in their Complaint alleged that the §5 objections interposed by the Justice Department to Georgia's two proposed Congressional redistricting plans "represented an effort by individuals within the Justice Department to use the Voting Rights Act as a tool to forcibly implement their own redistricting policies rather than apply the Act according to its own terms" (Complaint at 8, paragraph 20). A bi-racial group of Eleventh District residents filed an Application for Intervention on February 7, 1994, asserting in their proposed Answer that the "State's consideration of race in its Congressional redistricting plan was proper and necessary in order to comply with §§2 and 5 of the Voting Rights Act" (Answer in Intervention, at 3). The Defendants-Intervenors are represented by the ACLU Foundation, Inc., the Georgia ACLU, and the NAACP Legal Defense and Education Fund, Inc. They took the position that the critical question is whether the sole motivation for reapportioning Georgia's Congressional districts was to segregate voters on the basis of race, and that a key factor in that inquiry is whether the State of Georgia likely would violate §2 of the Voting Rights Act if it had not created majority-black districts. The Defendants-Intervenors further asserted that the state is not likely to raise, much less vigorously advocate, defenses of the Georgia apportionment along these lines and "the state cannot be expected vigorously to argue, if at all, that voting in Georgia continues to be racially polarized, that existing structures, such as the statewide majority vote requirement, contribute to the dilution of minority voting strength, that elections have been characterized by subtle or overt racial appeals, or other factors probative of vote dilution which would justify the adoption of the existing Congressional districting plan." The Defendants-Intervenors also took the position that the Plaintiffs are seeking to advance interpretations of the Fourteenth and Fifteenth Amendments "that are hostile to black political opportunity and racial diversity in the Congressional delegation."

On February 22, 1994, the United States filed an Application to Intervene, which was thereafter granted by the Court, noting that the Plaintiffs had asserted that the United States Department of Justice had improperly administered §5 as part of the grounds for their claims that the challenged Georgia Congressional Redistricting Plan violated the Fourteenth and Fifteenth Amendments to the United States Constitution, and, in its Memorandum of Points and Authorities in Support of the Application of the United States to Intervene, stated:

> The Attorney General is charged with the primary responsibility for the administration and enforcement of the Voting Rights Act. In this action, the Attorney General's administration and enforcement of §5 serves as a basis for both Plaintiffs' claims, the expected defenses of the Defendants and the defenses asserted by the would-be Defendant-Intervenors. In addition, the Plaintiffs' allegations implicate the propriety and constitutionality of the Attorney General's administration of §5. Therefore, the Attorney General has a substantial interest in the subject matter of this case.

(Memorandum of Points and Authorities in Support of the Application of the United States to Intervene, at 1-2).

In its Memorandum of Points and Authorities, the United States, noting that it had precleared the challenged plan, took the position that the plan was constitutional

> because it is not so bizarre or irregular as to be unexplainable on grounds other than race. Moreover, even if plaintiffs can prove that the challenged plan does constitute a "racial gerrymander," as defined in *Shaw v. Reno*, 113 S.Ct. at 2826-28, the United States believes that the plan is narrowly tailored to serve the state's compelling interests in complying with the Voting Rights Act and in remedying the effects of past discrimination.

(Memorandum of Points and Authorities, *supra*, at 5-6).

160

The United States noted also that this case would be one of the first to interpret the equal protection claim outlined by the Supreme Court in *Shaw v. Reno*:

> The United States has a strong interest in participating in litigation that will shape the development of this area of the law and define the relationship between the Voting Rights Act and the Equal Protection Clause of the Fourteenth Amendment. The United States also is in a unique position to provide the Court with the benefit of our extensive involvement in redistricting litigation throughout the country and our experience with the administrative review of redistricting plans.

(Memorandum of Points and Authorities, *supra*, at 6).

On April 19, 1994, the Court in an Order signed by United States Circuit Judge J. L. Edmondson of the Eleventh Circuit Court of Appeals denied the preliminary injunction. In declining to issue a preliminary injunction, the Court stated:

> On this record and at this time, the Court cannot agree on Plaintiffs' likelihood of ultimate success on the merits. The merits of Plaintiffs' claim raise new and difficult questions that we will save for a full trial and a complete study of applicable case law. We deny the injunction chiefly because the Court unanimously agrees that the public interest would not be served by an injunction.

(April 19, 1994, Order, at 3).

Reasoning the courts are generally extremely reluctant to interfere with the sensitive interrelations that comprise the election process and all of its aspects, the Court further stated:

> Georgia and the public have a high interest in Georgia keeping to its usual voting schedule. For now, at least, we will maintain the status quo because we conclude that it is in the public's best interest.

(April 19, 1994, Order, at 3-4).

Representative Democracy: No Safe Seats

Race-based redistricting should be confined to redistricting plans which are narrowly tailored to the goal of avoiding retrogression in minority voting strength or similar sufficient justifications, and then only where proper regard is had for traditional districting principles such as compactness, contiguity and respect for maintaining the integrity of political subdivisions. Any other resort to racial gerrymandering or any other form of race-based redistricting will irreconcilably conflict with the democratic ideal embodied in our system of representative democracy.

Resolution and correction of the fundamental problems that have been highlighted above does not require abandonment of or even restrictions on the fundamental goals and objectives of the Voting Rights Act. Even though the United States Supreme Court's decision in *Shaw v. Reno* may be perceived as the beginning of a long-term scale-back in the more extreme applications of the Act, in the context of both liability and remedy, the federal judiciary must of necessity deal with these issues on a case-by-case basis, whereas Congress can address these problems and concerns in a more systematic manner, through the legislative process, including committee hearings such as the present one, in which a broad-based legislative factfinding process, tempered by the pluralistic interests that are reflected in our elected Representatives and Senators, can ultimately guide the Voting Rights Act back to its original goals of open, fair and equal electoral access and opportunity to participate in the political process on the part of racial and ethnic minority groups.

Need for Colorblind Approach

It is simply wrong to assume that blacks cannot properly or adequately represent whites, just as it is wrong to assume that whites cannot properly or adequately represent blacks. It is wrong to assume that blacks need black officeholders to represent them properly, just as it is wrong to assume that blacks as a distinct group need their "own" representatives. Dense academic musings over the lack of "authenticity" of black officials who are elected in part with white votes implicitly let race define the content our character. Race-driven redistricting should not be allowed to lead to the creation of a system of "safe" or reserved seats for members of different racial or ethnic groups, thereby insuring proportionate representation. Such is the antithesis of a colorblind society and a colorblind constitution, and it leads to creation of a political system in which race is the only thing that matters.

Undue Emphasis on Racial Division

Our federal government, whether through District Court action or through the Justice Department's administrative interpretation and enforcement of the Voting Rights Act, should not substitute a rigid form of group rights for that of individual representation. As Professor Abigail Thernstrom has so ably pointed out, this is in effect pasting racial labels on voters and assuming only racial identity matters for purposes of districting and other electoral arrangement. Judicially sanctioned or administratively encouraged maximization of minority voting strength through racial gerrymandering will indeed balkanize jurisdictions into competing racial factions. It will make the racially divided society that Governor Otto Kerner described in 1967 even more so, by hardening racial lines, racial classifications and racial stereotyping.

It is just as wrong to assume black solidarity as it is to assume white solidarity, and it is just as wrong to assume that blacks will share the same interests and will have more in common with one another than they do with any whites, stereotyped patterns which are grounded on an almost religious belief in black victimization. Such race-conscious policies indeed have high costs.

Basic Political Liberty

Alexander Hamilton in the Federalist No. 35 made it clear that a right to proportional representation or group representation is not recognized in our Constitution, and that it would indeed endanger our basic political liberty:

> It is said to be necessary that all classes of citizens should have some of their own number in the representative body in order that their feelings and interests may be better understood and attended to. But we have seen that this will never happen under any arrangement that leaves the votes of the people free.

Congress included the proportional representation disclaimer in §2 when the 1982 amendments were finally enacted. Neither the Courts nor the Justice Department should be allowed to come through the back door and impose proportional representation either as a standard for determining liability or as the basis for assessing the adequacy of a remedy. To do otherwise would not only make a mockery of the §2 disclaimer but would be repugnant to the democratic principles upon which our American society is based.

Conventional Wisdom or Hardening of Intellectual Arteries?

Finally, the older "conventional wisdom" about the causal relationship between socioeconomic disparities and minority political participation is no longer free from challenge. Cf. *League of United Latin American Citizens v. Clements*, 999 F.2d 831, 866 (5th Cir. 1993) ("The Voting Rights Act responds to practices that impact *voting*; it is not a panacea addressing social deficiencies."). The views of such political scientists as Steven J. Rosenstone and John Mark Hansen, authors of Mobilization, Participation, and

Democracy in America (Macmillan Pub. Co., 1993), are providing a better understanding of the role of mobilization in participation differences and voter turnout, suggesting that the level of political participation by blacks and whites is more a factor of mobilization—that is, the level of efforts on the part of candidates to mobilize voters, to energize competitive campaigns, to ask people to vote—than it is the level of resources. S. Rosenstone and J. Hansen, Mobilization, Participation and Democracy in America 35, 219 (Macmillan Pub. Co., 1993).

Conclusion

In conclusion, we submit that the "guilt" established in 1965 (triggered by the existence of literacy tests) should not justify distinctive treatment thirty years later without a competent substantial record of continued racial unfairness. Racial progress can be measured by an intensely local appraisal carried out by a local federal court. The time has come to permit local federal courts to decide §5 preclearance issues. Southern states need no longer remain in bondage to the United States District Court for the District of Columbia as an expensive, burdensome and problematical alternative to the unbridled administrative discretion of the §5 Unit of the Civil Rights Division's Voting Section. Just as constitutional issues under the Fourteenth and Fifteenth Amendments and issues under §2 of the Voting Rights Act have been effectively litigated in local federal courts, §5 preclearance issues can properly be adjudicated on the local level.

The need for eliminating racial separation from our basic political structure and positively encouraging coalition-building are key elements to racial fairness in the political arena.

Bill Clinton, in his inaugural address as Chairman of the Southern Growth Policies Board, said in 1985 what is even more apparent in 1994:

> If we have learned anything in the South better than the rest of the country, it is that we are going up or down together as a people. Because of our history and because of the progress we have already made, we should take upon ourselves the commitment to prove that our country can achieve excellence with equity. I am absolutely convinced that it can be done and it ought to be done in the South, better than and before any other region.[*]

---

[*]Charge to the Board in establishing the 1986 Commission on the Future of the South, June 1985, Atlanta, Georgia, p.5, Report of the 1986 Commission on the Future of the South "Halfway Home and a Long Way to Go" (Southern Growth Policies Board 1986).

In The United States District Court
for the District of Maryland

<table>
<tr><td>HONIS W. CANE, JR. et al.,
Plaintiffs,</td><td>)
)
)
)</td><td></td></tr>
<tr><td>٠.</td><td>)
)</td><td>Case No. Y92-3226</td></tr>
<tr><td>WORCESTER COUNTY, MARYLAND, et al.,
Defendants</td><td>)
)
)
)</td><td></td></tr>
</table>

State of North Carolina
County of Durham

AFFIDAVIT

DONALD L. HOROWITZ, being duly sworn, deposes and says:

1.   I am a lawyer and political scientist, currently the James B. Duke Professor of Law and Political Science at Duke University.   I have specialized principally in the politics of ethnic and racial relations for nearly three decades.

2.   A list of my publications is contained in the attached curriculum vitae.   My books have received a number of prizes, including the 1992 Ralph J. Bunche Award of the American Political Science Association for the best work on ethnic and cultural pluralism.   I have also held a variety of competitive fellowships and grants, served on editorial boards, and lectured on ethnic and racial politics at universities around the world.

3.   In approaching issues of ethnic and racial politics, I have worked on the relations between electoral systems and the politics of ethnic and racial relations.   I have researched, written, and spoken on such questions (including the impact of

plurality systems, list-system proportional representation, the single transferable vote, distribution systems, and the alternative vote) for many years.

4.   Earlier this month, I was retained by Benjamin E. Griffith, counsel for the defendants in the above-captioned case to assess the consequences likely to follow from the imposition of a system of cumulative voting for the County Commissioners of Worcester County.

5.   Among the materials I read in preparing this affidavit were the Court's opinions and orders in the instant case and a good deal of the testimony taken at trial, including that of the expert witnesses for both sides and the testimony of County Commissioners.

6.   In addition to the materials relating to this litigation, I also consulted a wide range of studies bearing on the likely impact of cumulative voting in Worcester County. These studies are based on research on cumulative voting systems in effect in this country and elsewhere in the world.

7.   Cumulative voting (CV) is a semi-proportional system of electing representatives. Its central feature is to permit a voter in a multimember constituency to cast more than one vote for a single candidate. Usually, the voter is able to cast as many votes for a single candidate as there are candidates running for office, so that if there are, for example, three candidates, a voter could allocate one, two, or three votes to a single candidate and fewer or none to the others. This feature permits voters to cumulate their votes for particularly favored candidates, thereby permitting

individual voters to express the intensity of their preferences for favored candidates and permitting candidates who are intensely preferred by only a minority of voters to add to their vote totals by virtue of multiple votes from individual voters.

8.   Cumulative voting is referred to as a semi-proportional system because it lowers the threshold of exclusion, the fraction of the total vote that is required for a candidate to secure election. If there are five seats contested in a multimember constituency under CV, it takes merely one-sixth of all votes cast for a candidate to be guaranteed a seat.[1] Because of this feature, CV has been advocated enthusiastically in recent years by some who are skeptical of the effects of the Anglo-American plurality system of election, including some who have provided expert testimony for plaintiffs in voting rights cases[2] and others who are skeptical of majoritarian political institutions more generally.[3] They suggest that CV offers a way for geographically dispersed minorities to

---

[1]For general descriptions, see REIN TAAGEPERA AND MATTHEW SHUGART, SEATS AND VOTERS 13 (1989); ENID LAKEMAN AND JAMES D. LAMBERT, VOTING IN DEMOCRACIES: A STUDY OF MAJORITY AND PROPORTIONAL ELECTORAL SYSTEMS 79 (3d ed. 1970). For the mechanics of the operation of CV, see Richard L. Engstrom, *Modified Multi-Seat Election Systems as Remedies for Minority Vote Dilution*, 21 STETSON L. REV. 743, 749-51 (1992).

[2]See, e.g., Engstrom, *supra* note 1; Bernard Grofman, *Alternatives to Single-Member Plurality Districts: Legal and Empirical Issues*, 9 POLICY STUDIES J. 875, 888-89 (1981).

[3]See LANI GUINIER, THE TYRANNY OF THE MAJORITY 16, 95, 107-08, 122, 151-52 (1994); Lani Guinier, *The Triumph of Tokenism: The Voting Rights Act and the Theory of Black Electoral Success*, 89 MICH. L. REV. 1077, 1143 n. 309 (1991); Lani Guinier, *No Two Seats: The Elusive Quest for Political Equality*, 77 VA. L. REV. 1413 (1991); Rob Richie, *Cumulative Voting Captures Imagination of Electoral Reformers*, 82 NATIONAL CIVIC REV. 72 (Winter 1993).

secure representation (in the sense of officeholding) that would
otherwise be denied them and for geographically conCentrated minorities Comprising majorities in particular areas to secure representation without denying representation to those who comprise in
turn a minority in those areas.[4]

9.   In my judgment, the likely benefits of CV have been exag-
gerated, and the likely costs have been largely ignored. One reason for this is that CV is not merely an exotic system in this
country; it has rarely been used anywhere. The longest experiments
with CV in this country--in the Illinois House of Representatives
and on corporate boards, where its use is declining[5]--did not involve attempts to secure representation for racial minorities but
for minority political parties and minority shareholders. It thus
takes some extrapolation to derive and apply the pertinent lessons.

10.   In continental Europe, where enthusiasm for proportional
systems has been infinitely greater than it has in the United
States or Great Britain, CV is used in a few very small countries
to mitigate some of the effects of list-system proportional representation. In Switzerland and Luxembourg, a voter can allocate up
to two votes to each candidate on a party list; in local elections
in Norway, a voter can cancel, add, or repeat (that is cumulate) a

---

[4]GUINIER, THE TYRANNY OF THE MAJORITY, *supra* note 3, at 152;
Richard Engstrom, Delbert A. Taebel, and Richard L. Cole, *Cumula-
tive Voting as a Remedy for Minority Vote Dilution: The Case of
Alamogordo, New Mexico*, 5 J. LAW & POLICY 469, 472 (1989).

[5]Frank H. Easterbrook and Daniel R. Fischel, *Voting in Corporate Law*, 26 J. LAW & ECONS. 395, 409 (1983).

name on a list.[6] In Britain, CV has been used in local   school board elections.[7]

The history of CV in this country is equally thin. It was adopted in Illinois for elections to the lower house in 1870 and repealed in a referendum in 1980. In other states, proposals to adopt CV in legislative elections have repeatedly failed, although CV was widely required or permitted in corporate charters for elections to boards of directors. For some decades after 1937, West Virginia used CV for election to boards drafting home rule charters for local governments.[8] Apart from the recent adoption of CV in a number of relatively small jurisdictions, generally in settlements of voting rights cases, there is little experience to go on. It is, however, clear that, given a choice, American electorates have usually rejected CV.[9]

11. In view of this sparse experience, it is not surprising that cumulative voting "is uncertain in its operation."[10] Never-

---

[6]See CHRISTOPHER HUGHES, THE PARLIAMENT OF SWITZERLAND 38 (1962); WOLFGANG BIRKE, EUROPEAN ELECTIONS BY DIRECT SUFFRAGE 47 (1961); Audun Offerdal, *Kumulering, Ressursar og Representasjon*, 15 TIDSSKRIFT FOR SAMFUNNSFORSKNING 29-49 (1974).

[7]LAKEMAN AND LAMBERT, *supra* note 1, at 80.

[8]See Paul D. Stewart, *West Virginia Uses Cumulative Voting*, 47 NAT'L MUNICIP. REV. 577 (1958).

[9]Whitney Campbell, *The Origin and Growth of Cumulative Voting for Directors*, 10 BUS. LAWYER 3, 6-7 (April 1955). A few municipalities had utilized cumulative voting in the second half of the nineteenth century, but they invariably repealed the experiments after a short time. See Charles W. Dunn, *Cumulative Voting Problems in Illinois Legislative Elections*, 9 HARV. J. LEGISL. 627, 629-30 (1972).

[10]LAKEMAN AND LAMBERT, *supra* note 1, at 79.

theless, there are ways of thinking systematically about electoral systems that permit informed evaluations of their likely effects. It is quite true that "the effect of a particular voting system can be understood only in the context of the politics in which it is embedded."[11] Extrapolations from the experience of CV need to take this caution into account.

12.   The Illinois CV experiment has been studied carefully, and the results reveal rather profound effects in patterns of political competition. The original aim of CV was to permit Republicans in the southern part of the state, where they were then a minority, to elect some representatives and to permit Democrats to do the same in the northern parts of the state, where they in turn were a minority.[12] The purpose was, therefore, to mitigate geographic polarization in representation and the sectional divisiveness that followed the Civil War.

13.   This aim was achieved immediately. In most three-member constituencies all over the state, the minority party was able to elect one representative. On the other hand, where the majority party put up candidates for all three seats, cumulative voting often allowed the minority party to elect candidates from two of the three seats, despite its minority status. In those cases, the majority vote was split, whereas the minority vote could be cumulated or concentrated on two candidates. As a result, it soon became customary for the majority party in an area to limit itself

---

[11]Grofman, *supra* note 2, at 889.

[12]Dunn, *supra* note 9.

to two candidates, while the minority party listed only one. A modus vivendi was achieved.

14. These tacit agreements to limit competition, referred to as "sweethearting," often involved blatant collusion, including having the candidates of one party speak in favor of those of the other.[13] By requiring each party to nominate at least two candidates for each three-member district, a constitutional amendment in 1970 reduced explicit arrangements of this kind but failed to produce significantly increased interparty competition. From 1966 to 1976, in some 354 elections involving three seats each, not once did any party win all three seats. Although forced to run two candidates, party committees refused to run full slates for fear of spreading votes too thinly when the other party could cumulate votes for fewer candidates.[14]

15. Cumulative voting therefore produced dramatically reduced interparty competition, and as a result it also gave more power to party leaders who chose nominees in an environment of scarcity of candidacies. As interparty competition declined, so did the electoral accountability of representatives. Safe seats and long ten-

---

[13]*Ibid.*, Joseph F. Zimmerman, *Alternative Electoral Systems*, 79 NAT'L CIVIC REV. 23, 28-29 (Feb. 1990). George H. Hallett, Jr., *Proportional Representation with the Single Transferable Vote*, in CHOOSING AN ELECTORAL SYSTEM: ISSUES AND ALTERNATIVES (Arend Lijphart and Bernard Grofman eds. 1984), 113, 116; Leon Weaver, *Semi-Proportional and Proportional Representative Systems in the United States*, in *ibid.*, 191, 198-99.

[14]Charles W. Wiggins and Janice Petty, *Cumulative Voting and Electoral Competition: The Illinois House*, 7 AM. POL. Q. 345, 355, 358, 360, 362 (1979).

ure in office increased, since most candidates ran unopposed for election and reelection.[15]

16. Cumulative voting thus "provided many incumbents with a free ride to reelection."[16] When the legislature approved a salary increase for itself in 1978, it ignited a storm of opposition in the form of a referendum to reduce the size of the House of Representatives and to substitute single-member for multimember districts. The referendum passed overwhelmingly in 1980, ending CV in Illinois.[17]

17. To assess the likely impact of an electoral change in a given jurisdiction, it is necessary to ask how the incentives set up by the new electoral system interact with electoral demography and patterns of political competition in that jurisdiction. In the light of the structure of cumulative voting and the Illinois experience, the probable effect of cumulative voting in Worcester County seems clear.

18. The principal effect that could be anticipated would be increased racial polarization. The incentive system set up by cumulative voting pushes strongly in this direction. Cumulative voting allows voters to express "a stronger choice"[18] for one

---

[15]Dunn, supra note 9, at 634-35, 639, 646-48, 648-49.

[16]DAVID KENNEY AND BARBARA BROWN, BASIC ILLINOIS GOVERNMENT 58 (1993).

[17]Ibid. at 57-59. The statement that the referendum abolishing CV had "little or nothing to do with support/opposition to cumulative voting," Grofman, supra note 2, at 889, is inaccurate. Cumulative voting produced safe seats, which facilitated the salary increase, which produced the voter reaction.

[18]TAAGEPERA AND SHUGART, supra note 1.

candidate than for others. For a minority candidate to insure his or her election, it is necessary to cumulate votes. Minority candidates are likely to believe that their best chance of gaining multiple votes from individual voters rests on the existence of divisive racial issues. African Americans are a minority of less than 20 percent of the voting-age population in Worcester County, and the threshold of exclusion (the minimum share of the vote required to assure a seat) in a five-member council is 16.67 percent, which is very close to the black voting-age percentage. Consequently, black candidates are likely to plot their strategy on the assumption that they will need multiple votes from all black voters, especially if the white crossover vote is generally not large, as was suggested by Dr. Theodore Arrington, plaintiffs' expert witness at the trial. Cumulative voting encourages very small groups--those whose aggregate numbers are under the threshold of exclusion--to join with others to exceed the threshold and win a seat, but it also provides no such incentives for larger groups that can elect candidates by slim margins.[19] The latter would be the case in Worcester County.

19. This is by no means a one-sided affair. White candidates, too, will be likely to engage in racial appeals, especially if they anticipate or observe that black candidates will do so, for white candidates also benefit from cumulation. Cumulation of votes, as we have seen, is a function of intensities of preference.

---

[19]Note, *Alternative Voting Systems as Remedies for Unlawful At-Large Systems*, 92 YALE L.J. 144, 154 (1982).

Intense preferences are fostered by polarized environments. Under these circumstances, cumulative voting is likely to produce centrifugal pulls in the electoral system.[20] Electoral systems, of course, are not merely receptacles for preexisting voter sentiment. They help to shape and channel voter opinion, and one way they do so is to set up incentives for candidate behavior in election campaigns. In the name of remedying racial polarization, cumulative voting would be likely to entrench it.

20. The Illinois system, it has been noted,[21] was set in the context of a strong two-party system, and so it did not proliferate single-issue candidates or parties. This is quite true, but the Illinois constituencies each contained only three seats and therefore had a significantly higher threshold of exclusion than does the five-seat Worcester County Commission. All else equal, the lower the threshold of exclusion, the less necessary is it for candidates to avoid single-issue politics.

21. I am familiar with decisions under section 2 of the Voting Rights Act holding that a minority electorate need not be required to enter into cross-racial coalitions to elect the candidate of its choice, and I am not suggesting that the likely effect I have identified for Worcester County can be defined as simply the absence of a need to form such coalitions. The effect is rather to

---

[20]Commenting on the effect of cumulative voting among corporate shareholders, Easterbrook and Fischel, *supra* note 5, at 410, note that cumulation increases the risk of "multipeaked preferences," which is to say that it fosters incompatible or centrifugal claims.

[21]Grofman, *supra* note 2, at 889.

create a positive incentive for racial appeals. Contrast the case
in which a blaCk electorate has a two-thirds majority in a given
single-member district and a white electorate has the same two-
thirds majority in a different single-member district. These can
be characterized as racially safe seats. The criticism levelled
against suCh arrangements has Considerable force--namely, that
black candidates in the first district can often ignore the interests of their white constituents, who form a one-third minority,
and that white candidates in the second district can likewise
ignore the interests of their black constituents who form a similar
minority. But with cumulative voting, there is a different
problem, for no seat is necessarily safe. All candidates run
against each other as they try to gain one of the five seats by
receiving a vote tally among the top five candidates. The Illinois
experience shows very clearly that a few wasted (that is,
noncumulated) votes can easily lead to defeat if one's opponents
are diligently cumulating votes among their supporters.

22. In short, under these circumstances, cumulative voting is
likely to lead to something analogous to an arms race: an attempt
by each candidate to insure that all of his or her supporters give
all of their votes to him or her.

23. In Illinois, nothing like this happened, partly, as
noted, because of the high threshold of exclusion, which aided only
the two parties, but also because there was perfect symmetry and
reciprocity between the parties when they made the bargains that
restrained competition. For every district with a Republican

minority there was an equal and opposite district with a Democratic
one. The basis for such reciprocity is absent in Worcester County,
which now has considerable volatility in party support (Republicans
having swept all five seats in 1990, a dramatic change). In any
case, parties are no longer the main actors. Racial groups are
also important actors in politics. Needless to say, absence of
competition was hardly a benign force in Illinois, but to the
extent that comparable "sweetheart" arrangements might mitigate
racial tensions in Worcester County's CV system, it is difficult to
imagine that the underlying conditions would be present.

24. Nevertheless, let us assume that the parties in Worcester
County were to reach a modus vivendi, and certain seats were left
uncontested in the general election for the County Commission,
which is indeed conducted along party lines, as it must be by law
in Maryland. The effect would not be to reduce the prospect of
racial polarization but simply to push it back into the primary
contests within the parties. Wiggins and Petty have shown
convincingly that this was the effect of the dampening of
interparty competition and the resulting safe seats in Illinois:
the less the competition between parties at the general election,
the greater the competition between candidates of the same party in
the primary election. Illinois had, in fact, an above-average
level of primary contests under CV.[22]

25. I am scarcely the first person to suggest that CV is a
system conducive to polarization. It has often been remarked that

_____

[22]Wiggins and Petty, *supra* note 14, at 349-50.

CV may lead to extremism or polarization within legislative bodies[23] or that it increases the risk of "inConsistent or illogical decisions" in corporations as a result of incompatible agendas.[24] In Worcester County, the centrifugal effects of CV might extend beyond racial polarization and into other issues as well. Testimony at the trial indicates that, although a small county, Worcester is a heterogeneous and complex area.[25] Pocomoke sees itself as a cosmopolitan, industrial, and progressive town, closely tied to adjacent areas of Virginia. Snow Hill, the county seat, is in a rural area, inward looking, agrarian, and conservative. Berlin is oriented toward its history and toward tourism based on that history. Ocean City is a retirement area, with migrants from other places. The county has a significant north-south split. The Commission chairman justified at-large elections on the basis of the need to bridge these regional divisions. Ironically, CV, adopted by the Court to preserve the single at-large constituency, might well foster the same conflicts the Commission sought to bridge. As things stand under the preexisting electoral system, candidates must receive support from all over the county. Under CV, that need no longer be the case. A system with a low threshold of exclusion, which rewards the expression of intense preferences, is conducive to the strong representation of a variety of intense

---

[23]Note, *Alternative Voting Systems as Remedies for Unlawful At-Large Systems*, 92 YALE L.J. 144, 156 (1982); Weaver, *supra* note 13, at 195.

[24]Easterbrook and Fischel, *supra* note 5, at 410.

[25]Tr. 772-73, 122-24.

preferences and special interests that might otherwise be confined to lobbying activity. Concomitantly, it makes the aggregation of interests, one of the main functions of legislatures, more difficult.

26. "Many of the arguments in favor of cumulative voting simply look at one favorable consequence and conclude that the system is good. . . . Important negative consequences, however, induced by cumulative voting . . . are either overlooked or underestimated."[26] There are two recent studies of cumulative voting that have an advocacy flavor to them and seem vulnerable to this objection. These studies concern elections conducted under CV systems adopted as a result of voting rights litigation settlements.

27. The first deals with an election in North Dakota in which a Sioux candidate managed to cumulate 94.7 percent of the votes cast by Sioux to win election to a local school board.[27] The survey conducted after the election concluded the voters understood the electoral system and could operate it easily.[28] A common objection against CV--that it is too complex for the electorate--is, therefore, without foundation, a conclusion with which I agree completely. The problem with CV is not that it is too complex for

---

[26]Dunn, *supra* note 9, at 643. For some particularly extravagant and unsupported claims, see GUINIER, THE TYRANNY OF THE MAJORITY, *supra* note 3, at 16, 95. For another glowing account, see Richard H. Pildes, *Gimme Five*, THE NEW REPUBLIC, March 1, 1993, at 16-17.

[27]Richard L. Engstrom and Charles J. Barrilleaux, *Native Americans and Cumulative Voting: The Sisseton Wahpeton Sioux*, 72 Soc. Sci. Q. 388 (1991).

[28]*Ibid.* at 391.

voters. The study notes in passing that this new system "stimulated
a special effort at mobilizing the potential native American electorate,"[29] which cumulated its votes at the 93.4 percent level.[30]
The study makes no comment on the implications of maximal cumulation.

28. The second case, involving a New Mexico city council, is
more pertinent to Worcester County, because it suggests that polarization need not always result from CV elections.[31] Two elections
were studied, in 1987 and 1990. In both, a Hispanic woman won, principally but not exclusively on the basis of cumulated Hispanic votes.
The cumulation feature was used by increasing fractions of voters in
the second election, and a great many more voters voted all three of
their votes for one candidate the second time around.[32] The
Hispanic candidate, however, also received a significant share of
Anglo votes, negating any notion of inevitable polarization. She had
campaigned as "a conservative candidate who will not vote for higher
taxes."[33] Clearly, she chose to make centripetal appeals and was
able to do so with impunity. CV does not require increased ethnic or

---

[29]*Ibid.* at 391 n. 5.

[30]*Ibid.* at 391. Anglo voters cumulated at much lower levels,
at least in the first election, though the incentives to counter-
mobilization are lower there than in Worcester, for in the South
Dakota case the Sioux population is considerably above the
threshold of exclusion, and so its seat seems very safe. The
opposite is true in Worcester County.

[31]Richard L. Cole and Delbert A. Taebel, *Cumulative Voting in
Local Elections: Lessons from the Alamogordo Experience*, 73 Soc.
Sci. Q. 194 (1992); Richard L. Cole, Delbert A. Taebel, and Richard
L. Engstrom, *Cumulative Voting in a Municipal Election: A Note on
Voter Reactions and Electoral Consequences*, 43 West. Pol. Q. 191
(1990).

[32]Cole and Taebel, *supra* note 31, at 197-99.

[33]Engstrom, Taebel, and Cole, *supra* note 4, at 486.

racial tension, but it is still a system that provides incentives toward that end if the environment is otherwise conducive.

29.   It is worth adding that all forecasts, including the present one, are hazardous.   While electoral systems depend for their operation on preexisting cleavages and patterns of political competition, they also can change these variables. The configuration of political competition is especially vulnerable to change in a new system which alters electoral incentives so sharply. If, for example, white voters prove to be less cohesive than they were depicted by Dr. Arrington at the trial, African American voters may prove to be less cohesive as well.   All else equal, the more widely spread votes are among various candidates in a CV system, the smaller the number of votes required to secure a seat.   Consequently, maximum cumulation would be less important.   In a racially divided society, the less the need for below-maximum cumulation, the less the electoral system ends up fostering racial tension. As things now stand, however, the rather close approximation of the threshold of exclusion to the black percentage of voting-age population makes maximum cumulation the safest strategy to guarantee a seat.

30.   A system that sets up such incentives can scarcely be commended.   Certainly such a system ought not be adopted without full consideration of the interplay among variables.   This is particularly so when the voting-age population of a group is so close to the threshold of exclusion that a small degree of lack of voting cohesion threatens the loss of the seat and so creates incentives for in-group

17

candidates to raise the stakes and for out-group candidates to countermobilize to attempt to wrest the seat away. This is the situation created by the Court's order in Worcester County.

31. Finally, I should point out that my own inclinations are by no means hostile to novel electoral systems. In scholarly writing and in consulting with governments, I have recommended unfamiliar electoral systems to ameliorate tensions in severely divided societies. But no serious student of this subject can be unaware of the need to ask exactly what incentives a remedial order sets up.

_____
Donald L. Horowitz

Sworn to and subscribed before me this _22_ day of April, 1994,

_____
Notary Public

My commission expires

_11/15/98_____

CURRICULUM VITAE

Donald L. Horowitz

Born June 27, 1939   Married, three children

Home
Address:
2501 Wrightwood Avenue
Durham, North Carolina 27705
Telephone: (919) 489-1017

Present
Position:
James B. Duke Professor of Law and
    Political Science

Office
Address:
School of Law
Duke University
Durham, North Carolina 27706
Telephone: (919) 684-6039
Facsimile: (919) 684-3417

Education:
A.B., Syracuse University, 1959
LL.B., Syracuse University, 1961
LL.M., Harvard University, 1962
M.A., Harvard University, 1965
Ph.D., Harvard University, 1968

Professional
Experience:
Law Clerk to Hon. Joseph S. Lord, III,
    Chief United States District Judge,
    Philadelphia, Pennsylvania, 1965-66

Research Associate, Center for International
    Affairs, Harvard University, 1967-69

Attorney, Department of Justice,
    Civil Division, Appellate Section,
    Washington, D.C., 1969-71

Fellow, Council on Foreign Relations and
    Woodrow Wilson International Center for
    Scholars, 1971-72

Research Associate, The Brookings Institution,
    1972-75

Senior Fellow, Research Institute on Immigra-
    tion and Ethnic Studies, the Smithsonian
    Institution, 1975-81

Duke University since 1980; Charles S. Murphy
    Chair, 1988-93

James B. Duke Chair since 1994

Curriculum Vitae   -2-   Donald L. Horowitz

<table>
<tr><td>

Part-Time
Teaching:

</td><td>

Lecturer, George Washington University, 1972-73

Professorial Lecturer, Johns Hopkins University School of Advanced International Studies, 1976-81

</td></tr>
<tr><td>

Memberships
and
Professional
Activities:

</td><td>

Chairman, American Academy of Arts and Sciences Planning Group on Ethnicity, 1984-89; Co-Chairman, American Academy-Ecole Normale Supérieure FrenCh-American Ethnicity Project, 1988-91

Chairman, North Carolina Advisory Committee to the U.S. Commission on Civil Rights, 1985-88

Principal Consultant on Ethnic Issues in Asia and Africa, The Ford Foundation, 1977-82

Panel of Arbitrators, American Arbitration Association: Labor, Commercial, and Community Dispute Panels

Bars of New York, the District of Columbia, the United States Supreme Court, and the United States Court of Appeals for various circuits

Consultant to the General Counsel, U.S. Department of Transportation, 1980

Editorial Board, Ethnicity, 1974-82

Editorial Board, Law and Contemporary Problems, 1983-84 and since 1989

Editorial Board, Law and Society Review, 1979-82

Editorial Board, Public Interest Law Review, since 1988

Editorial Board, Journal of Democracy, since 1993

International Editorial Board, Nations and Nationalism, since 1994

National Science Foundation Review Panel on AID Entrepreneurship Project, 1982-86 (including field evaluation in Malawi, 1985-86)

</td></tr>
</table>

Order of the Coif

Advisory Commission on Intergovernmental Re-
    lations, Advisory Board on Federalism and
    the Federal Courts, 1985-87

Council on the Role of the Courts, a Study
    Group of Lawyers, Judges, and Social
    Scientists under the auspices of the
    Department of Justice, 1978-84

Board of Directors, Private Adjudication
    Center, 1984-92

Member of the Program Committee for the 1989
    Annual Meeting of the American Political
    Science Association

Member, Council on Ethnic Accord, Project on
    Ethnic Relations [in Eastern Europe],
    since 1991

External Examiner, Faculty of Economics and
    Administration, University of Malaya,
    1990-93

External Examiner, Faculty of Law, Universiti
    Kebangsaan Malaysia, 1992

Member, Advisory Board, Series on Constitu-
    tionalism and Democracy, University Press
    of Virginia, since 1992

Chairman, Advisory Board, Ethnicity Program,
    Woodrow Wilson Center, since 1992

Member, Advisory Board, Project on Nationalism
    and Ethnic Conflict Management in the
    Former Soviet Union, sponsored by the In-
    stitute of Ethnology and Anthropology,
    Russian Academy of Sciences, and Conflict
    Management Group (CMG), Cambridge, Mas-
    sachusetts

Member, Advisory Board, Project on Genocide,
    World Without War Council--Midwest, since
    1993

Member, Borneo Research Council, since 1993

Honors and
Awards:

Louis Brownlow Prize of the National Academy
of Public Administration for the best book
in public administration, 1977 (for The
Courts and Social Policy)

Finalist, C. Wright Mills Book Award of the
Society for the Study of Social Problems,
1978 (for The Courts and Social Policy)

McDonald-Currie Memorial Lecturer, McGill
University, Montreal, 1980

Outstanding Academic Book, Choice magazine,
1987 (for Ethnic Groups in Conflict)

Maurice Webb Memorial Lecturer, Natal
University, 1989

Ralph J. Bunche Award of the American
Politicial Science Association for the
best book on ethnic and cultural
pluralism, 1992 (for A Democratic South
Africa?)

Finalist, Herskovits Award of the African
Studies Association, 1992 (for A
Democratic South Africa?)

Fellow, American Academy of Arts and Sciences,
since 1993

Sondermann Lecturer, Colorado College,
Colorado Springs, Colorado, 1994

Fellowships
and
Visiting
Appointments:

Harvard University Graduate Fellowships,
1963-65

National Science Foundation Predoctoral and
Postdoctoral Fellowships, 1966-68

Woodrow Wilson Center Fellowship, 1971-72

Council on Foreign Relations Fellowship,
1971-72

Rockefeller Foundation Fellowship, 1976

Social Science Research Council Fellowship,
1977

Guggenheim Fellowship, 1980-81

185

National Humanities Center Fellowship, 1984

Visiting Fellow, Institute of Strategic and
International Studies, Malaysia, and Re-
search Associate, Faculty of Economics and
Administration, University of Malaya, 1984

Visiting Fellow, Wolfson College, Cambridge
University, 1988

Visiting Professor and Charles J. Merriam
Scholar, University of Chicago Law School,
Autumn 1988

Rockefeller Foundation Residency, Bellagio
Study Center, Lake Como, Italy, Summer
1990

Visiting Professor, Faculty of Law, Universiti
Kebangsaan Malaysia, Spring 1991

Publications: The Courts and Social Policy (Washington,
D.C.:   The Brookings Institution,
1977)

The Jurocracy: Government Lawyers, Agency
Programs, and Judicial Decisions (Lexington, Mass.:   D.C. Heath & Co., 1977)

Coup Theories and Officers' Motives: Sri
Lanka in Comparative Perspective (Princeton: Princeton University Press, 1980)

Ethnic Groups in Conflict (Berkeley and Los
Angeles: University of California Press,
1985)

A Democratic South Africa? Constitutional
Engineering in a Divided Society (Berkeley
and Los Angeles: University of California
Press, 1991)

Coeditor, Immigrants in Two Democracies:
French and American Experience (New York:
New York University Press, 1992)

Special Editor of issue, Federal Regulation of
Work from Recruitment to Retirement, Law
and Contemporary Problems, Vol. 49, no. 2
(Spring 1986)

Special Editor of issue, Public Policy in
Developing Countries, Policy Sciences,
Vol. 22, nos. 3-4 (November 1989)

"Multiracial Politics in the New States:
Toward a Theory of Conflict," in Robert J.
Jackson and Michael B. Stein, editors,
Issues in Comparative Politics (New York:
St. Martin's Press, 1971), pp. 164-80

"Three Dimensions of Ethnic Politics," World
Politics, Vol. 23, no. 2 (January 1971),
pp. 232-44

"Color Differentiation in the American Systems
of Slavery," Journal of Interdisciplinary
History, Vol. 3, no. 3 (Winter 1973),
pp. 509-41

"Direct, Displaced, and Cumulative Ethnic Ag-
gression," Comparative Politics, Vol. 6,
no. 1 (October 1973), pp. 1-16

"Ethnic Identity," in Nathan Glazer and Daniel
P. Moynihan, editors, Ethnicity: Theory
and Experience (Cambridge: Harvard University Press, 1975), pp. 111-40

"The Courts as Guardians of the Public Interest," Public Administration Review, Vol.
37, no. 2 (March-April 1977), pp. 148-54

"Cultural Movements and Ethnic Change," The
Annals, Vol. 433 (September 1977), pp. 6-
16

"About-Face in Africa: The Return to Civilian
Rule in Nigeria," Yale Review, Vol. 68,
no. 2 (December 1978), pp. 192-206 . . . .

"Civil-Military Relations in a Multiethnic Society: The Case of Sri Lanka (Ceylon),"
Asian Affairs, Vol. 3, no. 1 (Fall 1978),
pp. 157-69

"The Worldwide Resurgence of Ethnicity," in
U.S. International Communication Agency
Emerging Issues series, no. 78-F-125 (June
1978)

"Overcoming Barriers to the Use of Social
Research in the Courts," in Michael Saks
and Charles Baron, editors, The
Use/Misuse/Non-use of Applied Social
Research in the Courts (Cambridge: Abt
Books, 1980), pp. 148-54

"Patterns of Ethnic Separatism," Comparative
Studies in Society and History, Vol. 23,
No. 2 (April 1981), pp. 65-95

"Foreword" to Robert G. Wirsing, editor, Protection of Ethnic Minorities: Comparative
Perspectives (New York: Pergamon Press,
1981)

"The Judiciary: Umpire or Empire?" Law and
Human Behavior, Vol. 6, no. 2 (September
1982), pp. 129-43

"Racial Violence in the United States," in
Nathan Glazer and Ken Young, editors,
Ethnic Pluralism and Public Policy:
Achieving Equality in the United States
and Britain (London: Heinemann, 1983),
pp. 187-211, abridged in the Bulletin of
the American Academy of Arts and Sciences
(December 1983)

"Decreeing Organizational Change: Judicial
Supervision of Public Institutions," Duke
Law Journal, Vol. 1983, no. 6 (December
1983), pp. 1265-1307

"Conflict and Accommodation: Mexican Americans in the Cosmopolis," in Walker Connor,
editor, Mexican Americans in Comparative
Perspective (Washington: The Urban
Institute Press, 1985), pp. 58-103

"Justification and Excuse in the Program of
the Criminal Law," Law and Contemporary
Problems, Vol. 49, no. 3 (Summer 1986),
pp. 109-26

"Foreword: The Deprivatization of Labor Relations Law," Law and Contemporary Problems,
Vol. 49, no. 4 (Autumn 1986), pp. 1-8

"Is the Presidency Failing?" _The Public Interest_, no. 88 (Summer 1987), pp. 3-27

"The Constitution and the Art of Compromise," in J. Jackson Barlow _et al._, editors, _The New Federalist Papers_ (1988)

"The Voting Rights Act," in J. Jackson Barlow _et al._, editors, _The New Federalist Papers_ (1988)

"Immigration and Ethnicity in Europe and America," _Revue Européenne des Migrations Internationales_, Vol. 5, no. 1 (2ème trimestre 1989), pp. 47-61

"Incentives and Behavior in the Ethnic Politics of Sri Lanka and Malaysia," _Third World Quarterly_, Vol. 11, no. 4 (October 1989), pp. 18-35

"Cause and Consequence in Public Policy Theory: Ethnic Policy and System Transformation in Malaysia," _Policy Sciences_, Vol. 22, nos. 3-4 (November 1989), pp. 249-87

"Is There a Third-World Policy Process?" _Policy Sciences_, Vol. 22, nos. 3-4 (November 1989), pp. 197-212

"Ethnic Conflict Management for Policy-Makers," in Joseph V. Montville and Hans Binnendijk, editors, _Conflict and Peace-Making in Multiethnic Societies_ (Lexington, Mass.: Lexington Books, 1990)

"Making Moderation Pay: The Comparative Politics of Ethnic Conflict Management," in Joseph V. Montville and Hans Binnendijk, editors, _Conflict and Peace-Making in Multiethnic Societies_ (Lexington, Mass.: Lexington Books, 1990)

"Community Conflict: Policy and Possibilities," Centre for Conflict Studies, University of Ulster, Coleraine, Monograph Series, number one, 1990 (also translated into Romanian)

189

"Democracy, Presidential and Parliamentary,"
Journal of Democracy, Vol. 1, no. 4 (Fall
1990), pp. 73-79

"Irredentas and Secessions: Adjacent Phenomena, Neglected Connections," in Naomi
Chazan, editor, Irredentism and International Politics (Boulder: Lynne Rienner,
1991)

"How to Begin Thinking Comparatively About
Soviet Ethnic Problems," in Alexander J.
Motyl, editor, Thinking Theoretically
About Soviet Nationalities: History and
Comparison in the Study of the USSR (New
York: Columbia University Press, 1992)

"Ethnic and Nationalist Conflicts," in Michael
Klare, editor, World Security (New York:
St. Martin's Press, 1991; 2d ed., 1993)

"Existe-t-il un modèle européen d'intégration?" in Didier Lapeyronnie, editor,
L'intégration des minorités immigrées en
Europe (Paris: Agence pour le Développe-
ment des Relations Interculturelles,
1991), vol. 1, pp. 183-86

"The Helping Professions and the Hurting Con-
flicts," East Lansing: Michigan State
University Center for Advanced Study of
International Development, Distinguished
Speaker Series, monograph no. 10, 1992

"Immigration and Group Relations in France and
America," in Donald L. Horowitz, coeditor,
Immigrants in Two Democracies: French and
American Experience (New York: New York
University Press, 1992), pp. 3-35

"Democracy in Divided Societies," Journal of
Democracy, vol. 4, no. 4 (October 1993),
pp. 18-38

"Conflict and the Incentives to Political
Accommodation," in Dermot Keogh and
Michael H. Haltzel, editors, Northern
Ireland and the Politics of Reconciliation
(Cambridge and Washington, D.C.:
Cambridge University Press and Woodrow
Wilson Center Press, 1993)

"The Qur'an and the Common Law: Islamic Law
Reform and the Theory of Legal Change,"
manuscript submitted to law reviews (128
pp. + footnotes)

Various articles, on legal institutions and on
ethnic relations, in the New Republic,
Commentary, the Washington Post, the Los
Angeles Times, Le Monde, the New Leader,
Africa Update, Development Digest,
Problèmes Politiques et Sociaux (Paris),
and the Wall Street Journal

**Works in
Progress:**

"The Deadly Ethnic Riot" (book manuscript)

**Unpublished
Papers:**

"Ethnic Secession and the 'Bigness Bias': A
Dissent," Woodrow Wilson International
Center for Scholars (January 1972)

"Achieving Minorities and Ethnic Conflict," a
Report to the Ford Foundation (July 1977)

"Ethnic Conflict: Designing a Research Program," a Report to the Ford Foundation
(August 1978)

"Ethnic Conflict: Focusing the Research Program," a Report to the Ford Foundation
(December 1978)

"Area Specialization and the Problems of
Cross-Areal Research and Teaching: Preliminary Reflections" (March 1979)

"Policies to Reduce Ethnic Tensions in Three
African Countries," a Report to the Ford
Foundation (February 1980)

"Policies to Reduce Ethnic Tensions in South
and Southeast Asia," a Report to the Ford
Foundation (June 1980)

"Ethnicity and Development: Policies to Deal
With Ethnic Conflict in Developing
Countries," a Report to the Agency for
International Development (March 1981)

"Policies of Ethnic Preference: A Brief Introduction," presented at the Ford Foundation Workshop on Preferential Policies,
Trincomalee, Sri Lanka (March 1982)

"Research on Ethnicity," A Report of a Meeting
at the Woodrow Wilson International Center
for Scholars (August 1991)

"A Harvest of Hostility: Ethnic Conflict and
Self-Determination After the Cold War"
(August 1992)

"Territorial Aspects of Ethnicity: Secession
and the Right of Self-Determination"
(November 1992; published in Romanian and
in Russian: Bucharest and Moscow, 1993)

Congressional   Statement on the Voting Rights Act, prepared
Testimony: for the Senate Judiciary Committee,
                 Subcommittee on the Constitution (February
                 12, 1982), in Voting Rights Act, Hearings
                 Before the Subcommittee on the
                 Constitution, Committee on the Judiciary,
                 U.S. Senate, 97th Cong., 2d Sess., on S.
                 53 and Other Bills, vol. 1, pp. 1307-32
                 (1983)

                 Statement on Ethnic Problems in the Soviet
                 Union, prepared for the Senate Committee
                 on Foreign Relations (April 12, 1989),
                 101st Cong., 1st Sess.

Listings: Who's Who in America
                 Who's Who in American Education
                 Who's Who in American Law
                 International Authors and Writers Who's Who

STATEMENT OF ALLAN J. LICHTMAN, PROFESSOR OF HISTORY, AMERICAN UNIVERSITY

Mr. LICHTMAN. Thank you very much, Mr. Chairman, Mr. Hyde.

There has indeed been a political revolution in America over the last 25 years, a quiet revolution that has transformed the face of American politics, increasing by fivefold the number of black elected officials in the United States. As evidenced indeed by the example of Mississippi, a critical factor in this revolution has been litigation and settlement at every level of government under the Voting Rights Act.

As critical as this revolution has been, however, it is not new. We had a revolution during the Reconstruction period of the 1860's and the 1870's that brought voting rights to newly freed slaves and that elected black officials throughout the South. But that revolution, as you know, was lost and wasn't remedied for another hundred years.

Part of that loss was, of course, attributed to the so-called white redeemers in the South who sought to restore white government. But a deeper reason for the loss during Reconstruction were supporters of black rights who came to believe that somehow during the Reconstruction period the Federal Government had gone too far in support of black rights and that somehow Federal intervention was now an obstacle to a race-neutral society.

So, too, today we are beginning to see a backlash against black elected officials. The attack today is not on black voting as it was in the post-Reconstruction era but on black and other minority districts that are still the backbone of black representation, and, again, the real problem is with people of goodwill, supporters of the Voting Rights Act, who have somehow come to believe that somehow we have gone too far and that vigorous enforcement of the Voting Rights Act is antithetical to a race-neutral or colorblind society.

I would argue—and I hope we discuss this today—that that view rests on a series of fundamental misconceptions about the Voting Rights Act and black districts. Let me just mention a few of them.

There has been talk about the creation of so-called apartheid districts, and yet the district that engendered the *Shaw* v. *Reno* decision in North Carolina is one of the most racially diverse districts in the United States, just 53 percent black in its voting age population.

We have heard the argument that the creation of these black districts somehow balkanizes and separates ourselves. In fact, the opposite is true. Black districts are created to deal with the problem of polarized voting, and, once elected, black elected officials like Mike Espy, former Congressman from Mississippi, today Secretary of Agriculture, have been able to put together interracial coalitions.

Finally, we have heard these districts are solely based on race. Yet, in fact, analysis of the districts in North Carolina show that they unite people on bases other than race. For example, they unite the less affluent who have been divided and separated previously.

So I think when we begin to go beyond the rhetoric and see what is going on in black districts, people of goodwill will this time come together in support of and not in retreat from minority voting rights.

[The prepared statement of Mr. Lichtman follows:]

STATEMENT OF ALLAN J. LICHTMAN
ON THE VOTING RIGHTS ACT
CONGRESSIONAL RESEARCH SERVICE, LIBRARY OF CONGRESS
SUBCOMMITTEE ON CIVIL AND CONSTITUTIONAL RIGHTS
COMMITTEE ON THE JUDICIARY
UNITED STATES HOUSE OF REPRESENTATIVES
MAY 11, 1994

Allan J. Lichtman
Professor of History
The American University
Washington, D.C. 20016

202-885-2411

A quiet revolution has transformed American politics during the past 25 years, increasing by five-fold the number of black elected officials in the United States. Expanded black officeholding has enriched policy debates and provided a voice for citizens with minimal access to government. More than ever before in American history, government is now responsive to the range of diversity in American life.

But black elected officials are experiencing a backlash similar to that which shattered black officeholding after Reconstruction. As in the 1870s, critics are winning support for the charge that government has gone "too far" in protecting black voting rights.

Although there is little danger today that black officeholding will again be wiped out, it is possible that a combination of shifting legal doctrine and adverse public opinion will erode the gains so painstakingly achieved during the last generation.

It took one hundred years to remedy the inequities following the collapse of Reconstruction. The nation can ill afford yet another period of retrenchment and rectification.

Of the strides made by African-Americans following the Civil War, black officeholding was most dismaying to whites, including Republican supporters of Reconstruction. Diarist Mary Logan, wife of Union General and Republican Senator John Logan, confessed "that when I first visited Richmond and saw the negro members of the House and Senate of the Virginia legislature occupying the places that were once filled by the great men of Virginia, the spectacle was repulsive to me."

Prior to the collapse of Reconstruction in 1876, blacks served in congress from several of the former confederate states. But an assault on black voting rights by white "redeemers" eventually eliminated the black ballots that had elected black officeholders.

In 1901, George White of North Carolina became the last black representative of the nineteenth century to leave congress. In his farewell address, titled "A Defense of the Negro Race," White said: "This, Mr. Chairman, is perhaps the Negroes' temporary farewell to the American Congress; but let me say, Phoenix-like he will rise up some day and come again. These parting words are in behalf of an outraged, heart-broken, bruised, and bleeding, but God-fearing people, faithful, industrious, loyal people -- rising people, full of potential force." Not until the restoration of voting rights for black individuals and the creation of black-majority districts in the 1960s and 1970s, would African-Americans again serve in congress from southern states.

During Reconstruction, as today, critics professed race neutrality and conjured fears of discrimination against whites. In 1866, President Andrew Johnson, vetoed the nation's first civil rights bill, writing: "they establish for the colored race safeguards which go infinitely beyond any that the General Government has ever provided for the white race. In fact, the distinction of race and color is made by the bill to operate in favor of the colored and against the white race."

By the 1870s, the northern public had become reluctant to

sustain black voting rights. "The whole public are tired out with these annual autumnal outbreaks in the South ... and are ready now to condemn any interference on the part of the Government," wrote President Ulysses Grant in 1875.

Post-Reconstruction redeemers attacked black voting. Today, the attack has shifted to black districts: still the primary base of black elected officials. Last summer, in Shaw v. Reno, a challenge to North Carolina's congressional districts, the Supreme Court ruled that a district so bizarrely shaped as to have no apparent basis other than race could violate the Equal Protection Clause of the Fourteenth Amendment. A trial on the merits of the North Carolina claim was held in early April of 1994 and a ruling is pending from the district court.

A district court in Louisiana recently extended the Shaw doctrine in a decision striking down the black-majority district represented by first-term African-American congressman Cleo Fields. The Hays v. Louisiana ruling suggested that any intentionally created minority district could be an unconstitutional "racial gerrymander" that must be justified as narrowly designed to meet a compelling state interest.

Ironically, the Hays decision sanctions the drawing of white ethnic or religious districts, no matter what their shape. Only minority districts are suspect, because minorities are protected by the Fourteenth Amendment. Thus is history inverted and an Amendment crafted to empower minorities turned to their detriment. Lawsuits have since challenged minority congressional districts in Georgia,

Florida, and Texas.

The critique of minority districts, whether in courts of law or public opinion, rests on several misconceptions. First, most minority districts (for congress and other offices) are not oddly shaped, and some of the nation's most bizarre districts were crafted to protect white incumbents.

Second, even oddly shaped districts may unite communities of interest on a basis other than race. The challenged Louisiana and North Carolina districts combine low income blacks and whites who had previously been fragmented into more affluent districts. A North Carolina survey, conducted for the Shaw litigation, shows that whites in the challenged districts are as ideologically compatible with blacks in those districts as with whites in the more affluent white district included in the study.

Third, despite comparisons to "apartheid" practices or "balkanization," the districts now challenged as racial gerrymanders are among the most racially mixed in the nation. The North Carolina district that engendered the Shaw decision, for example, is only 53 percent black in voting age population.

Fourth, minority districts do not promote racially polarized voting. Rather, such districts are remedies for a white bloc vote that denies minorities the opportunity to elect candidates of their choice. Candidates elected in racially polarized elections from such districts have often been able to form interracial coalitions in their reelection campaigns. A case in point is Secretary of Agriculture Michael Espy, elected to Congress in a black-majority district in Mississippi. Initially elected with support from only about 10 percent of white voters, Espy's ability to attract strong interracial support in reelection campaigns helped make him a national political figure.

The North Carolina survey provides additional evidence that the election of minority officials can diminish racial divisions and racial stereotypes. The survey showed that there was no relationship between the race of a member of congress and the race of constituents contacting that member.

Fifth, despite the Voting Rights Act, African-Americans (about 12 percent of the population) are not overrepresented in office. African-Americans constitute about 8 percent of the membership of the House of Representatives and only 1 percent of the membership of the Senate. Nationwide African-Americans constitute only 1.5 percent of all elected officials, national, state, and local.

In their attack on minority districts, it is the opponents of civil rights that are stirring racial discord. Unless the civil rights community effectively counterattacks, there will once more be diminished opportunities for racial minorities to participate in American political life.

Depending on the denouement of current disputes over the Shaw doctrine, congressional action may well be warranted. It may become necessary for Congress to specify the compelling national interest in remedying voting discrimination and to indicate that this interest transcends that geographical configuration of remedial districts.

OPINION/ESSAYS

Defending the Second Reconstruction

Attacks on 'gerrymandered' districts twist the 14th Amendment

By Allan J. Lichtman

IN the years following the post-Civil War Reconstruction, "redeemers" strongly discouraged voting by blacks. Today the attack has shifted to black districts, still the primary base of black elected officials.

Last summer in Shaw v. Reno, a suit challenging North Carolina's congressional districts, the United States Supreme Court ruled that a district so bizarrely shaped as to have no apparent basis other than race could violate the Equal Protection Clause of the 14th Amendment. A district court will shortly decide the fate of the North Carolina plan.

A district court in Louisiana recently extended the Shaw doctrine in a decision striking down the black-majority district represented by first-term African American Rep. Cleo Fields. The Hayes v. Louisiana ruling suggested that any intentionally created minority district could be an unconstitutional "racial gerrymander" that would have to be justified as narrowly designed to meet a compelling state interest.

Ironically, the Hayes decision sanctions the drawing of white ethnic or religious districts no matter what their shape. Only minority districts are suspect because minorities are protected by the 14th Amendment. Thus is history inverted; an amendment crafted to empower minorities is turned to their detriment. Lawsuits have since challenged minority districts in Georgia, Florida, and Texas.

The critique of minority districts, whether in courts of law or public opinion, rests on several misconceptions. First, many minority districts (for Congress and other offices) are no more oddly shaped than white districts, and some of the nation's most bizarre districts were crafted to protect white incumbents. Only after redistricting had begun to provide opportunities for minority voters did federal courts become concerned with the shape of districts.

Second, oddly shaped districts may unite communities of interest on a basis other than race. The challenged Louisiana and North Carolina districts combine low-income blacks and whites who had previously been scattered in more affluent districts. A survey conducted for the Shaw litigation shows that blacks and whites in the challenged districts have more in common with one another ideologically than blacks and whites in the most geographically compact district in the state. Despite the usually wide racial differences in opinion, the survey shows that whites in the challenged districts are about as compatible ideologically with blacks in the districts as with whites.

Third, despite comparisons to "apartheid" practices or "balkanization," the districts now challenged as racial gerrymanders are among the most racially mixed in the nation. The North Carolina district that engendered the Shaw decision is only 53 percent black

in voting age population.

Fourth, minority districts do not promote racially polarized voting. Rather, such districts are remedies for a preexisting white-bloc vote that denies minorities the chance to elect candidates of their choice. Prior to the creation of minority districts, no Southern state had elected a black member of Congress in the 20th century. Nationwide, blacks now constitute fewer than 10 percent of US House members and only 1 percent of Senate members.

By showing that minorities can represent both minorities and whites, the election of minority officials has diminished racial divisions. The North Carolina survey shows that white constituents are about as likely to contact a black as a white member of Congress. Minority officials elected with token white votes have gained considerable white support in reelection campaigns.

The argument over racial gerrymandering is being manipulated for political ends. In the hope of draining Democratic votes from neighboring districts, the Republican Party supported the creation of heavily concentrated minority districts. After this strategy failed, Republicans joined the attack on minority districts, hoping to undo plans crafted by Democratic legislatures. The Republican National Committee is an intervening plaintiff in Shaw v. Reno.

During Reconstruction, as today, critics made inroads into public opinion by professing race neutrality and conjuring fears of discrimination against whites. Then, as now, even defenders of civil rights grew weary of maintaining the vigilance needed to preserve minority rights.

The opponents of civil rights are stirring racial discord. Unless the civil rights community effectively counterattacks, there will again be diminished opportunities for racial minorities to participate in American political life.

Allan J. Lichtman is professor of history at American University in Washington and an expert witness for defendants in Shaw v. Reno and Hayes v. Louisiana.

Mr. EDWARDS. Thank you.

May I interrupt to welcome the gentleman from North Carolina, Congressman Howard Coble.

Mr. COBLE. Thank you, Mr. Chairman.

Mr. EDWARDS. Mr. Lund.

Mr. LUND. In the interests of time, I will waive my right to make a statement, sir.

STATEMENT OF BERNADINE ST. CYR, NEW ROADS, LA

Ms. ST. CYR. Thank you very much.

I am Bernadine St. Cyr, and I am pleased to be here, and I appreciate the opportunity to come.

I was born in New Roads, LA. I have lived in Louisiana all of my life. I finished high school in 1965. That summer I walked in many picket lines seeking the integration of schools and other public offices. Shortly after, I began my involvement in politics. I worked in the campaign when the first black ran for city council and lost. I have been politically involved ever since. I have, however, seen some progress but believe we have a long way to go. I also believe that in many areas we are losing ground. Progress comes so slow, and discrimination is still alive and well.

I was brought up in an atmosphere of discrimination and have faced many racist situations. However, it is 1994 and there are still lingering effects of racism. We still have an all-white Falls River Academy, a nearly all-black Rosewall Elementary School, a nursing home which places white patients on one wing and black on another, an all-white city council with a 56.7 black voter registration.

I am a two-time candidate for New Roads City Council. The election system is a 95-year-old at-large system with a majority vote requirement, a system in which whites have been able to consolidate their votes against other black candidates. I ran in 1989 and 1992. Although I lost both races, I am clearly the candidate of my race. The second campaign was most difficult because I was a plaintiff in *Rodney* v. *McKeithen,* a police jury reapportionment lawsuit which we won. Now we have four black jurymen out of 12 rather than 2 out of 12 who have been elected since 1980.

One thing is clear to me as a community activist, an NAACP legal redress officer, a two-time candidate for the New Roads City Council, a plaintiff in *Major* v. *Treen* which created the first majority black congressional district in New Orleans, *Rodney* v. *McKeithen* which created five majority districts rather than two, and as a member of a group of black voters who tried to intervene in *Hays* v. *Louisiana* but was denied the opportunity to do so by a Shreveport, LA, court judge. *Hays* v. *Louisiana* has brought us some hope, and I am a member of the Fourth District.

It is clear to me that the Voting Rights Act is a necessary vehicle. The Voting Rights Act is not self-enforcing. The lack of enforcement weakens the Act. The police juror case demonstrates how it works, while the city of New Roads, LA, all-white council demonstrates that the act has not been tough enough.

Where I am from, whites are not likely to vote for a black candidate, and when you speak out for equality and justice, you become an undesirable candidate. Vote buying, indebtedness, fear, and poor economic conditions play a strong role in the political process and make it extremely difficult to be elected. In some cases, it seems impossible.

Through my work with the Louisiana Hunger Coalition and the Louisiana Survivor Coalition, both statewide advocacy and legislative networks founded by Annie Smart, the only black woman to run against Russell Long, I understand how important the political and legislative process is. It would be difficult to run this country without the implementation of that process. That is how important the Voting Rights Act is. From a grassroots level, I have seen the difference it can make, and to retreat from it would be a grave mistake. Without the Voting Rights Act and stronger enforcement of the Act, I believe that we would again relive the days of the sixties.

[The prepared statement of Ms. St. Cyr follows:]

STATEMENT OF BERNARDINE ST. CYR
BEFORE THE SUBCOMMITTEE ON CIVIL AND CONSTITUTIONAL RIGHTS
OF THE UNITED STATES HOUSE OF REPRESENTATIVES
COMMITTEE ON THE JUDICIARY
VOTING RIGHTS ROUNDTABLE DISCUSSION
MAY 11, 1994

GOOD MORNING MR. CHAIRMAN, MEMBERS OF CONGRESS, VOTING RIGHTS ACTIVISTS, AND CONCERNED CITIZENS. IT IS A PRIVILEGE AND AN HONOR FOR ME TO PARTICIPATE IN THIS ROUNDTABLE DISCUSSION, AND I THANK YOU FOR INVITING ME TO JOIN YOU TODAY.

I WAS BORN IN NEW ROADS, LOUISIANA, AND I HAVE LIVED IN EITHER NEW ROADS OR NEW ORLEANS, LOUISIANA MY ENTIRE LIFE. I ATTENDED SEGREGATED LOUISIANA SCHOOLS FOR TWELVE YEARS, AND I GRADUATED FROM AN ALL-BLACK HIGH SCHOOL IN NEW ROADS IN 1964. AS A STUDENT, I WALKED IN MANY PICKET LINES SEEKING THE INTEGRATION OF SCHOOLS AND PUBLIC FACILITIES IN NEW ROADS, AND ELSEWHERE IN LOUISIANA. I GREW UP IN AN ENVIRONMENT OF STATE-IMPOSED DISCRIMINATION AND, LIKE MANY BLACK CITIZENS OF LOUISIANA, I HAVE FACED NUMEROUS OBSTACLES BECAUSE OF MY RACE.

MY FIRST INVOLVEMENT IN ELECTORAL POLITICS WAS AS A VOLUNTEER IN THE CAMPAIGN OF THE FIRST BLACK CANDIDATE FOR NEW ROADS CITY COUNCIL. THE BLACK CANDIDATE LOST THE ELECTION, EVEN THOUGH HE HAD THE SUPPORT OF THE OVERWHELMING MAJORITY OF BLACK VOTERS IN NEW ROADS. I HAVE BEEN POLITICALLY INVOLVED EVER SINCE THAT

CAMPAIGN. FORTUNATELY, I HAVE LIVED TO WITNESS AND ENJOY THE BENEFITS OF MANY OF THE STRUGGLES FOR CIVIL RIGHTS IN THE 1960S, INCLUDING THE MANY ADVANCES THAT CAN BE CREDITED TO THE ENFORCEMENT OF THE VOTING RIGHTS ACT OF 1965. HOWEVER, I BELIEVE THAT FOR ALL OF THE PROGRESS OF THE LAST THREE DECADES, IN SOME AREAS WE ARE LOSING GROUND, IN MANY OTHERS PROGRESS COMES TOO SLOWLY, AND DISCRIMINATION IS STILL ALIVE AND WELL. WE HAVE A LONG WAY TO GO.

EVEN IN 1994, THERE ARE STILL LINGERING SIGNS OF RACISM AND EFFECTS OF DISCRIMINATION IN NEW ROADS. WE STILL HAVE THE ALL-WHITE FALSE RIVER ACADEMY, WHICH WAS CREATED AFTER THE 1954 <u>BROWN v.</u> <u>BOARD OF EDUCATION</u> DECISION, PARTIALLY WITH STATE FUNDS, TO AVOID INTEGRATION OF THE LOCAL PUBLIC SCHOOLS. ROSENWALD ELEMENTARY SCHOOL, WHICH I ATTENDED AS A CHILD, IS STILL NEARLY ALL BLACK, AS IT WAS WHEN I ATTENDED. AS LEGAL REDRESS CHAIR OF THE NEW ROADS BRANCH OF THE NAACP. I HAVE RECEIVED, AND BEGUN TO INVESTIGATE COMPLAINTS THAT A LOCAL NURSING HOME PLACES ITS WHITE PATIENTS ON ONE WING OF THE HOME, AND ITS BLACK PATIENTS ON ANOTHER. AND, ALTHOUGH BLACKS ARE A MAJORITY OF THE POPULATION OF NEW ROADS, NO MORE THAN ONE AFRICAN-AMERICAN HAS EVER SERVED ON THE FIVE-MEMBER CITY COUNCIL, AND NONE SERVE ON THE COUNCIL TODAY.

IN 1993, THE INCUMBENT AFRICAN-AMERICAN COUNCILMAN DECIDED TO

STEP DOWN AFTER 20 YEARS OF SERVICE. I WAS ONE OF THREE BLACK CANDIDATES IN THE 1993 CITY COUNCIL RACE, AND ALL THREE OF US WERE DEFEATED. AS A RESULT, FOR THE FIRST TIME IN TWENTY YEARS, AN ALL-WHITE NEW ROADS CITY COUNCIL TOOK OFFICE ON JANUARY 1 OF THIS YEAR, AND WILL SERVE UNTIL JANUARY 1 OF 1999.

I RAN FOR CITY COUNCIL IN 1989 AND IN 1993 UNDER AN AT-LARGE SYSTEM, WITH A MAJORITY VOTE REQUIREMENT. IN BOTH ELECTIONS I WAS ONE OF THE TOP VOTE-GETTERS IN THE PRIMARY, AND WOULD HAVE EASILY WON A SEAT ON THE COUNCIL IF A PLURALITY, RATHER THAN A MAJORITY OF VOTES WAS REQUIRED FOR ELECTION. IN BOTH RACES, I WAS ONE OF THE MOST POPULAR CANDIDATES, LARGELY BECAUSE OF THE STRONG SUPPORT THAT I RECEIVED FROM BLACK VOTERS IN NEW ROADS. HOWEVER, IN BOTH ELECTIONS, I LOST IN THE RUN-OFF (OR "SECOND PRIMARY") ELECTION BECAUSE, UNDER NEW ROADS' AT-LARGE ELECTION SYSTEM WITH A MAJORITY VOTE REQUIREMENT, IF WHITES CHOOSE TO CONSOLIDATE THEIR VOTES AGAINST BLACK CANDIDATES AND INSTEAD CONCENTRATE THEIR SUPPORT FOR WHITE CANDIDATES, THEY ARE USUALLY ABLE TO DETERMINE THE OUTCOME OF THE ELECTIONS.

ALTHOUGH I LOST THE 1989 AND 1993 COUNCIL RACES I WAS CLEARLY THE CANDIDATE OF CHOICE OF NEW ROADS' BLACK VOTERS. I HAD ENORMOUS DIFFICULTY, THOUGH, IN GAINING SIGNIFICANT WHITE SUPPORT FOR MY CANDIDACY. FOR EXAMPLE, I AM A BUSINESSWOMAN, AND WHEN I RAN FOR

CITY COUNCIL IN 1989, I WAS A VERY ACTIVE MEMBER OF THE LOCAL CHAMBER OF COMMERCE. NEVERTHELESS, WHEN I SOUGHT THE CHAMBER OF COMMERCE'S SUPPORT FOR MY CANDIDACY, I WAS UNSUCCESSFUL, EVEN THOUGH THEY TRADITIONALLY SUPPORTED THEIR MEMBERS IN CAMPAIGNS FOR ELECTED OFFICES. WHEN I CAMPAIGNED IN WHITE AREAS, I WAS FREQUENTLY RECEIVED WITH HOSTILITY. AS A VOLUNTEER FOR OTHER BLACK CANDIDATES, I HAVE ENCOUNTERED SIMILAR HOSTILITY WHILE CAMPAIGNING IN WHITE AREAS.

MY SECOND CAMPAIGN WAS EVEN MORE DIFFICULT BECAUSE BY THEN I HAD BECOME A PLAINTIFF IN RODNEY V. MCKEITHEN, A LAWSUIT THAT CHALLENGED THE REAPPORTIONMENT OF THE POINTE COUPEE PARISH POLICE JURY, AND I HAD BEEN OUTSPOKEN IN MY SUPPORT FOR A CHANGE FROM THE AT-LARGE CITY COUNCIL ELECTION SYSTEM TO A SINGLE-MEMBER DISTRICT ELECTION SYSTEM IN NEW ROADS. MANY WHITES IN LOUISIANA ARE UNWILLING TO VOTE FOR BLACK CANDIDATES UNDER ANY CIRCUMSTANCES. BLACK CANDIDATES WHO SPEAK OUT FOR EQUALITY AND JUSTICE ARE EVEN MORE UNPOPULAR AND UNDESIRABLE FROM THE PERSPECTIVE OF WHITE VOTERS. ECONOMIC COERCION AND OTHER FORMS OF INTIMIDATION OF BLACK VOTERS COMBINE WITH POOR ECONOMIC CONDITIONS IN THE PARISH TO STRONGLY INFLUENCE THE LOCAL POLITICAL PROCESS AND MAKE IT EXTREMELY DIFFICULT FOR BLACK CANDIDATES TO BE ELECTED OUTSIDE OF DISTRICTS WHERE BLACKS ARE AN EFFECTIVE MAJORITY OF THE VOTING

POPULATION. UNDER THESE CIRCUMSTANCES, IT HAS BEEN EXTREMELY DIFFICULT, AND AT TIMES NEARLY IMPOSSIBLE, FOR BLACKS TO BE ELECTED UNDER NEW ROADS' AT-LARGE ELECTION SYSTEM, COMBINED WITH THE MAJORITY VOTE REQUIREMENT WHICH APPLIES TO LOUISIANA ELECTIONS.

ONE THING IS CLEAR TO ME AS A COMMUNITY ACTIVIST; NAACP LEGAL REDRESS OFFICER; A TWO-TIME CANDIDATE FOR THE NEW ROADS CITY COUNCIL; A PLAINTIFF IN MAJOR v. TREEN, WHICH CREATED THE FIRST MAJORITY BLACK CONGRESSIONAL DISTRICT IN LOUISIANA SINCE RECONSTRUCTION; A PLAINTIFF IN RODNEY v. MCKEITHEN, WHICH CREATED 5 BLACK-MAJORITY POLICE JURY DISTRICTS INSTEAD OF THE 2 THAT EXISTED BEFORE THE LAWSUIT; AND AS A MEMBER OF A GROUP OF BLACK VOTERS WHO TRIED TO INTERVENE IN DEFENSE OF THE FOURTH CONGRESSIONAL DISTRICT OF LOUISIANA IN HAYS v. LOUISIANA, BUT WERE DENIED THE OPPORTUNITY TO DO SO BY THE THREE-JUDGE FEDERAL COURT THAT TRIED THE CASE: THE VOTING RIGHTS ACT HAS BEEN A KEY TO PROVIDING BLACK VOTERS AN EQUAL OPPORTUNITY TO PARTICIPATE IN THE POLITICAL PROCESS THROUGHOUT THE STATE OF LOUISIANA. HOWEVER, THE VOTING RIGHTS ACT IS NOT SELF-ENFORCING, AND STRONG SUPPORT FOR ENFORCEMENT BY PRIVATE CITIZENS AND ORGANIZATIONS AS WELL AS FEDERAL GOVERNMENT ENFORCEMENT OF THE ACT, ARE BOTH ESSENTIAL COMPONENTS OF FULL ENFORCEMENT OF THE ACT. THE INCREASING EXPENSE AND DIFFICULTY ASSOCIATED WITH BRINGING A SUCCESSFUL VOTING RIGHTS CASE MAKES PRIVATE ENFORCEMENT FAR

MORE DIFFICULT. ULTIMATELY, EITHER WEAK PRIVATE ENFORCEMENT OR WEAK GOVERNMENT ENFORCEMENT WILL SERIOUSLY UNDERMINE THE EFFECTIVENESS OF THE ACT.

THE CREATION OF LOUISIANA'S SECOND MAJORITY-BLACK CONGRESSIONAL DISTRICT, THE FOURTH CONGRESSIONAL DISTRICT, WHICH I AM A RESIDENT OF, REPRESENTED REAL PROGRESS IN VOTING RIGHTS IN LOUISIANA. THE HAYS v. LOUISIANA DECISION WAS A SETBACK TO VOTING RIGHTS, BUT HOPEFULLY IT WAS ONLY A TEMPORARY SETBACK. THE OPPORTUNITY TO ELECT A REPRESENTATIVE OF MY CHOICE IN CONGRESSIONAL ELECTIONS IS VERY IMPORTANT TO ME, AS I BELIEVE IT IS FOR MANY BLACK VOTERS WHO LIVE IN THE FOURTH CONGRESSIONAL DISTRICT. IT WAS MY CONCERN ABOUT THE PRESERVATION OF THE DISTRICT THAT PROMPTED ME TO TRY TO INTERVENE IN THE HAYS v. LOUISIANA LAWSUIT.

THE CURRENT POINTE COUPEE PARISH POLICE JURY ALSO ILLUSTRATES THE STRENGTH OF THE VOTING RIGHTS ACT WHEN IT IS PROPERLY ENFORCED. THE JUSTICE DEPARTMENT REFUSED TO ALLOW THE PARISH TO IMPLEMENT RACIALLY DISCRIMINATORY REDISTRICTING PLANS ADOPTED BY THE PARISH POLICE JURY OVER THE OBJECTION OF ITS BLACK MEMBERS. THE RODNEY v. MCKEITHEN LAWSUIT LED TO THE POLICE JURY'S ADOPTION OF A PLAN THAT ALLOWED THE ELECTION OF FOUR BLACK POLICE JURY MEMBERS -- DOUBLE THE NUMBER OF BLACK REPRESENTATIVES ELECTED UNDER THE OLD REDISTRICTING PLAN, AND THE LARGEST NUMBER OF BLACK REPRESENTATIVES

6

EVER ELECTED TO THE PARISH POLICE JURY IN THE HISTORY OF THE PARISH. UNDER THE NEW REDISTRICTING PLAN, BLACKS ARE ALSO THE MAJORITY OF THE POPULATION IN ANOTHER DISTRICT, MAKING A TOTAL OF FIVE DISTRICTS IN WHICH BLACK VOTERS HAVE A REALISTIC OPPORTUNITY TO ELECT CANDIDATES OF THEIR CHOICE.

ON THE OTHER HAND, THE CITY OF NEW ROADS, LOUISIANA, WITH AN ALL-WHITE COUNCIL GOVERNING A BLACK-MAJORITY POPULATION, DEMONSTRATES THAT THE ACT IS STILL NOT FULLY ENFORCED, AND IT IS NOT SELF-ENFORCING.

THROUGH MY WORK WITH THE LOUISIANA HUNGER COALITION AND LOUISIANA SURVIVAL COALITION -- A STATEWIDE ADVOCACY AND LEGISLATIVE NETWORK FOUNDED BY ANNE SMART, THE ONLY BLACK WOMAN TO RUN AGAINST RUSSELL LONG -- I UNDERSTAND HOW IMPORTANT THE POLITICAL AND LEGISLATIVE PROCESS IS. I UNDERSTAND THAT THERE IS A RELATIONSHIP BETWEEN HOW REPRESENTATIVES ARE ELECTED AND THEIR SENSE OF ACCOUNTABILITY TOWARDS THE PEOPLE WHO HAVE ELECTED THEM. FROM A GRASSROOTS LEVEL, I HAVE SEEN THE IMPACT THAT THE VOTING RIGHTS ACT CAN HAVE ON BLACK VOTERS' OPPORTUNITIES TO PARTICIPATE IN ELECTIONS AND TO ELECT CANDIDATES OF THEIR CHOICE. FUNDAMENTALLY, I BELIEVE THAT THE ACT -- BY MAKING THE PROCESS MORE OPEN AND ALLOWING VOTERS TO ELECT REPRESENTATIVES FROM MORE DIVERSE POINTS OF VIEW -- HAS BENEFITTED NOT ONLY BLACK VOTERS, BUT IN FACT HAS IMPROVED OUR

SYSTEM OF GOVERNMENT OVERALL. I BELIEVE THAT IT WOULD BE DIFFICULT TO RUN THE COUNTRY NOW WITHOUT THE DIVERSE REPRESENTATION THAT HAS BEEN MADE POSSIBLE LARGELY THROUGH THE ENFORCEMENT OF THE VOTING RIGHTS ACT. THAT'S HOW IMPORTANT THE VOTING RIGHTS ACT IS.

CONGRESSMEN, I HAVE SEEN FIRSTHAND THE DIFFERENCE THAT THE VOTING RIGHTS ACT CAN MAKE. ON A GRASSROOTS LEVEL I KNOW THE IMPORTANT CONTRIBUTION THAT THE VOTING RIGHTS ACT HAS MADE. THE VOTING RIGHTS ACT HAS TRULY SUCCEEDED BY MAKING GOVERNMENT AT EVERY LEVEL BETTER REFLECT THE DIVERSITY OF THE PEOPLE WHO ARE GOVERNED, AND BY MAKING ELECTED OFFICIALS MORE ACCOUNTABLE TO THEIR CONSTITUENTS. WITHOUT THE VOTING RIGHTS ACT, I FEAR A RETURN TO THE WORLD OF DISCRIMINATION AND SEGREGATION THAT I GREW UP IN. WE ONLY NEED TO LOOK BACK TO THE DAYS OF EXCLUSION OF BLACK VOTERS FROM THE POLLS, PURGING BLACK VOTERS FROM ELECTIONS LISTS, AND DEVELOPING OTHER DEVICES TO PREVENT FULL POLITICAL EQUALITY AMONG BLACKS AND WHITES, TO KNOW THAT TURNING THE CLOCK BACK ON VOTING RIGHTS WOULD BE AGONIZING, DANGEROUS, AND WRONG. NOW IS NOT THE TIME TO RETREAT FROM THE ACT -- THE ACT IS A SUCCESS. INSTEAD, I HOPE THAT THIS SUBCOMMITTEE WILL EXAMINE WAYS OF STRENGTHENING ENFORCEMENT OF THE VOTING RIGHTS ACT AND GIVE SERIOUS ATTENTION TO MAKING THE ACT EVEN MORE EFFECTIVE.

I LOOK FORWARD TO CONTINUING THIS DISCUSSION OF THE VOTING

RIGHTS ACT, AND AGAIN I THANK YOU FOR THIS OPPORTUNITY TO PARTICIPATE IN THIS VOTING RIGHTS ROUNDTABLE DISCUSSION.

Mr. EDWARDS. Thank you.

Let me interrupt to introduce and welcome Barney Frank, Congressman from Massachusetts.

Barney, do either you or Howard want to make a statement?

Mr. FRANK. Only that I think this is important an issue as we have before us, the question of adapting the Voting Rights Act to various trends, and I am pleased to listen.

Mr. EDWARDS. Thank you. Mr. Taylor.

STATEMENT OF STUART TAYLOR, JOURNALIST, LEGAL TIMES

Mr. TAYLOR. Mr. Chairman, Mr. Ranking Minority Member, my name is Stuart Taylor. I am a working journalist. As such, I am flattered to be included in such distinguished company, and as such I must apologize for jumping up periodically and running into the hallway, making phone calls to see if the White House will ever make up its mind about appointing a Supreme Court Justice.

I would like to——

Mr. EDWARDS. Are you a candidate?

Mr. TAYLOR. I volunteered my services a year ago in print, but I haven't heard from them. That was after Governor Cuomo, Chief Judge Kaye, and various others had turned them down, including William Kunstler. I thought, if William Kunstler turns them down, why not me? I think he was volunteering his turndown though, I don't believe he was requested.

I would like to speak in very broad brush terms. I don't consider myself a particular expert in this area. I have written about it, and I hope maybe I make up in objectivity to some extent what I lack in expertise.

As I see it, we have a very serious problem, racial bloc voting, which is serious first because it leads in many parts of the country still to the exclusion of blacks, Hispanic-Americans, and perhaps Asian-Americans from winning elective office in anything like proportionate numbers, and I think generally speaking it would be nice if we had roughly proportionate representation as long as it came about through natural means. It doesn't seem to come about through natural means.

The second problem I see with racial bloc voting is that it perpetuates what divides us. We have a primary solution that our courts and the Congress have developed to that particular problem. Typically, it is to find ways of drawing majority minority districts. Sometimes it is very easy if you have concentrations of population. Sometimes it involves considerable stretching and bizarre gerrymandering, as occurred in the district in question in *Shaw* v. *Reno*.

I think the problem that solution raises is not racial preference in the usual sense, and for that reason I disagree with those who see *Shaw* v. *Reno* as an assertion of white rights against black rights. I think it demonstrates the problem that racial gerrymandering as a remedial device poses when it is carried to extremes is twofold.

One, it perpetuates racial polarization by encouraging politicians of all races to appeal only or primarily to members of their own race. If you put people in a district where they only need to appeal to members of their own race, that is what they are likely to do, whites and blacks alike, and when we stretch too hard to draw majority minority districts, an inevitable side effect is to create whiter districts in the surrounding area. That too, it seems to me, leads to racial polarization.

I think this particular remedy also has a tendency to entrench racial bloc voting, to perpetuate it perhaps ad infinitum, by putting the law's imprimatur on the notion that it is natural and expected. I am reminded of a phrase Justice Scalia used many years ago in another context, "the disease as cure," and for those reasons, I am troubled as the Supreme Court was in *Shaw* v. *Reno* by extremes of racial gerrymandering.

At the same time, I am not sure that anybody has proposed a very adequate alternative to race-conscious redistricting when we do need some kind of remedy for the type of racially polarized voting that has an exclusionary effect, as it does.

This leads me to think, and I think it is leading the Supreme Court to think, that some kind of muddled moderate compromise— you can gerrymander a little bit but not too much—may be the lesser evil here.

Lani Guinier, of course, and others have proposed cumulative voting as a creative alternative to gerrymandering, to racial gerrymandering. I think cumulative voting has one salient attraction in that regard which is that people who choose to concentrate their votes behind one candidate for reasons partially of race at least are doing so by individual choice, they are not doing so because the districts were manipulated in a way to make them do that.

I am concerned that cumulative voting may also have a tendency to perpetuate divisions and it may have unanticipated consequences. We may find that not only are racial minorities benefiting from cumulative voting as candidates but also perhaps the David Dukes of the world will be benefiting, or prochoice people or antichoice people or any number of ideological groups, focused groups, single issue groups.

I think that *Shaw* v. *Reno* was a badly written opinion in a good cause. I don't believe the Court intends to carry it to the extreme of ruling out all race-conscious redistricting. Although I am afraid Justice O'Connor's opinion might lend itself, some aspects of it, to that interpretation, I don't think it is the most natural reading of her interpretation.

I think we are going to learn a lot more about the Court's intentions in this regard this spring when the two voting rights cases now pending before the Court are decided, in particular the *Grandy* v. *Johnson,* the south Florida case, which deals with the proposition which many lower courts have assumed to be valid, that whenever a majority minority district can be drawn, it must be drawn.

I believe that proposition will be put to the test before the Supreme Court. I believe the Court will reject that proposition, and I hope that the Court will muddle its way toward a reasonable compromise in this area without any great necessity for further legislation.

Thank you.

Mr. EDWARDS. Thank you, Mr. Taylor.

Mr. Markman.

STATEMENT OF STEVEN MARKMAN, MILLER, CANFIELD, PADDOCK & STONE, DETROIT, MI

Mr. MARKMAN. Thank you very much, Mr. Chairman. I appreciate the opportunity to be here and participate in this round table.

If I understood Mr. Durbin correctly at the outset, he indicated that one of the issues here is how you take race into account, and that is a problem. I agree with that, and, in fact, I think it is an intractable problem. Trying to take race into account has been a problem that has plagued our country for the past 200 years, and I would respectfully submit· that there is no possible social equilibrium when you do have a policy that takes race into account as aggressively as the Voting Rights Act Amendments of 1982.

The result of section 2, as amended, in 1982 is to make meticulous racial calculations the law of the land, and this is the stuff of ordinary debate in courtrooms around the country. The intensity and the preoccupation with racial statistics and racial details is quite extraordinary, and this kind of debate takes place as a routine basis in cases brought under section 2 around the country.

But the issue is not merely proportional representation, although that is clearly the inevitable starting point, notwithstanding the disclaimer in section 2, because there is no other alternative benchmark other than proportional representation by which to calculate whether or not a jurisdiction is in compliance with the Voting Rights Act.

But the problem goes beyond proportional representation, it goes to the question of optimization, and, as Mr. Taylor indicated, the issue there is if it is possible or conceivable to create more districts, do you have an obligation to do so?

In the case that I am participating in, in Michigan, the basic argument in the complaint is that the State has not created as many districts as it is possible to do and we acknowledge that, in fact, is true, but the question is whether or not there is an obligation under the Voting Rights Act to create as many majority minority districts, effective majority minority districts, as one can possibly create.

In fact, the argument there is that in the Detroit metropolitan area where most of the black concentration in the State of Michigan exists, you have to create greater than proportional representation in order to compensate for scatterings of black individuals who live around the rest of the State who aren't sufficiently concentrated to allow the election of a member. So it is the idea that you have to compensate for scattered enclaves of blacks throughout the rest of the State by providing greater than proportional representation in those areas in which it is possible to elect a black representative.

The Voting Rights Act, in my judgment, has moved inevitably in this direction. I would disagree with Mr. Griffith that it is judicial abuse. I would suggest it is a more fundamental problem in that it derives directly from the fact that the language and the syntax and the grammar of section 2 is really quite confusing and quite— I don't think anybody has been able to suggest a core meaning, a core principle of what section 2 means, and as a result you have judges basically deciding what they think is more important. One judge over here will decide that he thinks the essential meaning of section 2 is equality of opportunity. The next judge will say he thinks it is equality of results.

The compromise that was engineered in 1982 is not like the compromise between levels of spending in an appropriation or authorization bill, it is a compromise between two fundamentally untenable and inconsistent concepts. In fact, I think the untenability of the section and the lack of standards in section 2 is reflected by the fact that Lani Guinier, whom I respect for her abilities, can argue seriously that cumulative voting which would effect a tremendous political, a revolutionary political overhaul of our system, is somehow compelled by section 2.

Was this within the contemplation of the Congress back in 1982, that cumulative voting would have to be the law of the land? I think not, but Lani Guinier can reasonably deduce from the language that perhaps cumulative voting is required.

Shaw v. *Reno*, I think, is only a manifestation of the problem. It is a sexy part of the problem because it involves an extraordinarily convoluted district. But the core problem with section 2 of the Voting Rights Act is not that kind of district, it is the quite regularly shaped district, the aesthetically pleasing district that nevertheless is the result of nothing but racial preoccupation, the idea that one group of Americans among many have to have their electoral interest optimized.

The Voting Rights Act is transforming America, and I do think it is time for the partisan debate that we have seen in the Voting Rights Act in the past with Republicans and Democrats trying to calculate whether the act is in their interests to be replaced by some calculation of a long-term national interest.

I would respectfully submit that when we look at what our Nation has become in the year 2020, a Lebanonized, segregated, racially preoccupied society, we will be able to look back upon the 1982 amendments to section 2, if they are not changed, as an enormous factor contributing to those circumstances.

In conclusion, I think that Congressman Frank is correct. There is no more important issue to what our Nation is all about and what its values are, and again I commend this committee for taking the time to set up this round table.

Thank you.

Mr. EDWARDS. Thank you. Ms. Karlan.

STATEMENT OF PAMELA KARLAN, PROFESSOR OF LAW, UNIVERSITY OF VIRGINIA SCHOOL OF LAW

Ms. KARLAN. Thank you very much, Mr. Chairman, ranking minority member.

I think there is nothing sadder than hearing people talk about the Voting Rights Act as if it is going to turn the United States into the Balkans or Lebanon. It would be funny if it weren't so sad, because really what the Voting Rights Act has done for America is to integrate minorities into the political process with less violence than has taken place anywhere in the world.

In 1982 in the Senate report accompanying the 1982 amendments, the report stated that blaming the Voting Rights Act for racial polarization in America is like blaming the thermometer for the fever, and I think that is true. It is not the Voting Rights Act which led the Louisiana congressional leadership in 1981 to lock blacks literally out of the room when they drew the districts. It is not the Voting Rights Act that led the white members of the Etowah County Commission to vote when the black member wasn't even there and to tell him that, alone among county commissioners, he would have no road supervision authority, no hiring authority, and no spending authority.

That is not the Voting Rights Act, that is a more intractable problem, and it seems to me that one of the real geniuses of the Voting Rights Act is that it has allowed Congress and the President, the political branches of this Government, to enter into bargaining.

Of course, some of that bargaining comes from partisan interests, but that is one of the great things about the Voting Rights Act. It has given blacks the same kind of bargaining chip in the political process that all sorts of other identifiable groups have had.

What bothers me about *Shaw* v. *Reno*, what bothers me about *Presley* v. *Etowah County Commission*, is that the Court is stepping in to overturn what the national political branches have recognized as an accommodation of competing race interests in a country in which, as W.E.B. DuBois noted at the beginning of the century, the central problem is the color line. I don't think we can abandon that, and I think when Justice O'Connor quotes Justice Stewart on pornography to explain why appearances matter or when Judge Wiener in the fifth circuit compares the intent of the legislature and of the Bush Justice Department in compelling the drawing of a second black congressional district to the kind of intent that murderers have under the homicide statute, something is clearly very wrong in this country. It seems to me that the political branches have shown enough commitment to the Voting Rights Act both in Republican and Democratic administrations that we should let politics take care of this problem and not let the Supreme Court dismantle what I think, Representative Edwards, you rightly refer to as the most significant civil rights statute in this country's history.

[The prepared statement of Ms. Karlan follows:]

SCHOOL OF LAW
UNIVERSITY OF VIRGINIA

Pamela S. Karlan
Professor of Law

MEMORANDUM

TO: Members of the Subcommittee on Civil and Constitutional Rights and Other
               Participants in the Voting Rights Roundtable Discussion

        I have attached to this memorandum four items which respond to the questions raised
by the Voting Rights Round Table Issues List for May 11, 1994

- the first item is a memorandum prepared for an American Sociological
  Association retreat that provides a framework for thinking about issues related
  to majority-minority districts and to so-called "third generation" issues: the sort
  presented by *Presley v. Etowah County Commission*, 112 S.Ct. 820 (1992)

- the second item is a brief piece written for The Nation that argues that the
  Supreme Court and several lower federal courts seem intent on dismantling or
  at least narrowing the reach of the Voting Rights Act

- the third item is an article published in the Texas Law Review that both sets
  out a theoretical framework for thinking about voting rights questions and
  argues that current legal doctrine, combined with a variety of procedural
  considerations incident to litigation, has produced confusion and an opportunity
  both for partisan "capture" of the Voting Rights Act and for a politicized
  federal judiciary to interfere with the political process

- the final item is a forthcoming article in the Supreme Court Review that
  analyzes the Court's three voting rights cases from the 1993 Term. Of
  particular salience, I criticize the Court's opinion in *Shaw v. Reno*, 113 S.Ct.
  2816 (1993), and argue that it may represent the opening salvo in an attempt
  by the Court to seize control over the accommodation of minority and majority
  interests in the political process from the political branches of the federal
  government. In this piece, pages 277-87 are of particular relevance.

I hope this materials will be helpful to your consideration and would be delighted to discuss
any of them with you at greater length.

580 Massie Road
CHARLOTTESVILLE, VIRGINIA 22903-1789
(804) 924-7810
Fax (804) 924-7536
Internet psk7e@virginia.edu

MEMORANDUM

To: Participants in the ASA's "Rethinking the Urban Agenda"
           Retreat

FROM: Pam Karlan, University of Virginia School of Law

Re: Voting Rights Issues: Racial Bloc Voting; Majority-Black
           Districts; and Third-Generation Issues

The "right to vote" is not a unitary concept. It actually embodies a constellation of concepts:

- **Participation**: the entitlement of individuals to cast ballots and have those ballots counted

- **Aggregation**: the ability of a voter to combine her vote with those of other voters to elect the candidate of her choice

- **Governance**: the voter's participation, through her elected representatives, in the process of representative decisionmaking

The so-called "first generation" of enforcement under the Voting Rights Act of 1965 dealt with the right of black Americans to participate fully and freely in the electoral process. On the eve of the Act's passage, black voters throughout the South were largely disenfranchised by discriminatory practices such as poll taxes, "good character" tests, and literacy requirements (often unfairly enforced). As to these first generation issues, the Act has been a stunning success. A majority of black Americans are registered to vote, and Congress and the states have steadily dismantled most of the remaining legal barriers to full participation.

But simply giving black voters the formal right to participate did not mean that they were able to elect candidates responsive to their concerns. The most pervasive set of aggregation rules in American politics concerns the geographical allocation of voters among electoral jurisdictions. The way in which districts are drawn often determines which voters will be able to elect their preferred candidates and which voters will have their preferences go unsatisfied.

There are basically three ways in which geographic aggregation rules might impair a voter's ability to elect her preferred candidate -- the euphonious trio of cracking, stacking, and packing. Cracking occurs when a political group is split between two or more districts, in each of which it forms an ineffective minority. Stacking occurs when a group that would be large enough to form an effective majority in a district is placed within a multimember district in which hostile opponents constitute the majority and control election to all the available positions. Finally, packing occurs when a distinctive group is overconcentrated into a few districts; its opponents concede victory in those districts but leave group members in surrounding districts politically impotent.

The mechanism behind all these dilutive effects is bloc voting. If blacks form a minority within a particular jurisdiction or district and they vote differently from the white majority, then candidates can ignore black interests.

The "second generation" of voting rights litigation has attacked dilutive districting. Here, the Act has been relatively successful, although not in so dramatic a sense as with respect to first generation participation claims. At-large elections and multi-member districts (which both lead to stacking) have largely been eliminated in areas where significant, geographically defined black communities had previously been unable to elect candidates of their choice. And majority-black single-member districts have been created for congressional, state, and local offices. In districts where blacks form a majority of the electorate, racial bloc voting no longer prevents them from electing their preferred candidates.

But the creation of majority-black districts raises at least two possible practical problems, in addition to raising the normative political question whether race ought to be taken into account in drawing district lines. First, in a deeply polarized society, electing black representatives may simply move the locus of discrimination from the voting booth to the legislative chamber. Second-generation aggregation lawsuits might, for example, permit black voters to elect one black commissioner to a seven-member commission, but if he then gets consistently outvoted by the six members elected from majority-white districts, blacks may be no better off. Second, a plan that maximizes the number of representatives a group directly elects could produce a generally unfriendly elected body. For example, the creation of majority-black districts may enable black voters to elect some representatives to an assembly but may result in the election of hostile delegates from the remaining, majority-white districts. Again, if the black community's representatives are consistently outvoted within the legislature, the black community may have achieved its aggregation interest at the expense of a real role in governance.

So-called "third generation" voting rights issues deal with the first problem: legislative exclusion of representatives from the black community. That there is a problem seems clear from recent testimony before the civil rights subcommittee of the House Judiciary Committee. Sometimes, white officials meet without notifying their black colleagues; sometimes proposals advanced by black representatives is totally ignored. But I think it would be mistaken to overestimate the problem. In many legislative and local bodies, representatives from the black community have been extraordinarily successful at advancing their constituents' agenda. Black legislators often attain seniority, and the committee chairmanships that accompany it, thereby gaining substantial informal power. Black legislative caucuses often successfully horsetrade their collective votes to obtain support on issues of particular importance to their communities. Devices such as rotation of chairmanships or committee assignments can accelerate the process of political integration. Moreover, the face-to-face ongoing relationships within governmental bodies mean that prejudices and stereotypes may break down more quickly within such groups than in the general populace.

The hard question in "third generation" issues is how to create standards for assessing full participation in governance. There is no consensus on how often a group that constitutes, say, 25 percent of the population should get its preferences satisfied in the legislative process. This is especially true given the deeply majoritarian rhetoric of American politics. To the extent that democracy is equated with pure majority rule, third generation governance claims are problematic because they seem to involve the assertion by a numerical (as well as racial) minority that it deserves to win some of the time.

Actually, however, third generation issues are simply a species of an ongoing American quandary stemming back to the foundation of the Republic: the need to tame the power of factional politics. The Framers did a pretty good job of devising institutional arrangements to "break and control the violence of faction[s]" based on economic and regional interests. But nothing in those institutional arrangements has effectively restrained "the superior force of an interested and over-bearing [racial] majority" from ignoring the interests of racial minorities and their claims to equal respect and treatment in the governance process. A central task of the third generation will be to develop remedies that can break apart the monolithic majority bloc in order to put minorities, and the officials who represent them, in a position where their votes mean something because they can be used to construct winning electoral and governing coalitions. There is no blanket categorical answer, however, since solutions will be as localized as the problems.

Just as important, one way of reducing the effects of racially identifiable factions and hence persistent minority exclusion is to break down racial bloc voting. The question of how to do this is complex, since it involves trying to change individual voters' attitudes, attitudes that the First Amendment protects.

The empirical evidence suggests that the single factor most

likely to lead white voters to support candidates sponsored by the black community is incumbency. In other words, black incumbents gain a higher percentage of the white vote than either black candidates competing for open seats or black candidates challenging white incumbents. Moreover, black candidates who succeed at lower-level offices are more likely to attract white support when they run for higher office than blacks without such prior experience. These data suggest that majority-black districts perform a function beyond simply enhancing the opportunities for black inclusion in particular bodies. Such districts also increase the willingness of white voters to build biracial coalitions or support candidates from the black community. And they increase the willingness of white voters to consider these officials when they compete for offices beyond the boundaries of the majority-black districts.

By contrast, there is little hard data that once majority-black districts are created, representatives elected from white districts necessarily become less likely to support items of special interest to black voters. First, it was often the case, because of racial polarization, that representatives elected from 25 or 35 percent black districts ignored the views of the black community anyway. Second, the opportunity for horsetrading mentioned above often outweighs any diminution in direct support for the black community's agenda.

This is not, however, to say that majority-black districts are the ultimate solution to the political exclusion of black Americans. Such districts do not give every black voter a full chance to participate in the process; black voters who continue to live in majority-white districts may be marginalized. And as a greater proportion of the black middle and professional classes moves into racially mixed neighborhoods, this problem may grow. Moreover, to the extent that "safe" racial districting provides for safe incumbent districting, it may not promote grass-roots political mobilization. Lani Guinier made trenchant criticisms along these lines in her much-attacked Michigan and Virginia Law Review pieces. Alternatives that promote cross-racial coalition building within the electorate as well as inside the council chamber -- such as cumulative and limited voting -- should thus be explored in order to see whether they can fully serve black voters' aggregative interests while increasing their participation in governance.

The Nat

May 23, 1994 $2.25 U.S./$2.75 Canada

Broken Promise

Brown v. Board of Education Forty Years Later

PATRICIA J. WILLIAMS
•
TERRY WILLIAMS
AND
THE HARLEM
WRITERS CREW
•
ROGER WILKINS
•
JONATHAN KOZOL
•
PAMELA S. KARLAN
•
DERRICK BELL

Linda Brown Thompson, 1994

PHOTO BY VIRGINIA BLAISDELL

ly." The white doctor who treated my family in Boston, where I grew up, "used to treat us in such a completely offhand way. But after *Brown*, he wanted to discuss it with us, he asked questions, what I thought. He wanted my opinion and I suddenly realized that no white person had ever asked what I thought about anything."

Perhaps as people like my father and the doctor have permitted those conversations to become more and more straightforward, the pain of it all, the discomfort, has been accompanied by the shutting down, the mishearing, the turning away from the euphoria of *Brown*. "It has become unexpectedly, but not unpredictably, hard. The same thing will probably have to happen in South Africa," sighs my father.

When Frederick Douglass described his own escape from slavery as a "theft" of "this head" and "these arms" and "these legs," he employed the master's language of property to create the unforgettable paradox of the "owned" erupting into the category of a speaking subject whose "freedom" simultaneously and inextricably marked him as a "thief." That this disruption of the bounds of normative imagining is variously perceived as dangerous as well as liberatory is a tension that has distinguished racial politics in America from the Civil War to this day. Perhaps the legacy of *Brown* is as much tied up with this sense of national imagination as with the pure fact of its legal victory; it sparkled in our heads, it fired our vision of what was possible. Legally it set in motion battles over inclusion, participation and reallocation of resources that are very far from resolved. But in a larger sense it committed us to a conversation about race in which all of us must join—particularly in view of a new rising Global Right.

The fact that this conversation has fallen on hard times is no reason to abandon what has been accomplished. The word games by which the civil rights movement has been stymied— in which "inner city" and "underclass" and "suspect profile" are racial code words, in which "integration" means "assimilation as white," in which black culture means "tribalism," in which affirmative action has been made out to be the exact equivalent of quota systems that discriminated against Jews— these are all dimensions of the enormous snarl this nation has been unraveling, in waves of euphoria and despair, since the Emancipation Proclamation.

We remain charged with the task of getting beyond the stage of halting encounters filled with the superficial temptations of those "my maid says blacks are happy" or "whites are devils" moments. If we could press on to an accounting of the devastating legacy of slavery that lives on as a social crisis that needs generations more of us working to repair—if we could just get to the enormity of that unhappy acknowledgment, then that alone might be the paradoxical source of a genuinely revivifying, rather than a false, optimism.

The most eloquent summary of both the simplicity and the complexity of that common task remains W.E.B. Du Bois's essay "On Being Crazy":

> After the theatre, I sought the hotel where I had sent my baggage. The clerk scowled.
> "What do you want?" he said.
> Rest, I said.
> "This is a white hotel," he said.

I looked around. Such a color scheme requires a great deal of cleaning, I said, but I don't know that I object.
"We object," said he.
Then why, I began, but he interrupted.
"We don't keep niggers," he said, "we don't want social equality."
Neither do I, I replied gently, I want a bed. □

VOTING RIGHTS AND THE COURT

End of the Second Reconstruction?

PAMELA S. KARLAN

We lived many lives in those swirling campaigns ... yet when we achieved, and the new world dawned, the old men came out again and took our victory to remake in the likeness of the former world they knew. ... We stammered that we had worked for a new heaven and a new earth, and they thanked us kindly and made their peace.   —Lawrence of Arabia

Brown v. Board *of Education* is justly recognized as one of the Supreme Court's finest moments. In *Brown* the Court expressed a sweeping vision of racial equality. But when we celebrate *Brown*, we need to remember that the Supreme Court is not always the special champion of black Americans. Indeed, if history is any guide, the Court is as likely to choke off an American Reconstruction as to precipitate one. In the 1870s and 1880s the Court gutted the First Reconstruction by invalidating or misconstruing a series of critical Congressional protections of black political and economic rights. Last year in *Shaw v. Reno* the High Court cast an ominous shadow over the centerpiece of the Second Reconstruction: the Voting Rights Act, which after nearly thirty years had finally begun to integrate the political process. And next, in any one of a plethora of post-*Shaw* voting rights cases currently percolating up through the system, the Court may take the opportunity to gut the act altogether.

The Voting Rights Act is unquestionably the most successful civil rights statute in American history. On the eve of the act's passage a decade after *Brown*, blacks were still completely excluded from the rolls in large parts of the South, and economic and physical harassment kept even those blacks who had managed to register from actually casting ballots. Within five years, nearly as many blacks had been added to the rolls as had managed to register in the preceding century. The bill's first great victory was thus its enfranchisement of black Americans.

The Voting Rights Act's second triumph was to delineate a view of the right to vote that included an equal opportunity actually to elect candidates of the voter's choice. If the votes

Pamela S. Karlan is a professor of law at the University of Virginia Law School.

of a politically cohesive black community are overwhelmed, election after election, by the ballots of antagonistic white voters, the right to vote loses much of its meaning. One of the central principles of the act is that equality here and now matters: discriminatory motivations are simply beside the point. The act has been used to dismantle the two major devices that historically have prevented black communities from electing representatives: at-large elections and multimember legislative districts. Before the Voting Rights Act, there were virtually no black elected officials in the South and fairly few in the North. Now there are thousands, most of whom have been elected from majority nonwhite constituencies. And these elected officials have played a critical role in fighting for a variety of progressive policies, ranging from free kindergartens in Mississippi to increased pressure on South Africa to end apartheid.

The act's third great achievement was its creation of a national political consensus in favor of equal political opportunity. A broad spectrum of Democratic and Republican legislators—from Charles Grassley and Bob Dole to Don Edwards and Ted Kennedy—have fought to amend and extend the bill's protections. And with the exception of eight years of deep hostility under Reagan, both Democratic and Republican administrations have used the power of "pre-clearance" granted the federal government under the act—requiring states with a history of low minority participation to get approval from the Justice Department before they change their election laws—to guarantee black voters the same chance white voters have to elect representatives of their choice.

Of course, this support reflects the calculated self-interest of the two major political parties as much as it does moral commitment. But the fact that majority politicians horse-trade with the black community is a sign that because of the Voting Rights Act, politics, broadly defined, is working.

Apparently, it is working too well for the Supreme Court and a coterie of hostile lower court judges. The white plaintiffs in *Shaw v. Reno* challenge a reapportionment compromise, hammered out by a majority-white North Carolina General Assembly and the Bush Justice Department, that gave black North Carolinians their first chance since 1901 to elect representatives to Congress. The districts North Carolina drew were, to be sure, oddly shaped—largely to create two majority black districts while protecting the seats of incumbent white Democrats. But oddly shaped districts—meeting the interests of the political parties and machines that control legislatures—are a staple of American politics; the late Representative Phil Burton referred to the Congressional districting plan for California as "my contribution to modern art."

In 1986, Justice Sandra Day O'Connor argued that a Republican gerrymander in Indiana was entirely immune from judicial scrutiny. But in *Shaw* this same Justice O'Connor wrote an opinion that perversely used the equal protection clause of the Fourteenth Amendment to make it harder for blacks to reap the benefits of reapportionment available to other cohesive groups. O'Connor's opinion was packed with heated rhetoric. The North Carolina plan, she said, "bears an uncomfortable resemblance to political apartheid" and "may balkanize us." How a 55 percent black district might reflect apartheid is beyond comprehension. And the idea that the three-way political compromise among black state legislators, their white colleagues and a Republican-led Justice Department civil rights division is in any way analogous to the kind of slaughter occurring in the Balkans would be ludicrous if it were not so sad. In *Shaw* the Court seemed willing to elevate the aesthetic interests of the five white plaintiffs—two of whom did not even live in the challenged districts and none of whom claimed any dilution of his or her right to vote—above the interests of more than 1 million black North Carolinians in having an integrated Congressional delegation.

The Court sent the North Carolina plan back to the lower court for a trial on whether the redistricting was "so extremely irregular on its face that it rationally can be viewed only as

★ **Eric Drooker**

an effort to segregate the races for purposes of voting, without regard for traditional districting principles and without sufficiently compelling justification." What precisely this means is anyone's guess. The Court simply asserted that "reapportionment is one area in which appearances do matter," citing former Justice Potter Stewart's famous remark about pornography: "I know it when I see it." Apparently, the appearance of an all-white legislative delegation in a multiracial society is less troubling than the appearance of a district drawn to give black and white voters equal opportunities to see their preferred candidates win. And what if the irregularity is partially the result of pure political gerrymandering? Is that enough to satisfy the Court? Would complying with a Congressional mandate to equalize political opportunity be a sufficient justification? The Court's opinion provides no real guidance. But the use of the phrase "compelling justification" is ominous; the phrase is normally used to trigger so-called "strict scrutiny": the kind of rationale that little short of a wartime emergency can satisfy.

Whatever the ultimate result in *Shaw*—which was retried in April and will almost certainly return to the Supreme Court sometime next year—the Court's decision has unleashed a flood of similar lawsuits, challenging many of the other majority nonwhite districts created in the wake of the 1990 census. Louisiana's plan was the first to hit the dirt. Judge Jacques Wiener of the Fifth Circuit Court of Appeals went so far as to draw an analogy between the intent behind the legislature's decision to draw majority-black districts and the intent of willful murderers.

In all these cases, the courts act as if they are protecting the political process. In fact, they are substituting their narrow vision of voting rights for the more progressive choices made by the political branches, which, for all their flaws, continue to make substantial strides in integrating minorities into the government. In Texas, for example, the Fifth Circuit upset a settlement between the state and black and Latino plaintiffs who were challenging the state's system of electing trial judges. The settlement would have enabled black voters in Houston and Latino voters in several other jurisdictions finally to have some say in who sits on the bench.

The Voting Rights Act is in danger not from a lack of political will but from a surfeit of judicial willfulness. When black voters came to the Supreme Court in 1903 asking it to order Alabama to place them on the voting rolls, the Court, per the great Justice Oliver Wendell Holmes, refused to help them. For the Court, Holmes stated that "relief from a great political wrong, if done . . . by the people of a state and the State itself, must be given by them or by the legislative and political department of the government of the United States" rather than by the courts. The Voting Rights Act is the product of precisely the civil rights movement's sustained campaign to enlist Congress and the President in the cause of full black enfranchisement. Why white voters—who have participated fully and equally in the election of state officials as well as of the Congress and the President—have greater standing to invoke judicial protection than their black counterparts, who were the intended beneficiaries of the Reconstruction amendments, is a mystery, to put it charitably.

Or perhaps it's really not a mystery. In the past fifteen years, the Supreme Court has relentlessly chipped away at the foundations of the Second Reconstruction. (In *Patterson v. McLean Credit Union*, a case challenging racial harassment, it even went back to a venerable statute from the First Reconstruction and radically restricted its scope.) Sixteen times, Congress has had to overrule the Court's cramped interpretation of the civil rights laws. What worries me most about *Shaw* is that the Court hinted that North Carolina's districts might be invalid as a matter of constitutional law—something Congress cannot overrule. And so, forty years after *Brown*, the danger is that the Supreme Court will hold back the political branches, state and federal, from giving full voice to the aspirations of black Americans to participate equally in national life. □

■ 'I DIDN'T EXPERIENCE THAT'

The World of
Brown's Children

As the fortieth anniversary of Brown v. Board of Education *approached, a group of young intellectuals—members of the Harlem Writers Crew—gathered around the dining-room table of Terry Williams, a sociologist, in his apartment on 116th Street. The crew began keeping journals and meeting as teenagers five years ago. In anticipation of this meeting about Brown, the crew members had been thinking and reading about school integration and the many ways race issues figure in their daily experience. They were joined by William Kornblum, a longtime friend and research colleague of Williams.*

The crew members, each of whom figures in Williams and Kornblum's new book, The Uptown Kids: Struggle and Hope in the Projects *(Putnam's), include: Tina Ipeleng Kgositsile, 24, a freelance writer; Dexter Errol James, 20, currently involved with the Children's Defense Fund Black Student Leadership Network; Marisa Charece Sanders, 24, a college student and struggling freelance writer; Paco Alejandro Smith, 23, a production assistant for a film company; and Sheena (last name withheld by request), 20, who is working on a book about the life of a Harlem girl.*

TERRY WILLIAMS AND
THE HARLEM WRITERS CREW

Terry: Is a segregated society an unjust society?

Tina: A segregated society is only an unjust society when the groups that are separated are not treated equally. At times, I don't think a segregated society is the most unjust society in the world. Look at, for example, the roles that black colleges played at one point and how rich they were academically. They certainly helped train a lot of people who are making a difference in this and past generations.

Sheena: I believe a segregated society is unjust. I believe it's unjust because it's a matter of someone controlling whether

Reprinted from

Texas Law Review

From the Symposium on
Regulating the Electoral Process:

The Rights To Vote:
Some Pessimism About Formalism

Pamela S. Karlan

The Rights To Vote: Some Pessimism About Formalism

Pamela S. Karlan[*]

Chief Justice Warren called *Reynolds v. Sims*[1] his most important opinion "because it insured that henceforth elections would reflect the collective public interest—embodied in the 'one-man, one-vote' standard— rather than the machinations of special interests."[2] Measured against that ambition, *Reynolds* has been a spectacular failure. Advances in the technology of districting have stripped the substantive principles of one-person, one-vote of any real constraining force. Nonetheless, *Reynolds* remains critical for a procedural reason: Its essentially empty substantive rule interacts with the decennial census to mandate periodic redistricting.[3]

Much of *Reynolds*'s initial appeal lay in its simplicity. The one-person, one-vote rule seemed to afford each citizen an equal opportunity

---

[*] Professor of Law, University of Virginia. B.A. 1980, M.A. 1984, J.D. 1984, Yale University. Many of the ideas in this essay are drawn from a series of conversations I have had over the years with Jim Blacksher, Lani Guinier, Sam Issacharoff, and Eben Moglen. Every time I write about the Voting Rights Act, I realize what a debt I owe them. Earlier drafts of this paper were presented at the *Texas Law Review* symposium, *Regulating the Electoral Process*, in November 1992, as well as at faculty workshops at the University of Pennsylvania Law School and the Benjamin N. Cardozo School of Law. All three times I benefited tremendously from suggested revisions and observations. In addition, several colleagues during my year away from Virginia, particularly Bruce Ackerman, Jack Balkin, Paul Gewirtz, Burke Marshall, and David Richards, helped me to refine my ideas. Finally, Jonathan Weissglass was an invaluable research assistant. In the interest of full disclosure, I should note that I was counsel for one of the parties or *amici* in two of the cases discussed in the text, Presley v. Etowah County Commission, 112 S. Ct. 820 (1992), and Voinovich v. Quilter, 113 S. Ct. 1149 (1993).

1. 377 U.S. 533 (1964).

2. G. EDWARD WHITE, EARL WARREN: A PUBLIC LIFE 337 (1982); *cf.* Chandler Davidson, *The Voting Rights Act: A Brief History, in* CONTROVERSIES IN MINORITY VOTING: THE VOTING RIGHTS ACT IN PERSPECTIVE 7, 7 (Bernard Grofman & Chandler Davidson eds., 1992) (reporting that Lyndon B. Johnson viewed the passage of the Voting Rights Act as "his greatest accomplishment and his happiest moment during his tenure").

3. The Court expressly contemplated the prospect that one-person, one-vote would require decennial reapportionment. *See Reynolds*, 377 U.S. at 583 ("Decennial reapportionment appears to be a rational approach to readjustment of legislative representation in order to take into account population shifts and growth."). Population shifts within jurisdictions mean that reapportionment may often be required even when there has been little change in a jurisdiction's total population. *See, e.g.,* Quilter v. Voinovich, 794 F. Supp. 695, 706, 705-06 (N.D. Ohio 1992) (three-judge court) (Dowd, J., dissenting) (noting that although Ohio experienced only a 50,000 person gain in its total population of approximately 10 million, significant population shifts meant that "the majority of the 1981 configured districts in [all] major urban counties had to be reconfigured to meet the population requirements" of the Ohio Constitution), *rev'd*, 113 S. Ct. 1149 (1993).

to participate in the political process, while at the same time limiting the courts' incursion into the political thicket to a mathematical, surgical strike on entrenched interests.[4] It soon became clear, of course, that one or the other of these aims had to yield. Advances in the technology of districting, particularly the increasing use of computers, made it quite feasible to comply with the requirement of equipopulous districts while continuing to eviscerate the political strength of identifiable groups of voters. Thus, the Court was forced to face questions of qualitative, as well as quantitative, vote dilution. It resolved this tension in a somewhat half-hearted and disingenuous fashion: It recognized the justiciability of constitutional claims of group vote dilution by both racial minorities and identifiable political groups, but set such exacting standards of proof that most constitutional dilution claims were foreclosed.[5]

---

4. *See* James U. Blacksher & Larry T. Menefee, *From* Reynolds v. Sims *to* City of Mobile v. Bolden: *Have the White Suburbs Commandeered the Fifteenth Amendment?*, 34 HASTINGS L.J. 1, 18 (1982) (contrasting the Court's willingness to intervene to prohibit malapportionment, where there is an easily quantifiable standard, with its reluctance to protect racial minorities from qualitative vote dilution through the use of at-large elections); Jan G. Deutsch, *Neutrality, Legitimacy, and the Supreme Court: Some Intersections Between Law and Political Science*, 20 STAN. L. REV. 169, 248 (1968) (arguing that a formula such as one-person, one-vote was virtually inevitable given the Court's institutional constraints and its desire for apparent neutrality); *cf.* Sanford Levinson, *Gerrymandering and the Brooding Omnipresence of Proportional Representation: Why Won't It Go Away?*, 33 UCLA L. REV. 257, 259-60, 266 (1985) (explaining how a similar simplifying imperative might drive the Court toward a mathematical proportionality standard in gerrymandering cases).

5. In cases involving racial vote dilution, the Court required proof that the challenged practice had either been adopted or maintained for the precise purpose of diluting minority voting strength and that the practice was actually operating to deny or dilute minority voting strength. *See* Rogers v. Lodge, 458 U.S. 613, 617 (1982) (holding that "a showing of discriminatory intent has long been required in *all* types of equal protection cases charging racial discrimination" (emphasis in original) (citations omitted)); City of Mobile v. Bolden, 446 U.S. 55, 65-71 (1980) (plurality opinion) (holding that despite the existence of disproportionate effects on minority voters, a voting practice would not constitute a violation of the Equal Protection Clause absent a showing of purposeful discrimination). While plaintiffs were often able to demonstrate that the operation of a particular practice diluted their collective voting strength, the purpose requirement was extraordinarily difficult for plaintiffs to satisfy. *See* S. REP. No. 417, 97th Cong., 2d Sess. 37-39 (1982), *reprinted in* 1982 U.S.C.C.A.N. 177, 215-17 [hereinafter "Senate Report"] (explaining that an amendment to § 2 of the Voting Rights Act was needed to shift the focus of statutory voting rights challenges from "protracted, burdensome inquiries into the racial motivations of lawmakers" to examinations of the "present ability of minority voters to participate equally in their political system").

The test in political gerrymandering cases is almost the inverse of the test in racial vote-dilution cases, despite the fact that both claims invoke the same constitutional provision, the Equal Protection Clause. In political gerrymandering cases, discriminatory intent is virtually presumed. *See* Davis v. Bandemer, 478 U.S. 109, 129 (1986) (holding that "[a]s long as redistricting is done by a legislature, it should not be very difficult to prove that the likely political consequences of the apportionment were intended"). Yet discriminatory impact is virtually unprovable, because the plaintiffs must show not merely that they are unable to elect their preferred candidates, but also that "the electoral system is arranged in a manner that will consistently degrade a voter's or a group of voters' influence on the political process as a whole." *Id.* at 132; *see also infra* text accompanying notes 40-46 (discussing the slipperiness of these doctrines).

The 1982 amendments to Section 2 of the Voting Rights Act of 1965[6] essentially exploded this resolution with regard to claims of racial vote dilution. The amendments established a result-oriented test,[7] thereby confronting the courts with literally thousands of challenges to election schemes that did not fairly reflect the voting strength of minority communities. Moreover, because Congress expressly eschewed any universal, abstract formula, the results test required courts to grapple with local political reality in assessing minority voters' claims.[8] Finally, in conjunction with one-person, one-vote, Section 2 guaranteed repeated judicial involvement in local politics: The nearly universal replacement of multimember systems by single-member districts meant that electoral structures would be subject to judicial oversight after each census.[9]

This Paper explores the interaction between substantive conceptions of the right to vote and judicial devices for adjudicating voting rights lawsuits. The latest round of reapportionment and the ensuing litigation suggests that partisan political exploitation of the procedural strand of one-person, one-vote poses a serious threat to careful consideration of the substantive values regarding minority voting rights that are embodied in the Voting Rights Act. One-person, one-vote provides a vehicle for parties to invoke judicial oversight but provides no brakes on the substantive decisions of an increasingly partisan judiciary. Faced with these lawsuits, the courts have adopted understandings of the Voting Rights Act that are "partial" in both senses of the word.

In Part I of this Paper, I develop a taxonomy of voting rights. The Supreme Court often speaks as if there were a single framework for assessing voting rights claims. I show, however, that the Court's cases reflect three discrete, yet ultimately linked, conceptions of voting. First,

---

6. Voting Rights Act Amendments of 1982, Pub. L. No. 97-205, sec. 2, § 3, 96 Stat. 131, 134 (1982) (amending 42 U.S.C. § 1973 (1976)).

7. The language of § 2 requires courts to consider whether, "under the totality of the circumstances," members of the minority group "have less opportunity than other members of the electorate to participate in the political process and to elect representatives of their choice." 42 U.S.C. § 1973(b) (1988).

8. The legislative history of § 2 delineated a variety of factors the courts were to consider in applying the results test. These ranged from socioeconomic disparities between minority group members and their nonminority counterparts to the electoral success of minority candidates and the level of racial bloc voting. See Senate Report, supra note 5, at 28-29, reprinted in 1982 U.S.C.C.A.N. at 206-07. Taken together, these factors require "'an intensely local appraisal of the design and impact' of the contested electoral mechanisms" that is "peculiarly dependent upon the facts of each case" and upon "indigenous political reality." Thornburg v. Gingles, 478 U.S. 30, 79 (1986) (citations omitted).

9. At-large elections by definition weigh each voter's vote equally because every voter participates in the election of every representative. See Lucas v. Forty-Fourth Gen. Assembly, 377 U.S. 713, 750 (1964) (Stewart, J., dissenting) (arguing that if the goal of legislative apportionment is equally weighted votes, districts should be abolished and replaced with an at-large election system). The geographic distribution of residents within the jurisdiction thus is irrelevant. At-large systems did not require periodic readjustment of district boundaries, essentially because there were no districts.

Texas Law Review [Vol. 71:1705

voting involves *participation*: the formal ability of individuals to enter into the electoral process by casting a ballot. Second, voting involves *aggregation*: the choice among rules for tallying individual votes to determine election outcomes. Finally, voting involves *governance*: It serves a key role in determining how decisionmaking by elected representatives will take place. I end this Part by discussing the relationship among these conceptions.

Part II begins by showing that the Court's failure to acknowledge the distinctive elements of these different conceptions has often led it to respond to one sort of claim with an analysis that rests on a different conception of voting. Standing alone, this doctrinal confusion could give litigants and the increasingly politicized lower federal judiciary an opportunity to distort the Voting Rights Act. But several structural aspects of voting rights litigation exacerbate the danger that the Act—like its constitutional forebears—will be "commandeered," or at least domesticated, by partisan white interests.[10] One-person, one-vote provides a wedge for partisan participation in the litigation process, permits a variety of forum-shopping stratagems, and, in combination with remedial doctrines, provides opportunities for the two major political parties to advance conceptions of the Act that serve their partisan ends. Democratic incumbents and party officials advance, although they do not call it this, a governance-driven model of minority voting rights: They claim that blacks and (at least some) Hispanics would maximize their voting strength by seeking legislatures whose overall composition is most favorable to minority interests (*i.e.*, majority-Democratic bodies). This can best be accomplished by drawing districts in which minority voters contribute to the victory base of a broad range of (largely white) Democratic candidates. Recently, Republicans have countered with an exclusively aggregation-driven model. They claim that minorities are best off when they can elect individual candidates of their choice from districts where they control, rather than influence, outcome. Like the Democratic model, which is aimed at creating Democratic-controlled bodies, the Republican model will, the Republicans hope, lead to Republican-controlled legislatures.

Having explored these conceptual and structural explanations for the current disorder, Part III analyzes the conditions that call for judicial involvement in the political process. Unlike earlier participation- or aggregation-based claims, contemporary voting rights problems do not admit of easy, abstract judicial solutions. Rather, they demand close attention to the historical context in which issues of full political

---

10. *See* Blacksher & Menefee, *supra* note 4, at 1 ("In 1964, [in *Reynolds v. Sims*] citizens of Birmingham, Mobile and Gadsden, Alabama, convinced the United States Supreme Court that the Constitution guarantees equal voting rights for white people.").

participation are embedded. In some critical respects, the Voting Rights Act has worked wonderfully well and has given minority voters leverage within the process to seek political solutions for the political problems of redistricting. Federal courts must therefore take care not to disturb the products of a nascent but nonetheless real integration of minorities into the give-and-take of politics as usual.[11] At the same time, the courts must be alert to situations in which minority voters and the officials they have elected continue as members of a permanent, excluded faction and must seek out context-sensitive ways for effectively integrating them into the process of governance.

I. Three Conceptions of the Right To Vote

The Supreme Court's repeated references to *"the* right to vote"[12] and its attempt to ground its one-person, one-vote cases in earlier decisions involving such disparate practices as ballot-box stuffing, white primaries, and racial gerrymandering,[13] obscure the extent to which its decisions in fact operate to protect very different types of interests. To understand both the current doctrinal confusion and, ultimately, the opportunities this confusion affords for manipulating the voting rights system, we must first consider the complex role that voting plays in the American political process.

A. Voting as Participation

To begin, the right to vote involves *participation*: the right to cast a ballot that is counted. This participatory right has been implicated by a variety of restrictions on the franchise, including white primaries,[14]

---

11. *Cf.* Senate Report, *supra* note 5, at 12, *reprinted in* 1982 U.S.C.C.A.N. at 189 (noting that "[s]ophisticated rules regarding elections may seem part of the everyday rough-and-tumble of American politics" but that Congress and the courts should be sensitive to the danger that in some circumstances such rules may represent "efforts to perpetuate the results of past voting discrimination and to undermine the gains won under . . . the Voting Rights Act").

12. In Shaw v. Reno, 113 S. Ct. 2816, 2819 (1993), for example, Justice O'Connor describes the case as involving "the meaning of the constitutional 'right' to vote," suggesting by her quotation marks around the word "right" that it involves a single, unified concept.

13. *See* Reynolds v. Sims, 377 U.S. 533, 555 (1964) (supporting its treatment of malapportionment with examples including Gomillion v. Lightfoot, 364 U.S. 339 (1960) (racially exclusionary gerrymandering); Terry v. Adams, 345 U.S. 461 (1953) (white primaries); Smith v. Allwright, 321 U.S. 649 (1944) (white primaries); and United States v. Classic, 313 U.S. 299 (1941) (election fraud)).

14. In a series of decisions known collectively as the White Primary Cases, the Court overturned a variety of stratagems by the State of Texas, the Democratic Party, and a subgroup of the Democratic Party that were intended to keep blacks from participating in primary elections. The decisions include Nixon v. Herndon, 273 U.S. 536 (1927); Nixon v. Condon, 286 U.S. 73 (1932); Smith v. Allwright, 321 U.S. 649 (1944); and Terry v. Adams, 345 U.S. 461 (1953).

de-annexation,[15] poll taxes and literacy tests,[16] durational residency requirements,[17] and, most recently, the power to cast write-in votes.[18] The fact that many of the early cases involved claims by blacks who had been disenfranchised for racially discriminatory reasons may mask an essential feature of the claims: The right to participate is wholly outcome-independent. Put somewhat differently, in the early cases the Court did not ask whether blacks and whites, or literate and illiterate people, or long-term residents and newcomers were likely to vote differently. Indeed, in several contexts, the Court squarely rejected the idea that outcome effects *could* form a permissible reason for limiting participation.[19]

The primary value underlying the participation cases, then, is an aspect of what I have called civic inclusion: "a sense of connectedness to the community and of equal political dignity; greater readiness to acquiesce in governmental decisions and hence broader consent and legitimacy."[20]

---

15. *See Gomillion*, 364 U.S. at 341 (involving the "Tuskegee gerrymander," in which the Alabama state legislature redrew the boundaries of Tuskegee, Alabama, to remove virtually all black residents from the jurisdiction).

16. *Compare* Lassiter v. Northampton County Bd. of Elections, 360 U.S. 45, 51 (1959) (upholding a literacy test because it was rationally related to the state's legitimate interest in promoting "intelligent use of the ballot") *with* Harper v. Virginia State Bd. of Elections, 383 U.S. 663, 670 (1966) (applying strict scrutiny and striking down a poll tax as unconstitutional under the Equal Protection Clause because "wealth or fee paying has . . . no relation to voting qualifications").

17. *See* Marston v. Lewis, 410 U.S. 679, 680 (1973) (holding that Arizona's 50-day residency and registration cutoff "pass[ed] constitutional muster" because it was "supported by sufficiently strong local interests," such as the preparation of accurate voter lists); Dunn v. Blumstein, 405 U.S. 330, 358 (1972) (striking down Tennessee's one-year residency requirement because the relationship between the state's interest in an informed electorate and the residency requirement was too attenuated to be deemed compelling).

18. *See* Burdick v. Takushi, 112 S. Ct. 2059, 2066 (1992) (upholding Hawaii's absolute ban on write-in voting in general elections).

19. *See, e.g.*, *Dunn*, 405 U.S. at 355 (rejecting the argument that short-term residents could be excluded from voting in state elections because they might not have local interests sufficiently in mind and holding that the exclusion constituted an impermissible attempt to regulate voting based on differences of opinion); Carrington v. Rash, 380 U.S. 89, 94 (1965) ("'Fencing out' from the franchise a sector of the population because of the way they may vote is constitutionally impermissible.").

In one particularly notable application of this principle in the context of race discrimination, the Fifth Circuit invalidated an election in which black voters had been forced to use segregated booths if they wanted to participate at all, despite the fact that it was a mathematical impossibility for the excluded voters to have changed the outcome. *See* Bell v. Southwell, 376 F.2d 659, 662 (5th Cir. 1967) (setting aside election because "there are certain discriminatory practices which, apart from demonstrated injury or the inability to do so, so infect the process of the law as to be stricken down as invalid").

Moreover, from the perspective of the individual voter, it would be downright *irrational* to take an outcome-dependent perspective. *See* Paul E. Meehl, *The Selfish Voter Paradox and the Thrown-Away Vote Argument*, 71 AM. POL. SCI. REV. 11, 30 (1977) (noting that it is extraordinarily unlikely that any person's vote will influence the outcome of an election).

20. Pamela S. Karlan, *Maps and Misreadings: The Role of Geographic Compactness in Racial Vote Dilution Litigation*, 24 HARV. C.R.-C.L. L. REV. 173, 180 (1989); *see also* Kathryn Abrams, *"Raising Politics Up": Minority Political Participation and Section 2 of the Voting Rights Act*, 63 N.Y.U. L. REV. 449, 476-77 (1988) (discussing voting as a means of expression and interaction with fellow citizens); Ronald Dworkin, *What Is Equality? Part 4: Political Equality*, 22 U.S.F. L. REV. 1, 4 (1987) (arguing that by giving an individual the right to vote, "[t]he community confirms an

Thus, participation claims invoke assertions of *anonymous* equality: whatever the plaintiff's individual characteristics, she is entitled to participate fully in community governance by casting a ballot.[21]

The Court's decision to employ strict scrutiny in assessing participation claims[22] has had two effects. First, of course, in cases that the Court puts within the participation rubric, the application of strict scrutiny has resulted in universal invalidation of the challenged restrictions. But more importantly, the fatality of strict scrutiny has led the Court to strain to exclude certain types of claims from the core right to participate. So, for example, the Court has assumed the validity of restricting the franchise to citizens,[23] bona fide residents,[24] and adults,[25] even when claimants out-

---

individual person's membership, as a free and equal citizen"); Lani Guinier, *The Triumph of Tokenism: The Voting Rights Act and the Theory of Black Electoral Success*, 89 MICH. L. REV. 1077, 1084-85 (1991) (discussing how voting, particularly in support of black candidates, served the civil rights movement's goals of "affirmation of self-worth and human dignity"); Frank I. Michelman, *Conceptions of Democracy in American Constitutional Argument: Voting Rights*, 41 FLA. L. REV. 443, 451 (1989) (discussing a "constitutive" vision of politics whereby citizens define themselves through their participation); Daniel D. Polsby & Robert D. Popper, *The Third Criterion: Compactness as a Procedural Safeguard Against Partisan Gerrymandering*, 9 YALE L. & POL'Y REV. 301, 315 (1991) (arguing that voting is not an act of utilitarian self-interest but one of "self-expression, a means to affirm the philosophy of popular sovereignty"); Note, *The Disenfranchisement of Ex-Felons: Citizenship, Criminality, and the "Purity of the Ballot Box,"* 102 HARV. L. REV. 1300, 1304-06 (1989) (discussing the community-defining aspects of enfranchisement and disenfranchisement).

21. See CHARLES R. BEITZ, POLITICAL EQUALITY: AN ESSAY IN DEMOCRATIC THEORY 8-9 (1989) (discussing the anonymity condition).

22. The first case in which the Supreme Court explicitly applied strict scrutiny was Harper v. Virginia State Bd. of Elections, 383 U.S. 663 (1966), although it was not entirely clear in that case that the trigger for strict scrutiny was the status of voting as a fundamental right rather than the suspect nature of classifications based on wealth. By the time the Court decided Kramer v. Union Free School District No. 15, 395 U.S. 621 (1969), and Dunn v. Blumstein, 405 U.S. 330 (1972), however, it was clear that it was the nature of the right infringed, rather than the characteristics of the class affected, that required heightened scrutiny. See *Kramer*, 395 U.S. at 626-28 (holding that voting classifications have the potential to invade fundamental rights and liberties and therefore must be closely scrutinized); *Dunn*, 405 U.S. at 337 (stating that "it is certainly clear now that a more exacting test is required for any statute that 'place[s] a condition on the exercise of the right to vote.'" (quoting Bullock v. Carter, 405 U.S. 134, 143 (1972)) (brackets in original)).

23. See Gerald L. Neuman, *"We Are the People": Alien Suffrage in German and American Perspective*, 13 MICH. J. INT'L L. 259, 292 (1992) (noting that "it appears to be settled doctrine that, so far as the federal Constitution is concerned, alien suffrage is entirely discretionary—neither compelled nor constitutionally forbidden"); see also Sherman v. United States, 155 U.S. 673, 682 (1855) (listing alienage as one reason that a person may be disqualified from voting); Breedlove v. Suttles, 302 U.S. 277, 282 (1937) (mentioning in passing that aliens are not permitted to vote).

24. See *Dunn*, 405 U.S. at 343 ("We have in the past noted approvingly that the States have the power to require that voters be bona fide residents . . . ."); *Kramer*, 395 U.S. at 625 (assuming the validity of citizenship, age, and bona fide residence requirements). Lower court decisions, however, indicate that nonresident voting is permissible in some situations. See, e.g., Brown v. Board of Comm'rs, 722 F. Supp. 380, 399 (E.D. Tenn. 1989) (finding generally valid a Tennessee provision that permitted nonresident property owners to vote in municipal elections but striking it down as applied, on the ground that it allowed nonresidents who owned a trivial amount of property to vote); see also Glisson v. Mayor of Savannah Beach, 346 F.2d 135, 137 (5th Cir. 1965) (upholding nonresident voting in a summer vacation community because there could be a "logical and sensible reason for permitting nonresidents owning property . . . to vote in the municipal elections").

25. The Twenty-Sixth Amendment provides constitutional protection against age discrimination

side these categories have strong reasons for seeking to participate.[26] And once these claims are excluded from the core right to participate and the Court applies rational-relationship scrutiny, disenfranchising restrictions survive challenge.

Moreover, by severing the link between the public inclusion of an individual voter and the product of her inclusion—an untraceable vote—the Court has rendered problematic the analysis of a class of participation-based claims that focus on voter choice. In *Burdick v. Takushi*,[27] for example, the Court upheld a Hawaiian ban on casting write-in votes. It rejected the argument that strict scrutiny should be applied, asserting that Burdick's right to vote had been only minimally affected by the requirement that he vote for one of the candidates who had qualified for the general election ballot or not at all. The right to vote involves the right to choose among already nominated, bona fide candidates, the Court said, rather than "a more generalized expressive function."[28] In short, the right to participate takes for granted the general contours of existing electoral arrangements.

B. Voting as Aggregation

The primary function of voting, however, is not simply to delineate the boundaries of the political community. Rather, it is to combine individual preferences to reach some collective decision, such as the selection of representatives.[29] Voting therefore involves *aggregation*, and each

---

with regard to voting, but only for "citizens of the United States, who are eighteen years of age or older." U.S. CONST. amend. XXVI, § 1; *see* Wesley v. Collins, 605 F. Supp. 802, 813 (M.D. Tenn. 1985) (holding that although nothing bars states from extending the franchise to persons younger than eighteen, the Constitution does not compel such an extension), *aff'd*, 791 F.2d 1255 (6th Cir. 1986); Gaunt v. Brown, 341 F. Supp. 1187, 1189 (S.D. Ohio) (rejecting claim by plaintiffs who would be eighteen in time for the general election that they had a right to participate in primary elections held before their eighteenth birthdays), *aff'd*, 409 U.S. 809 (1972).

26. For a particularly powerful example, see Holt Civic Club v. City of Tuscaloosa, 439 U.S. 60 (1978). *Holt Civic Club* involved residents of Tuscaloosa's statutorily defined police jurisdiction who lived outside the municipal boundaries. The Court held that denial of the right to vote did not violate the Fourteenth Amendment, observing that "a government unit may legitimately restrict the right to participate in its political processes to those who reside within its borders." *Id.* at 68-69. *See also* Michelman, *supra* note 20, at 474-80 (criticizing the majority in *Holt Civic Club* for its reliance on arbitrary geographical boundaries).

27. 112 S. Ct. 2059 (1992).

28. *Id.* at 2066. *But cf.* Allen v. State Bd. of Elections, 393 U.S. 544, 570 (1969) (holding that changes in the procedure for casting write-in votes are subject to the preclearance requirements of § 5 of the Voting Rights Act because such changes could be motivated by a discriminatory intent to dilute minority voting strength or could result in such dilution).

29. The particular concerns raised by noncandidate voting—for example, voting on referenda or bond issues—are largely beyond the scope of this Paper. For discussions of some of these issues, particularly as they relate to aggregation issues and minority interests, see Lynn A. Baker, *Direct Democracy and Discrimination: A Public Choice Perspective*, 67 CHI.-KENT L. REV. 707, 712-15 (1991); Bruce E. Cain, *Voting Rights and Democratic Theory: Toward a Color-Blind Society?*, in

voter has an interest in the adoption of aggregation rules that enable her to elect the candidate of her choice.

Unlike participation claims, aggregation claims are essentially outcome-regarding: They rest upon assertions that the voter has been denied a fair opportunity to elect her preferred representative. While it is of course possible for a voter to raise a purely individual aggregation claim,[30] aggregation claims are largely group-based: They involve claims by individual voters that they are part of a discrete *group* of voters whose direct preferences have been unfairly ignored.[31] Moreover, although a variety of groups might conceivably raise aggregation claims, the conjunction of the two-party system, American history, and the near-universal use of geographic electoral districts has meant that aggregation claims are normally brought on behalf of identifiable racial groups or the members of political parties.[32]

There are, broadly speaking, two kinds of aggregation claims. The first focuses on electoral boundaries: A group whose members share distinctive electoral preferences claims that its ability to elect its preferred candidate has been impaired because its votes have been overwhelmed by the votes of a hostile majority. This submergence might be due to the use of at-large elections, with their tendency toward winner-take-all outcomes, or it might be due to gerrymandering, that is, a districting plan that fractures the group among several districts and then submerges the votes

---

CONTROVERSIES IN MINORITY VOTING, *supra* note 2, at 261, 274-75; Julian N. Eule, *Judicial Review of Direct Democracy*, 99 YALE L.J. 1503, 1551-58 (1990).

30. In Gordon v. Lance, 403 U.S. 1 (1971), for example, the Court confronted a West Virginia statute that required a supermajority (*i.e.*, a 60% affirmative vote) for passage of bond issues. *Id.* at 2. The plaintiffs claimed that this requirement violated one-person, one-vote because it gave negative votes more weight than affirmative votes. *Id.* at 6. The Court rejected this argument, in part because it could "discern no independently identifiable group or category that favors bonded indebtedness over other forms of financing. Consequently no sector of the population may be said to be 'fenced out' from the franchise because of the way they will vote." *Id.* at 5 (citing Carrington v. Rash, 380 U.S. 89, 94 (1965)).

31. This is not to say that the Court has always been clear on this point. *See* Samuel Issacharoff, *Polarized Voting and the Political Process: The Transformation of Voting Rights Jurisprudence*, 90 MICH. L. REV. 1833, 1840-41 (1992) (describing the Court's ambivalence in Whitcomb v. Chavis, 403 U.S. 124 (1971), as to whether dilution involved an individual- or group-based deprivation).

32. *But cf.* United Jewish Orgs., Inc. v. Carey, 430 U.S. 144, 168 (1977) (denying relief to Hasidic Jews who claimed that their community was improperly split between two districts in order to maximize safe seats for black voters). In deciding early aggregation claims, the Court seemed not to distinguish between the claims that could be brought by racial groups and those that could be raised by political blocs. *See, e.g.*, Gaffney v. Cummings, 412 U.S. 735, 751-52 (1973) (discussing districting that may violate the Fourteenth Amendment by minimizing the voting strength of racial groups or political parties); Fortson v. Dorsey, 379 U.S. 433, 439 (1965) (mentioning that certain apportionment schemes may operate to minimize the voting strength of "racial or political elements of the voting population"); *see also infra* notes 40-46 and accompanying text (describing the later divergence of the equal protection analysis applied to claims brought by minority groups and those brought by political parties).

of a now-fragmented community in several majority-controlled districts.[33] The second sort of claim focuses on structural rules within an electoral jurisdiction: Majority-vote runoff requirements may raise aggregation concerns by denying some groups the voting power that other equally sized groups enjoy,[34] and numbered-post[35] or anti-single-shot provisions[36] may enhance the winner-take-all aspects of at-large elections.[37] One of the precursors to the one-person, one-vote apportionment cases involved this sort of structural rule: Under the Georgia county unit system, ballots not cast for the candidate who finished first were ignored in allocating the county's unit votes, and it was therefore possible for a candidate to win the election even though he received fewer popular votes than his opponent.[38]

To assess the claim that an aggregation rule unfairly dilutes a group's voting strength requires, of course, having some baseline notion of the results that a fair aggregation would produce, and this baseline problem has bedeviled the Supreme Court for a generation. Early on, the Court rejected the baseline of proportionality—the premise that a group should succeed in electing candidates in proportion to its presence in the electorate.[39] But

---

33. *See, e.g.*, Thornburg v. Gingles, 478 U.S. 30, 46 n.11 (1986); Allan J. Lichtman & J. Gerald Hebert, *A General Theory of Vote Dilution*, 6 LA RAZA L.J. 1, 3-4 (1993) (both explaining submergence); Frank R. Parker, *Racial Gerrymandering and Legislative Reapportionment, in* MINORITY VOTE DILUTION 85, 86-99 (Chandler Davidson ed., 1984) (describing techniques of racial gerrymandering).

34. *See* Pamela S. Karlan, *Undoing the Right Thing: Single-Member Offices and the Voting Rights Act*, 77 VA. L. REV. 1, 25-28 (1991) (explaining that when there are majority-vote runoff requirements and racial bloc voting, a black candidate may garner a plurality of votes in the primary, but will lose in the runoff when white voters coalesce behind a white candidate).

35. Numbered post provisions require each candidate to limit her candidacy to only one of the available seats. Karlan, *supra* note 34, at 17 n.54. For example, in an election for a three-member county commission, a numbered-post provision would designate the three seats as "Position 1," "Position 2," and "Position 3." Each candidate would seek only one position and each voter would have one vote for each seat. Numbered posts increase the likelihood of head-to-head contests between minority- and majority-sponsored candidates and in jurisdictions with racial bloc voting, this will cause the defeat of minority candidates. *See* ROY E. YOUNG, THE PLACE SYSTEM IN TEXAS ELECTIONS 20-22 (1965) (arguing that numbered-post provisions were adopted in Texas to reduce the political influence of racial minorities).

36. Anti-single-shot provisions work similarly; by requiring voters to cast as many votes as there are available seats, they preclude a minority from denying its support to any of the majority's candidates and from thereby increasing the share of the total vote cast that supports the minority's candidate. For a more detailed discussion of anti-single-shot provisions, see Karlan, *supra* note 34, at 17 n.54.

37. *See* City of Rome v. United States, 446 U.S. 156, 183-84 (1980); Chandler Davidson, *Minority Vote Dilution: An Overview, in* MINORITY VOTE DILUTION, *supra* note 33, at 6 (both describing how such provisions can exacerbate the discriminatory impact of racial bloc voting).

38. *See* Gray v. Sanders, 372 U.S. 368, 372 (1963) (noting that counties having only one-third of Georgia's population controlled a majority of the unit votes; thus a candidate could win the election by winning in those counties even if he lost overwhelmingly in the rest of the state).

39. *See* White v. Regester, 412 U.S. 755, 765-66 (1973) (holding that the plaintiffs' burden is not satisfied merely by a showing that a minority group has failed to win legislative seats in proportion to its voting potential and requiring instead a showing that the nomination and election process was not equally open to the minority group in question); Whitcomb v. Chavis, 403 U.S. 124, 149 (1971)

having rejected this mechanical benchmark, the Court needed some other device to keep itself from becoming enmeshed in the normative political thicket of evaluating competing group claims. Although the Court held out a formal guarantee of fair aggregation, it forestalled aggregation claims as a practical matter by setting standards of proof that essentially could not be met.

In cases involving claims of racial vote dilution, the Court focused on the *racial* aspect of the cause of action, which allowed it to borrow the discriminatory purpose requirement from general equal protection doctrine. This meant that, regardless of how a challenged practice affected a minority group's ability to elect its preferred representatives, the practice was invalid only if it had been adopted or maintained with the specific purpose of diluting the minority's votes.[40] The Court rejected the idea that strict scrutiny should apply because a fundamental right—the right to vote—had been implicated.[41] This stringent purpose requirement was extraordinarily difficult for plaintiffs to meet.[42] By contrast, when the Court was faced with a claim of political gerrymandering, in *Davis v. Bandemer*,[43] it could hardly use the purpose requirement to pretermit the claim; given the overtly partisan nature of the redistricting process, nearly *every* districting scheme was intended to maximize the election of members of the redistricting party at the expense of other parties' candidates.[44] So, in the area of political gerrymandering, the Court developed a heightened effects requirement: Even a voter's permanent inability to elect her preferred candidates did not unconstitutionally impair her right to vote, as long as she was not

---

(holding that "the fact that the number of ghetto residents who were legislators was not in proportion to ghetto population" could not support a finding of "invidious discrimination absent evidence and findings that ghetto residents had less opportunity" than other voters to "participate in the political process").

40. *See* Rogers v. Lodge, 458 U.S. 613, 617 (1982) (holding that multimember legislative districts are unconstitutionally discriminatory only if they are "conceived or operated as purposeful devices to further racial discrimination"); City of Mobile v. Bolden, 446 U.S. 55, 66 (1980) (plurality opinion) (stating that multimember districts "could violate the Fourteenth Amendment [only] if their purpose were invidiously to minimize or cancel out the voting potential of racial or ethnic minorities").

41. *See Bolden*, 446 U.S. at 113-14 (Marshall, J., dissenting) (claiming that the Court had erroneously treated the *Bolden* plaintiffs' claim as resting on the suspect classification prong, rather than the fundamental rights prong, of strict-scrutiny equal protection analysis); *see also* Blacksher & Menefee, *supra* note 4, at 48 (criticizing the Court for giving the equivalent of strict scrutiny to one-person, one-vote claims, while giving only rational relationship review to claims of racial vote dilution).

42. *See* Senate Report, *supra* note 5, at 26-27, *reprinted in* 1982 U.S.C.C.A.N. at 203-04 (noting the "dramatic" impact of the discriminatory purpose requirement on pending cases and finding that "litigators virtually stopped filing new voting dilution cases" as a result of the requirement); *id.* at 36-39, *reprinted in* 1982 U.S.C.C.A.N. at 214 (mentioning the "difficulty often encountered in meeting the [discriminatory] intent test").

43. 478 U.S. 109 (1986).

44. *See id.* at 129 (plurality opinion); *cf.* Gaffney v. Cummings, 412 U.S. 735, 738-39 (1973) (involving a "bipartisan" gerrymander designed to give each of the two major parties a proportional share of the state legislative seats).

cut off from "influence on the political process as a whole."[45] This test, like the purpose test in racial vote dilution cases, was virtually impossible to meet.[46]

The *Bandemer* Court's treatment of a qualitative aggregation claim implicitly recognized that aggregation cannot provide a stable stopping point for a theory of voting rights. Once we embrace a conception of the right to vote that looks at electoral outcomes rather than at entry into voting booths, it becomes clear that the election of representatives represents only an intermediate point along the path to the determination of policies that are voted on within the elected body. And with regard to that determination, the critical question for an individual cannot simply be whether *she* can elect *her* preferred candidate. Rather, it must focus on whether the system for selecting the entire governmental body gives her an effective opportunity to participate in policymaking.[47]

C. Voting as Governance

The individual's concern with the makeup of the legislature embodies a third conception of voting rights: voting as an integral part of *governance*, the practice of decisionmaking through representatives. Thinking about voting in this way requires abandoning the view of voting as a declaratory event—the act of pulling a lever on Election Day—and replacing it with an image of voting as part of an ongoing conversation.[48]

---

45. *Bandemer*, 478 U.S. at 132 (plurality opinion).

46. *See infra* note 79 (discussing Badham v. Eu, 694 F. Supp. 664 (N.D. Cal. 1988) (three-judge court), *aff'd per curiam*, 488 U.S. 1024 (1989)).

47. *See Bandemer*, 478 U.S. at 127 (plurality opinion) (characterizing the plaintiffs' claim as one challenging the statewide composition of the legislature, even though each voter could participate directly only in the election of representatives from her district); BEITZ, *supra* note 21, at 153 (arguing that political equality exists when each voter stands a fair chance of satisfying her preferences for political decisions).

48. Leading proponents of this view include James Blacksher, Lani Guinier, and Kathryn Abrams. Blacksher has used this expansive understanding of voting rights to develop a litigation strategy in such cases as Bolden v. City of Mobile, 542 F. Supp. 1050 (S.D. Ala. 1982) and Presley v. Etowah County Commission, 112 S. Ct. 820 (1992). In *Bolden*, the remedy included the adoption of supermajority voting rules within the city council that were aimed at giving representatives of the black community an effective voice in governmental decisionmaking. *See* Karlan, *supra* note 20, at 246-47 (discussing the *Bolden* remedy). In *Presley*, Blacksher challenged post-election changes in the powers and responsibilities of county commissioners that stripped a newly elected black commissioner of his ability to represent fully his constituents. *Presley*, 112 S. Ct. at 829; *see also infra* text accompanying notes 80-90 (discussing *Presley*).

Abrams and Guinier also see voting as part of a broader process of political participation. *See*, *e.g.*, Abrams, *supra* note 20, at 489 (describing a more accurate model that treats political participation "not as a single electoral event, but as a process that beg[ins] with reflection on, and discussion of, preferences and conclude[s] with the enactment of substantive policies" and that "acknowledge[s] those occasions on which processes of aggregation [make] choices final, but . . . also highlight[s] . . . interactive activities"); Kathryn Abrams, *Relationships of Representation in Voting Rights Act Jurisprudence*, 71 TEX. L. REV. 1409, 1417-18 (1993) (reasoning that the Voting Rights Act should

Because the voter's horizon extends beyond the moment of representative selection to various opportunities for collective decisionmaking by assembled legislators, she necessarily will be concerned both with who serves as the representative(s) of her district, and just as centrally, with the overall composition of the governing body.[49] She will, in short, be interested in the degree of both her direct and her virtual representation. Moreover, she will be concerned with aggregation rules *within* the legislature because these rules can determine the practical effectiveness of the representatives who champion her interests.[50]

The conception of voting as governance has both constitutional and statutory underpinnings. To my mind, *Reynolds* was ultimately a governance case. The Court implicitly recognized that all of the plaintiffs had an unfettered right to participate in the formal election process[51] and although it found that the votes of citizens in the more populous districts were diluted,[52] this dilution did not implicate any particular voter's ability to elect the actual legislators of her choice. In my view, the real injury in *Reynolds* was that once the elected representative arrived in the legislature, her constituents' effective voting power *in the legislature* would be unfairly minimized because their representative could be outvoted by representatives of smaller groups of constituents. Put somewhat differently, *Reynolds* sought to protect the governance rights of the *majority*, which was unable to elect a legislature whose overall composition reflected its preferences.[53]

---

protect the relationships of minority constituents with their representatives because citizen participation in the political process continues after election day); Lani Guinier, *No Two Seats: The Elusive Quest for Political Equality*, 77 VA. L. REV. 1413, 1458-93 (1991) [hereinafter Guinier, *No Two Seats*] (arguing in favor of a conception of vote dilution that focuses on attaining a fair share of legislative outcomes through "interest representation"); Guinier, *supra* note 20, at 1080-91 (discussing the civil rights movement's theory of political participation as embodying grass-roots mobilization of the black community, promoting a social and economic agenda, and electing responsive officials).

49. *See* JEAN-PIERRE BENOIT & LEWIS A. KORNHAUSER, VOTING SIMPLY IN THE ELECTION OF ASSEMBLIES 27 (1991) (C.V. Starr Center for Applied Economics Working Paper) (observing that although in many elections, "citizens choose among candidates that then constitute assemblies rather than choose among the [potential] assemblies directly[,] . . . the voter's preferences over assemblies, not candidates, are fundamental").

50. *See, e.g.*, Guinier, *No Two Seats, supra* note 48, at 1442 (describing the way in which majority-rule voting within a legislative body may submerge the voice of minorities who are not part of the "ruling coalition"); Karlan, *supra* note 20, at 236-48 (arguing that "legislative exclusion" denies elected black officials practical political power).

51. *See* Reynolds v. Sims, 377 U.S. 533, 555-56, 557, 562-63 (1964) (recognizing the plaintiffs' claim as one of dilution rather than outright denial).

52. *Id.* at 563.

53. The early parts of the Court's opinion stressed the individual nature of the right to an equally effective vote. *See id.* at 561 (quoting United States v. Bathgate, 246 U.S. 220, 227 (1918), for the proposition that "[t]he right to vote is personal"). By the middle of the opinion, however, the Court's focus shifted from the injury suffered by individual voters to the disempowerment of the majority. *See id.* at 565 ("[A] majority of the people of a State [should be able to] elect a majority of that State's legislature."). Moreover, the Court's recognition that the right to vote for representatives is bound up

Despite the Court's individualist rhetoric, the system it overturned was one that systematically biased the overall legislative complexion in favor of identifiable groups—white rural voters[54]—rather than one in which atomistic individuals were arbitrarily deprived of equal voting power.[55]

Reynolds was a tempting case in which to protect the governance component of the right to vote: One-person, one-vote provided a relatively self-executing, clearly judicially manageable standard for assessing governance claims.[56]   Put simply, the Court was able to use an aggregation rule—voters must be put in districts with essentially equal populations—to achieve a more fair governance outcome.   But although majoritarian governance claims could be substantially protected by one-person, one-vote, *Reynolds* provides no guidance to courts faced with claims by numerical minorities that their ability to influence the legislative process has been impaired.

Given the privileged position of majoritarianism in American political theory,[57] it would be difficult to develop mathematical rules for assessing

---

with the "inalienable right [of every citizen] to full and effective participation in the political processes of his State's legislative bodies," *id.*, further shows that its concern extends temporally far beyond mere participation in the selection of a single legislator. For further discussion of this more expansive conception of voting rights, see *supra* note 48 and accompanying text.

54. *See Reynolds*, 377 U.S. at 542 n.7 (noting that Alabama's existing legislative apportionment scheme overweighted rural votes while particularly underweighting suburban votes). Blacksher and Menefee note an ironic consequence of *Reynolds*: It stripped Alabama's rural, predominantly black counties of their legislative influence virtually on the eve of the massive black enfranchisement brought about by the Voting Rights Act of 1965. Had the 1901 reapportionment remained in effect until 1982, blacks would have controlled a higher percentage of the seats in the Alabama Legislature (18% of the House and 20% of the Senate in a state with a 25% black population) than they controlled as a result of the protections against dilution provided by § 2 and § 5 of the Voting Rights Act. Blacksher & Menefee, *supra* note 4, at 39 n.261; *cf.* Davidson, *supra* note 2, at 31 (noting that *Reynolds* destroyed the traditionally available option of racial vote dilution through malapportionment).

55. Perhaps the one-person, one-vote case that most clearly illustrates the governance-driven aspect of the doctrine is Board of Estimate v. Morris, 489 U.S. 688 (1989). There, the Court invalidated New York City's use of a body consisting of the five borough presidents and three citywide elected officials to make budgetary and land-use decisions. *Id.* at 690. Although voters in Brooklyn, the city's most populous borough with a population of roughly 2.2 million, were able to elect the borough president of their choice, their preferences could be canceled out by the vote cast by Staten Island's borough president, who represented only 350,000 people. *See id.* at 700 n.7. *But see* Issacharoff, *supra* note 31, at 1858 (claiming that *Reynolds* was concerned essentially with individual voting rights); Polsby & Popper, *supra* note 20, at 321-26 (claiming that one-person, one-vote and political gerrymandering claims are in fact individual-based rather than group-based).

56. *See* Blacksher & Menefee, *supra* note 4, at 14 ("[T]he simplicity of the population equality rule was precisely what attracted the Court's majority."); Samuel Issacharoff, *Judging Politics: The Elusive Quest for Judicial Review of Political Fairness*, 71 TEX. L. REV. 1643, 1648 (1993) (observing that the appeal of one-person, one-vote lay in its "numerical standards · · · drawn from unassailable empirical data," the fact that it could be "readily managed by the courts," and its promise of preventing gerrymandering through the use of "objective measures").

57. For a trenchant critique of this assumption, see James U. Blacksher, In Search of a Legitimate Politics of Ethnicity: An American's View of Canada's Experience (1992) (unpublished LL.M. thesis, Dalhousie University).

minority governance claims. Instead we need, in Jim Blacksher's phrase, to create a politics "that favors what is particular and provisional over what is universal and enduring."[58] That, in some measure, is what the 1982 amendments to Section 2 of the Voting Rights Act sought to do. The legislative history of the amendments directs courts applying the totality-of-the-circumstances test to look at such factors as a particular jurisdiction's history of denying minorities the right "to register, to vote, *or otherwise to participate in the democratic process*,"[59] and "whether there is a significant lack of responsiveness on the part of elected officials to the particularized needs of the members of the minority group."[60]

D. The Right to Vote As a Continuum

The three conceptions of voting that I have set forth in this Part form a continuum. The participatory right, to cast a ballot and have it counted, is a necessary precondition to the ability to elect. Similarly, the aggregative right, to elect, is what distinguishes self-governance, in which groups participate through their representatives in the formation of policy, from civic republican charity, in which individuals depend on the kindness of Platonic guardians. Just as importantly, the denial of effective inclusion can reverberate backward through the narrower conceptions of voting discouraging minorities from even casting ballots.[61]

I do not mean to suggest that these three conceptions of voting will always fit together smoothly in the real world, especially in a society as

---

58. *Id.* at 7.

59. Senate Report, *supra* note 5, at 28, *reprinted in* 1982 U.S.C.C.A.N. at 206 (emphasis added).

60. *Id.* at 29, *reprinted in* 1982 U.S.C.C.A.N. at 207; *see* Issacharoff, *supra* note 31, at 1845 (noting that the factors mentioned in the Senate Report "look[ ] both backward from the electoral process, to examine the historical circumstances leading to its establishment, and forward to determine the outcome of policy decisions by legislative bodies elected under such electoral arrangements"). Other commentators argue that even the original Voting Rights Act was intended to embody a broad view of the electoral process. Pamela S. Karlan & Peyton McCrary, *Without Fear and Without Research: Abigail Thernstrom on the Voting Rights Act*, 4 J.L. & POL. 751, 756 (1988) (reviewing ABIGAIL M. THERNSTROM, WHOSE VOTES COUNT? AFFIRMATIVE ACTION AND MINORITY VOTING RIGHTS (1987)) (rejecting Thernstrom's view that the sole aim of the Act was black enfranchisement and asserting that supporters of the Act saw the ballot as a means by which black voters would gain full inclusion in political decisionmaking); *cf.* J. Morgan Kousser, *The Voting Rights Act and the Two Reconstructions*, *in* CONTROVERSIES IN MINORITY VOTING, *supra* note 2, at 135, 136 (observing that the broad view of voting prevailed as early as Reconstruction, when voting was seen as providing "opportunity, education, fair play, right to office and elbow room" (quoting abolitionist Wendell Phillips)). I am in the process of thinking through the role that findings of nonresponsiveness should play in § 2 lawsuits, but a fuller articulation will have to await my work now in progress.

61. *See* Guinier, *supra* note 20, at 1111 (suggesting that the lack of an effective role in governance experienced by representatives who are elected from majority-black constituencies but are later isolated in the legislature may depress black political mobilization); Kousser, *supra* note 60, at 174 ("[D]isfranchisement and vote dilution are not pure concepts. They not only merge into each other, they are complementary, each increasing the other's force . . . .").

Texas Law Review

racially riven as contemporary America.[62] The current preoccupation with the election of representatives as the only measure of a minority's protected political strength has generated criticism from both the right and the left.[63] "Narrow constructionists"—who would largely limit constitutional and statutory protections of the right to vote to guarantees of formal participation—argue that the creation of "safe" majority-black or majority-Latino districts maximizes the number of representatives elected solely by minority-group members at the expense of sacrificing minority participation in the selection of a larger number of representatives, thereby reducing the minority-group's influence within the legislature.[64] In short, they argue that the focus on aggregation actively undercuts effective governance by creating legislatures whose overall makeup is less favorable to minority interests. At the other end of the spectrum, "expansive constructionists"—who are concerned with effective minority empowerment—argue that while direct control over some representatives is a necessary component of the right to vote, it remains insufficient if those representatives are consistently outvoted or excluded from winning coalitions within the legislature.[65] Put somewhat differently, they argue that the exclusive focus on aggregation actively undercuts effective governance by blinding observers to post-election behavior within the legislature. Of course, these competing arguments have not occurred in a vacuum. Before we can even begin to resolve the debate, we need to consider more carefully the procedural framework within which at least the legal answer to these questions will be worked out.

II. Doctrinal Chaos and Doctrinal Manipulation: Playing Games with Voting Rights

The Supreme Court's failure to acknowledge that its cases reflect more than one "right to vote" creates both a danger of doctrinal chaos at the Supreme Court level and a risk of doctrinal manipulation by the lower courts. In this Part, I begin by describing several conspicuous instances

---

62. For an extensive discussion of the role of racial bloc voting in Voting Rights Act jurisprudence, see generally Issacharoff, *supra* note 31.

63. *See* Davidson, *supra* note 2, at 45-48 (summarizing the critiques offered by "narrow constructionists" on the right and "expansive constructionists" on the left); *see also infra* notes 128-33 and accompanying text (discussing in greater depth the emphasis on aggregation as the measure of minority political success).

64. *See, e.g.*, ABIGAIL M. THERNSTROM, WHOSE VOTES COUNT? AFFIRMATIVE ACTION AND MINORITY VOTING RIGHTS 242-43 (1987) (claiming that a minority voting district plan runs the risk of sacrificing minority influence on a governmental body in return for guaranteed seats).

65. *See, e.g.*, Guinier, *No Two Seats*, *supra* note 48, at 1477-84 (arguing that black citizens' votes are unfairly diluted even if they can elect some members of a governmental body if their representatives' influence is minimized or canceled out by the actions of a permanent, hostile white legislative majority).

of the former problem. I then show how several structural features of voting rights litigation exacerbate the danger of partisan capture of the voting rights debate.

A. Rock, Paper, Scissors: The Supreme Court's Mischaracterization of Voting Rights Claims

Far from treating the differing conceptions of the right to vote as a progressive continuum, the Supreme Court seems to have viewed *each* conception as potentially trumping claims advanced under alternative conceptions. In addition to its effects at the Supreme Court level, this inconsistent ordering creates the doctrinal situation that allows lower courts to elevate their preferred conception to a position of primacy.

In *City of Mobile v. Bolden*,[66] for example, the Supreme Court rejected a challenge by Mobile's black voters to the use of at-large elections to select the city commission. The core of the lawsuit was the allegation that the aggregation rule unfairly submerged the votes of a large, geographically and politically distinctive minority group, thereby denying its members the opportunity to elect the candidates of their choice.[67] Justice Stewart's plurality opinion began by limiting the Fifteenth Amendment's protection of the right to vote so that it guaranteed only a right to participation: Because Mobile's black voters were able to register and cast ballots "without hindrance," their Fifteenth Amendment right to vote was not implicated by the electoral system.[68]

When he turned to their Fourteenth Amendment rights, which did extend to aggregation claims,[69] Justice Stewart rejected the plaintiffs' claim because they had not shown a racially discriminatory purpose.[70] Just as he had earlier refused to look beyond formal participation to ask whether aggregation rules unfairly abridged blacks' voting rights, here Justice Stewart refused to consider how aggregation rules played into larger issues of governance. The plurality essentially disregarded evidence that the commission was unresponsive to the black community, that is, that blacks were excluded from governance:

> If [elected officials are unresponsive,] those discriminated against may be entitled to relief under the Constitution, albeit of a sort quite different from that sought in the present case. The Equal Protection

---

66. 446 U.S. 55 (1980).

67. *Id.* at 58.

68. *Id.* at 64-65 (plurality opinion). To Justice Marshall, what the plurality was protecting was a "right to vote [that] provides the politically powerless with nothing more than the right to cast meaningless ballots." *Id.* at 104 (Marshall, J., dissenting).

69. *See id.* at 65 (plurality opinion).

70. *See id.* at 70-74 (plurality opinion).

Clause proscribes purposeful discrimination because of race by any unit of state government, whatever the method of its election. But evidence of discrimination by white officials in Mobile is relevant only as the most tenuous and circumstantial evidence of the constitutional invalidity of the electoral system under which they attained their offices.[71]

Standing alone, *Bolden* could perhaps be viewed as a cramped, but coherent, reconciliation of the three rights: That is, the core constitutional interest is the ability to participate, methods of aggregation are limited by only the prohibition on intentional discrimination, and governance decisions lie essentially outside the ambit of voting rights jurisprudence. But the Court's subsequent cases show that *Bolden* is part of a larger analytic failure, in which the Court has misconceived participation, aggregation, and governance claims.

In *Burdick v. Takushi*,[72] for example, the Court upheld Hawaii's total ban on write-in voting. Although Burdick's claim was essentially participational—he sought to cast and have counted a ballot that would be "meaningful" to him[73]—the Court's response rested on the view that voting serves an aggregative purpose:

> [T]he function of the election process is to "winnow out and finally reject all but the chosen candidates," not to provide a means of giving vent to "short-range political goals, pique, or personal quarrel[s]." Attributing to elections a more generalized expressive function would undermine the ability of States to operate elections fairly and efficiently.[74]

The Ninth Circuit had taken an even firmer stand. For it, the right to vote involved a "right to cast one's vote *effectively*,"[75] and because write-in votes virtually never affected electoral outcomes, their elimination did not implicate the right to vote.

---

71. *Id.* at 73-74 (plurality opinion). *But cf.* Shaw v. Reno, 113 S. Ct. 2816, 2827 (1993) (suggesting that the danger that officials elected from deliberately created majority-minority districts will "believe that their primary obligation is to represent only the members of that group, rather than their constituency as a whole" is one reason strict scrutiny of such districting is required).

72. 112 S. Ct. 2059 (1992).

73. *Id.* at 2065.

74. *Id.* at 2066 (citations omitted) (quoting Storer v. Brown, 415 U.S. 724, 735 (1974)). *But cf. Shaw*, 113 S. Ct. at 2824 (noting that although the plaintiffs did not claim their votes had been diluted, they nonetheless could claim a denial of a "constitutional right to participate in a 'color-blind' electoral process").

75. Burdick v. Takushi, 937 F.2d 415, 418 (9th Cir. 1991) (emphasis added), *aff'd*, 112 S. Ct. 2059 (1992); *see id.* at 420 ("[T]he fact that Burdick cannot cast a write-in vote does not place any substantial burden on his *fundamental right to participate equally in the election of those who will make or administer the laws*." (emphasis added)).

In an analogous fashion, *Davis v. Bandemer*[76] transformed an aggregative political gerrymandering lawsuit into a governance claim in order to defeat the plaintiffs' challenge. The plaintiffs in *Bandemer* were Democratic voters who, as a result of a Republican-orchestrated apportionment of the state legislature, were unable to elect their preferred candidates. The Court, however, rejected their aggregation claim because they had failed to show that their governance interests had been impaired. First, the Court stated that "[a]n individual or a group of individuals who votes for a losing candidate is usually deemed to be adequately represented by the winning candidate and to have as much opportunity to influence that candidate as other voters in the district."[77] Notably, the Court did not explain why, if this is so, the formal, individual, participatory right to vote is protected so strongly. Second, the Court held that the test for assessing unconstitutional political vote dilution looks at "a voter's or a group of voters' influence on the political process as a whole,"[78] *including* the virtual representation of their interests by legislators elected from other districts in the state. In short, as long as the overall distribution of power fairly reflects the political composition of the state and thereby offers fair governance, the use of aggregation rules that deliberately preclude some subgroups of voters from directly electing their preferred candidates does not invalidate the apportionment scheme.[79]

Finally, in *Presley v. Etowah County Commission,*[80] the Court seemingly held that the right to vote is not implicated at all by post-election allocations of power among elected officials. In 1986, a conventional

---

76. 478 U.S. 109 (1986).

77. *Id.* at 132 (plurality opinion).

78. *Id.*

79. For a particularly striking example of this logic, consider the judicial response to a challenge to the 1980 California congressional apportionment. That the apportionment was a deliberate political gerrymander was hardly contested or for that matter contestable. *See generally* Frederick K. Lowell & Teresa A. Craigie, *California's Reapportionment Struggle: A Classic Clash Between Law and Politics,* 2 J.L. & POL. 245, 246 (1985). Although the reapportionment had reduced the Republicans' share of the state's delegation from 21 of 43 to 17 of 45, the three-judge district court found no discriminatory effect, in part because

> California has a Republican governor, and one of its two senators is Republican. Given also that a recent former Republican governor of California has for seven years been President of the United States, we see the fulcrum of political power to be such as to belie any attempt of plaintiffs to claim that they are bereft of the ability to exercise potent power in "the political process as a whole" because of the paralysis of an unfair gerrymander.

Badham v. Eu, 694 F. Supp. 664, 672 (N.D. Cal. 1988) (three-judge court), *aff'd per curiam,* 488 U.S. 1024 (1989). For a further discussion of *Badham* as a governance case involving de facto ticket balancing, see Karlan, *supra* note 34, at 34-36 (discussing how the insight of *Badham*—that elective power is properly measured by considering all of the available political positions—underlies the well-known practice of balanced tickets, where a party divides political posts between different minority groups in order to motivate individuals to vote for the entire party slate).

80. 112 S. Ct. 820 (1992).

Section 2 aggregation-focused lawsuit filed in Alabama resulted in the
adoption of a single-member districting plan for the Etowah County Commission and the election of the county's first black commissioner.
Immediately afterward, the white holdover commissioners passed a series
of resolutions that, according to the plaintiffs, transferred all effective
power from the individual commissioners to the commission as a whole
and then essentially stripped the black commissioner of the traditional
powers of his office.[81] The plaintiffs in *Presley* argued that these resolutions were subject to preclearance under Section 5 of the Voting Rights Act
because they represented changes "with respect to voting."[82] The challenged resolutions, they argued, were merely the latest and most subtle
effort to assure complete white control of the county.[83]

The Supreme Court rejected that position. Although it recognized that
"in a real sense every decision taken by government implicates voting,"[84]
it feared that the broad conception of voting advanced by the plaintiffs
would embroil the courts in oversight of a limitless number of local decisions.[85] Moreover, the Court confronted what it saw as the essential
standardlessness of such an inquiry: How can one assess the fairness of
legislative outcomes?[86] And so the Court sought to detach the struggle
for effective governance from the right to vote: "Congress meant . . . what
it said when it made [Section] 5 applicable to changes 'with respect to

---

81. *See id.* at 825-26 (describing how the white holdover commissioners gave themselves control
over the repair, maintenance, and improvement of the roads in the new commissioner's district—control
previously exerted by each commissioner with respect to his own district—as well as how they switched
from the separate allocation of funds for roads in individual districts to a common fund for road
repairs).

82. *Id.* at 824. Section 5 of the Voting Rights Act provides, in pertinent part, that certain
jurisdictions with a history of disenfranchisement and depressed political participation must obtain
federal approval before they "enact or seek to administer any voting qualification or prerequisite to
voting, or standard, practice, or procedure with respect to voting" different from those previously in
force. 42 U.S.C. § 1973c (1988).

83. In this sense, the move from participation to aggregation to governance mirrors the analytic
evolution of so-called first-, second-, and third-generation voting rights claims. *See, e.g.*, Guinier,
supra note 20, at 1093-94, 1102, 1116, 1135 (discussing the change of focus in voting rights
jurisprudence from direct impediments to indirect structural barriers and advocating a greater focus on
the inability of minority legislators to "infiltrate the decisionmaking process"); Issacharoff, *supra* note
31, at 1839 (noting the shift from first-generation voting rights claims based on individual rights to
second-generation challenges based on group rights of certain minority groups); Karlan, *supra* note 20,
at 183-84, 236-39 (describing the three generations of problems); Binny Miller, *Who Shall Rule and
Govern? Local Legislative Delegations, Racial Politics, and the Voting Rights Act*, 102 YALE L.J. 105,
138-50 (1992) (discussing the evolution of these challenges from claims of formal barriers to vote
dilution to exclusionary activity in the post-election period).

84. *Presley*, 112 S. Ct. at 829.

85. *See id.*

86. *See id.* at 829 ("Appellants and the United States fail to provide a workable standard for
distinguishing between changes in rules governing voting and changes in the routine organization and
functioning of government."); *The Supreme Court, 1991 Term—Leading Cases*, 106 HARV. L. REV.
163, 375 (1992) (describing the Court's desire for a "workable standard").

voting' rather than, say, changes 'with respect to governance.'"[87] In short, Etowah County's black citizens enjoyed a complete right to vote because the rules for selecting county commissioners gave them an equal opportunity to elect a candidate to the commission. Whether they enjoyed any effective access to commission decisionmaking fell outside the scope of their right to vote.

There is a rich irony behind the Court's unwillingness to recognize that the voting rights of Etowah County's black citizens were impaired when their elected representative was denied an appropriate share of the power to determine legislative outcomes. In *Reynolds*,[88] the Court had accorded expansive constitutional protection to an essentially identical claim by *white* citizens in the Etowah County municipality of Gadsden, holding that their right to vote had been unconstitutionally diluted because they were unable to exercise, through their elected representatives, a fair share of the state's legislative power.[89] Undoubtedly, part of the explanation for this divergence lies in the Court's racially selective indifference, not to mention its privileging of majoritarian political values.[90] But the divergence is equally rooted, I think, in the Court's enduring misgivings about entering the political thicket for anything but the most antiseptic and surgical of incursions. *Reynolds* offered a clean oversight rule; *Presley*, on the other hand, required an intimate, functional appraisal of political reality. If the Court were not forced to confront such fundamentally political and intractable claims, it would have every incentive to exclude them from its definition of voting.

The 1982 amendments to the Voting Rights Act, however, require precisely this form of judicial engagement. Congress has expressly directed courts to consider whether racial and ethnic minority groups have an equal opportunity "to *participate in the political process* and to elect representatives of their choice."[91] And while the statute does not provide a clear

---

87. *Presley*, 112 S. Ct. at 832.

88. Reynolds v. Sims, 377 U.S. 533 (1964).

89. *Id.* at 575; *see also* Blacksher & Menefee, *supra* note 4, at 1 (stating that the plaintiffs in *Reynolds* "convinced the United States Supreme Court that the Constitution guarantees equal voting rights for white people").

90. *See* Karlan, *supra* note 34, at 9-14, 39-45 (discussing the nonmajoritarian and countermajoritarian strains of the Voting Rights Act and the judiciary's discomfort with these perspectives).

91. 42 U.S.C. § 1973(b) (emphasis added). As Kathy Abrams and Sam Issacharoff have pointed out, the three-part test developed by the Supreme Court in Thornburg v. Gingles, 478 U.S. 30, 43 (1986), represents an attempt to simplify and rigidify the contextual test created by the 1982 amendments. *See* Abrams, *supra* note 20, at 452 (arguing that the approach suggested in *Gingles* threatens to rigidify into an approach that uses a misleadingly simple measure of political effectiveness); Issacharoff, *supra* note 31, at 1834 (stating that the *Gingles* Court adopted a simpler test than the one set forth in the Voting Rights Act amendments). Under the three-part test created in *Gingles*, a minority group must first "demonstrate that it is sufficiently large and geographically compact to

benchmark for assessing aggregation claims, let alone governance issues, its "political process" language forces courts to address these questions on the merits. The doctrinal confusion I have just sketched out, however, renders the lower courts analytically ill-equipped to undertake this task. In the next Part, I show how this analytic poverty interacts with several structural features of voting rights litigation to undermine the Voting Rights Act's central aim of fully integrating historically excluded minorities into the political process as that process is broadly understood.[92]

B. Capture the Flag: Litigation Structure and Strategy and the "Commandeering" of the Voting Rights Act

Technology has largely marginalized the substantive impact of one-person, one-vote. Computers allow plan drafters to devise a wide variety of "equipopulous gerrymanders": apportionment schemes that satisfy one-person, one-vote while significantly distorting the relationship between a group's share of the electorate and its share of the elected officials.[93] Nonetheless, one-person, one-vote continues to play a substantial role in voting rights litigation. In this subpart, I trace how the procedural incidents of voting rights litigation have shaped substantive voting rights law.

1. The Race to the Courthouse.—One-person, one-vote claims are not only doctrinally privileged; they are temporally privileged as well. Once the decennial census figures are released, virtually every existing apportionment scheme becomes instantly unconstitutional because of a decade of population shifts. This means that challenges based on one-person, one-vote can be brought *before* reapportionment occurs.[94] And the Supreme Court's individualist rhetoric in *Reynolds* and its progeny

---

constitute a majority in a single-member district. . . . [It then must] show that it is politically cohesive[, and finally must] demonstrate that the white majority votes as a bloc" such that the minority group's preferred candidate will normally be defeated. *See Gingles*, 478 U.S. at 50-51.

92. *See supra* note 48 and accompanying text (examining the broad view of the political process); *see also* H.R. Rep. No. 227, 97th Cong., 1st Sess. 14 (1981) (stating that the Voting Rights Act was intended to combat the "observable consequences of exclusion from government to the minority community," such as "failure to secure a share of local government employment" and "disproportionate allocation of funds, location and type of capital projects").

93. For discussion of the computer revolution, see Issacharoff, *supra* note 56, at 1695-1702; Polsby & Popper, *supra* note 20, at 303 & n.15.

94. *See* ELLEN SPEARS, THE REPUBLICANS GO TO COURT: A REVIEW OF REPUBLICAN LEGAL STRATEGIES ON MINORITY RIGHTS IN THE AREA OF THE VOTING RIGHTS ACT 6-7 (1992) (noting, among other examples, that Republicans in Florida filed suit on the first day of the legislative session, "claiming the Legislature *would* fail" to adopt timely plans" (emphasis added)); *see also State Redistricting Activities*, REDISTRICTING NEWS UPDATE (Leadership Conf. Educ. Fund, Wash., D.C.), Spring 1992, at 1, 4 [hereinafter REDISTRICTING NEWS UPDATE] (setting out the background of Florida reapportionment).

gives an essentially limitless number of voters standing to bring such a case.[95]   In short, one-person, one-vote essentially licenses a race to the courthouse.

Moreover, the overlapping regulation of voting rights offers a wide choice of courthouses to which plaintiffs can race. In addition to their jurisdiction over purely state-law apportionment-related claims, state courts have concurrent jurisdiction over most federal voting rights laws.[96] The ability to choose state court, particularly in states where judges are selected in partisan elections,[97] provides potential leverage to a plaintiff group that can appear before a sympathetic court. This is particularly true where the court, as it usually does, goes beyond striking down the existing plan to supervise the design of a replacement. Thus, the most recent round of reapportionment litigation has witnessed parallel state and federal proceedings in a number of hotly contested states, including Illinois,[98] Ohio,[99]

---

95. The novel, "analytically distinct" constitutional cause of action recognized by Shaw v. Reno, 113 S. Ct. 2816, 2830 (1993)—that it violates the Equal Protection Clause for a state to adopt reapportionment legislation that, "though race neutral on its face, rationally cannot be understood as anything other than an effort to separate voters into different districts on the basis of race" unless the state can provide "sufficient justification," id. at 2828—of course creates an entire new population of potential plaintiffs to challenge newly enacted reapportionment plans. Essentially, every voter, regardless of the district to which she has been assigned, can bring a Shaw claim.

96. See Hathorn v. Lovorn, 457 U.S. 255, 265-70 (1982) (holding that a state court had the power and the duty to decide whether preclearance was needed for a change in voting procedure). The one clear exception involves § 5 preclearance proceedings, which can be litigated only in the United States District Court for the District of Columbia. See 42 U.S.C. § 1973l(b) (1988). But even under § 5, a court hell-bent on implementing, albeit only temporarily, a plan that has not received preclearance can do so by using such a plan as the basis for interim judicial relief. See McDaniel v. Sanchez, 452 U.S. 130 (1981) (holding court-fashioned remedial plans do not require preclearance).

97. For a catalog of state judicial election practices, see John M. Roll, Merit Selection: The Arizona Experience, 22 ARIZ. ST. L.J. 837, 845-47 (1990). Because Roll's list focuses only on appellate courts, it actually may understate the level of partisan politics involved. New York, for example, has a merit panel-nominated, gubernatorially appointed Court of Appeals (the state's highest court), but has a trial bench chosen through partisan elections. N.Y. CONST. art. VI, § 2(e); see also Davidson, supra note 2, at 42 (observing that 41 states elect some or all of their judges).

98. See REDISTRICTING NEWS UPDATE, supra note 94, at 7 (describing how Illinois Republicans litigated a challenge to the state's congressional districts in federal court, while Democrats pursued a parallel state supreme court challenge because that court had a 4-3 Democratic majority).

99. Ohio's apportionment plan was drawn by a Republican-dominated state apportionment board. See Voinovich v. Ferguson, 586 N.E.2d 1020, 1037 (Ohio 1992) (Resnick, J., dissenting). The Ohio Supreme Court upheld the plan against a state-law challenge in a vote that divided its members along party lines, see id. at 1022, but the two-judge Democratic majority on a three-judge federal district court struck down the plan, finding that it violated the Voting Rights Act. See Quilter v. Voinovich, 794 F. Supp. 695, 701-02 (N.D. Ohio 1992) (three-judge court), rev'd, 113 S. Ct. 1149 (1993); see also Reapportionment Legal Battle Continues, UPI, Nov. 21, 1991, available in LEXIS, Nexis Library, Wires File (setting out the political affiliations of the various judges). For a more detailed discussion of the Ohio experience, see infra notes 134-47 and accompanying text (discussing Voinovich).

Pennsylvania,[100] Minnesota,[101] California,[102] and New York.[103]

Even with regard to federal court, multidistrict states afford an opportunity for some limited degree of forum shopping, because a lawsuit can be brought in virtually any district.[104] The greatest potential impact of

---

100. As a result of the 1990 Census, Pennsylvania lost 2 of its 23 congressional seats. The Democrat-controlled state house proposed a plan it claimed would cause each of the parties to lose one seat, but the Republican-controlled state senate rejected the plan, leading to political deadlock. Democrats then brought suit in state court, seeking implementation of their plan. Ultimately, the Commonwealth Court recommended a plan devised by state senate Democrats. *See* Hugh Bronstein, *Commonwealth Court Backs Democratic Plan*, UPI, Feb. 24, 1992, *available in* LEXIS, Nexis Library, UPI File; *Federal Panel Upholds Decision for Pennsylvania Congressional Districting*, PR Newswire, Aug. 17, 1992, *available in* LEXIS, Nexis Library, Wires File. Republicans, however, were dissatisfied with their prospects for success in front of a court consisting of seven Democrats and one Republican, so they filed a lawsuit in the Middle District of Pennsylvania, "hoping for better treatment from federal Judge Sylvia Rambo, a Republican." Bronstein, *supra*. In the end, a three-judge federal court rejected the Republicans' motion to enjoin the state proceeding. *See Federal Panel Upholds Decision for Pennsylvania Congressional Districting, supra*.

101. For a discussion of the relationship between the state and federal lawsuits in Minnesota, see Growe v. Emison, 113 S. Ct. 1075, 1085 (1993). *See also infra* text accompanying notes 119-21 (discussing *Growe*).

102. California's Republican governor vetoed congressional and state legislative districting plans that had been drawn by the Democratically controlled state legislature. In light of the ensuing legislative deadlock, the Republican-dominated California Supreme Court agreed, at the governor's request, to take charge of drawing legislative and congressional districts. *See* Wilson v. Eu, 816 P.2d 1306 (Cal. 1991); REDISTRICTING NEWS UPDATE, *supra* note 94, at 3. In response, the Democratic members of California's congressional delegation brought suit in federal district court. California Democratic Congressional Delegation v. Eu, 790 F. Supp. 925, 928 (N.D. Cal. 1992). The three-judge court, however, refused to enjoin the state-court proceeding or to enjoin the actual districts approved by the state, *id.* at 929, and eventually, in a 2-1 decision with two Reagan appointees in the majority and a Carter nominee in dissent, allowed the California Supreme Court's plan to stand. *Id.* at 933.

103. For discussions of the parallel state and federal proceedings (which included simultaneous lawsuits in both the Eastern and Western Districts of New York), see Puerto Rican Legal Defense and Educ. Fund, Inc. v. Gantt, 796 F. Supp. 677, 677-78 (E.D.N.Y. 1992) (three-judge court) (per curiam); Daniel Wise, *Congressional Redistricting Battle Continues on 2 Fronts*, N.Y. L.J., May 15, 1992, at 1; Sam H. Verhovek, *Political Notes*, N.Y. TIMES, May 17, 1992, Metro Section, at 41.

The three-judge court in the Eastern District attempted, under the All Writs Act, 28 U.S.C. § 1651 (1988), to enjoin the state court from proceeding to devise its own plan. *Gantt*, 796 F. Supp. at 680. Its order, however, was stayed by the Supreme Court of the United States. Gantt v. Skelos, 112 S. Ct. 1926 (1992). Further judicial conflict was avoided when the legislature approved the plan that had been developed by the state court, thereby devising a "legislative" solution. Act of June 11, 1992, ch. 137, 1992 N.Y. Laws 690; *see* Kevin Sack, *G.O.P. Leader Supports State Court District Plan*, N.Y. TIMES, June 3, 1992, at B4 (noting that the state court plan was generally seen as more beneficial to incumbents than the federal plan). Although that plan was precleared by the Department of Justice and used for the 1992 general election, it is still the subject of litigation because the Puerto Rican Legal Defense and Education Fund claims that the plan violates § 2 of the Voting Rights Act by failing to draw an additional majority-Latino congressional district. Kenneth J. Cooper, *Battle Lines Drawn on Voting Districts in 4 More States*, WASH. POST, July 18, 1993, at A6.

104. *See Gantt*, 796 F. Supp. at 678 (observing that parallel challenges to the same New York apportionment plan were filed in both the Eastern and Western Districts of New York, as well as in state court); *cf.* Appellants' Record Excerpts at 21, 24, City of Scottsboro v. Battles, No. 88-7674 (11th Cir. appeal dismissed Nov. 26, 1990) (observing that attorneys for a city that faced potential litigation in the Middle District of Alabama, before a judge whom the city viewed to be unsympathetic to its use

the federal litigation system does not, however, arise from the plaintiffs' choice of forum. Rather, it arises from the distinctive kind of court before which congressional and state legislative cases are heard. Precisely because these cases intrude on the state's political processes, these lawsuits are heard by three-judge district courts composed of two district judges and one court of appeals judge.[105] But the decision as to *which* judges are to serve on three-judge courts is completely unconstrained by statute—it is left entirely to the chief judge of the court of appeals. The appointment of particular judges to three-judge courts thus presents a significant opportunity for a result-oriented chief judge to stack the court. In the 1960s, for example, the chief judge of the Fifth Circuit was widely believed to have deliberately assigned progressive circuit judges to three-judge courts in controversial civil rights cases.[106]   Moreover, the use of three-judge courts eliminates review by the courts of appeals, substituting in its place theoretically mandatory appellate review by the Supreme Court.[107] Although the Court has noted probable jurisdiction in a substantial number of the appeals that have already reached it, it has summarily disposed of a number of other, equally controversial, lower court decisions.[108] And this practical unreviewability is also fostered because a range of critical conclusions are subject to the "clearly erroneous" standard of review.[109]

   2.   *The Availability of Favorable Remedies.*—Of course, the real reason for this race to the courthouse is not simply to invalidate the

---

of at-large elections, filed a declaratory judgment action in the Northern District of Alabama).

   105. *See* 28 U.S.C. § 2284 (1988). Congress originally created three-judge courts because states feared that federal judges were indiscriminately enjoining the enforcement of state statutes. *See* S. REP. No. 204, 94th Cong., 1st Sess. 4-5 (1975), *reprinted in* 1976 U.S.C.C.A.N. 3160, 3163-64. Congress in 1976 eliminated the use of three-judge courts in most situations, but retained them for reapportionment "because it is the judgment of the committee that these issues are of such importance that they ought to be heard by a three-judge court." *Id.* at 9, *reprinted in* 1976 U.S.C.C.A.N. at 3168; *cf.* Napoleon B. Williams, Jr., *The New Three-Judge Courts of Reapportionment and Continuing Problems of the Three-Judge-Court Procedure*, 65 GEO. L.J. 971, 975-79 (1977) (discussing proper construction of the § 2284 requirement concerning the use of three-judge courts).

   106. For a discussion of this controversy and its resolution (as well as a critical appraisal of the evidence), see JACK BASS, UNLIKELY HEROES 233-47 (1981).

   107. *See* 28 U.S.C. § 1253 (1988).

   108. *See, e.g.*, Arizona Hispanic Community Forum v. Symington, 113 S. Ct. 454 (1992), *aff'g* Arizonans for Fair Representation v. Symington, 1992 U.S. Dist. LEXIS 21227 (D. Ariz. Apr. 30, 1992) (three-judge court) (raising questions regarding interim use of plans objected to under § 5); Pope v. Blue, 113 S. Ct. 30, *aff'g* 809 F. Supp. 392 (W.D.N.C. 1992) (three-judge court) (raising claims regarding gerrymandering); Turner v. Arkansas, 112 S. Ct. 2296 (1992), *aff'g* 784 F. Supp. 553 (E.D. Ark. 1991) (three-judge court) (involving assertion of "influence district" claim); Anne Arundel County Republican Cent. Comm. v. State Admin. Bd. of Election Laws, 112 S. Ct. 2269 (1992), *aff'g* 781 F. Supp. 394 (D. Md. 1991) (three-judge court) (involving issues of incumbency protection, partisan line drawing, and minority safe districting).

   109. *See* Thornburg v. Gingles, 478 U.S. 30, 79 (1986) (stating that a finding of vote dilution is subject to a clearly erroneous standard of review).

existing plan. Because a nearly limitless number of plans can satisfy equipopulous districting criteria, the choice among them becomes crucial. One-person, one-vote lawsuits are essentially "vehicle law·suits,"[110] empty of any real content but pregnant with the possibility of persuading a court to adopt a favorable new plan.

As a doctrinal matter, once a federal court has overturned an apportionment scheme, it must give the defendant jurisdiction an opportunity to propose a new plan; moreover, the court must defer to the defendant's proposal as long as it fully cures the violation and does not itself violate federal law.[111] But this remedial doctrine is undercut by the structure of voting rights litigation.

To begin with, it is not entirely clear to whom this opportunity and accompanying deference must be given. In some states, reapportionment is entrusted to the legislature and governor working in tandem.[112] In others, the process is controlled by a designated group of elected officials.[113] In yet others, the legislature can reapportion without any executive input.[114] But the state legislature is virtually never an actual party to preemptive voting rights lawsuits. Instead, such lawsuits often involve only an executive officer in his official capacity.[115] This detachment of the real parties in interest from formal party status offers opportunities for collusive lawsuits. In Alabama, for example, a Republican governor induced the Republicans to file a lawsuit against him in an

---

110. Cf. Davis v. Bandemer, 478 U.S. 109, 114 n.2 (1986) (noting that the Indiana reapportionment process used "vehicle bills," that is, bills with no content that are referred to committee for actual drafting).

111. See Wise v. Lipscomb, 437 U.S. 535, 540 (1978) ("[I]t is . . . appropriate, whenever practicable, to afford a reasonable opportunity for the legislature to meet constitutional requirements by adopting a substitute measure . . . ."); Chapman v. Meier, 420 U.S. 1, 27 (1975) ("[R]eapportionment is primarily the duty and responsibility of the State through its legislature or other body, rather than of a federal court."); Tallahassee Branch of NAACP v. Leon County, Fla., 827 F.2d 1436, 1438 (11th Cir. 1987) ("Only when the state is unable or refuses to reapportion itself in accordance with federal law will a federal district court undertake reapportionment."), cert. denied, 448 U.S. 960 (1988).

112. In Alabama, for example, congressional district boundaries are codified. ALA. CODE § 17-20-1 (1988 & Supp. 1992). As such, any attempt at reapportionment must pass the legislature and be submitted to the governor for approval. See ALA. CONST., art. V, § 125. The most recent version of this act, 1992 Ala. Acts 63, § 1, however, went into effect when the legislature overrode the governor's veto. See REDISTRICTING NEWS UPDATE, supra note 94, at 1.

113. See, e.g., ARK. CONST. art. VIII, §§ 1, 4 (establishing a "board of apportionment" consisting of the governor, secretary of state, and attorney general); OHIO CONST. art. XI, § 1 (establishing a panel consisting of specified executive officials and designees of legislative leadership).

114. See, e.g., CONN. CONST. art. III, § 6 (requiring a two-thirds supermajority in each house for reapportionment and providing no role for the governor unless there is a deadlock).

115. See, e.g., Thornburg v. Gingles, 478 U.S. 30, 34 (1986) (involving a state attorney general as the defendant in a lawsuit that challenged a redistricting plan enacted by the state general assembly). Interestingly, the state's governor supported the plaintiffs' position. See id. at 34 (footnote listing parties before the Court).

attempt to avoid being faced with a plan created by the Democrat-dominated state legislature.[116]   A comparable end run occurred in Houston, Texas, where the city sought to avoid the federal preclearance process by counterclaiming against its own citizens.[117] The broad doctrinal rule allowing defendants to propose their own plans thus provides no guidance to a court faced with a handful of plans, each with very different aggregative effects, each of whose proponents claim that their plan is entitled to presumptive adoption. Thus, it is hardly surprising that courts have resorted to special masters.[118] Moreover, the opportunity to short-circuit partisan redistricting altogether provides some political actors with an incentive to stonewall in the hope that a judicially created plan will be more favorable than the plan that the group can obtain in the normal apportionment process.

The Supreme Court's recent decision in *Growe* v. *Emison*[119] adds an interesting dimension to this problem. In *Growe*, the Court held that federal courts must "defer" to state court reapportionment proceedings in two ways. First, they must "defer" in the sense of *postpone*; as long as the state, "through its legislative *or* judicial branch, has begun to address [the] highly political task [of redistricting] itself,"[120] federal courts should not interfere or impose remedies. Second, they must "defer" in the sense of *respect*; if a state court imposes a reapportionment plan, the federal court must abide by that plan unless the plan independently violates federal law.[121] *Growe* may thus cut off one form of judicial circumvention—by preventing federal courts from immediately jumping into the reapportionment fray when state courts are already involved—only to open up a new avenue of circumvention by encouraging litigants to pitch their cases in state courts rather than state legislatures, even when, under state law, judges are not part of the redistricting apparatus.

If the only question were whether a proposed plan satisfies the one-person, one-vote rule, answering the question would be easy, and partisanship would be essentially unconstrained. But the concurrent requirement

---

116. *See* SPEARS, *supra* note 94, at 11-12 (discussing the backdrop to and litigation of Wesch v. Hunt, 785 F. Supp. 1491 (S.D. Ala.), *aff'd sub nom.* Camp v. Wesch, 112 S. Ct. 1926 (1992), *and aff'd sub nom.* Figures v. Hunt, 113 S. Ct. 1233 (1993)).

117. *See* Campos v. City of Houston, 776 F. Supp. 304, 305-06 (S.D. Tex. 1991), *vacated and remanded*, 968 F.2d 446 (5th Cir. 1992), *cert. denied*, 113 S. Ct. 971 (1993).

118. *See* REDISTRICTING NEWS UPDATE, *supra* note 94, at 2, 4 (noting the appointment of special masters to devise districting plans in California and Florida following legislative deadlock); *see also* Quilter v. Voinovich, 794 F. Supp. 756, 757 (N.D. Ohio 1992) (three-judge court) (appointing a special master in an Ohio state legislative reapportionment case), *rev'd on other grounds*, 113 S. Ct. 1149 (1993).

119. 113 S. Ct. 1075 (1993).

120. *Id.* at 1080 (emphasis in original).

121. *See id.* at 1082, 1085.

that plans satisfy Section 2 adds a remarkably complicating factor. First, Section 2 protects the votes of racial minorities from wastage, either through cracking or packing;[122] no such protection exists for political opponents. This protection of minority votes limits the range of valid plans and therefore constrains the level of partisan advantage that the drafters of redistricting plans can obtain. Second, the "parties problem" emerges here as well: Who should speak for the minority community? Although racial vote dilution claims are inherently group-based, individual minority voters have standing to participate in the litigation process, and the political parties will enlist at least some members of the relevant groups to advance their views of the "best" accommodation of Section 2.[123]

At this point, the doctrinal confusion described in Part I becomes critical. What approach should a court take in deciding whether a particular plan fairly protects the ability of minority voters to participate in the political process and to elect the candidates of their choice? On the one hand, a purely aggregative approach would demand the maximum number of safe districts, and might even require a substantial amount of "packing," because in areas with significant racial bloc voting, a minority voter could hope to elect the candidate of her choice only if she were placed in a district composed primarily of minority-group members. On the other hand, to the extent that minority voters were concerned with the overall composition of the legislature, packing would undermine their collective interest in governance. They would thus be concerned not only—and, some commentators have argued, not even primarily[124]—with the creation of safe seats, but also with maximizing minority influence on the legislative process through the use of "influence districts."[125]

---

122. *See* Thornburg v. Gingles, 478 U.S. 30, 46 n.11 (1986) (explaining that vote dilution may be caused either "by the dispersal of blacks into districts in which they constitute an ineffective minority of voters," (cracking), or "from the concentration of blacks into districts where they constitute an excessive majority" (packing)).

123. *See, e.g.*, Quilter v. Voinovich, 794 F. Supp. 695, 695 (N.D. Ohio 1992) (three-judge court) (describing certain plaintiffs in a suit decided on § 2 grounds as "Democratic electors and state legislators, some of whom are members of a protected class under the Voting Rights Act"), *rev'd*, 113 S. Ct. 1149 (1993); *cf.* Wright v. Rockefeller, 376 U.S. 52, 53-54 (1964) (involving an attack on New York City congressional districts by black voters who claimed they were unconstitutionally "packed" into a single district and intervention in the litigation by Representative Adam Clayton Powell and other black leaders who defended the plan).

124. *See, e.g.*, THERNSTROM, *supra* note 64, at 11-30, 232-44 (discussing the evolution of the Voting Rights Act and arguing that packing minorities into safe districts dissipates their influence over the process as a whole); Peter H. Schuck, *What Went Wrong With the Voting Rights Act*, WASH. MONTHLY, Nov. 1987, at 51, 55 (arguing that minority voters are better served by a return to the Act's original vision of equal political opportunity than by a "paternalistic policy of electoral apartheid"); Abigail M. Thernstrom, *'Voting Rights' Trap*, NEW REPUBLIC, Sept. 2, 1985, at 21, 23 (arguing that safe minority districts do not necessarily serve either long-term or immediate black political interests and that resegregated politics is an undesirable effect of the current policy).

125. For discussions of influence district claims, see, for example, Armour v. Ohio, 775 F. Supp. 1044, 1052, 1059-60 (N.D. Ohio 1991) (three-judge court); BERNARD GROFMAN ET AL., MINORITY

3. The Battle for the Voting Rights Act.—Given this combination of
doctrinal confusion, substantial lower-court independence from review, and
opportunities for procedural manipulation, the Voting Rights Act is ripe for
partisan capture. Indeed, that possibility is suggested both by the specific
history of how white majorities "commandeered" the constitutional protections of voting rights, set out in Jim Blacksher and Larry Menefee's
influential article,[126] and by the more general interest-convergence
hypothesis advanced by Derrick Bell, which predicts that the judicial
system will adopt a conception of minority rights only to the extent that the
conception also promotes majority interests.[127]

That both major political parties are in fact trying to commandeer the
Voting Rights Act seems evident. In the litigation context, for example,
Republicans have advanced a pure aggregation model of voting rights, assuming that the creation of majority-black districts will deprive white
Democrats of a critical element of their base of support and thereby allow
Republicans to win elections in predominantly white districts.[128] This
convergence of their aggregative interests with those of minority voters led
them to provide technical assistance to minority groups seeking to draw
plans that would increase the number of minority seats.[129] Several

---

REPRESENTATION AND THE QUEST FOR VOTING EQUALITY 117-18 (1992); Guinier, *No Two Seats*,
supra note 48, at 1452 n.146, 1457-58. The Supreme Court has twice dodged the question of influence
districts this past Term. *See* Voinovich v. Quilter, 113 S. Ct. 1149, 1155 (1993) ("We have not yet
decided whether influence-dilution claims . . . are viable under § 2, nor do we decide that question
today." (citations omitted)); Growe v. Emison, 113 S. Ct. 1075, 1084 n.5 (1993) (refusing to consider
the impairment of the minority's ability to influence election results because the district court had not
considered the issue).

126. *See* Blacksher & Menefee, *supra* note 4.

127. *See* Derrick A. Bell, Jr., *Brown v. Board of Education and the Interest-Convergence
Dilemma*, 93 HARV. L. REV. 518, 523 (1980) ("The interest of blacks in achieving racial equality will
be accommodated only when it converges with the interest of whites."). For applications of the
interest-convergence hypothesis to the area of voting rights, see DERRICK A. BELL, JR., AND WE ARE
NOT SAVED: THE ELUSIVE QUEST FOR RACIAL JUSTICE 73 (1987); Guinier, *No Two Seats*, *supra* note
48, at 1416-17; Guinier, *supra* note 20, at 1123-24. *See also* Karlan, *supra* note 34, at 41-43 (arguing
that "[a]s long as blacks are a numerical minority within the jurisdiction, the white majority can retain
control" and perpetuate majority predominance in the political process).

128. *See* Hugh D. Graham, *Voting Rights and the American Regulatory State*, in CONTROVERSIES
IN MINORITY VOTING, *supra* note 2, at 177, 188 ("[I]t seems likely in the 1990s that a proliferation
in urban areas of single-member electoral districts, where federal policy requires that boundaries be
drawn to maximize the electoral chances of blacks and Hispanics, would displace white voters into
suburban districts where Republican prospects would brighten."); Carol Matlack, *Questioning Minority-
Aid Software*, 22 NAT'L J. 1540, 1540 (1990) (observing that Republicans "have an interest in
concentrating minority voters in a few districts because the remaining districts will become more
heavily white—and, GOP strategists figure, more likely to vote Republican"); SPEARS, *supra* note 94,
at 6-13 (discussing Republican involvement in recent Voting Rights Act lawsuits).

129. *See* Gregory A. Caldeira, *Litigation, Lobbying, and the Voting Rights Bar*, in
CONTROVERSIES IN MINORITY VOTING, *supra* note 2, at 230, 249 n.50 (reporting that the Republican
National Committee funded the development of a redistricting software package and database to be used
by minority groups).

commentators trace the Department of Justice's insistence during the Reagan and Bush administrations that districting plans seek to maximize the number of minority districts to these partisan concerns.[130] Moreover, Republicans have funded a number of ostensibly minority-generated challenges to plans drawn by Democrats.[131]

On the other side, Democrats, who in fact have relied for roughly a quarter century on black votes to provide the margin of victory for many white Democratic candidates,[132] seek to advance an at least partially governance-driven model of minority voting rights. They argue that minority voters ultimately will benefit more from legislatures in which the overall legislative composition is sympathetic to minority concerns than from polarized legislatures composed of progressive black Democrats and conservative white Republicans.[133]

The clash of these alternative perspectives has been evident in a variety of cases. *Voinovich v. Quilter*,[134] the recent Ohio state legislative apportionment case, provides an illustrative example.[135] The Republican-controlled Apportionment Board developed a plan that created a substantial

---

130. *See, e.g.*, Charles Lane, *Ghetto Chic: New York's Redistricting Mess*, NEW REPUBLIC, Aug. 12, 1991, at 14 (claiming that Justice Department insistence on more minority districts for the New York City Council was part of a Republican strategy); Abigail M. Thernstrom, *A Republican-Civil Rights Conspiracy: Working Together on Legislative Redistricting*, WASH. POST, Sept. 23, 1991, at A11 (describing "the role of the Justice Department in furthering RNC aims" through requiring more safe minority districts).

131. *See* Richard L. Berke, *Strategy Divides Top Republicans*, N.Y. TIMES, May 9, 1991, at A17; Linda Chavez, *Party Lines: The Republicans' Racial Quotas*, NEW REPUBLIC, June 24, 1991, at 14.

132. *See, e.g.*, John W. Mashek, *Southern Democrats Face Dilemma on Thomas Nomination*, BOSTON GLOBE, Aug. 11, 1991, at 16 (noting that five Southern Democratic Senators first elected in 1986 "would never have packed their bags for Washington if they [had not gotten] the overwhelming majority of black votes"). For a more historical discussion of Democratic dependence on black votes, see Edward G. Carmines & Robert Huckfeldt, *Party Politics in the Wake of the Voting Rights Act*, in CONTROVERSIES IN MINORITY VOTING, *supra* note 2, at 117, 125-29.

133. *See, e.g.*, Lane, *supra* note 130, at 14 ("Rather than strengthening minority political power, the system arguably undermines it by confining minority influence to a single, concentrated area. And safe race-based districts, in which candidates need only take account of the interests of their own group, are a potential breeding ground for extremists of all races."). For a more pointed criticism of the limits of the "black electoral success model," in which the election of some "fair" number of black representatives serves as the ultimate aim of the Voting Rights Act, see Guinier, *No Two Seats*, *supra* note 48, at 1447-58 (arguing that increasing the number of black representatives through single-member district voting will not ensure that blacks will have effective representation); Guinier, *supra* note 20, at 1101-34 (concluding that "the black electoral success empowerment model fails to provide a realistic enforcement mechanism for establishing either leadership accountability within the black community or representational effectiveness within the legislative deliberation and coalition-building process"). Notably, unlike the more simplistic Democratic commentators, Guinier does not view the choice as a trade-off between black representation and black influence. Rather, she argues for developing political structures that permit *both* aspects of full participation. In the terms of this Paper, she is arguing for participation plus aggregation plus governance.

134. 113 S. Ct. 1149 (1993), *rev'g* 794 F. Supp. 695 (N.D. Ohio 1992).

135. For a detailed discussion of *Voinovich* and its relationship to theories of vote dilution, see Lichtman & Hebert, *supra* note 33, at 22-24.

number of majority-black districts. The plan's architect claimed that this result was required by the Voting Rights Act and that it enhanced black voting strength.[136] Of course, the plan also promised substantial partisan benefits to the Republican Party. The plan was challenged in federal district court, ostensibly by minority voters claiming that they had been discriminatorily "packed" into a few majority-black districts, thus minimizing their influence on the legislature as a whole.[137] In reality, the minority plaintiffs were Democratic activists, advancing a competing conception of voting rights that would maximize the party's legislative strength. By the time the case arrived at the Supreme Court, the Court was faced with the curious phenomenon of the national voting rights litigators weighing in with a defense of the Republican approach.[138]

The lower court essentially "crosonized"[139] the reapportionment process: It held that race-conscious "safe districting" is permissible only when the failure to draw such districts would itself violate the Voting Rights Act, and that the drawer of the districting plan must justify such districting by building the kind of record that a court faced with a Section 2 challenge would construct.[140] Such an outcome turns the Supreme Court's voting rights jurisprudence on its head; it forces upon the political branches a constrained form of fact-finding, one that was originally adopted precisely to prevent the courts from engaging in the freewheeling choice in which the political branches were *supposed* to engage. And its implicit resolution of the tension between electoral success and post-election legislative influence is no more satisfactory than the partial solution offered by the Supreme Court in *Davis v. Bandemer*.[141]

---

136. *See Voinovich*, 113 S. Ct. at 1153.

137. *See id*. As the lower court noted, plaintiffs sought to show that representatives who were responsive to the minority community, measured in terms of their voting records on "bills related to minority issues," had been elected from districts that were roughly one-third to one-half black. *Voinovich*, 794 F. Supp. at 698.

138. *See* Brief Amici Curiae in Support of Appellees of the NAACP Legal Defense and Educational Fund, Inc., the Mexican American Legal Defense and Educational Fund, Inc., the National Asian Pacific American Legal Consortium, the Lawyers' Committee for Civil Rights Under Law, and the Puerto Rican Legal Defense and Education Fund, Inc., at 4.5, 14.16, Voinovich v. Quilter, 113 S. Ct. 1149 (1993) (No. 91-1618). Although the *amici* supported the Republican approach of drawing majority-minority districts, they argued in favor of affirmance of the district court's invalidation of the plan on the independent ground that the population deviations among districts were not sufficiently justified. *See Voinovich*, 113 S. Ct. at 1159-60 (remanding the case for a determination of whether the population deviations among districts were justifiable).

139. In City of Richmond v. J.A. Croson Co., 488 U.S. 469 (1989), the Supreme Court struck down a minority set-aside program adopted by Richmond, Virginia, in part because the city had not established with sufficient specificity the factual predicates for race-conscious affirmative action, and without such a finding, race-conscious policies could not be justified. *See id*. at 498-500.

140. *See Voinovich*, 794 F. Supp. at 696, 700-01 (concluding that findings based on data that were not subjected to statistical analysis, or even memorialized, constituted "such a casual analysis of voting returns" that it did not "rise to the level of proof of racially polarized voting").

141. 478 U.S. 109 (1986); *see supra* text accompanying notes 43-47.

Justice O'Connor's unanimous opinion for the *Voinovich* Court rejected the lower court's crosonization.[142]   And it implicitly recognized the potential tension between claims for influence districts and claims for safe seats,[143] wisely concluding that the effect of the choice between the two approaches will depend "entirely on the facts and circumstances of each case."[144] In light of the fact that "Ohio does not suffer from 'racially polarized voting,'"[145] the Court basically consigned to the political process the choice whether to draw safe or influence districts.[146] Although the Court disposed of this point in a short paragraph, the underlying rationale for this approach must rest on the notion that absent legally significant racial bloc voting, the decision how to distribute black voters among districts is no different from decisions about how to distribute any other group of voters; the regular give-and-take of politics will enable them to advance their interests effectively.[147]

But the same Court that willingly relegated the claims of *black* voters—the classic beneficiaries of the Fourteenth and Fifteenth Amendments, as well as the Voting Rights Act—to the regular political process soon showed itself distressingly eager to intervene on behalf of *white* voters who did not like the results of that same process. In *Shaw v. Reno*,[148] the Court resuscitated a lawsuit by five voters in North Carolina who opposed the state legislature's deliberate creation of two majority-black congressional districts. The *Shaw* lawsuit was indeed, as the Court noted, "analytically distinct" from the sorts of claims the courts had entertained in the past.[149] Unlike the plaintiffs in the participation cases, the *Shaw*

---

142. *See Voinovich*, 113 S. Ct. at 1156 (noting that "surely Congress could not have intended the State to prove the invalidity of its own [preexisting] apportionment scheme," and thus holding that "requiring [the State] to justify the creation of majority-minority districts" before plaintiffs have shown a § 2 violation "depart[s] from the statutorily required allocation of burdens"). Later in the Term, however, Justice O'Connor's opinion in Shaw v. Reno, 113 S. Ct. 2816 (1993), raised the specter that although § 2 does not require "crosonization" to justify the deliberate creation of majority-black districts, the *Constitution* might. *See id.* at 2830-31. The relationship between *Shaw*'s constitutional cause of action and § 2 is too tangled to be fully explored in this Paper. I plan to offer a more extensive analysis in Pamela S. Karlan, *All Over the Map: The Supreme Court's Voting Rights Trilogy*, 1993 SUP. CT. REV. (forthcoming).

143. *See Voinovich*, 113 S. Ct. at 1155-56.

144. *Id.* at 1156.

145. *Id.* at 1158 (quoting Quilter v. Voinovich, 794 F. Supp. at 700-01). In Thornburg v. Gingles, 478 U.S. 30 (1986), the Supreme Court held that proof that "the white majority votes sufficiently as a bloc to enable it . . . usually to defeat the minority's preferred candidate" was one of three essential preconditions of a § 2 lawsuit. *Id.* at 51.

146. For a more detailed analysis of the significance of racial bloc voting to analysis of the Ohio plan, see Lichtman & Hebert, *supra* note 33, at 22-24.

147. I return briefly to this point in the final Part of this Paper. I intend to offer a fuller elaboration in a later paper, tentatively titled *Political Deference and the Voting Rights Act*.

148. 113 S. Ct. 2816 (1993).

149. *Id.* at 2830.

plaintiffs were all able to vote "without hindrance."[150] Unlike the plaintiffs in the aggregation cases, the *Shaw* plaintiffs did not claim they were unable to elect the candidates of their choice.[151] Nor, of course, was the *Shaw* complaint cast as a governance claim: nothing in the record before the Court suggested that the *Shaw* plaintiffs were excluded from equal participation in the state's decisionmaking process.

In light of the Court's general hostility to constitutional voting claims that do not depend on easy-to-apply mathematical standards,[152] *Shaw* represents a puzzle, for it demands that lower courts address a host of nebulous questions: When is a district's shape so "bizarre" or "extremely irregular on its face"[153] that it can rationally be viewed only as a device to segregate voters on account of race? What *are* "traditional districting principles" in a nation of pervasive partisan gerrymandering, and how much deviation is too much?[154] What sorts of justifications permit what sort of race-consciousness in a process that the Court concedes can never truly be "color blind," since the "legislature always is *aware* of race when it draws district lines"?[155] These questions threaten to enmesh the judiciary in precisely the political theory quagmire that thirty years of the Court's constitutional case law seemed intended to avoid.[156]

III. Beyond Judicial Control of Politics and Political Control of Judges: Beginning to Rethink Voting Rights

One of the striking features of the papers and comments in the *Texas Law Review* symposium[157] is an emerging sense that courts often serve as an obstacle, rather than the solution, to problems of minority political empowerment. In part, this perception results from the politicization of the federal judiciary, which threatens to saddle us with conservative activists in the federal courthouse even as the Voting Rights Act produces more diverse, representative, and progressive local, state, and federal legislators[158] and state court judges.[159] In part, it is a function of judicial

---

150. This terminology was used by the Court in City of Mobile v. Bolden, 446 U.S. 55, 65, 64-65 (1980) (plurality opinion).

151. *Shaw*, 113 S. Ct. at 2824. Indeed, three of the five plaintiffs were not even residents of the challenged district. *See id.* at 2821. And the Supreme Court had already summarily affirmed the dismissal of a political dilution attack on the North Carolina plan. Pope v. Blue, 113 S. Ct. 30 (1992).

152. *See supra* text accompanying notes 5 and 40-46.

153. *Shaw*, 113 S. Ct. at 2825.

154. *Id.* at 2824.

155. *Id.* at 2826 (emphasis in original).

156. For a more complete analysis of *Voinovich, Growe,* and *Shaw,* see Karlan, *supra* note 142.

157. Symposium, *Regulating the Electoral Process,* 71 TEX. L. REV. 1409 (1993).

158. *See* Lani Guinier, *Lines in the Sand,* 72 TEX. L. REV. (forthcoming 1994) (reviewing CHARLES FRIED, ORDER AND LAW: ARGUING THE REAGAN REVOLUTION: A FIRST-HAND ACCOUNT (1991)).

159. The first Voting Rights Act lawsuits challenging the methods of electing state court judges

reluctance to address claims of political exclusion that do not have neat, mathematical solutions.[160] If anything, the Court's decision in *Shaw v. Reno* can only strengthen this sentiment.

Whatever the cause, the solution must start from the realization that the cure for (judicial) politics is more (legislative) politics. That is a lesson the past three decades should already have taught us. For all the Supreme Court's protection of minority voting rights from *Nixon v. Herndon*[161] through *Louisiana v. United States*,[162] it was not until Congress empowered the federal executive branch to register voters and to use Section 5 to block new disenfranchising and dilutive tactics that blacks were effectively enfranchised.[163] Moreover, minority citizens obtained from Congress what they could not acquire from the Supreme Court: the recognition of a results standard, rather than a purpose test, for assessing claims of racial vote dilution.[164] Enforcement of Section 2, therefore, should not be viewed as an undemocratic judicial intrusion into the political process. Rather, Section 2 reflects the views of the "national political culture" in which minorities have begun to exercise some real influence.[165] Much

---

judicial elections until 1991. *See* Chisom v. Roemer, 111 S. Ct. 2354, 2368 (1991); Houston Lawyers' Ass'n v. Attorney Gen., 111 S. Ct. 2376, 2380 (1991). Between 1990 and 1991, the number of black elected state-court judges increased by 10%. *See* JOINT CTR. FOR POLITICAL AND ECONOMIC STUDIES, BLACK ELECTED OFFICIALS: A NATIONAL ROSTER, 1991, at xv (1992).

160. *See supra* notes 85-91 and accompanying text. The fact that federal courts may be unwilling to develop and implement a more capacious understanding of voting rights should not, however, bar either legislators or state-court judges from acting on such a theory. *See* Lawrence G. Sager, *Fair Measure: The Legal Status of Underenforced Constitutional Norms*, 91 HARV. L. REV. 1212, 1221-26 (1978) (arguing that when the lack of judicially manageable standards keeps federal judges from enforcing a constitutional value, nonfederal judicial officials remain empowered to enforce the value).

161. 273 U.S. 536 (1927). I count *Nixon*, which declared unconstitutional under the Fourteenth Amendment a Texas statute providing that "in no event shall a negro be eligible to participate in a Democratic party primary election," *see id.* at 540-41, as marking the beginning of modern *judicial* solicitude for the right to vote. In an earlier case, *Guinn v. United States*, the Court had invalidated the Oklahoma grandfather clause in the context of a federally initiated civil-rights prosecution of Oklahoma election officials, but I suspect that, were it not for the involvement of the United States, the case could have been decided the other way. *Compare* Guinn v. United States, 238 U.S. 347 (1915) *with* Giles v. Harris, 189 U.S. 475, 486-88 (1903) (refusing to entertain a challenge brought by black voters against a similarly crafted Alabama disenfranchisement policy).

162. 380 U.S. 145, 156 (1965) (striking down Louisiana literacy, character, and understanding tests as purposefully discriminatory).

163. *See* Davidson, *supra* note 2, at 21-22 (noting that in the five years after passage of the Act, almost as many blacks registered to vote in Alabama, Georgia, Louisiana, North Carolina, and South Carolina as in the entire century before 1965).

164. As Jim Blacksher has often noted, the 1982 amendments and extensions of the Voting Rights Act are themselves a powerful illustration of the political strength of even an only partially empowered minority community: Without the increased political effectiveness of black voters in the period from 1965 to 1980, there would have been far less support in Congress for further expansion of statutory protections. *Cf.* Kousser, *supra* note 60, at 151 (noting a correlation between expansion of the franchise during the second Reconstruction and greater support by Southern members of Congress for voting rights legislation).

165. *See* Karlan, *supra* note 34, at 13, 13-14 (arguing that judicial oversight under the Voting Rights Act does not present countermajoritarian conflicts and that any such argument is merely an effort

of that influence has come from the presence of black elected officials with votes to trade within the halls of Congress, and it is important to remember that they usually owe the creation of their districts not to the courts directly, but to the exercise of pressure that Congress vested in the executive branch through creation of the preclearance requirement[166] and to the horse trading of black legislative caucuses within state legislatures.

Seen in this light, *Presley v. Etowah County Commission*[167] takes on a very different cast. The Supreme Court was not being asked for a dramatic judicial expansion of the scope of Section 5. Rather, it was being asked to enforce the executive branch's understanding of the power confided in it by Congress. The Civil Rights Division of the Department of Justice, headed by an experienced politician,[168] recognized that the Common Fund and Road Supervision Resolutions[169] were attempts to perpetuate indirectly what had been openly achieved by disenfranchisement and dilution from the turn of the century through 1986: the exclusion of Etowah County's black citizens from county governance. Thus, *Presley* drives home the aridity of a view of voting rights that stops short of grappling with the reality of the black political experience in America. Only by essentially ignoring the county's multifarious strategy for disempowering its black inhabitants could the Court treat the challenged resolutions as disconnected from voting rights. Similarly, *Shaw v. Reno*'s invocation of this nation's tragic history of political exclusion of black Americans as a justification for perhaps unseating the first black Representatives elected from North Carolina in this century,[170] and its use of such terms as "deliberate segregation,"[171] "apartheid"[172] and "balkaniz[ation]"[173] reflects a court that in T.S. Eliot's famous phrase, "had the experience but missed the meaning."[174]

---

to "dress up a discredited federalism concern in majoritarian clothing"); *see also* RONALD DWORKIN, LAW'S EMPIRE 377 (1986) (discussing the constitutional fairness of subjugating local majorities to the national political culture).

166. Of course, administrative preclearance takes place in the shadow of the courts, given that the scope of the preclearance requirement is judicially interpreted, and that jurisdictions retain the possibility of obtaining judicial preclearance even if administrative preclearance is denied. *See* 42 U.S.C. § 1973c (1988). But the judicial process is so costly, time-consuming, and at least influenced by administrative construction of the statutory standard that jurisdictions often find it more practical simply to modify their plans to obtain Department of Justice approval.

167. 112 S. Ct. 820 (1992); *see supra* notes 80-87 and accompanying text (discussing the facts and holding of *Presley*).

168. John Dunne, then the Assistant Attorney General in charge of the Division. was a former state legislator from New York. *See* OFFICE OF THE FED. REGISTER, NAT'L ARCHIVES AND RECORDS ADMIN., THE UNITED STATES GOVERNMENT MANUAL 1992/1993, at 371 (1992).

169. *See Presley*, 112 S. Ct. at 825-26.

170. *See* Shaw v. Reno, 113 S. Ct. 2816, 2843 (1993) (Blackmun, J., dissenting).

171. *Id.* at 2824 (majority opinion).

172. *Id.* at 2827.

173. *Id.* at 2832.

The core problem that voting rights theory and case law must face today is the persistence of permanent racial faction. Avoiding the threats factionalism poses was a central animating principle in designing the American political system.[175] The Founders did a pretty good job of devising institutional arrangements to "break and control the violence of [economic and regional] faction."[176] But nothing in those institutional arrangements has effectively restrained "the superior force of an interested and over-bearing [white] majority"[177] from ignoring the interests of racial minorities and their claims to equal respect and treatment in the governance process. In Etowah County and many other parts of the country, blacks and whites have remained two distinct and permanent factions.

The central task of modern voting rights law must be to control the effects of this polarization. Thus, any theory of voting rights must ultimately encompass what Ronald Dworkin has called a "dependent conception" of democracy: an arrangement of political rights that yields "results that treat all members of the community with equal concern,"[178] rather than relegating a discrete group to a position of permanent marginalization. As long as the theoretically equal votes of black citizens can be overwhelmed by the votes of antagonistic white voters in racially polarized elections, or the theoretically significant votes of elected officials chosen by black voters can be ignored in the determination of governmental policy, blacks have not achieved the *political* equality that the Voting Rights Act promised.[179]

The remedies for the political subordination of minorities must be as multifaceted as the schemes that have disenfranchised them. They must be responsive to the political realities of individual jurisdictions. Unlike the one-person, one-vote, or *Gingles*-based Section 2 lawsuits that transformed the political landscape in a relatively wholesale fashion, the next round of remedies for minority political exclusion will have to be constructed at the retail level. And the central task will be to develop remedies that can break apart the monolithic majority bloc in order to put minorities, and the officials who represent them, in a position where their votes mean something because they can be used to construct winning electoral and governing coalitions.

---

175. *See* THE FEDERALIST NO. 10, at 77-84 (James Madison) (Clinton Rossiter ed., 1961); THE FEDERALIST NO. 51, *supra*, at 325 (James Madison).

176. THE FEDERALIST NO. 10, *supra* note 175, at 77.

177. *Id.*

178. Dworkin, *supra* note 20, at 3, 4.

179. *See* BEITZ, *supra* note 21, at 134-35 (contrasting the idea of *electoral* success—managing to achieve the election of one's preferred candidate—with the idea of *political* success—"seeing [one's] policy preferences satisfied").

PAMELA S. KARLAN

ALL OVER THE MAP:
THE SUPREME COURT'S
VOTING RIGHTS TRILOGY

So quick bright things come to confusion. Midway through the 1992 Term, the Supreme Court issued two unanimous decisions that clarified the role of federal courts in the decennial redistricting process. *Growe v Emison*[1] and *Voinovich v Quilter*[2] reflected the maturation of the voting rights system the Court had begun to construct three decades before with *Gomillion v Lightfoot*,[3] *Reynolds v Sims*,[4] and *Harper v Virginia Board of Elections*.[5] *Growe* and *Voinovich* recognized that state governments were largely capable of implementing the quantitative and qualitative constraints imposed by the Fourteenth Amendment and the Voting Rights Act and that minority citizens were now effectively integrated into the political process, at least in some jurisdictions.

Pamela S. Karlan is Professor of Law, University of Virginia.

AUTHOR's NOTE: I thank Chris Eisgruber, Lani Guinier, Sam Issacharoff, Mike Klarman, Eben Moglen, Rick Pildes, Mark Rush, and Larry Sager for many thoughtful comments. I also received many helpful suggestions from participants in a roundtable sponsored by the American Political Science Association, the NYU Constitutional Theory Colloquium, and the Georgetown Constitutional Law Discussion Group. In the interest of full disclosure, I note that I served as counsel for amici curiae in *Voinovich v Quilter*, 113 S Ct 1149 (1993), and as counsel for one of the parties in several cases cited in the footnotes.

[1] 113 S Ct 1075 (1993).
[2] 113 S Ct 1149 (1993).
[3] 364 US 339 (1960).
[4] 377 US 533 (1964).
[5] 383 US 663 (1966).

But on the last day of the Term, in *Shaw v Reno*,[6] the Court plunged itself and the lower federal courts into a previously unexplored and particularly tangled precinct of the "political thicket." *Shaw* identified a new, "analytically distinct,"[7] constitutional cause of action: a reapportionment plan violates the Equal Protection Clause if, "though race-neutral on its face, [it] rationally cannot be understood as anything other than an effort to separate voters into different districts on the basis of race, and . . . the separation lacks sufficient justification."[8] But although the Court scattered its opinion with voting rights rhetoric, *Shaw* turns out not really to be a case about the right to vote, at least not the right the Court had identified in its earlier decisions. Rather, *Shaw* forms an integral piece of an ongoing struggle between the Supreme Court and the political branches over how to address the enduring problems of race in America.

The 1960s, 1970s, and 1980s together worked what has been called the "reapportionment revolution."[9] The revolution began with the declaration of a constitutional command to reapportion and with a set of quantitative constraints on permissible districting schemes. Soon, the Court and Congress turned their attention to the qualitative dimension of reapportionment, ultimately requiring that apportionments fairly respect the voting strength of identifiable racial and political groups. But as Robert Frost once remarked, "[T]he trouble with a total revolution . . . [i]s that it brings the same class up on top."[10] In this sense, *Shaw v Reno* may well be signaling the completion (or perhaps the abandonment) of the ongoing reapportionment revolution that has engaged the Court for the past thirty years.[11]

---

[6] 113 S Ct 2816 (1993).

[7] Id at 2830.

[8] Id at 2828.

[9] See generally Gordon E. Baker, *The Reapportionment Revolution: Representation, Political Power, and the Supreme Court* (Random House, 1966); Gordon E. Baker, *Whatever Happened to the U.S. Reapportionment Revolution?* in Bernard Grofman and Arend Lijphart, eds, *Electoral Laws and Their Political Consequences* (Agathon, 1986); Gordon E. Baker, *The Unfinished Reapportionment Revolution*, in Bernard Grofman, ed, *Political Gerrymandering and the Courts* 11 (Agathon, 1990).

[10] Robert Frost, *A Semi-Revolution*, in Edward Connery Lathem, ed, *The Poetry of Robert Frost* 363 (Holt, Rinehart & Winston, 1969).

[11] For one particularly neat example, compare *Reynolds*, 377 US at 562, 580 ("Legislators represent people, not trees or acres. . . . [P]eople, not land or trees or pastures, vote.") with *Shaw*, 113 S Ct at 2826 ("A reapportionment statute typically does not classify persons at all; it classifies tracts of land, or addresses.").

The 1993 voting rights trilogy raises fundamental questions about the American voting rights system. Part I of this essay sets out a framework for thinking about these questions. First, what does "the 'right' to vote" mean?[12] Despite Justice O'Connor's use of the singular person in *Shaw*, the right actually embodies a constellation of concepts: participation—the entitlement of individuals to cast ballots and have those ballots counted; aggregation—the choice among rules for tallying individual votes to determine election outcomes; and governance—the structure in which representative decision making takes place.[13] Reapportionment questions occupy a precarious position on the border between aggregation and governance.

Second, how should control over the voting rights system be allocated among various state and federal actors?[14] This question has both a vertical and a horizontal dimension. The former concerns the relationship between different levels of government, namely, federal and state. The latter concerns the relationship among different branches of government. It asks to what extent the judiciary may revise the choices reached by other branches, as well as to what extent the judiciary can intervene to resolve conflicts among other branches.

Using this framework, Part II examines *Growe* and *Voinovich*. These cases confronted the Court with a central failure of the existing system: its generation of pervasive, redundant, partisan litigation. The Court responded by adjusting the relationship among reapportionment institutions and by clarifying the prerequisites for federal intervention. *Growe*'s requirement that federal courts defer to state judicial proceedings serves two functions: it clearly establishes state courts as the primary judicial police of reapportionment and, by treating state courts as an integral part of an opaque state political process, manages to avoid federal involvement in state interbranch conflicts. And *Growe* and *Voinovich* together limited intervention under the Voting Rights Act to situations characterized by racial bloc voting and the ensuing process failure, thus providing a firm doctrinal basis for displacing the political process.

---

[12] *Shaw*, 113 S Ct at 2819.

[13] See Pamela S. Karlan, *The Rights to Vote: Some Pessimism About Formalism*, 71 Tex L Rev 1705, 1708 (1993).

[14] Compare Essay, *Voting Rights and the Role of the Federal Government: The Rehnquist Court's Mixed Messages on Minority Vote Dilution Cases*, 27 USF L Rev 627, 628 (1993) (drawing a distinction between the court's "right" cases and its "role" cases).

Shaw takes a diametrically opposite position, and in Part III, I focus on this turnabout. *Shaw* abandons the Court's previous circumspection about involving itself in questions of governance. The plaintiffs who challenged North Carolina's congressional districting raised neither participation nor aggregation claims. Instead, they raised what can best be described as a meta-governance claim. In order to address this claim, the Court turned its back on the entire fabric of standing law. The Court then proceeded to upset well-settled doctrines in equal protection law as well. Perhaps just as significant, *Shaw* may herald a new response to questions of how power over the voting rights system ought to be allocated among the branches of the federal government. Indeed, *Shaw*'s odd analytic path may represent the opening volley in a judicial attempt to control national, political resolution of the problem of minority exclusion.

I. The Voting Rights System

The current voting rights system is the product of three decades of judicial and congressional revision of the principles governing voting rights and the allocation of political power. This revision has proceeded antiphonally, as reconceptions of the meaning of the right precipitated more extensive federal involvement in state redistricting activity and the prospect of even greater federal involvement began to shape the contours of the right.

A. THREE RIGHTS TO VOTE

The "right" to vote actually embraces the separate, yet complementary, interests in participation, aggregation, and governance.[15] First, individual citizens have an interest in taking part in the formal electoral process by casting a ballot that gets counted. This ability to participate serves both a symbolic and an instrumental function. The symbolic function is to proclaim an individual's full membership in the political community. This aspect of voting, at least with regard to the core electorate—adult resident citizens—was firmly established as a fundamental individual right early

---

[15] This taxonomy is developed at greater length in Karlan, 71 Tex L Rev at 1709–20 (cited in note 13).

on.[16] The individualistic focus has an important corollary: outcome-independence. In determining whether an individual is entitled to participate, the Court has avoided asking what effect her participation might have on electoral results.[17]

But as soon as we move beyond this largely symbolic purpose, voting loses its purely individual character.[18] The instrumental purpose of voting—having one's preferences taken into account in choosing public officials—necessarily involves aggregating the votes of individuals to achieve a collective outcome. There are many ways to aggregate votes; an individual will of course prefer the electoral system most likely to result in the satisfaction of her preferences. Perhaps the most pervasive set of aggregation rules in American politics concerns the geographical allocation of voters among electoral jurisdictions. The way in which districts are drawn often determines which voters will be able to elect their preferred candidates and which voters will have their preferences go unsatisfied.

There are basically three ways in which geographic aggregation rules might impair a voter's ability to elect her preferred candidate—the euphonious trio of cracking, stacking, and packing.[19]

---

[16] Thus, restrictions on the franchise are subject to strict scrutiny. See, for example, *Dunn v Blumstein*, 405 US 330, 337 (1972); *Kramer v Union Free School Dist. No. 15*, 395 US 621, 626-28 (1969); *Harper v Virginia State Bd of Elections*, 383 US 663, 670 (1966). At least with respect to black voters, however, it was Congress' authorization of federal voting rights examiners, and not the Supreme Court's formal pronouncements about the centrality of the right to participate, that provided an effective right to participate. See Chandler Davidson, *The Voting Rights Act: A Brief History*, in Bernard Grofman and Chandler Davidson, eds, *Controversies in Minority Voting: The Voting Rights Act in Perspective* 7, 21-22 (Brookings Institution, 1992) (federal registrars registered more black voters in the South in the five years following passage of the Voting Rights Act than had been registered in the entire preceding century).

Although the formal entitlement to participation is well established, there remain significant barriers to full participation. The most pervasive of these are various registration requirements. See Frances Fox Piven and Richard A. Cloward, *Why Americans Don't Vote*, 178-80 (Pantheon, 1988). The desirability of removing the obstacle posed by these sorts of requirements has been a source of substantial controversy, as the tortured history of the so-called "Motor Voter" bill, which contains a variety of nearly automatic registration provisions, suggests. See Michael Wines, *Accord Reached on Easing Voter Registration*, NY Times (Apr 29, 1993), at A-16.

[17] See Karlan, 71 Tex L Rev at 1710 (cited in note 13).

[18] See id at 1713. In fact, Alex Aleinikoff and Sam Issacharoff go further in a recent article to argue that "an individual-rights based view" has very little relevance at all to voting rights issues since the very essence of voting in a democratic system is its group-oriented character. See T. Alexander Aleinikoff and Samuel Issacharoff, *Race and Redistricting: Drawing Constitutional Lines After Shaw v Reno*, 92 Mich L Rev 588, 600-601 (1993).

[19] For a more detailed account of these dilutive practices, see Frank R. Parker, *Racial Gerrymandering and Legislative Reapportionment*, in Chandler Davidson, ed, *Minority Vote Dilution* 85, 89-99 (Howard Univ Press, 1984).

267

Cracking occurs when a political group is split between two or more districts, in each of which it forms an ineffective minority. Stacking occurs when a group that would be large enough to form an effective majority in a district is placed within a multimember district in which hostile opponents constitute the majority and control election to all the available positions. Finally, packing occurs when a distinctive group is overconcentrated into a few districts; its opponents concede victory in those districts but leave group members in surrounding districts politically impotent.

The two major legal constraints on aggregation rules are the Fourteenth Amendment and the Voting Rights Act of 1965.[20] Unlike participation claims, which are subject to strict scrutiny under the fundamental rights strand of equal protection doctrine, constitutional aggregation claims are subject to strict scrutiny only when the plaintiffs can show both a discriminatory intent and a discriminatory effect.[21] In political gerrymandering cases, intent is essentially presumed, but the requisite effect—"consisten[t] degrad[ation of] a voter's or group of voters' influence on the political process as a whole"[22]—is in practice impossible to prove. By contrast, in racial vote dilution cases, the requirement that plaintiffs prove a racially discriminatory purpose often proves an insuperable obstacle even when minority voters have consistently been unable to elect their preferred candidates.[23]

Originally, the liability standard under the Voting Rights Act dovetailed with the constitutional standard. But in 1982 the Act was amended to eliminate the requirement that plaintiffs show a discriminatory purpose; proof of a dilutive effect is enough.[24] This

---

[20] There are two relevant substantive provisions of the Act. Section 2, which applies nationwide, forbids any state or political subdivision from using a voting procedure that results in minority voters having "less opportunity that other members of the electorate to participate in the political process and to elect representatives of their choice." 42 USC § 1973(b) (1988). Section 5, which applies only to specified jurisdictions with a history of depressed political participation (largely the Deep South, Southwest, and parts of New York City), requires jurisdictions to obtain federal approval, either from the Attorney General or the federal district court in Washington, D.C., before making any change in their existing election laws. To obtain such approval, they must convince the federal authorities that the proposed change will have neither the purpose nor the effect of diluting minority voting strength. See 42 USC § 1973c (1988)

[21] See City of Mobile v Bolden, 446 US 55, 112–14 (1980) (Marshall dissenting) (criticizing the court's failure to accord strict scrutiny).

[22] Davis v Bandemer, 478 US 109, 132 (1986) (plurality opinion).

[23] See Karlan, 71 Tex L Rev at 1715–16 (cited in note 13).

[24] The purpose behind the 1982 amendments is set out in Voting Rights Act Extension, Sen Rep No 97-417, 97th Cong, 2d Sess 15-30 (1982) ("Senate Report").

shift has had two effects. First, plaintiffs in racial vote dilution cases now normally seek relief under the more favorable statutory standard, rather than the constitutional one. Second, the relatively favorable treatment accorded racial vote dilution claims creates an incentive for partisan groups either to recast their claims to fall under the Voting Rights Act or to use plaintiffs protected by the Act as stalking horses.[25]

Even aggregation, however, serves only as a midpoint in the political process. Voters elect representatives with an eye toward having those representatives participate in official decision making.[26] Voting is a means for derivatively taking part [post-election] *governance*. The extent to which a voter's policy preferences will be satisfied often depends as much on the overall composition of an elected body as well as on her direct election of a single representative to that body. Thus, although voters choose among candidates who then constitute elected bodies, rather than choosing among alternative elected bodies directly, a voter's preferences about the overall complexion of the assembly can be as important as her preference among candidates running from her district.[27]

Despite the individualistic, participation-oriented rhetoric, the slogan "one-person, one-vote" in fact reflects a concern with governance.[28] Plaintiffs in quantitative malapportionment cases do not invoke the participatory strand of the right to vote: they are not claiming that they are disenfranchised or that their ballots are ignored. Nor, in fact, are they really claiming that their aggregation interests have been impaired: they are not claiming that the candidates they support are being defeated at the polls. Their real complaint is that their voice is diluted at the post-election process of official decision making. Similarly, packing claims may ultimately be as much about governance as aggregation: after all, the group members who are packed into the conceded districts are able to

---

[25] See Karlan, 71 Tex L Rev 1732 (cited in note 13).

[26] See *Reynolds*, 377 US at 565 ("[R]epresentative government is in essence self-government through the medium of elected representatives of the people, and each and every citizen has an inalienable right to full and effective participation in the political processes of his State's legislative bodies. Most citizens can achieve this participation only as qualified voters through the election of legislators to represent them.").

[27] See Jean-Pierre Benoit and Lewis A. Kornhauser, *Voting Simply in the Election of Assemblies* 27 (1991) (C. V. Starr Center for Applied Economics Working Paper); Pamela S. Karlan, *Maps and Misreadings: The Role of Geographic Compactness in Racial Vote Dilution Litigation*, 24 Harv CR-CL L Rev 173, 235–48 (1989).

[28] See Karlan, 71 Tex L Rev at 1717–18 (cited in note 13).

elect the candidate they prefer; only the group members left out of the packed district have a pure aggregation claim.[29]

⌐ The Court's entertainment of malapportionment and packing claims illustrates its willingness to consider governance interests if they can be achieved through the development of a rule about aggregation. But in general, the Court's voting rights cases have been quite reluctant to address questions of governance. In *Presley v Etowah County Commission*,[30] for example, the Court recognized that "in a real sense every decision taken by government implicates voting,"[31] but drew an explicit line between "voting" and "governance,"[32] holding that the Voting Rights Act provides no authorization for federal judicial intervention in post-electoral allocations of voting power. The background assumption seems to be that post-election judicial supervision is somehow too intrusive on self-government.

The process of decennial reapportionment lies on the boundary between aggregation and governance. How and where district lines are drawn will powerfully affect both which voters are able to elect the candidates of their choice (an aggregation interest) and the likelihood that those candidates will be members of elective bodies friendly to the group's legislative agenda (a governance interest). Ideally, a group will be able to achieve both goals simultaneously. For example, black voters might favor a plan that both creates majority-black districts in the urban areas where they live and draws districts in overwhelmingly white suburban and rural areas to favor the election of candidates likely to be sympathetic to black citizens' concerns. But aggregation and governance interests do not always point toward the same plan. A plan that maximizes the number of representatives a group directly elects could produce a generally unfriendly legislature. For example, the creation of majority-black districts may enable black voters to elect some rep-

---

[29] The fact that "packing" claims are often litigated by a class of minority plaintiffs some of whom live inside and some of whom live outside the packed district shows as much; if aggregation were the sole basis for such claims, presumably the voters who have been packed into the district would have no standing to sue, since they cannot claim that *their* ability to elect their preferred candidate has been impaired. Indeed, it has if anything been enhanced. The gravamen of their complaint is that their votes could be more influential elsewhere, where they might provide the margin of victory to a candidate who will otherwise lose.

[30] 112 S Ct 820 (1992).

[31] Id at 829.

[32] Id at 832.

resentatives to an assembly but may result in the election of hostile
delegates from the remaining, majority-white districts; if the black
community's representatives are consistently outvoted within the
legislature, the black community may have achieved its aggregation
interest at the expense of a real role in governance.[33] Thus, apportionment poses fundamental "choices about the nature of representation"[34] and the right to vote.

B. TWO ISSUES OF CONTROL

The problem of who is to control these fundamental choices
has vexed the contemporary voting rights system since the very
beginning. The Court's initial answer, in *Colegrove v Green*,[35] was
to consign these issues entirely to nonjudicial actors—the state
legislatures and, in the face of their default, Congress. Federal
courts, Justice Frankfurter declared, "ought not to enter this political thicket."[36]

The Court's initial foray into the redistricting arena—the proclamation of one-person, one-vote in *Wesberry v Sanders*[37] and *Reynolds
v Sims*[38]—attempted to respond to this danger by enunciating a
straightforward quantitative rule that could be easily understood
and applied. But the rule had the perverse effect of actually guaranteeing repeated visits to the "thicket." The requirement of decennial reapportionment meant the political system's answers to questions of how to allocate political power were necessarily subject to
decennial reconsideration and attack.[39]

The thicket metaphor obscures as much as it reveals, for the
Court's continued disclaimers that *this* judicial intervention would
not plant the Court within the dread "political thicket" suggested
the existence of neutral, apolitical standards for allocating political

[33] Some commentators have argued that interpretations of the Voting Rights Act that compel the creation of majority-black districts have had exactly this effect. See Abigail M. Thernstrom, *Whose Votes Count? Affirmative Action and Minority Voting Rights* 242–44 (Harv U Press, 1987); Carol Matlack, *Questioning Minority-Aid Software*, 22 Natl J 1540, 1540 (1990).

[34] *Burns v Richardson*, 384 US 73, 92 (1966).

[35] 328 US 549 (1946).

[36] Id at 556.

[37] 376 US 1 (1963).

[38] 377 US 533 (1964).

[39] See Karlan, 71 Tex L Rev at 1705 (cited in note 13).

power. But no such standards exist. Every rule has identifiable aggregative and governance consequences; every rule benefits some groups and disadvantages others. A judicial decision *not* to adjudicate voting rights claims will have distinctive political consequences, since it effectively freezes into place the resolution obtained by a particular political faction.[40] The real question is not whether federal courts ought to enter the thicket but how they should treat the handiwork of the other denizens they discover there.

~~While~~ announcing broad principles—such as the requirement of equipopulous districting or the prohibition of intentional political or racial vote dilution—the Court has sought to delegate the responsibility for putting those principles into effect to actors it views as more appropriately "political." The Court's first line of response has been to stress the primacy of state institutions in deciding apportionment issues. Originally, the Court treated its justiciability decision in *Baker v Carr*[41] and its announcement of one-person, one-vote in *Wesberry* and *Reynolds* as simply devices for triggering pre-existing state reapportionment mechanisms. The Court backed up this commitment by requiring that states be given an additional opportunity for self-apportionment even in the face of a voting rights violation.[42] Only when the state process fails completely ought federal courts step in and do the reapportionment themselves.

The Court's second line of response has been to recognize a prominent role for Congress and the executive branch in policing the voting rights system. *South Carolina v Katzenbach,*[43] *Katzenbach*

---

[40] This seems to have been Justice Clark's point in his concurrence in *Baker v Carr,* 369 US 186, 259 (1962) (noting that because of Tennessee's sixty-year failure to reapportion, "[t]he majority of the voters have been caught up in a legislative strait jacket . . . the legislative policy has riveted the present seats in the Assembly to their respective constituencies, and by the votes of their incumbents a reapportionment of any kind is prevented.").

[41] 369 US 186 (1962).

[42] See *Wise v Lipscomb,* 437 US 535, 540 (1978); *Chapman v Meier,* 420 US 1, 27 (1975). See also *Tallahassee Branch NAACP v Leon County,* 827 F2d 1436, 1438 (11th Cir 1987), cert denied, 488 US 960 (1988). As Sam Issacharoff once noted, there is something more than a little ironic about deferring to the political branches' views in vote dilution cases since "the vindication of voting rights can hardly be trusted to the very representatives whose election is the result of the alleged vote dilution." Note, *Making the Violation Fit the Remedy: The Intent Standard and Equal Protection Law,* 92 Yale L J 328, 346 (1982). This point is of course less true in contemporary cases involving quantitative malapportionment: presumably the legislature's composition was constitutional at the time it was last redistricted.

[43] 383 US 301 (1966) (upholding federal voter registration, suspension of literacy tests, and imposition of preclearance on specified jurisdictions with a history of minority disenfranchisement).

v Morgan,[44] *Oregon v Mitchell,*[45] and *Thornburg v Gingles*[46] approved
a system for safeguarding minority rights that explicitly went beyond what the Court itself was willing to guarantee. Section 5 of
the Voting Rights Act confers on the Department of Justice practi-
cally unreviewable power to adjudicate voting rights controversies
in large parts of the Nation;[47] *Mitchell* and *Gingles* effectively overruled, on statutory grounds, the Court's constitutional rulings regarding participation and aggregation rights.

But like the Court's different conceptions of the right to vote,
its different conceptions of institutional deference can collide. In
addition to empowering the federal executive to deal directly with
state and local governments, Congress created a set of legally en-
forceable entitlements that require federal courts to review state
reapportionment activities. Thus, the Court confronts a string of
institutional questions. To what extent ought it recognize and enforce constitutional rights itself? To what extent ought it defer to
congressional interpretations of constitutional provisions? To what
extent ought it condone nonjudicial federal intervention in a state's
internal process of self-governance? All these questions were presented by last Term's voting rights cases, and, as might be expected
in light of a thirty-year track record of inconsistent approaches,
the Court answered them in a somewhat confused fashion.

II. The Means of Voting Rights Enforcement: Growe and Voinovich

The round of reapportionment that followed the 1990 census was the first to be subject from the very outset to the overlapping constraints of one-person, one-vote and amended Section 2 of
the Voting Rights Act.[48] It was also the first to involve widespread

---

[44] 384 US 641, 652–56 (1966) (upholding Congress' power under § 5 of the Fourteenth Amendment to suspend New York's English-language literacy test for citizens educated in certain Spanish-language schools).

[45] 400 US 112 (1970) (upholding nationwide suspension of literacy tests).

[46] 478 US 30 (1986) (implicitly upholding Congress' power to prohibit dilutive practices regardless of the intent behind their passage or maintenance).

[47] See *Morris v Gressette,* 432 US 491 (1977).

[48] After the passage of the 1982 amendments, plaintiffs did successfully use the new results standard to challenge post-1980 census congressional and legislative plans. See, for example, *Gingles,* 478 US 30 (North Carolina legislative districts); *Major v Treen,* 574 F Supp 325 (ED La 1983) (three-judge court) (Louisiana congressional districts); *Jeffers v Clinton,* 730 F Supp 196 (ED Ark 1989) (three-judge court), and 740 F Supp 585 (ED Ark 1990) (three-judge court) (Arkansas legislative districts), summarily aff'd, 498 US 1019 (1991).

use of sophisticated computer technology.[49] The combination turned out to be an infelicitous one for the operation of the voting rights system. Sophisticated redistricting software enabled interested groups to flood the market with plans that complied with one-person, one-vote, while at the same time enabling rather effective equipopulous political gerrymandering. The primary constitutional constraint thus had little constraining effect on the ultimate choice of a plan.

What it did do was provide a vehicle for short-circuiting the state's routine redistricting procedures. Immediately following the 1990 census, factions that foresaw defeat (or the denial of victory) within the state reapportionment process rushed into court to challenge the pre-existing, 1980, apportionments.[50] A decade of population shifts had inevitably rendered *those* apportionments unconstitutional. The real point of these lawsuits, however, was not to establish the unconstitutionality of the 1980 plans. Rather, it was to maneuver one's faction into the best position for influencing the successor plans. At a minimum, filing a lawsuit would channel judicial review into the most favorable forum; a truly fortunate plaintiff might find a court whose judges would be moved to outright partisan activity.[51]

Once the existing plan has been struck down, the Voting Rights Act comes into play. In contrast to one-person, one-vote, the Voting Rights Act often does impose quite decisive constraints on the range of permissible plans. But in the context of partisan-driven litigation, it has often been conscripted into use as yet another weapon for factional advantage, used to knock out constitutionally acceptable but politically disadvantageous plans.

---

[49] See generally Samuel Issacharoff, *Judging Politics: The Elusive Quest for Judicial Review of Political Fairness*, 71 Tex L Rev 1643 (1993).

[50] For representative accounts of this phenomenon, see Ellen Spears, *The Republicans Go to Court. A Review of Republican Legal Strategies on Minority Rights in the Area of the Voting Rights Act* (S Regional Council, 1992); Leadership Conf Educ Fund, *Redistricting News Update*, Spring 1992.

[51] Federal District Judge James Nowlin, a former Republican member of the Texas House of Representatives, was one member of a three-judge court in a case involving the reapportionment of the Texas State Senate. Before the district court issued its plan, he contacted one Republican state senator *ex parte* and asked that senator to help him draw the new district lines. Ultimately, when this activity came to light, Judge Nowlin was reprimanded by the Fifth Circuit and, after lengthy litigation seeking his disqualification, recused himself. See Mark Langford, *Nowlin Withdraws from Texas Redistricting Case*, UPI (July 22, 1992), available in LEXIS, Nexus Library, Wires File, see also Issacharoff, 71 Tex L Rev at 1686 n 217 (cited in note 49) (discussing Judge Nowlin's behavior).

Both *Growe* and *Voinovich* confronted the Court with this messy reality. In particular, the litigation history of both the Minnesota and Ohio apportionments revealed a set of widespread assumptions about partisan partiality within the federal judiciary that sharply undercut the Supreme Court's conception of federal judicial intervention as a limited, principled incursion into the political process.

A. THE LIMITED DOMAIN OF THE FEDERAL COURTS

Minnesota's state legislative reapportionment offered a textbook illustration of dysfunctional political litigation.[52] Minnesota performs reapportionment through conventional lawmaking: the legislature passes a bill that is sent to the governor; if he vetoes the bill, the legislature must override the veto or the existing apportionment remains in effect. In 1991, the Democratic-Farmer Labor Party (DFL) controlled the Minnesota Legislature while a Republican occupied the governorship.

In January 1991—without waiting either for the release of final census figures or for the state legislature to begin the redistricting process—a group of voters allied with the DFL filed suit in state court claiming that the existing legislative districts were malapportioned ("*Cotlow*").[53] Within a month, the parties had agreed that

[52] The following account of the procedural background is based on information contained in the following sources: Brief for the United States as Amicus Curiae, *Growe v Emison*, 113 S Ct 1075 (1993); Brief of Appellants, *Growe v Emison*, 113 S Ct 1075 (1993) ("*Growe* Appellants' Brief"); Robert Whereatt, *State Redistricting Rift Goes Before U.S Supreme Court*, Minneapolis Star Tribune (Nov 2, 1992), at 1B ("Whereatt, *State Redistricting Rift*"), Robert Whereatt, *Federal Judges Tell State Panel to Stop Its Work on Redistricting*, Minneapolis Star Tribune (Dec 6, 1991), at 2B ("Whereatt, *Federal Judges Tell State Panel to Stop*"), Robert Whereatt, *DFL Wins Round in Redistricting Fight; 3 Judges Say Revised Map Must Be Based on '91 Law*, Minneapolis Star Tribune (Oct 2, 1991), at 3B ("Whereatt, *DFL Wins Round*").

[53] Subsequently, a group of plaintiffs claiming to represent Republican interests intervened in *Cotlow*. See *Growe* Appellants' Brief (cited in note 52). These intervenors were represented by the same counsel who represented the plaintiffs in *Emison* See id.

The *Cotlow* plaintiffs also challenged the existing configuration of Minnesota's congressional districts. Both the legislative and the congressional lines had been drawn by a federal district court following the state's failure to enact acceptable plans following the 1980 census. See *Lacomb v Growe*, 541 F Supp 145, 147–48 (D Minn) (three-judge court) (congressional districts), aff'd 456 US 966 (1982); *Lacomb v Growe*, 541 F Supp 160, 162 (D Minn 1982) (three-judge court) (state legislative districts). Minnesota seems to have been going for a triple crown of sorts—its post-1970 reapportionment also landed in federal court. See *Beens v Erdahl*, 336 F Supp 715 (D Minn) (three-judge court), vacated sub nom *Sixty-seventh Minnesota State Senate v Beens*, 406 US 187 (1972).

In the text of this article, I focus on the litigation concerning Minnesota's state legislature rather than its congressional districts for three reasons. First, Voting Rights Act considerations apparently played no part in the congressional case since it was impossible to draw a majority nonwhite congressional district. Second, the federal district court enjoined the state court's activities with respect to congressional redistricting at an earlier stage, and thus

the existing apportionment was now unconstitutional, whereupon
the Minnesota Supreme Court appointed a three-judge special
panel (two of whose members had DFL backgrounds) to preside
over the remedial process. Shortly thereafter, a second group of
voters, affiliated with the Republican Party, filed a separate lawsuit, this time in federal court ("*Emison*").[54] The *Emison* plaintiffs
argued both that the existing plan was malapportioned and that it
diluted the voting strength of blacks in Minneapolis and Native
Americans on two reservations.

The *Cotlow* court acted first. It asked the parties to propose
new plans, but it directed them to use a 1991 DFL-generated,
Republican-opposed plan as their starting point.[55] The state court
then released preliminary versions of its plans and announced its
intention to put them into effect unless the legislature acted by
mid-January 1992.

The federal panel viewed the state court's action as an attempt
to end-run the political process: "The premature issuance of [a
judicially created] plan prevented the occurrence of any possible compromise or negotiation which might have brought a divided state government to some form of agreement on redistricting."

---

there was no state judicial plan actually on the table. Finally, the Supreme Court's opinion
in *Growe* largely focused on the shared issues by discussing the legislative redistricting.

[54] Of the seven original named plaintiffs, three were white, one was black, one was a
Native American, one was Hispanic, and one was "Asian" (presumably an American citizen). They came from counties across the state. See *Emison v Growe*, 782 F Supp 427, 429
(D Minn 1992) (three-judge court), rev'd 113 S Ct 1075 (1993). They filed the lawsuit on
behalf of all similarly situated voters, but what these voters had in common beyond their
dissatisfaction with the likely outcome of the state redistricting process is unclear. The
Emison plaintiffs were represented by the same lawyers who represented the Republican
intervenors in *Cotlow*. To complete the circle, the *Cotlow* plaintiffs also intervened in *Emison*.

[55] The DFL had managed to enact that plan, over heated Republican opposition and a
botched veto attempt by the governor. But the plan was so riddled with technical errors,
such as noncontiguous districts and double representation, that it would have been unconstitutional to use it.

The *Cotlow* opinion thus served as a sort of *deus ex machina* for the DFL's otherwise
unusable plan. See Whereatt, *DFL Wins Round* (cited in note 52) ("John French, a lawyer
for the DFL-controlled House and Senate, said, 'In a preliminary and tentative way, it's a
favorable result from the standpoint of the Legislature.' But others were more direct. 'It's
all over. We won,' said Todd Johnson, a DFL House staff member who worked on the
original redistricting plan and has followed the complex lawsuit."). Compare the reactions
when the federal court enjoined further state activity. See Whereatt, *Federal Judges Tell State
Panel to Stop* (cited in note 52) (The attorney who represented DFL interests "called the
injunction stopping the state court action 'a political decision' that 'shows a gross disrespect
for the federal system and the integrity of a coequal sister court. Were this permitted to
stand, the losers would be the citizens of this state who did not elect these two judges,' while
a Republican legislator termed the action 'a great victory for the people of Minnesota'.")

[56] In order to protect what it saw as Minnesota's inter-branch allocation of redistricting authority, the federal court granted the *Emison* plaintiffs' request to enjoin all further state court proceedings and stayed all of the orders issued by the *Cotlow* court.[57]

After a DFL-sponsored plan was again passed by the Legislature but this time effectively vetoed by the Republican governor, the state court—reasoning that the legislature had not managed to enact a plan—issued a final order adopting its own previously announced plan. Two days later, the federal court held that the state court's failure to create a majority nonwhite state senate district in Minneapolis violated Section 2 of the Voting Rights Act. Moreover, it declined even to use the DFL-sponsored/state court adopted scheme as its starting point because the governor's veto showed that it had "been rejected as state policy" by an executive official who "has a constitutionally recognized role in redistricting in Minnesota."[58] Accordingly, it adopted plans created by its own special masters and permanently enjoined interference with their implementation.[59]

A unanimous Supreme Court reversed. Federal courts, Justice Scalia's opinion declared, must "defer consideration of disputes involving redistricting where the State, through its legislative *or* judicial branch, has begun to address that highly political task itself."[60] In holding that the district court "erred in not deferring to the Minnesota Special Redistricting Panel's proceedings,"[61] the Court meant two things. First, federal courts must defer in the sense of "stay[ing their] hands"[62] or "postponing consideration of [the] merits"[63] as long as some state entity is addressing the responsibility to redistrict. Second, as the Court's discussion of "what ought to have happened" shows,[64] federal courts must defer in

---

[56] *Emison*, 782 F Supp at 433.

[57] The Supreme Court vacated this injunction in January 1992. *Cotlow v Emison*, 112 S Ct 855 (1992).

[58] *Emison*, 782 F Supp at 442.

[59] Id at 448. Once again, the Supreme Court stayed the district court's injunction. See *Growe v Emison*, 113 S Ct at 1080 (stay granted by Blackmun in chambers).

[60] Id (emphasis in original).

[61] Id at 1080.

[62] Id (quoting *Railroad Comm'n v Pullman Co.*, 312 US 496, 501 (1941)).

[63] Id at 1080 n 1.

[64] Id at 1082.

the sense of *respecting* or *yielding to* the state court's choice among permissible plans, "rather than treating [the state court's scheme] as simply one of several competing legislative redistricting proposals available for the district court's choosing."[64] Thus, *Growe*'s statement that "state courts have a significant role in redistricting"[65] goes beyond their simply being responsible for enforcing the constitutional requirement of one-person, one-vote. *Growe* treated state courts as an integral part of the state political process, as well as an agent under the federal Constitution.

This approach has substantial appeal. If federal courts involve themselves at the outset of the apportionment process, they will often be left with no guidance on how to choose among acceptable plans in the event the state process does not coalesce behind a single one. The black-letter rule that federal courts must give defendants in reapportionment lawsuits a fair opportunity to develop a new plan does not answer the question of to *whom* a federal court should defer.[66] According deference to the Minnesota House of

---

[64] Id. This interpretation may also underlie the court's reference to "the mistaken view that federal judges need defer only to the Minnesota Legislature and not at all to the State's courts." Id at 1081. To recast a distinction once made by the Minnesota Supreme Court, *Growe* held that the state *process* to which federal courts must yield includes actions by all state *entities*, whatever the role accorded them by positive state law. See *Duxbury v Donovan*, 272 Minn 424, 432–33, 138 NW 2d 692, 698 (1965).

There is more than a little irony in Justice Scalia's celebration of the "legitimacy of state *judicial* redistricting," *Growe*, 113 S Ct at 1081 (emphasis in original), given his assertion in *Chisom v Roemer*, 111 S Ct 2354 (1991), that Section 2 of the Voting Rights Act should not apply to state judicial elections because judges are not "representatives" who act for the people. See id at 2372 (Scalia dissenting).

Moreover, the phrase "legislative redistricting proposals" contains a double entendre. Of course, Justice Scalia was referring to proposals for redistricting legislatures. But there is a long line of cases in which the Supreme Court has used the phrase "legislative plans" to refer to plans that are entitled to federal deference because they are plans that reflect legislative, that is, political, judgments. See, for example, *McDaniel v Sanchez*, 452 US 130, 138 (1981) ("we have recognized important differences between legislative plans and court-ordered plans"); *Wise v Lipscomb*, 437 US 535, 543–46 (1978) (White); id at 547–49 (Powell concurring in part and concurring in the judgment). This dual meaning may lead to problems in administering the preclearance scheme of Section 5 of the Voting Rights Act, because plans imposed by federal courts are not subject to preclearance. If redistricting litigation gets funneled into state courts in covered jurisdictions, are plans imposed by state courts "legislative" under *Growe* and therefore subject to federal preclearance or are they "court-ordered" and therefore exempt?

[65] *Growe*, 113 S Ct at 1081.

[66] See Karlan, 71 Tex L Rev at 1730 (cited in note 13). It is hard to advance any coherent reason why, for example, a court should defer to the nominal defendant in *Growe*—the Minnesota Secretary of State, who essentially performs ministerial functions connected with the electoral process. Under state law she plays absolutely no role in deciding legislative district boundaries. Why should the fortuity of litigation give her views greater weight?

Representatives and Senate would distort the reapportionment process by reducing the Legislature's incentive to compromise with the governor.[68] If a federal court cannot defer to either the legislature or the governor, what criteria would enable it to choose between the competing plans as long as both complied with one-person, one-vote and neither violated the Voting Rights Act?

B. THE CENTRAL ROLE OF THORNBURG V GINGLES

Having thus sharply limited federal judicial intervention, the Court turned to the substantive disagreement between the *Emison* and *Cotlow* courts—whether Section 2 of the Voting Rights Act of 1965 required creating a majority nonwhite state senate district in Minneapolis.[69] Here, too, the Court sought to clarify and limit

[68] As the *Emison* district court noted, the Legislature's knowledge that it could not obtain the legislative plan it wanted through the political process—because the governor would veto the plan—would encourage it to hold out and refuse to compromise. See *Emison*, 782 F Supp at 433; see also Whereatt, *Federal Judges Tell State Panel to Stop* (cited in note 52) (following the federal injunction against further state-court proceedings, one Republican legislator "said the federal panel's order will force DFLers who control the House and Senate to *negotiate* new congressional and district boundary maps") (emphasis added).

[69] The court could have simply reversed the district court's judgment and remanded the case with instructions to dismiss the complaint. Instead, the court apparently felt obliged to address the district court's reasoning—essentially for the purpose of reviewing the Minnesota Supreme court's judgment. This may be because the court ignored the larger implications of its requirement of federal district court deferral. *Grove* suggests that the Minnesota Supreme court reached and resolved the Voting Rights Act implications of its plan. See *Grove*, 113 S Ct at 1079; see also *Grove* Appellants' Brief (cited in note 52) (claiming the state redistricting panel "reviewed [the DFL proposal] to ensure that it met the requirements of [Section 2]" and "[u]pon its own examination, . . . after full review of the parties' submissions, held that [it] did not violate the Voting Rights Act"). If this is correct, then there is a question under the *Rooker-Feldman* doctrine, see *District of Columbia Court of Appeals v Feldman*, 460 US 462 (1983); *Rooker v Fidelity Trust Co.*, 263 US 413 (1923), whether the district court would have been free to revisit that issue. *Rooker-Feldman* suggests that the sole forum for federal review of a state court determination is the U.S. Supreme Court, not the initiation of a new lawsuit in federal district court.

The *Rooker-Feldman* question is further clouded by the temporal relationship between the two Minnesota reapportionment cases. On the one hand, the fact that *Emison* was pending when the *Cotlow* court issued its judgment may suggest that it was not precluded from reaching the Voting Rights Act issues. Otherwise, federal deferral will in fact become federal abstention despite Justice Scalia's footnote to the contrary. See *Grove*, 113 S Ct at 1080 n 1. On the other hand, the fact that *Cotlow* was already pending when the *Emison* complaint was filed, and the ability of the *Emison* plaintiffs to intervene in *Cotlow*, strengthens the case for precluding federal district court review, particularly since a contrary holding would vitiate *Grove's* practical effect. (Parties dissatisfied with their prospects in state court could simply wait until the state court's proceedings were over and then file a new lawsuit challenging the now-in-place state court-created plan in federal court.) And even if *Rooker-Feldman* is not controlling, considerations of full faith and credit, res judicata, and collateral estoppel may lead to the same conclusion. (Indeed, one of the questions presented by the *Grove* appellants was "Was the federal court barred by the Full Faith and Credit Act and

the conditions that justify federal intervention. The mechanism it used was the extension of the *Gingles* test for assessing claims of dilution through submergence—in particular, the insistence on proof of racial bloc voting—to all claims of geographically based vote dilution.

Thornburg v Gingles[70] was the Supreme Court's first encounter with amended Section 2. There, the Court held that North Carolina's use of multimember state legislative districts unlawfully diluted black voting strength in several parts of the state. But rather than engaging in the multifactor, impressionistic, "totality of the circumstances" analysis that Congress had described, the *Gingles* Court articulated three "necessary preconditions" for finding dilution. First, the minority group must show that it is "sufficiently large and geographically compact to constitute a majority in a single-member district"; second, it must show that it is "politically cohesive"; and third, it must show "that the white majority votes sufficiently as a bloc to enable it . . . usually to defeat the minority's preferred candidate."[71] The critical concept underlying the test is one of causation: does the current system deny minority voters a fair opportunity to elect the candidates of their choice, and is there an alternative system which *would* provide that opportunity?[72]

In the half-dozen years following *Gingles*, the lower courts had come to treat the *Gingles* test as a bright-line threshold for weeding

---

the doctrines of collateral estoppel and mootness from adopting a legislative redistricting plan that was directly contrary to a prior state court legislative redistricting judgment?" See *Growe* Appellants' Brief (cited in note 52).)

Thus, the Supreme Court's conclusion that "[w]e must review [the *Emison* court's] analysis because, if it is correct, the District Court was right to deny effect to the state-court legislative redistricting plan," *Growe*, 113 S Ct at 1083, may well assume too much. *Emison's* analysis would in fact be sheer dicta if the district court had had no power to pass on the state court's plan in the first place.

[70] 478 US 30 (1986).

[71] Id at 50–51.

[72] See *Growe*, 113 S Ct 1084 (the first prong establishes "that the minority has the potential to elect a representative of its choice in some single-member district," while the second two prongs show "that the challenged districting thwarts a distinctive minority vote by submerging it in a larger white voting population"). See also *Dillard v Baldwin County Bd. of Educ.*, 686 F Supp 1459, 1461 (MD Ala) (the *Gingles* preconditions frame the inquiry into whether the difficulty a minority experiences in electing its preferred candidates is "in some measure attributable to the challenged election feature, or, to put it another way, that the minority has the *potential* to elect representatives in the absence of the challenged feature") (emphasis in original), aff'd, 862 F2d 878 (11th Cir 1988).

out "marginal" Section 2 lawsuits.[73] *Growe* endorsed that threshold approach,[74] at least with respect to the second and third factors, which, taken together, establish racially polarized voting.[75] Since the record was entirely barren of any evidence of bloc voting,[76] Section 2 provided no warrant for the federal courts to upset the state's apportionment.

Growe thus further tightened the test for assessing claims of racial vote dilution by extending *Gingles* to single-member districts—the most prevalent form of legislative and congressional districting—and by emphasizing the centrality of racial bloc voting even within the *Gingles* analysis.[77]

---

[73] *McNeil v Springfield Park Dist*, 851 F2d 937, 942–43 (7th Cir 1988) (Although "the *Gingles* criteria might conceivably foreclose a meritorious claim, in general they will ensure that violations for which an effective remedy exists will be considered while appropriately closing the courthouse to marginal cases. In making that trade-off, the *Gingles* majority justifiably sacrificed some claims to protect stronger claims and promote judicial economy."); see *East Jefferson Coalition v Parish of Jefferson*, 926 F2d 487, 491 (5th Cir 1991) (*Gingles* factors are "necessary preconditions"); *Neal v Coleburn*, 689 F Supp 1426, 1434 (ED Va 1988) (*Gingles* factors are "essential elements"). Compare *Solomon v Liberty County*, 899 F2d 1012 (11th Cir 1990) (en banc) (evenly divided on whether proof of the *Gingles* factors establishes liability outright or merely serves as a threshold determination), cert denied, 498 US 1023 (1991). See also Samuel Issacharoff, *Polarized Voting and the Political Process: The Transformation of Voting Rights Jurisprudence*, 90 Mich L Rev 1833, 1834–35 (1992) (describing the evolution of more bright-line dilution standards); Kathryn Abrams, *"Raising Politics Up": Minority Political Participation and Section 2 of the Voting Rights Act*, 63 NYU L Rev 449, 450–52 (1988) (same).

[74] See *Growe*, 113 S Ct at 1084 ("Our precedent requires that . . . a plaintiff must prove three threshold conditions.").

[75] The court explicitly left open the question whether a plaintiff could bring a so-called "influence" claim when the group to which she belonged was not large enough to actually control the outcome of an election but was sufficiently large so that an alternative to the present system would give it greater *influence* over the selection of public officials. See *Growe*, 113 S Ct at 1084 n 5; *Gingles*, 478 US at 46–47 n 12 (also leaving open that question). See also *Voinovich v Quilter*, 113 S Ct 1149, 1155 (1993) (assuming, without deciding, that such a claim may be brought). For more detailed discussions of influence district claims, see Bernard Grofman, Lisa Handley, and Richard G. Niemi, *Minority Representation and the Quest for Voting Equality* 117–18 (Cambridge U Press, 1992); J. Morgan Kousser, *Beyond Gingles: Influence Districts and the Pragmatic Tradition in Voting Rights Law*, 27 USF L Rev 551 (1993); Allan J. Lichtman and J. Gerald Hebert, *A General Theory of Vote Dilution*, 6 La Raza L J 1 (1993).

[76] See *Growe*, 113 S Ct at 1085. Indeed, there was substantial evidence before the district court showing that minority candidates had been elected from majority-white jurisdictions across the state. See *Growe* Appellants' Brief (cited in note 52). The plaintiffs' inability to meet the latter two prongs of the test enabled the court to leave open the question whether the first prong applies to all claims of racial vote dilution. See *Growe*, 113 S Ct at 1085.

[77] See generally Issacharoff, 90 Mich L Rev at 1845–91 (cited in note 73) (discussing the emergence and rationale for the centrality of the racial bloc voting inquiry).

C. THE BROAD DOMAIN OF STATE POLITICAL RESOLUTION

Growe answered the question of when a federal court could require majority-nonwhite districts. *Voinovich* addressed the converse
issue: when can federal courts prohibit them? Once again, racial
bloc voting emerged as the critical factor.

A heatedly partisan, Republican-controlled, reapportionment
process produced a plan ("the Tilling Plan") for the Ohio House
of Representatives that contained eight majority-black districts, an
increase of four over the 1981 plan.[78] It also produced a flood of
state and federal court litigation.[79]

The plaintiffs in the federal lawsuit were characterized by the
district court as "Democratic electors and state legislators, some of
whom are members of a protected class under the Voting Rights
Act."[80] Their complaint alleged that the 1991 plan violated the
Voting Rights Act, the Fourteenth and Fifteenth Amendments'
prohibitions on racial discrimination, and the Fourteenth Amendment's prohibition of political vote dilution through gerrymandering. After an extremely expedited process in which it gave each
party three hours to present its evidence, the federal district court
ruled that the Tilling Plan's deliberate creation of majority-black
districts violated Section 2 of the Voting Rights Act. The plan,
the district court held, unnecessarily and impermissibly "packed"
black voters into a few districts, wasting minority votes in the
packed districts and diluting minority voting strength in surrounding areas where black voting strength had concomitantly

---

[78] The following account is taken from *Quilter v Voinovich*, 794 F Supp 756 (ND Ohio 1992) (three-judge court), rev'd 113 S Ct 1149 (1993) ("*Quilter II*"); *Quilter v Voinovich*, 749 F Supp 695 (ND Ohio 1992) (three-judge court) (1992), rev'd 113 S Ct 1149 (1993) ("*Quilter I*"); *Voinovich v Ferguson*, 586 NE2d 1020 (Ohio 1992) ("*Ferguson II*"); *Voinovich v Ferguson*, 584 NE2d 737 (Ohio 1992) ("*Ferguson I*"); Brief for Appellants, *Voinovich v Quilter*, 113 S Ct 1149 (1993) ("*Voinovich* Appellants' Brief").

[79] The Ohio litigation was even more complex than Minnesota's. The Republicans filed an original-jurisdiction lawsuit before the Republican-dominated Ohio Supreme Court seek-ing a declaratory judgment that the Tilling Plan complied with Ohio law. The Democrats removed the case to federal court and counterclaimed, alleging the plan's invalidity under both the Ohio constitution and federal law. But when the case was remanded, the Democrats withdrew their counterclaims and filed their own lawsuit in federal court, alleging that the plan violated the US Constitution as well as the Voting Rights Act and the state constitution. The federal court sought, ultimately unsuccessfully, to enjoin the state court's proceedings; the state court judges went out of their way in their opinions to insist that they had resolved the federal issues as well and had thus foreclosed the federal court from addressing them.

[80] *Quilter I*, 794 F Supp at 695.

282

been diminished.[81] Moreover, the court explained, the process had been infected by a fatal legal error: while the deliberate creation of majority-black districts may be an "appropriate *remedy* under certain circumstances, [the Apportionment Board] here failed to make the requisite findings which demonstrate a violation of the Voting Rights Act, thereby permitting such a remedy."[82] The district court directed the state either to justify its deliberate creation of majority-black districts or to present a new, legally satisfactory plan. The state responded by slightly lowering the black concentrations in six house districts and presenting a variety of information designed to show that, under the totality of the circumstances as delineated in the legislative history to the 1982 voting rights amendments, its decision to draw majority-black districts was justified. The district court rejected the response, finding that the board's "analysis contains only meager information that was not previously before this Court."[83] In a later order, it noted "the absence of racial bloc voting, the [ability of black voters] to elect both black and white candidates of their choice," and the sustained electoral success of minority-sponsored candidates.[84] Thus, the district court held, "the Board fails once again to justify its wholesale creation of majority-minority districts, thus rendering the plan, as submitted, violative of the Voting Rights Act of 1965."[85] And it added an additional thought: "[W]e now proceed to decide that the plan as submitted is also violative of the Fifteenth Amendment of the United States Constitution."[86] That single sentence was the entirety of *Quilter*'s constitutional analysis.

Once again, the Supreme Court unanimously reversed. Justice O'Connor's opinion began by noting the importance of context in assessing districting schemes. Whether dispersal of a minority community among several districts constitutes impermissible "cracking" or concentration involves illegitimate "packing" will necessarily "depend[ ] entirely on the facts and circumstances of

---

[81] See id at 701.

[82] Id at 696 (emphasis added).

[83] *Quilter II*, 794 F Supp at 757.

[84] See *Voinovich*, 113 S Ct at 1154 (quoting from the unpublished order).

[85] *Quilter II*, 794 F Supp at 757.

[86] Id.

each case."[87] The appropriate composition of individual districts
will depend on the demographic character of the minority community as well as the level of bloc voting.[88] Accordingly, apportionment architects must walk a sometimes narrow path between cracking and packing.

But the Court emphasized that "Section 2 contains no *per se*
prohibitions against particular types of districts. . . . Only if the
apportionment scheme has the *effect* of denying a protected class
the equal opportunity to elect its candidate of choice does it violate
§ 2; where such an effect has not been demonstrated [Section] 2
simply does not speak to the matter."[89] Thus, Section 2 restricts
state autonomy only to the extent necessary to correct the process
failure caused by racial bloc voting.

The district court had found, however, that Ohio's political landscape was not blighted by racial polarization. It had stressed the

[87] *Voinovich*, 113 S Ct at 1156. For a more detailed explanation of these terms, see text accompanying note 10 above. Although majority-black districts give black voters an opportunity to elect their preferred candidates even in the face of racial bloc voting, a tipping point will eventually be reached at which putting additional minority citizens into already overwhelmingly black districts can diminish the overall voting strength of the minority community. For example, there might be enough black citizens within a given municipality to create two 97 percent black councilmanic districts. But using the same number of residents, it might also be possible to create three 65 percent black districts. Choosing the former configuration instead of the latter will not increase the electoral strength of any particular subset of black citizens and will diminish overall black influence on the composition of the council.

[88] With regard to the first question, the relatively greater dropoff between total population and voting-age population in black and Hispanic communities than in white ones, see, for example, *Whitfield v Democratic Party*, 686 F Supp 1365, 1380 (ED Ark 1988) (county was 53 percent black in total population but majority white in voting-age population), aff'd en banc by an equally divided court, 902 F2d 15 (8th Cir 1990), cert denied, 498 US 1126 (1991), combined with their lower rates of registration and turnout, see *UJO v Carey*, 430 US 144, 164 (1977), may require drawing a district with a nonwhite population "supermajority" to create a "toss-up" district on election day. See generally Grofman, Handley, and Niemi, *Minority Representation* at 120–21 (cited in note 75) (discussing the "so-called 65 percent rule" and the need for consideration of context). Thus, in a community blighted by pervasive bloc voting, a district that is less than, for example, 60 percent black, may never elect the black community's candidate.

By contrast, white crossover voting may mean that some majority-white districts nonetheless give minority voters a reasonable opportunity to elect the candidate of their choice. It is entirely possible, for example, that a 40 percent black district would give black voters an equal opportunity to elect candidates of their choice. If, for example, 90 percent of black voters vote for the candidate sponsored by the black community and 25 percent of white voters cross over, the black-sponsored candidate will win in a 40 percent black district (.90 × .40 + .25 × .60 = .36 + .15 = .51, or 51 percent of the votes), even though she would lose in a 30 percent black district (.90 × .30 + .25 × .70 = .27 + .175 = .445, or 44.5 percent of the vote).

[89] *Voinovich*, 113 S Ct at 1156 (emphasis in original).

"absence of racial bloc voting, the [ability of black voters] to elect both black and white candidates of their choice," and the sustained electoral success of minority-sponsored candidates.[90] In short, politics in Ohio was working. Blacks needed no more federal intervention than any other similarly sized group of citizens: in some places they elected representatives by themselves; in other areas, they built coalitions to attain a majority. Accordingly, the district court's inquiry under the Voting Rights Act should have come to an end.

Voinovich thus completed the ascension of bloc voting from one of seven optional "typical factors" indicating racial vote dilution[91] to one of three "necessary preconditions" in certain kinds of Section 2 cases[92] to the absolute centerpiece of Section 2 claims. This elevation promised to impose at least some order on Section 2 litigation, since it is at least possible to delineate fairly objective standards for assessing the degree and significance of bloc voting.[93]

In addition to identifying the district court's doctrinal misinterpretation, the Court also located a profound institutional failure in the district court's imposition on the state political process of a framework designed to curb federal *judicial* involvement. *Gingles's* identification of conditions of process failure provided congressional warrant for federal judicial intervention. But "precisely because it is the domain of the States, and not the federal courts, to

---

[90] Id at 1154 (quoting unpublished district court order).

[91] See Senate Report at 28 (cited in note 24) (terming "the extent to which voting in the elections of the state or political subdivision is racially polarized" one of seven "[t]ypical factors" tending to show dilution, but cautioning that "there is no requirement that any particular number of factors be proved" and stating that "[t]he failure of plaintiff to establish any particular factor, is not rebuttal evidence of non-dilution," id at 29 n 118).

[92] See *Thornburg v Gingles*, 478 US at 50 (describing racial bloc voting as one of the "necessary preconditions for multimember districts to operate to impair minority voters' ability to elect representatives of their choice"). See also id at 46 n 12 (noting that "we have no occasion to consider whether the standards we apply to [the] claim that multimember districts" violate Section 2 "are fully pertinent to other sorts of vote dilution claims, such as a claim alleging that the splitting of a large and geographically cohesive minority between two or more multimember or single-member districts resulted in the dilution of the minority vote"; since the first *Gingles* precondition still exists, this statement necessarily implies that it is the second and third—which together indicate racial bloc voting—that are uncertain).

[93] This is not to say, however, that the courts have in fact developed universally accepted standards. *Gingles* itself was divided on this point: Justice Brennan was unable to garner a majority for his analysis. None of the 1993 trilogy made any progress toward resolving this issue. For scholarly attempts to develop such standards, see Grofman, Handley, and Niemi, *Minority Representation* at 82–104 (cited in note 75); Issacharoff, 90 Mich L Rev at 1871–90 (cited in note 73).

285

conduct apportionment in the first place,"[94] states require no federal warrant to choose among districting plans. Essentially, the district court was hoist on its own petard. Rather than a Section 2 violation being a necessary precondition for a state's "remedy" of drawing majority-black districts, a Section 2 violation is a necessary precondition for the federal judicial remedy of overturning a state's affirmative choice to draw such districts.[95] In concluding that "surely Congress could not have intended the State to prove the invalidity of its own apportionment scheme" as a prelude to redistricting,[96] the Court rejected the lower court's attempt to "crosonize" the Voting Rights Act, that is, to require jurisdictions to set out a factual predicate for drawing majority-minority districts.[97]

Underlying that conclusion was the implicit recognition that *all* districts have a racial identity, at least in the sense that their racial composition can be readily described and readily perceived by any politically knowledgeable observer.[98] Thus, it is impossible to say that states must have a justification for consciously drawing racially identifiable districts without subjecting every state districting choice to federal review. But requiring special justification only for drawing majority-black districts reflects a deep normative indifference to racial vote dilution, for it assumes that majority-white districts have no racial identity even if black voters are submerged within them.[99] Since all districts in a biracial community must be either majority-white, majority-black, or evenly divided (and the last possibility will be attainable only if the starting point is an evenly split community), the state must either be compelled to draw districts which are all racial microcosms of the entire state or

---

[94] *Voinovich*, 113 S Ct at 1156.

[95] Because the court disposed of the Voting Rights Act issue in *Voinovich* on the question of racial bloc voting, it left open, as the *Growe* court had done, the question whether a protected group that is too small to form the majority in a fairly drawn single-member district can nonetheless prove a violation of Section 2. See *Voinovich*, 113 S Ct at 1155.

[96] Id at 1156.

[97] The reference is to *City of Richmond v J.A. Croson Corp*, 488 US 469, 498–506 (1989) See Karlan, 71 Tex L Rev at 1735 (cited in note 13) (discussing the "crosonization" question). In light of the court's decision in *Shaw v Reno*, 113 S Ct 2816 (1993), Alex Aleinikoff and Sam Issacharoff have suggested that perhaps the court is attempting to "*Bakke*-ize" [perhaps "*Bakke*-slide" would be more appropriate] voting rights questions. See Aleinikoff and Issacharoff, 92 Mich L Rev at 609–18 (cited in note 18).

[98] See *Shaw v Reno*, 113 S Ct 2816, 2826 (1993) ("the legislature always is aware of race when it draws district lines") (emphasis omitted).

[99] See Lani Guinier, *Groups, Representation, and Race-Conscious Districting: A Case of the Emperor's Clothes*, 71 Tex L Rev 1589, 1591 (1993).

be free to draw districts with a variety of complexions. The former possibility is very likely unattainable and would, given residential patterns, require grotesque gerrymandering and carving up of geographically cohesive minority communities. And to pretend that the latter possibility can be achieved through non-race-conscious districting is to ignore reality: as long as politicians familiar with local circumstances draw districts, they simply cannot be unaware of the racial makeup of the districts they draw. Given the explicit race-consciousness of the Voting Rights Act,[100] its imperative cannot be race-unconsciousness.

This recognition that race-consciousness is not the same thing as intentional racial discrimination formed the basis for rejecting the district court's constitutional analysis. As it had with regard to the statutory influence–district/dilution claim, the Court assumed, without deciding, that the plaintiffs had advanced an actionable theory under the Fifteenth Amendment.[101] But, the Court concluded, the district court's "finding of intentional discrimination was clearly erroneous."[102] Evidence in the record actually contradicted the district court's finding. "Tilling and the board relied on sources that were wholly unlikely to engage in or tolerate intentional discrimination against black voters, including the Ohio NAACP, the Black Elected Democrats of Ohio, and the Black Elected Democrats of Cleveland, Ohio. Tilling's plan actually incorporated much of the Ohio NAACP's proposed plan; the Ohio NAACP, for its part, fully supported the 1991 apportionment plan."[103]

The Court's discussion raised as many questions as it answered. Some of those questions were explicit. For example, the Court "express[ed] no view on the relationship between the Fifteenth

---

[100] Section 2 expressly provides that "the extent to which members of a protected class have been elected to office . . . is one circumstance that may be considered" in assessing a dilution claim. 42 USC § 1973(b) (1988).

[101] It is unclear why the district court decided this as a Fifteenth Amendment claim rather than a Fourteenth Amendment claim, especially given the plurality opinion in *City of Mobile v Bolden*, 446 US 55, 64–66 (1980), that the Fifteenth Amendment does not reach claims of racial vote dilution and the fact that the Fourteenth Amendment clearly does reach claims of racial vote dilution, see id at 65; *White v Regester*, 412 US 755, 765–66 (1973). The Supreme Court's decision to treat *Voinovich* as a Fifteenth Amendment case of course left the coast clear for its Fourteenth Amendment constitutional analysis in *Shaw v Reno*, 113 S Ct 2816 (1993).

[102] *Voinovich*, 113 S Ct at 1158.

[103] Id at 1158–59.

Amendment and race-conscious redistricting,"[104] although that, of course, was precisely the gravamen of the plaintiffs' Fifteenth Amendment claim. The Court elided the issue by assuming that if there were no racially discriminatory *effect*, by which the Court seemed to mean no disadvantageous electoral consequences, then race-consciousness alone would not violate either the Fifteenth Amendment or Section 2. Other unanswered questions were implicit. If, for example, the approbation of the NAACP and a group of black elected officials was sufficient to "directly contradic[t]" a finding of discriminatory intent, what does this say about the propriety of allowing two white Democratic members of the Apportionment Board and "various Democratic electors and legislators,"[105] some of whom almost fortuitously happened to be "members of a protected class under the Voting Rights Act,"[106] to use the Act essentially as a weapon in a straight partisan wrangle over redistricting? What, to be more precise, gives white politicians elected from majority-white jurisdictions standing to claim a violation of black voters' rights in entirely distinct districts? At the same time, what role should this sort of evidence about minority groups' extensive "opportunity . . . to participate in the political process"[107] of reapportionment and, by extension, of governance, play in Section 2 cases generally? But what *Voinovich* did clearly establish was the Supreme Court's commitment to keeping the Voting Rights Act within its own domain—cases where well-defined evidence showed minority exclusion from the political process.[108]

---

[104] Id at 1159.

[105] Id at 1153.

[106] *Quilter*, 794 F Supp at 695. This euphemism apparently refers to plaintiffs who are black, although that is nowhere stated in any of the courts' opinions. In fact, of course, *all* voters fall within that description, since Section 2 by its terms prohibits discrimination against white voters as well.

Had Justice O'Connor probed more deeply into the evidence before the district court, the essential absence of any black complainants from the case would have become even more obvious. The challenged plan actually involved *less* packing than its predecessor, which had been drawn by the Democratic plaintiffs' predecessors in interest. And the alternative plan proposed during the reapportionment process by the lead plaintiffs created only two fewer majority-black districts and only two more "influence" districts. Where the actual lines were drawn was thus no doubt a subject of intense *political* concern, but there seemed to be a consensus on the broad outlines of a fair *racial* allocation of legislative seats.

[107] 42 USC § 1973(b) (1988)

[108] Ultimately, the court disposed of *Voinovich* on an issue connected with one-person, one-vote. The total deviation in the Ohio plan (the sum of the percentage by which the least populous district fell below the ideal, that is, equipopulous, district size and the percentage by which the most populous district exceeded the ideal) was over 10 percent.

III. The Ends of Voting Rights Enforcement: Shaw v Reno

Growe and *Voinovich* offered a sensible response to attempted hijackings of Section 2 by the major political parties. *Shaw*, which came down the last day before the summer recess, was an entirely different story. The patent insufficiency of the Court's reasoning raises the question of the Court's real agenda in issuing such a confused and confusing opinion.

A. THE ROAD TO THE I-85 DISTRICT

CK ?

Shaw concerned North Carolina's congressional reapportionment. By now it should come as no surprise that *Shaw* was not the only litigation challenging the state's new lines. Democrats controlled both houses of the General Assembly; the lack of a veto left the state's Republican governor a bystander.[108] The North Carolina situation, however, introduced two wrinkles absent from the Minnesota and Ohio experience. First, there was no point in trying to upset the process through state-court litigation: the North Carolina judiciary was firmly in Democratic hands.[119] Second, and more important, North Carolina was subject to the preclearance regime of Section 5 of the Voting Rights Act: it could not hold

---

Thus, under existing case law, the plaintiffs had established a prima facie case of malapportionment. See *Brown v Thomson*, 462 US 835, 842–43 (1983) (explaining that "as a general matter, . . . an apportionment plan with a maximum population deviation under 10% falls within [the] category of minor deviations" that are "'insufficient to make out a prima facie case of invidious discrimination'," but that greater deviations among state legislative districts do require justification) (quoting *Gaffney v Cummings*, 412 US 735, 745 (1973)).

The *Quilter* court erred, however, in not giving the state the opportunity to show that the excessive deviation was justified as reasonably related to a rational and permissible state policy, in this case, preserving political subdivision boundaries. See *Voinovich*, 113 S Ct at 1159. Therefore, the Supreme Court remanded the case to give the state that opportunity. See id at 1159–60. But the court was careful not to give the district court another opportunity for excessive intervention: "[W]e . . . remand *only* for further proceedings on whether the plan's deviation from equal population among districts violates the Fourteenth Amendment." Id at 1154 (emphasis added).

[108] See *Pope v Blue*, 809 F Supp 392, 394 (WDNC) (three-judge court), summarily aff'd, 113 S Ct 30 (1992).

[110] A majority of the state supreme court were Democrats, several elected after fierce partisan contests. And the Fourth Circuit was only six months away from holding that the state Republican Party and its members had stated a claim of unconstitutional political gerrymandering with regard to the configuration of North Carolina's trial bench—on which only two Republicans had sat in the last century. See *Republican Party v Martin*, 980 F2d 943, 948 n 10, 958 (4th Cir), cert denied, 114 S Ct 93 (1993). *Republican Party v Martin* appears to be the first post-*Bandemer* case in which the complaint has not been dismissed for failure to state a claim.

elections until it had obtained federal approval for the new district configurations.[111] As a practical matter, this meant that North Carolina required Department of Justice approval for its congressional reapportionment.[112]

The 1990 census entitled North Carolina to twelve congressional seats, an increase of one over its post-1980 delegation. The change in the number of districts meant, of course, that more than some simple tinkering with existing lines was required. At the same time, in significant part as a result of *Thornburg v Gingles*,[113] the size and influence of the black state legislative contingent had grown dramatically, and representatives of the black community were demanding that the state, which was roughly 22 percent black and which had not elected a black to Congress since the turn of the century, draw some majority-black congressional districts. Finally,

---

[111] Jurisdictions are designated for preclearance on the basis of a triggering formula contained in section 4(b) of the Voting Rights Act, 42 USC § 1973b(b) (1988). Coverage is mandatory if the jurisdiction used a literacy test broadly defined (to include, for example, the use of English language–only election materials in a significantly non-English-speaking community) and voter registration or turnout in the 1964, 1968, or 1972 presidential elections dipped below 50 percent of voting age population. Currently, nine states and parts of seven others are "covered jurisdictions." See 28 CFR Part 51 App (1993). Forty North Carolina counties are covered and thus, as a practical matter, all statewide redistricting activity requires preclearance.

[112] As a formal matter, Section 5 provides both an administrative and a judicial mechanism for obtaining preclearance. The administrative process resembles the Book of the Month Club. A covered jurisdiction submits its change to the U.S. Attorney General. If she does not object within 60 days, the change can be implemented. The judicial process requires bringing a declaratory judgment action in the United States District Court for the District of Columbia before a three-judge court. Theoretically, the standard for preclearance is the same whichever avenue a jurisdiction seeks. See 28 CFR § 51.52(a) (1993) (the Attorney General "shall make the same determination that would be made by the court in an action for a declaratory judgment under Section 5: Whether the submitted change has the purpose or will have the effect of denying or abridging the right to vote on account of race, color, or membership in a language minority group"). A jurisdiction that fails to obtain administrative preclearance is still entitled to seek a declaratory judgment. See 42 USC § 1973c (1988).

As a practical matter, however, jurisdictions that fail to obtain administrative preclearance rarely seek judicial preclearance. The process is time-consuming, costly, not all that likely to achieve the desired result, and requires holding the changes in abeyance during the course of the litigation. Thus, although there have been roughly 60 congressional and legislative reapportionments subject to preclearance, and the Department of Justice has objected several dozen times, there are only five reported preclearance lawsuits. See *Texas v United States*, 802 F Supp 481 (DDC 1992) (three-judge court) (post-1990 state senate); *South Carolina v United States*, 589 F Supp 757 (DDC) (three-judge court) (post-1980 state legislature), cert dism'd, 469 US 875 (1984); *Busbee v Smith*, 549 F Supp 494 (DDC 1982) (three-judge court) (post-1980 Georgia congressional reapportionment), aff'd, 459 US 1166 (1983); *Mississippi v Smith*, 541 F Supp 1329 (DDC 1982) (three-judge court) (post-1980 congressional reapportionment), appeal dism'd, 461 US 912 (1983); *Mississippi v United States*, 490 F Supp 569 (DDC 1979) (three-judge court) (post-1970 state legislature), aff'd, 444 US 1050 (1980).

[113] 478 US 30 (1986).

the Democrats were concerned to protect Democratic incumbents in a state where Republicans, although still a decided minority, were increasing.[114]

The General Assembly's first plan created one majority-black district in the northeastern part of the state. The district nicely reflected the political situation that produced it; it was contorted to favor both the interest of a nearby white incumbent Democrat in protecting his political base and the ability of the black community to elect a representative of its choice.[115] But when North Carolina submitted its plan to the Department of Justice for preclearance, the Department objected. It was unable to conclude that the state's plan had neither a discriminatory purpose nor a discriminatory effect in light of its failure to draw a second majority nonwhite district and its suspicion that minority interests had been sacrificed to incumbent protection.[116]

the state's

the Department's

Accommodating both two majority-black districts and the needs of incumbent Democrats required a bit more artistry.[117] Instead of drawing another majority-nonwhite district in the southeastern part of the state, which the Department had identified as a possible location for such a district, the General Assembly drew the now-infamous "I-85" district in the north-central part of the state. The district was 160 miles long and, in some places, no wider than a single point. The voting age population of the district was 53.34 percent black and 45.21 percent white.[118]

[114] See *Pope v Blue*, 809 F Supp at 394.

[115] As the Department of Justice noted in its objection letter, "The unusually convoluted shape of that district does not appear to have been necessary to create a majority black district and, indeed, at least one alternative configuration was available that would have been more compact." But the contortion provided no basis for objecting under Section 5, since the Department "concluded that the irregular configuration of that district did not have the purpose or effect of minimizing minority voting strength in that region." Letter from John R. Dunne, Assistant Attorney General for Civil Rights, to Tiare B. Smiley, Special Deputy Attorney General of North Carolina, Dec 18, 1991 ("DOJ Objection Letter"), reprinted in Appendix to State Appellees' Brief, *Shaw v Reno*, 113 S Ct 2816 (1993) ("*Shaw* State Appellees' Brief").

[116] See DOJ Objection Letter (cited in note 115).

[117] The late Philip Burton reportedly referred to his egregious gerrymander of the California congressional districts, see *Badham v Eu*, 694 F Supp 664 (ND Cal 1988) (three-judge court), aff'd, 488 US 804 (1989), as his "contribution to modern art." Larry Liebert, *Burton-Style Remapping May Be a Thing of the Past*, SF Chron (Jan 9, 1992), at A19.

[118] *Shaw* State Appellees' Brief (cited in note 115). House District 1, the other majority-nonwhite district, was 53.40 percent black and 45.49 percent white in voting age population. The ten remaining districts had black voting age population percentages of between 4.94 and 20.90 percent. Id.

"The Attorney General did not object to the General Assembly's revised plan. But numerous North Carolinians did."[119] Their first line of attack was a political gerrymandering challenge.[120] In light of *Bandemer*'s declaration that "unconstitutional discrimination occurs only when the electoral system is arranged in a manner that will consistently degrade a voter's or group of voters' influence on the political process as a whole,"[121] the district court had no trouble granting the state's motion to dismiss for failure to state a claim: the plan created a number of "'safe' Republican seats"; there was no allegation that Republicans in Democratic districts were unable to influence their Representatives; and although Republicans had been excluded from the "political process . . . of redistricting," there was no evidence to suggest that "they have been or will be consistently degraded in their participation in the entire political process [as opposed to] the process of redistricting."[122] The Supreme Court summarily affirmed.[123]

B. THE ROAD TO THE SUPREME COURT

At the same time that *Pope* was being litigated in the Western District of North Carolina, five voters who lived in the Middle District filed a lawsuit in the Eastern District against the federal and state officials who had been involved in North Carolina's congressional reapportionment. Their complaint was more than a challenge to the particular plan enacted by the General Assembly; it was an assault on the constitutionality of the Voting Rights Act as well.[124] The plaintiffs argued that the Equal Protection Clause

---

In the November 1992 elections, both the First and Twelfth Districts elected black representatives.

[119] *Shaw*, 113 S Ct at 2821.

[120] *Pope*, 809 F Supp 392.

[121] *Davis v Bandemer*, 478 US 109, 132 (1986) (plurality opinion). Given that three justices did not think political gerrymandering claims were even justiciable, see id at 144 (O'Connor, joined by Burger and Rehnquist, concurring in the judgment), a plaintiff must, at a minimum, meet the plurality standard.

[122] *Pope*, 809 F Supp at 397-98. These items largely point to governance concerns—with the responsiveness of elected officials and the control over delegation composition.

[123] 113 S Ct 30 (1992). Only Justice Blackmun would have set the case for oral argument.

[124] Much of this assault was deflected by the district court's conclusion that it lacked subject matter jurisdiction over the plaintiffs' challenge to Section 2's constitutionality because Congress had vested exclusive jurisdiction over such proceedings in the United States District Court for the District of Columbia. See *Shaw v Barr*, 808 F Supp 461, 466-67 (EDNC 1992). See also 42 USC § 1973*l*(b) (1988) ("No court other than the District Court for the District of Columbia . . . shall have jurisdiction to issue . . . any restraining order or temporary or permanent injunction against the execution or enforcement of any provision

outlawed the intentional concentration of black voters in districts that are "in no way related to considerations of commpactness [*sic*], contiguousness and geographic or jurisdictional communities of interest,"[125] and that the Voting Rights Act was unconstitutional to the extent that it required such concentrations.

At the outset, the district court confronted what it termed a "puzzling" aspect of the plaintiffs' claim:

> They nowhere identify themselves as members of a different race than that of the black voters in whose behalf the challenged congressional districts allegedly (and concededly) were created. Nor, following this, do they plainly allege constitutional injury specific to their rights as members of a particular racial classification of voters. Indeed, in describing the constitutional injury allegedly caused by the race-conscious redistricting plan, they assert that it is injury suffered alike by "plaintiffs and all other citizens and registered voters of North Carolina—whether black, white, native American, or others."[126]

The district court repaired this "deliberate (and humanly, if not legally, laudable) refusal to inject their own race[s]" into the lawsuit by taking judicial notice of the plaintiffs' identity as white voters.[127]

But this repair in fact misled the district court into treating the plaintiffs' case as simply "some 'reverse' variety" of the traditional racial gerrymandering and vote dilution claims.[128] It enabled the court to make quick work of the plaintiffs' complaint. The claim that race-conscious redistricting was per se unconstitutional had been rejected by a fractured Supreme Court in *United Jewish Organizations v Carey*.[129] And when it came to an as-applied challenge,

---

of [this Act]"). The court also concluded, in perhaps a surfeit of caution, that it should dismiss the federal defendants on 12(b)(6) grounds because the Department's preclearance decisions are discretionary acts immune to judicial review. See *Shaw v Barr*, 808 F Supp at 467.

The Supreme Court disposed of the claims against the federal defendants in one sentence. See *Shaw*, 113 S Ct at 2823 ("In our view, the District Court properly dismissed appellants' claims against the federal appellees."). But near the end of its opinion was the suggestion, despite the lower court's holding that it lacked subject-matter jurisdiction over a challenge to Section 2's constitutionality, see *Shaw v Barr*, 808 F Supp at 466–67, that the issue of Section 2's unconstitutionally "remain[s] open for consideration on remand." *Shaw*, 113 S Ct at 2831.

[125] *Shaw v Barr*, 808 F Supp at 465–66 (quoting complaint).

[126] Id at 470 (quoting complaint).

[127] Id at 470.

[128] Id at 469 n 7.

[129] 430 US 144 (1977).

In a brief paragraph, the district court also rejected the claim that race-consciousness was permissible only to the extent that the creation of majority nonwhite districts was required by the Voting Rights Act—essentially along the same lines the Supreme Court was later

293

the plaintiffs had failed to allege either a discriminatory intent or a discriminatory effect. With regard to the former, they identified no "legislative intent to deprive white voters . . . of an equal opportunity with all other racial groups of voters—on a statewide basis—to participate in the political process and to elect candidates of their choice."[139] An intent to favor black voters was simply not the constitutional equivalent of an intent to injure white ones: "[t]he one intent may exist without the other."[131] And plaintiffs' concession that the state was simply trying to comply with the Voting Rights Act further fatally undermined any claim that it had acted with "the necessary invidious intent to harm [the plaintiffs]."[132]

With regard to the latter, the plaintiffs had alleged no discriminatory effect whatsoever. Only two of the five plaintiffs lived in one of the majority-black districts and neither, the district court held, would suffer any cognizable injury "if her or his particular candidate should lose by virtue of the district's racial composition."[133] Nor could the plaintiffs argue a general dilution of white voting strength: since whites constituted decisive majorities in 83 percent of the state's congressional districts (10 of 12), although they were only 75 percent of the state's population, "[t]he plan demonstrably will not lead to proportional underrepresentation of white voters on a statewide basis."[134] Only at the very end of its opinion did the district court, which had decided the orthodox questions entirely correctly, come to grips with the real heart of plaintiffs' challenge: the "political and social wisdom" of the General Assembly's plan.[135]

to use in *Voinovich:* the state's power to make districting decisions is not limited to remedying Section 2 violations. See *Shaw v Barr*, 808 F Supp at 472.

[139] Id at 472.

[131] Id at 473.

[132] Id. Compare *Voinovich*, 113 S Ct at 1158 (suggesting that "an inference of intentional discrimination" under the Fifteenth Amendment was rebutted by the finding that the race-conscious districting was undertaken in the belief it was required by the Voting Rights Act since "it demonstrates obedience to the Supremacy Clause of the United States Constitution.").

[133] *Shaw v Barr*, 808 F Supp at 473, relying on *UJO v Carey*, 430 US at 166 (plurality opinion) (stating that as long as white voters were fairly represented in the legislative body as a whole, individual white voters could not complain that they were unable to directly elect their preferred representatives, since "[s]ome candidate, along with his supporters, always loses"). In fact, nothing in the complaint alleged that any individual voter's aggregation interests were adversely affected by the redistricting plan.

[134] *Shaw v Barr*, 808 F Supp at 473.

[135] Id.

Their real point had very little to do, in fact, with voting rights, at least not in the sense of being concerned with who votes or who wins. Rather, the plaintiffs sought "to participate in a process for electing members of the House of Representatives which is color-blind";[136] apportionment was simply one arena in which they were playing out a broader commitment to the ideal of the "color-blind constitution."

C. THE SHAPES OF THINGS TO COME?

At least at the outset, it looked as if the Supreme Court was uninterested in confronting the broad questions the *Shaw* plaintiffs had tried to raise. In response to a jurisdictional statement that squarely challenged the state's power to draw majority black districts and the Attorney General's interpretation of the Voting Rights Act, the Court wrote its own question:

> Argument shall be limited to the following question, which all parties are directed to brief: "Whether a state legislature's intent to comply with the Voting Rights Act and the Attorney General's interpretation thereof precludes a finding that the legislature's congressional redistricting plan was adopted with invidious discriminatory intent where the legislature did not accede to the plan suggested by the Attorney General but instead developed its own."[137]

The answer to this question was obvious and probably could have been answered unanimously by a two-sentence *per curiam*.[138] The Attorney General's imprimatur could not possibly immunize an unconstitutional plan from attack. Moreover, by its very terms, Section 5 provides no "safe harbor" against constitutional challenge of a precleared plan.[139] But as is often the case, a confusing answer is what a confused question begets.

[136] Brief for Federal Appellees, *Shaw v Reno*, 113 S Ct 2816 (1993) (quoting complaint), available in LEXIS, Genfed Library, Briefs File ("*Shaw* Federal Appellees' Brief").

[137] *Shaw v Barr*, 113 S Ct 653 (1992).

[138] That comes pretty close to what the court did, in a paragraph buried toward the end of its opinion. See *Shaw*, 113 S Ct at 2837 ("Indeed, the Voting Rights Act and our case law make clear that a reapportionment plan that satisfies § 5 still may be enjoined as unconstitutional.").

[139] See 42 USC § 1973c (1988) ("Neither an affirmative indication by the Attorney General that no objection will be made, nor the Attorney General's failure to object, nor a declaratory judgment entered under this section shall bar a subsequent action to enjoin enforcement of such qualification, prerequisite, standard, practice, or procedure.").
The court's question contained a second misapprehension: the Attorney General does not "suggest" plans to covered jurisdictions. It is obviously the case that the tenor of her objec-

To be sure, the Court's answer *seemed* simple:

> [W]e conclude that a plaintiff challenging a reapportionment
> statute under the Equal Protection Clause may state a claim by
> alleging that the legislation, though race-neutral on its face,
> rationally cannot be understood as anything other than an effort
> to separate voters into different districts on the basis of race,
> and that the separation lacks sufficient justification.[140]

But although reapportionment may be an "area in which appearances do matter,"[141] reality should matter more, and despite the
Court's invocations of *Gomillion v Lightfoot*[142] and *Wright v Rockefeller*,[143] in reality, *Shaw* represents a dramatic departure from the
prior case law.

Perhaps the most remarkable departure is one that no one on the
Court seemed to notice: a complete disregard for standing requirements. What, precisely, was the "injury in fact" suffered by these
particular plaintiffs that made them appropriate parties to challenge
the districting scheme?[144] More particularly, what separated their
criticisms from "a generally available grievance about government—claiming only harm to [their] and every citizen's interest in
proper application of the Constitution and laws, and seeking relief
that no more directly and tangibly benefits [them] than it does the
public at large"?[145]

The plaintiffs did not claim that the reapportionment diluted
their votes.[146] Indeed, plaintiffs were in an ideological bind: it

tions to a previously submitted plan may influence a jurisdiction to produce a new plan
along particular lines more likely to obtain preclearance, but plans are always developed by
jurisdictions rather than the Department of Justice. See *Shaw* Federal Appellees' Brief (cited
in note 136).

[140] *Shaw*, 113 S Ct at 2828.

[141] Id at 2827.

[142] 364 US 339 (1960).

[143] 376 US 52 (1964).

[144] *Association of Data Processing Orgs. v Camp*, 397 US 150, 152 (1970).

[145] *Lujan v Defenders of Wildlife*, 112 S Ct 2130, 2143 (1992).

[146] See *Shaw*, 113 S Ct at 2824 ("In their complaint, appellants did not claim that the
General Assembly's reapportionment plan unconstitutionally 'diluted' white voting
strength."). This enabled the court to distinguish *Shaw* from its earlier decision in *UJO v
Carey*, 430 US 144 (1977), as well. See *Shaw*, 113 S Ct at 2829–30

The court's suggestion that the plaintiffs' claim resembled the one advanced in *Gomillion
v Lightfoot*, 364 US 339 (1960), see *Shaw*, 113 S Ct at 2825–27, is hard to take seriously.
The purpose and effect of the notorious Tuskegee gerrymander was to strip virtually all of
Tuskegee's black residents of their municipal citizenship (while keeping them subject to the
city's police powers, see Tr of Oral Arg at 7, *Gomillion v Lightfoot*, 364 US 339 (1960)) and
its few black voters (most eligible citizens having been effectively kept off the rolls) of their

would ill behoove people seeking "a 'color-blind' electoral process"[147] to claim that their votes had been rendered ineffective because they were placed in too black a district.[148] Their argument thus had to be based on considerations unrelated to electoral outcomes, or at least to their ability or inability to elect the candidate of their choice. Thus, as the Court explained:

> [R]eapportionment legislation that cannot be understood as anything other than an effort to classify and separate voters by race injures voters in other ways. It reinforces racial stereotypes and threatens to undermine our system of representative democracy by signaling to elected officials that they represent a particular racial group rather than their constituency as a whole.[149]

Of course, if *all* voters are equally injured, then the *Shaw* plaintiffs are invoking "citizen standing," a concept several members of the *Shaw* majority have repeatedly condemned.[150]

Just as troubling, the "injuries" Justice O'Connor identifies as cognizable in *Shaw* very closely resemble interests to which she and her compatriots in the *Shaw* majority have usually been quite impervious. Viewing her opinion in *Allen v Wright*[151] in light of *Shaw* makes the two look uncomfortably like photographic negatives of one another. A group of white voters suffer cognizable injury from the "reinforce[ment]" of racial stereotypes[152] when a democratically elected state government accedes to the wishes of black citizens to draw a majority-black district, but a group of black parents suffer no "judicially cognizable injury"[153] when they claim

---

right to vote in municipal elections. Of course, none of the *Shaw* plaintiffs was deprived of the right to cast a vote in a congressional election. The sole question along those lines concerned in *which* district they would vote.

[147] *Shaw*, 113 S Ct at 2824.

[148] Compare David A. Strauss, *The Myth of Colorblindness*, 1986 Supreme Court Review 99, 111 (the argument that race should be treated differently from other group characteristics is race-conscious, not colorblind).

[149] *Shaw*, 113 S Ct at 2828.

[150] For one particularly pointed example, see Antonin Scalia, *The Doctrine of Standing as an Essential Element of the Separation of Powers*, 17 Suffolk U L Rev 881, 881–82 (1983) ("[C]ourts need to accord greater weight than they have in recent times to the traditional requirement that the plaintiff's alleged injury be a particularized one, which sets him apart from the citizenry at large."). Apparently, that was then, *Shaw* is now. For another, see Justice O'Connor's opinion for the court in *Allen v Wright*, 468 US 737, 751 (1984).

[151] 468 US 737 (1984).

[152] *Shaw*, 113 S Ct at 2827.

[153] *Allen*, 468 US at 753.

"denigration" and "stigmatiz[ation]"[154] as a consequence of the Internal Revenue Service's complicity in invidious racial exclusion from private schools. The *Shaw* plaintiffs, but not the *Wright* plaintiffs, seem to enjoy standing based "simply on their shared individuated right" to a Government that obeys the Constitution.[155]

Nor can Justice O'Connor honestly claim, consistent with her position in *Davis v Bandemer*,[156] that the message race-conscious districting sends to elected representatives is "pernicious."[157] In *Bandemer*, Justice O'Connor agreed with the plurality's statement that "[a]n individual or a group of individuals who votes for a losing candidate is usually deemed to be adequately represented by the winning candidate and to have as much opportunity to influence that candidate as other voters in the district."[158] If this is so of Republican state legislators elected from districts deliberately drawn to ensure Democratic defeat, as she assumes it is in *Bandemer*, then she fails to explain anywhere in *Shaw* why it is not equally true of black Representatives elected from districts drawn in a way less likely to ensure white defeat and arguably drawn simply to give black and white voters an equal opportunity of seeing their preferred candidate prevail.[159] But if this is not so—if Representatives are in fact unresponsive to the interests of members of the racial minority within their district—then her earlier claim that "impermissible racial stereotypes" are at work becomes a bit more problematic, for now "the perception that members of the same racial group . . . think alike, share the same political interests, and will prefer the same candidates at the polls"[160] turns out to be true. And the decision not to draw any majority-black districts produces a congressional delegation in which *none* of the Representatives is responsive to the distinctive interests of this politically cohesive

---

[154] See id at 749, 754 (internal quotations omitted).

[155] Id at 754.

[156] 478 US 109 (1986).

[157] *Shaw*, 113 S Ct at 2827.

[158] 478 US at 132 (plurality opinion); see id at 152–53 (O'Connor concurring in the judgment) (agreeing with this position).

[159] Nowhere in the court's opinion, and buried in a single footnote in only one of the dissents, is any mention of the actual racial composition of House District 12. See *Shaw*, 113 S Ct at 2840 n 7 (White dissenting) (stating that the district is "54.71% African-American"). (Actually, 54.71 percent of the registered voters in the district are black, the district's total population is 56.63% black. See *Shaw* State Appellee's Brief (cited in note 115)).

[160] *Shaw*, 113 S Ct at 2827.

black community. The fact that Section 2 requires showing precisely this sort of political cohesion and racial bloc voting,[161] means,
moreover, that the Court cannot simply decline to take account of
such true racial generalizations—unless it is suggesting that Section
2 of the Voting Rights Act is unconstitutional. The Act reflects
Congress' judgment that the continued election of all-white congressional delegations from states with significant, historically dis-
empowered black communities "undermine[s] our system of representative democracy."[162]

Nor can Justice O'Connor sidestep this problem by claiming
that only when districts are "obviously created solely to effectuate
the perceived common interests of one racial group" will this message get through to elected officials.[163] As she earlier recognized,
"the legislature is always *aware* of race when it draws district
lines";[164] and if there is racial bloc voting, each elected official will
similarly be aware of which voters support her and which oppose
her. The message will be the same regardless of the shape of the
envelope in which it is sent.

Thus, neither of the "injuries" Justice O'Connor explicitly identifies can support the *Shaw* plaintiffs' cause of action. Instead, their
cognizable injury seems to stem from the Court's recognition of a
new, "analytically distinct claim that a reapportionment plan [vio-
lates the Constitution if it] rationally cannot be understood as anything other than an effort to segregate citizens into separate voting
districts on the basis of race without sufficient justification."[165] This
new cause of action contains two components. First, the court must
ask whether the plan "segregate[s]" voters on the basis of race.
Second, it must ask whether there is "sufficient justification" for
the segregation.[166]

If the Court had applied its newly discovered test to the undis-

---

[161] See *Gingles*, 478 US at 50–51.

[162] *Shaw*, 113 S Ct at 2828.

[163] See id at 2827.

[164] Id at 2826 (emphasis in original).

[165] Id at 2830.

[166] I phrase the issue this way because it is not entirely clear how the court proposed to
allocate the burdens of pleading and persuasion. It seems that a plaintiff must allege both
segregation and lack of justification, see *Shaw*, 113 S Ct at 2828 and 2830, but if she proves
segregation, the burden shifts to the defendant to articulate, and apparently to prove, a
justification.

puted record before it, it should simply have affirmed the district court's dismissal of the complaint for failure to state a claim. However race-conscious the General Assembly had been, and it concededly had drawn the plan with the intent to create two majority-black districts,[167] it had not in fact segregated the races into separate districts. Consider the racial composition of the two districts in which the *Shaw* plaintiffs lived. House District 2's population was 76.23 percent white and 21.94 percent black; House District 12's population was 41.80 percent white and 56.63 percent black.[168] To say that either district even remotely resembles "political apartheid"[169]—especially given that House District 2, where a majority of the *Shaw* plaintiffs lived, was a nearly perfect mirror of the state's overall racial makeup[170]—would be risible if it were not so pernicious.

Nor was the Court's discussion of the possible justifications more coherent. The Court identified several: compliance with Section 5's "nonretrogression" principle;[171] compliance with Section 2's prohibition of minority vote dilution; eradicating the effects of past discrimination; and ameliorating the effects of racial polarization.[172]

---

[167] The fact that North Carolina conceded race-consciousness raises the question why the court devoted so much space to explaining how a district's "bizarre," 113 S Ct at 2825, or "irregular," id at 2824, shape may enable a court to determine that it was drawn for race-conscious reasons. See id at 2825–27. Presumably, if the state conceded that a perfect square was drawn for the purpose of creating a majority-black district, this would satisfy the first prong of the new cause of action.

If, however, the court's point is that only proof of bizarreness will do, then *Shaw* elevates form over substance. The court's insistence that compactness or regularity is not constitutionally required, see id at 2827; see also *Wood v Broom*, 287 US 1, 6–7 (1932) (finding that Congress had deliberately deleted these requirements from the reapportionment statute), means that the bizarreness and irregularity are at most evidence of some other transgression. Compare *Bandemer*, 478 US at 157–58 (O'Connor concurring in the judgment) (chiding the plurality for using proportionality as a measure of political vote dilution when it did not operate as an independent constitutional requirement).

[168] *Shaw* State Appellees' Brief (cited in note 115). The ten other districts ranged from 5.46 to 57.26 percent black. Id. Notably, no one seemed to object—at least not enough to file a lawsuit—to the creation of three 90 percent white districts.

[169] *Shaw*, 113 S Ct at 2627.

[170] Whites are 75.56 percent of North Carolina's population. *Shaw* State Appellees' Brief (cited in note 115).

[171] The principle forbids preclearance if a change renders minorities worse off "with respect to their effective exercise of the electoral franchise." *Beer v United States*, 425 US 130, 141 (1976). Given the precise holding in *Beer*—that a change from a city council plan with no majority-black districts to a plan with one could not be retrogressive—this justification seems clearly foreclosed in *Shaw*. Even the perpetuation of a ninety-year tradition of no majority-black districts would leave blacks no worse off than they were before.

[172] See *Shaw*, 113 S Ct at 2831–32.

Notably absent from the Court's list was one quite plausible explanation for the configuration that had so troubled it: the General
Assembly's partisan desire to protect white Democratic incumbents. This omission is somewhat suspicious. What would happen
if, on remand, the state were to show that the shape of the challenged district[173] was the product of simultaneous desires to draw
a majority-black district and to conduct a partisan gerrymander?[174]
Even if political gerrymandering cannot serve as a justification for
race-consciousness, proof that it played a role in the choice among
configurations logically negates the first element of the plaintiffs'
case, namely, showing that the legislation "rationally cannot be
understood as anything other than an effort to separate voters."[175]
Given her endorsement of partisan gerrymandering in *Bandemer*,[176]

---

[173] For some reason, although the court early on described the First District as a "bug
splattered on a windshield," *Shaw*, 113 S Ct at 2820 (quoting Wall St J (Feb 4, 1992), at
A14), it proceeded on the assumption that the constitutionality of that district was not
placed in issue by the *Shaw* complaint. It is not entirely clear why. If white voters in the
Second District can challenge the configuration of the Twelfth District without claiming
that they should somehow be part of it, there is no reason to suppose they cannot challenge
the First as well. But compare *Davis v Bandemer*, 478 US at 153 (O'Connor concurring in
the judgment) (arguing that voters in one part of a state should not be able to challenge the
configuration of lines throughout the state because they can only vote in one district anyway
and suggesting the implication of a contrary position would be that "members of a political
party in one State should be able to challenge a congressional districting plan adopted in
any other State, on the grounds that their party is unfairly represented in the State's
congressional delegation, thus injuring them as members of the national party").
   In light of Justice O'Connor's reasoning in *Shaw*, though, it is unclear why even a resident
of Virginia would have any less standing than a citizen of North Carolina to challenge the
General Assembly's plan.

[174] Compare *Whitcomb v Chavis*, 403 US 124, 149–60 (1971) (suggesting that the use of a
multimember district cannot be viewed as invidiously discriminatory under the Equal Protection Clause if the fortunes of the black community's candidates rise and fall along with
those of other Democratic candidates).
   Incidentally, the court's distinction of districting schemes from at-large elections, on the
grounds that "[a]t-large and multimember schemes . . . do not classify voters on the basis
of race," *Shaw*, 113 S Ct at 2828, is yet another example of its historical ignorance. In fact,
at-large elections and multimember districts were often adopted *precisely* because of their
racially discriminatory effects, just as gerrymanders were. See J. Morgan Kousser, *The
Undermining of the First Reconstruction: Lessons for the Second*, in Chandler Davidson, ed, *Minority Vote Dilution* at 27, 32–33 (cited in note 19).

[175] *Shaw*, 113 S Ct at 2828, 2830. In this sense, proof of partisanship resembles the sort
of inquiry conducted under *Village of Arlington Heights v Metropolitan Housing Dev. Corp.*,
429 US 252, 266 (1977). There, the court stated that proof that race played a role in
governmental decision making required the defendant to show it would have undertaken
the same course of action without regard to race; here, proof of partisanship might be held
to require that the *plaintiffs* show that the state would have had to draw a bizarre shape
even in the absence of partisan concerns.

[176] "The opportunity to control the drawing of electoral boundaries through the legislative
process of apportionment is a critical and traditional part of politics in the United States,
and one that plays no small role in fostering active participation in the political parties at
every level." 478 US at 145 (O'Connor concurring in the judgment).

Justice O'Connor, at least, should be reluctant to strike down an apportionment whose irregular lines are the function of political, rather than racial, concerns. The Court having already held that the North Carolina plan complies with the relatively toothless prohibition on political vote dilution,[177] the North Carolina Legislature's decision to draw an irregular majority-black district rather than a conventionally shaped one should be left to the state political process, where the *Shaw* plaintiffs were fully and adequately represented.

When it came to the possible justifications it *did* mention, the Court's discussion was cryptic, providing virtually no guidance to the district court on remand or to other lower courts faced with what promises to be a stream of such cases. The Court's repeated condemnation of the Twelfth District's shape suggests that black and Hispanic plaintiffs will be unable to satisfy the first prong of the *Gingles* test—"the minority group must be able to demonstrate that it is sufficiently large and geographically compact to constitute a majority in a single-member district"[178]—by drawing districts the courts find "bizarre" or "irregular" or "uncouth."[179] Moreover, the fact that plaintiffs in Section 2 actions might not be able to establish liability under *Gingles* through identifying such potential districts does not mean that if plaintiffs were to establish liability by providing a court with relatively regular illustrative districts the defendant would be precluded from using an irregularly shaped district as a *remedy*, as long as the district provided minority citizens with a full and fair opportunity to participate in the political process and elect the representatives of their choice.[180] Thus, if Section 2 would obligate a defendant jurisdiction to draw *some* majority-black district—because racial bloc voting would otherwise unlawfully dilute the votes of a geographically compact, politically cohe-

---

[177] See text accompanying notes 120-23. p 274

[178] 478 US at 50. For extensive discussions of geographic compactness, see Karlan, 24 Harv CR-CL L Rev at 199-213 (cited in note 27); Richard H. Pildes and Richard G. Niemi, *Expressive Harms, "Bizarre Districts," and Voting Rights: Evaluating Election-District Appearances After Shaw v Reno*, 92 Mich L Rev 483, 527-59 (1993).   *Roman type*

[179] What these terms mean remains anyone's guess. For an attempt to give them some meaning, see Pildes and Niemi, 92 Mich L Rev at 575-86 (cited in note 178).

[180] For a particularly striking example of this, see *Dillard v Town of Louisville*, 730 F Supp 1546 (MD Ala 1990), where the court approved a defendant's proposal of a *non-contiguous* majority-black district. Indeed, as long as a defendant's plan fully remedies the proven violation, the plaintiffs' aesthetic preferences are irrelevant.

sive minority community—the jurisdiction's choice as to where to draw the lines should not trigger constitutional liability to white voters who would have preferred them drawn some other way.

In a similar vein, the Court never explained why a state's desire to dampen the effects of racial bloc voting does not override aesthetic considerations of compactness or regularity. The refusal of large numbers of white voters to vote for candidates sponsored by the black community results in the continuing exclusion of blacks from full participation in the political and governance processes. It may often reflect prejudiced or stereotypical thinking. In *Palmore v Sidoti*, the Court held that "[t]he Constitution cannot control such prejudices but neither can it tolerate them. Private biases may be outside the reach of the law, but the law cannot, directly or indirectly, give them effect. . . ."[181] In an analogous context, the Court has recognized that the government has "a fundamental, overriding interest in eradicating racial discrimination in education—discrimination that prevailed, with official approval, for the first 165 years of this Nation's constitutional history."[182] How this fundamental interest can be overridden by a preference for aesthetically pleasing districts in a system which tolerates all sorts of ugliness to benefit every sort of group but the original intended beneficiaries of the Fourteenth Amendment is hard to fathom.

D. COMING DOWN THE PIKE?

Shaw was not really a case about the right to vote, at least not as the Court had interpreted that right when the entitlements of black citizens were before it. No one was denied the ability to participate in congressional elections. No one's ability to elect her preferred candidate was impaired.[183] No allegations were made that the plaintiffs had been hindered in any way from participating fully in the governance process of reapportionment.

Shaw is, instead, a meta-governance case, because it raises ques-

---

[181] 466 US 429, 433 (1984); compare *Terry v Adams*, 345 US 461 (1953) (holding, on an extremely fractured set of rationales, that a private, whites-only pre-primary violated the Fifteenth Amendment).

[182] *Bob Jones Univ. v United States*, 461 US 574, 604 (1983) (footnote omitted).

[183] With regard to black voters' equal protection claims, the court has always required a showing of a discriminatory effect as well as some discriminatory intent. See Note, *The Constitutional Significance of the Discriminatory Effects of At-Large Elections*, 91 Yale L J 974, 976–77 (1982).

tions not merely about the composition of the North Carolina congressional delegation, but rather about the entire enterprise of the voting rights system. North Carolina's plan was the product of a General Assembly that, for the first time since Reconstruction, and as a direct consequence of prior litigation under the Voting Rights Act, contained significant numbers of legislators elected by black voters.[184] North Carolina's black citizens were also able to participate fully in the preclearance process. The political branches of the state and federal governments reached a political solution to a set of political concerns.

In *Shaw*, the same Supreme Court that had just told the lower courts not to interfere on behalf of the ostensible interests of black voters unless there was clear evidence that the political process had disregarded those interests thrust itself into the process on behalf of a group of voters who could not show that they had been discriminated against because of their race and who advanced no colorable claim that their right to vote had been impaired in any way. And by formulating a constitutional cause of action, the Court raised the specter that it was preparing itself for an all-out assault on the political branches' ability to preserve their resolution of competing claims. It is hard to escape the suspicion that the Court has learned a lesson from the sixteen times Congress has overruled its interpretations of civil rights statutes in the last fifteen years:[185] if it wants to impose its view of civil rights on the political branches, statutory interpretation is a weak tool. The Voting Rights Act has already worked too well: minority enfranchisement and voting strength has already given black Americans more influence in the political processes of reapportionment than they enjoy with the Supreme Court. *Shaw* at least raises the possibility that the Supreme Court will gut the Voting Rights Act and sharply limit Congress's authority to empower the executive branch and state governments to share in securing and enforcing the Fourteenth

---

[184] Compare *Gingles*, 478 US at 40 (prior to *Gingles*, less than 4 percent of North Carolina's state legislators were black) with Joint Center for Political and Economic Studies, *Black Elected Officials: A National Roster, 1991* at xxx (Joint Center for Political and Economic Studies Press 1992) (in January 1991, over 11 percent of North Carolina state legislators were black).

[185] See Eric Schnapper, *Statutory Misinterpretations: A Legal Autopsy*, 68 Notre Dame L Rev 1095, 1099 (1993).

Amendment's political rights.[186] And so, one-third of the way toward the next reapportionment, we find ourselves still within a dark wood where the straight way is lost.

---

[186] *City of Richmond v J.A. Croson Co.*, 488 US 469, 486–91 (1989), distinguished Richmond's minority set-aside program, which the court found invalid under the Equal Protection Clause, from a virtually identical federal program upheld in *Fullilove v Klutznick*, 448 US 448 (1980), because Congress had acted under its special enforcement powers. This distinction raises two questions. First, could *Congress* require states to engage in race-conscious districting under specified circumstances? Second, if it could do so directly, could it *delegate* the decision about how and when to do so to the states? See *Parker v Brown*, 317 US 341, 353–54 (1943) (in upholding a California raisin price-stabilization program against antitrust attack, the Court assumed that Congress's passage of the Agricultural Marketing Agreement Act of 1937 would have allowed the Secretary of Agriculture to devise such a program and decided that "[f]rom this, and the whole structure of the Act, it would seem that it contemplates that its policy may be effectuated by a state program either with or without the promulgation of a federal program by order of the Secretary."); Note, *City of Richmond v J.A. Croson Co.: A Federal Legislative Answer*, 100 Yale L J 451, 468 (1990) ("The court's determination that a state's race-based program is unconstitutional does not preclude congress from independently sanctioning a similar race-based program under its section 5 enforcement powers.").

STATEMENT OF RICHARD SAMP, GENERAL COUNSEL, WASHINGTON LEGAL FOUNDATION

Mr. SAMP. I also want to thank the committee for the opportunity to come before it today.

I think I agree with Professor Karlan 100 percent that we ought to let the political branches of government decide the problem. That is really, I think, one of the greatest beauties of the *Shaw* v. *Reno* decision. I don't think it is going to result in the dismantling of more than a handful of existing districts, but what the decision is going to do is to allow State legislatures to draw up districts the way they would like to.

Prior to the *Shaw* v. *Reno* decision, the basic assumption was that you had to maximize the number of majority/minority districts and that that was the overriding principle. And, regardless of what the legislature might want to do otherwise in terms of creating contiguous compact districts, that that simply was not to be permitted.

So I think that is the greatest legacy of the *Shaw* v. *Reno* decision, and I disagree with Professor Karlan that this is in any way a decision with the courts preempting the legislatures. If you talk to legislators around the country—I am sure Mr. Markman will tell you it is true in the Michigan Legislature—they would like to accommodate all groups and not have the threat of judicial review hanging over their head.

One other issue I want to address is not so much the question of equality of representation, because I think most people agree that there ought to be representation of some sort for all groups, and while many people are troubled by non-race-neutral approaches to it, certainly most people think that it is a better idea to have single-member districts rather than at-large districts.

I personally have no objection whatsoever to cumulative voting. I think at least within smaller areas it is probably a very good remedy.

I grew up in Cambridge, MA, which for the last 60 years has had the equivalent of cumulative voting, and it has worked very well at creating coalitions. I certainly agree with Mr. Griffith that it is a bad thing, however, for the courts to step in and tell the local jurisdictions that they have to adopt cumulative voting, but I think that it is a good solution if local jurisdictions would like it.

But the issue that bothers me is the newest focus on equality of substantive results, that it is not just enough for every group to have representation within a legislative body but also to be able to control the results at least on certain issues. What was most troubling, I think, to many conservatives with what Lani Guinier had to say was the whole idea of a minority veto over certain issues, and that is why I think that the Congress ought not to do anything to try to overrule the *Presley* decision which I think stands as a bulwark against this idea of equality of substantive results.

The *Presley* decision said that the Voting Rights Act is limited to changes in procedures with respect to voting. Therefore when a legislative body in the South decided that it wanted to change the substantive powers of members of that body, the Supreme Court said that is not what the Voting Rights Act addresses. If you say it addresses questions like that, then you would also have to say that every time that a legislative body cuts the budget, well, that is obviously reducing the power of the executive branch in that particular government and they have less opportunity to carry out their function. Are you going to say that every budget cut is going to need to get Justice Department preapproval? I don't think that this is a direction that Congress ought to be headed, and consequently the criticisms of the *Presley* decision simply are not well founded.

As the Court pointed out in its *Presley* decision, there are other remedies available if one can show that there was an intentional racial discrimination, and there certainly in the *Presley* case itself was significant evidence of that sort. But that is the way that the plaintiffs ought to proceed, they ought to bring a lawsuit claiming intentional racial discrimination, and if they can prove that, then they should get their remedy.

Thank you.

Mr. EDWARDS. Thank you, and we welcome Elaine Jones, whose impressive credentials have already been explained.

Elaine, do you have a quick statement?

STATEMENT OF ELAINE JONES

Ms. JONES. Thank you, Congressman Edwards.

I just want to emphasize a fact of historical and political life in this Nation. It is unfortunate, but it is true. We have a history of racially polarized voting in this country. I wish it were not so. I wish that we had lived up and could live up to our constitutional ideals and what we say in the Declaration of Independence and the Constitution.

We have had a 15th amendment to the Constitution since 1870 guaranteeing all of us a right to vote. Yet for African-Americans in this country the guarantee was not real until the Voting Rights Act was passed in 1965, and African-Americans have been voting in any significant numbers only for the past 30 years.

Now to look at the Voting Rights Act and to talk about racial apartheid in this country is to turn the act upside-down. If we don't have a mechanism and if Congress had not responded as it did in 1965 with the passage of this historic legislation, I dare say we would not have had as peaceful a democratic process in this Nation as we have had. The people responded through their elected representatives and understood that we had a national crisis, because we had significant minorities and especially the African-American community, excluded from our democratic processes.

Now race has played a role in redistricting, in our voting, and it has played a role that has been adverse to the interests of the African-American community. We can look back as recently as 1980 and see where districts were drawn in Louisiana, in New Orleans, how there was an affirmative effort to make sure that the black community in New Orleans was dismantled and broken up into pieces so that blacks could not elect representatives of their choice, and the reason given was, we have, quote, enough black big shots in this country.

Now we are beginning to recognize as part of our process that African-Americans have a right to elect representatives of their choice—and that does not mean elect African-Americans, African-Americans have been electing whites ever since we were voting because often there has only been whites on the ballot. It means that we ought to have a fair shot to be able to represent persons of our choosing.

Now we talk about districts and the shape of districts. I have looked at the shape of many of these districts and have looked at the shape of white districts. The shape of districts represented by incumbents, the shape of districts throughout the country—North Carolina, New York, Texas—what is interesting in terms of the majority black districts, the tentacles of the districts are reaching up to include white voters, and often the tentacles that reach into the majority black districts are those that pick out black voters for white Democratic incumbents in neighboring districts. So we cannot make judgments and constitutional judgments based on shape and bizarreness.

I simply want to urge that when we talk about political process, we should remember that *Presley* is a classic example where the rules change, when African-Americans and Hispanic-Americans start playing the game, and once they get elected, then all of a sudden all kinds of rules are imposed upon their being able to effectively represent their constituents. *Presley* needs to be amended.

Thank you very much.

Mr. EDWARDS. Moderator.

Mr. DURBIN. As the moderators, I just want to have one basic principle that we will follow. When you want to be recognized or make a rebuttal, please just raise your hand and give us some indication that you want to respond or you want to raise a question that should be discussed.

Ms. WHITAKER. Also at the same time, Tom and I would like to encourage all of you to have a free and flowing discussion, and also we have questions prepared, but we would also encourage all of you to pose questions to one another or to pose questions to the group that you would like the group to address so that we have as much input as possible.

Mr. DURBIN. You have an outline. It is a general outline. The first part is basically a general discussion of the Voting Rights Act, in particular the 1982 amendments. Obviously, the second part would be a discussion of majority/minority districts and then the future of the Voting Rights Act.

Obviously, all of this is going to mesh in, but if we can just sort of start with the first part and then enter into the second, but if we happen to get into the second at the same time it doesn't matter.

[The outline follows:]

Outline of Issues
Voting Rights Round Table
May 11, 1994

I.   Discussion of the Voting Rights Act of 1965

     A.   Purpose and goals of the 1965 Act: How broad is the
          Voting Rights Act?
     B.   Purpose and goals of the 1982 Amendments: How did the
          1982 legislation set the stage for the questions
          currently confronting the nation?

II. Majority-Minority Districts

     A.   The policy rationale and the problems surrounding
          majority-minority districts

     B.   Are majority-minority districts constitutional

          1.   What standards and factors have traditionally been
               considered in drawing congressional districts and
               is a "bizarre" shape a justifiable concern

          2.   Do majority-minority districts violate the equal
               protection rights guaranteed all citizens

          3.   Does the Voting Rights Act justify majority-
               minority districts

III. The Future of the Voting Rights Act

     A.   Interpretation of the Voting Rights Act in the present
          and into the 21st century: public sentiment, legislative
          bodies, and the courts

     B.   Should the Voting Rights Act be amended to clarify its
          purpose and scope

Mr. DURBIN. I now would like to ask if anybody wants to start this out by making a statement or issuing a rhetorical question that we can all use to discuss.

Yes, Professor Lichtman.

Mr. LICHTMAN. I would like to briefly address some of the issues that were raised that I think are crucial in this discussion.

First, we heard the expression "extreme racial gerrymandering," that somehow—and I believe Mr. Taylor pointed this out—the *Shaw* decision was in some senses benign because it would put a restraint on the kind of extreme racial gerrymandering, for example, that we saw in North Carolina.

I would like to raise the question on that issue: Why does two 53 percent African-American districts represent extreme racial gerrymandering when, under the previous plan, all districts were in the ranges of 65 to 70 percent white, and yet somehow that was not racial gerrymandering, when these virtually evenly divided districts were?

Similarly in Texas, the Hispanic district elected a white candidate. The black districts are approximately 50 percent black. Why are these extreme racial gerrymanders?

Second, the issue of proportionality. To hear the discussion today, you would think that the Voting Rights Act has been a wedge to somehow create proportional or even greater than proportional representation for minorities. Let us now put that in perspective. Minorities are 12 percent. Just look at African-Americans, 12 percent of the population, 11 percent of the voting age population, but they are 1.5 percent of elected officials.

In Mr. Markman's State of Michigan where this litigation is taking place, the population is about 13 percent African-American; they are less than 2 percent of elected officials. In no State in the United States are minorities anywhere close to their population proportion. Does the Dole compromise mean that we are supposed to freeze in overrepresentation for nonminorities?

Finally, there is an issue of racially polarized voting and there is somehow the unspoken assumption that the creation of 53 percent to 55 percent minority districts promotes racial polarization and promotes the notion that you only represent persons of one race. In fact you do not create these districts unless racial polarization is already proven to exist. The empirical evidence shows that, in fact, over time, when you create these districts and minority elected officials like Mike Espy in Mississippi, like Mel Watt in North Carolina, prove that they can represent both blacks and white, racial polarization goes down.

Mr. DURBIN. Yes, Congressman.

Mr. FRANK. Yes, that was one of the points that I wanted to ask about. Mr. Taylor said one of the problems is that people only appeal to one race or another. I must say that is contrary to all the experience I have ever had as a Representative or in watching other Representatives. There are a few people in my district whom I make a conscious effort not to represent, but I could give you their names, and it is personal in every case.

I think the overwhelming majority of us, frankly, spend a lot of time trying to conciliate people on the other side, and in particular with regard to our African-American colleagues from the South who are representing these mixed districts, every one of them, in my experience, works very hard in trying to reach out to the white voters. So I think there you just have an empirical error.

Second, when we get to item 2(b)(1): What standards and factors should judicially be considered in drawing congressional districts, and is a bizarre shape a justifiable concern? I would be interested in that. I have a district here that I want to show.

[The map follows:]

MASSACHUSETTS CONGRESSIONAL DISTRICTS

4th DISTRICT

Congressman: **Barney Frank (D)**
2404 Rayburn House Office Building, Washington, DC 20515 · Tel: (202) 225-5931
Newton: (617) 332-3920; New Bedford: (508) 999-6462; Fall River: (508) 674-3551;
Bridgewater: (508) 697-9325

BRISTOL COUNTY
Acushnet
Berkley
Dighton
Easton
  Pcts. 1, 2B, 3
Fairhaven
FALL RIVER
  Wd. 4: Pct. C
  Wd. 5
  Wd. 6: Pct. C
  Wds. 7, 8, 9
Freetown
Mansfield
  Pcts. 3, 4, 5B
NEW BEDFORD
Norton
Raynham
Rehoboth

MIDDLESEX COUNTY
NEWTON
Sherborn

NORFOLK COUNTY
Brookline
Dover
Foxborough
  Pcts. 2, 3
Millis
Norfolk
Sharon
Wellesley

PLYMOUTH COUNTY
Bridgewater
Carver
East Bridgewater
Halifax
Hanson
Lakeville
Marion
Mattapoisett
Middleborough
Pembroke
Plympton
Rochester
Rockland
  Pcts. 6, 7, 8
Wareham
West Bridgewater

Cities in CAPITALS

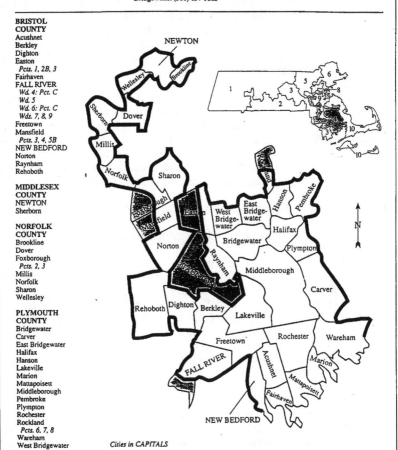

Mr. FRANK. Well, this part is a natural boundary, the rest of it is all drawn by the legislature, and it is a little misrepresentative because these junctures here are thicker on the paper than they really are, they are really much smaller.

But it is a rather bizarre district. It is mine. I didn't ask for it; it is what the legislature gave to me. And I guess I want to know— I mean is this OK because I am white? There is nothing racial about this. Anybody who thinks this happened by any general principle of representation or randomly is obviously quite wrong. This is the district the Massachusetts Legislature gave to me, and, as I said, only that is natural, everything else, all these other irregular borders border other Massachusetts communities, so they could have been different.

So I will be listening with particular interest when we get to bizarreness, because I think I am more bizarre than Mel.

Mr. EDWARDS. We are pleased to have been joined by Congressman Mel Watt of North Carolina, who has in his short time here made an enormous contribution on all issues and who, I might add, is one of six African-American Members of Congress in five States whose district is in danger because of our favorite decision, *Shaw* v. *Reno.*

Ms. WHITAKER. Congressman Watt, would you like to make a statement?

Mr. WATT. No. I just wanted to concur that Barney is more bizarre than me.

Mr. DURBIN. Professor Karlan.

Ms. KARLAN. I was fascinated by your district, Congressman Frank. I give a Rohrsach test in my voting rights class in which I give the students a set of different districts and I ask for their votes on which one they think is the most bizarre, and in many years they have voted for the State of Maryland as a whole as a bizarre district.

I think also the point that he raises is true, that probably the most bizarre district I can recall ever having seen was a district that the late Congressman Phil Burton drew and referred to as "my contribution to modern art," a district that was drawn purely for partisan reasons. This is part of what I think is so interesting: bizarreness or appearances have only come to be troubling to the courts when the appearance is in some part the function of trying to draw districts that represent different racial groups.

Justice O'Connor, for example, thought it was totally nonjudiciable in 1986 in the *Davis* v. *Bandemer* case that is mentioned on the time that we got. She thought it was totally nonjudiciable to draw bizarre shaped districts in Indiana so that Republicans could control the State legislature, and she recognized that even though there would be some Democratic voters put in districts where they could never elect a candidate of their choice, those people would be adequately represented because it was about fair allocation of political power on a statewide level.

It seems to me that if we are talking about appearances, that more troubling than the appearance of North Carolina District No. 12 or Louisiana District No. 4 is the appearance in a country that is a multiracial country of an all-white legislature. I think if we have to choose between some districts that are oddly shaped or having nobody but white people in Congress, I would prefer to have some oddly shaped districts.

Mr. DURBIN. Yes, sir?

Mr. MARKMAN. Again, I would repeat or state what I said in my opening argument, that bizarreness is not the issue, per se. The bizarreness of the geography appearance I don't think is the issue, per se. It is the issue of racial preoccupation. Is there an obligation on the part of a State districting authority to do everything it can to subordinate all other considerations to the one end of optimizing the political influence of one group of Americans necessarily at the expense of all other Americans? And if I could say just one word in defense of oddly shaped districts, including Congressman Frank's, it is that it is one thing to create an oddly shaped district for partisan reasons, it is an entirely different thing—our Constitution says so—to create such a district for racial reasons.

The amendment to our Constitution quite properly recognizes race as one of the great dividing issues of our country, and it deals with race, it doesn't deal with partisanship or anything else.

Ms. WHITAKER. Mr. Arthur Baer.

Mr. BAER. I just wanted to talk a little bit about proportionality and tie it into the question as well.

I think there is a misperception about the notion that the Voting Rights Act would lead to proportionality, although I am not sure I would say that that is a bad thing. The Voting Rights Act isn't a set-aside ruling. What the Voting Rights Act says: If there is racially polarized voting and there are segregated living conditions, then you are prohibited from excluding people based on drawing districts in a certain way to prevent people from getting elected.

So if there wasn't racially polarized voting, if society had progressed to the extent that there was no more racially polarized voting, or if there were no more segregated circumstances of geographic separation, then we wouldn't be having these claims under the Voting Rights Act.

So it is not a set-aside nor is it a proportionality based on just pure numbers. It is a proportionality which says we can't exclude people. It seems to me it is also an interesting thing that Mr. Markman points out, saying it is all right essentially to set aside districts for partisan reasons. In *Hays* v. *Louisiana* the Court said there is a commonality of interests and you are allowed to set aside districts for traditional criteria such as combining English, Scotch, Irish mainline Protestants and you are allowed to aggregate districts based on economic bases—that is, on whether or not there is petrochemical production or urban manufacturing. Also you are allowed to aggregate districts based on geography and topography. That is, you can elevate to a constitutional criteria the soil types of Louisiana, that is appropriate. But apparently you can't aggregate people based on race to remedy exclusion and to ensure people participate in a democratic process. I think that is a fundamental policy error. I think it is wrong.

I think that what we are saying is the Voting Rights Act, hopefully, is that transitional step between racially-polarized voting and no racially-polarized voting and that in the meantime people shouldn't be excluded from our halls of government to be able to effectuate public policy.

Mr. DURBIN. Yes, Mr. Samp.

Mr. SAMP. I certainly agree with Mr. Baer that we ought not to be excluding people. I think that Representative Frank pointed out that Members of Congress of all color go out of their way to not exclude their constituents. They do their very best to make sure that members of all races within their district do have representation, and I think that is a very good thing. So to say that members of a racial minority group are being excluded because their Member of Congress is not of the same color as them is really a wrong-headed approach.

Now Mr. Baer says that the Voting Rights Act doesn't require proportional representation, and he is correct. Indeed, it says right in the statute that this law is not intended to require proportional representation. What I think an awful lot of people complained about, however, is that that is precisely the way the courts have interpreted it. They have required that proportional representation be the ultimate outcome, because the way they measure exclusion is to say, "Is there a proportionality of results?" And if there are not, they call that exclusion.

And I am here to speak up against bizarre districts. I don't agree with Mr. Markman that bizarreness is not the problem, it is the problem. There is a lot to be said for compact districts, and I would hope that legislatures don't continue the kind of things that the Massachusetts Legislature has done in drawing up your district like that. I would like to see you with a more compact district. But the courts really can't step in, for all the sorts of reasons——

Mr. FRANK. Why not? Why would it be any harder in my case than in a racially done case?

Mr. SAMP. I don't believe it is in the Constitution that partisan gerrymandering is in any way unconstitutional, but I would hope you could speak to the Massachusetts Legislature and tell them not to do it next time.

Mr. FRANK. Well, it is the legislature and the Governor.

But I fail to understand. There were certainly principles in the Constitution that talk about equal representation and fairness, but you are saying your position would be that gerrymandering of any sort, while unattractive, is perfectly constitutional, it is only racial gerrymandering that is wrong constitutionally.

Mr. SAMP. The *Bandemer* case says that there is——

Mr. FRANK. I am asking you your own view.

Mr. SAMP. I would say that the courts in general shouldn't be stepping in except in rare circumstances.

Mr. FRANK. So that any gerrymandering other than race is OK?

Mr. SAMP. That is correct, and this is not a new idea of the Supreme Court. Both in *Gomillion* v. *Lightfoot* and *Wright* v. *Rockefeller* decision 30 and 40 years ago, the Supreme Court was stepping in to not permit racial gerrymandering.

Mr. FRANK. I understand.

I would hope we would have a twofold approach on this. One is—and I think, to be honest, this is what we all tend to do anyway—what does the Constitution say and what should it say, and there is obviously a problem you run into. You don't want to so push the Constitution to get a result you like in a particular case so that it has negative consequences in every other case.

But I would hope people wouldn't simply hide behind the Constitution. I hope we would also get some policy judgments, what should it say? I mean if that is, in fact, the result, should we try and change that? Is it a good thing in a society to say that you can have any kind of gerrymandering you want unless it is to deal with racial problems?

Mr. HYDE. Mr. Chairman; somebody.

Ms. WHITAKER. Congressman Hyde.

Mr. HYDE. Following up on what Mr. Samp has said, I have been involved in three reapportionments with the Illinois Legislature. They are relentlessly political. If the Democrats control the legislature, they are going to move lines, they are going to draw a map that gives the Democrats the maximum number of congressional seats. Similarly, if the Republicans control the legislature, they are going to draw a Republican map that is going to give the Republicans the majority of the seats, and you see that happen time and time again.

Now should the Court step in and say, "Wait a minute, there are too many Republicans," or, "There are too many Democrats here, you have politically gerrymandered?" I don't think so. I think that when you win elections you control the legislature. Certain things go along with that, and one of them is, every 10 years draw the maps for the congressional districts, and if they are not off the wall, so as to deny equal protection to people or some other egregious reason, I don't think it is the Court's function to step in and say——

Mr. FRANK. Can I ask a question?

Mr. HYDE. Just a second. Those are gerrymandered.

Now when you get to race, you open another problem that, well, we have the situation in Chicago to try and create a Hispanic district because there were a lot of Hispanics. Unfortunately, they lived on opposite sides of town, now one group here and one group here, and individually they didn't make enough to create a quote, "Hispanic district." So we made a set of earmuffs out of it, we connected it down a road, and it is one district, but we have a Hispanic district.

Mr. FRANK. The problem I have is this though, and maybe this is a way out in some ways. In the South in particular, race and partisanship correlate pretty good, so suppose you said well, we were drawing up this district which was a majority African-American, because we wanted to have democratic districts?

In other words, to some extent you are inviting people, it seems to me, to give an alternative rationale for the same district. Particularly in the South you could wind up drawing the exact same district, and apparently if you then said, "Oh, this is the only way a Democrat can win," it would be OK. The Court couldn't touch it. However if you said, "We are doing this because we want to help black people," it wouldn't be OK, but in fact in much of the South you might do the same way. That is a good way to count Democrats in some of these areas, would be to count African-Americans.

So that is, it seems to me, the result we are asking for, which is to say you can do the same thing but if you justify it in partisan terms you will be all right, and if you justify it in terms of dealing with racial justice, you won't be.

Mr. HYDE. Well, it is not just the South——

Mr. FRANK. But that is where all the suits are.

Mr. HYDE. The Democrat characterization applies in the North too.

Mr. FRANK. Yes, but in the North we have some white Democrats too, Henry. That is what we don't have in the South.

Mr. HYDE. I just would like to ask the question, can only a black represent blacks? Can only a white represent whites? Can only a woman represent women? Are only they capable of understanding the authentic experience? We seem to be moving in that direction, women representing women, blacks only representing blacks, whites representing whites.

I just want to point out, of the two most recent that I am familiar with on a congressional level, Senator Brook in Massachusetts and Gary Franks in Connecticut had largely white constituencies, and yet they did a pretty good job, particularly Congressman Franks, of representing their constituencies regardless of their color.

Ms. JONES. Congressman Hyde, to answer your question, you know, it is interesting to note that when the Voting Rights Act began to apply to that district I described in Louisiana, that majority black district sent Lindy Boggs back to Congress.

Also it is important to keep in mind that what we are talking about is a history here where white males have traditionally represented us all. Even at the Grand Convention in 1787 of the Founding Fathers, there were 55, and I am not saying that they didn't do the best job that they could do, but we all know now it would have been much better if Abigail Adams could have been a founding mother. She kept writing to join Adams, you know, and tried to say, "Please don't forget the ladies," which they promptly did.

Mr. HYDE. Her influence was profound, I am sure.

Ms. JONES. Yes, and had she been in the room, I think it would have reflected itself in the great document.

All I am saying is, it is very important that we get the diversity that we should have in our national bodies. I think you in the Congress would say you benefit from having colleagues across the aisle and on the same aisle of all stripes and both genders.

So what this is about is making sure we don't have State, local, and national bodies where everybody looks the same and that constituencies out there have a fair opportunity to elect representatives of their choice no matter what their color happens to be.

But the issue is in the electorate, that you have minorities in this country that have to believe and feel that we are part of this process, and it is very important that they can give political expression within our democratic system. That is why the Voting Rights Act was such a wise, wise measure.

Mr. HYDE. But Ms. Jones, a lot of blacks voted for John F. Kennedy. Was he not their President? Didn't they participate in the process? Didn't they say, "That's our man," and weren't they very satisfied with the job he did?

Did you say no?

Mr. FRANK. Right. As a matter of fact, John Kennedy approached the question of race quite gingerly, and in the first couple of years of the Kennedy administration race was not one of his priorities. I was glad John Kennedy got elected, but I think no, race was not one of his priorities, and if you go back to 1962——

Mr. HYDE. If the people voted for him didn't feel they——

Mr. FRANK. No. The answer was, Henry, that in 1962 you had a general sense that he was not doing nearly enough on civil rights as an historical fact.

Mr. HYDE. Well, we are moving away then from the notion of a colorblind society, we are moving to——

Mr. FRANK. When did we get there? We are not moving away from it, we have never been there.

Mr. HYDE. We are moving to a color-conscious, gender-conscious, ethnic-conscious and I want to know when the Italo-Americans are going to get their President or their county commissioner and when the Hungarian-Americans are going to get theirs, and the Jews, and the Catholics, and the Mormons.

Ms. KARLAN. They have always had the right to representation, and if you look at the balanced tickets in New York City, for 50 years you would have a Jewish person, a German, and an Irish person, and then when the Germans lost numbers you had an Italian, an Irish person, and a Jewish person, and nobody looked at that and said, "Oh, my God, America is falling apart."

Mr. HYDE. That is just smart slate making.

Ms. KARLAN. And why is it that black people were never on those slates? And how can you say that John F. Kennedy was the President of black southerners who were disenfranchised? Only 6 percent of the blacks in Mississippi could even register to vote in 1964. John Kennedy's first appointment to the bench was a judge who referred to blacks as chimpanzees, from the bench.

Mr. HYDE. Switch Kennedy for Carter, OK?

Ms. KARLAN. Yes, I think he was the choice of black people.

Mr. FRANK. But one point, and I am going to stop. Anybody who knows anything about State legislative redistricting, Henry, has to reject completely what you said. Ethnic considerations, Jewish, and Polish, and Italian, and Irish, have dominated and been very important in redistricting everywhere. To suggest that this is now the first time and to say oh, well, are Polish-Americans going to count, yes.

I will tell you in Massachusetts in 1970 when we redistricted, there was concern about the Italian seats and the Jewish seats and the Irish seats, and you know that, you know that very well.

Mr. DURBIN. Mr. Taylor, did you have something to say?

Mr. TAYLOR. Yes, I would like to respond. The point has been made that there has been a long history of gerrymandering for all kinds of reasons in this country, including bizarre gerrymandering, and it is a fair point. I would like to make a couple of responses on why there is reason for particular concern about the type of racial gerrymandering that was the issue in *Shaw*.

First, I think the Supreme Court—I disagree with Mr. Samp on this—I think the Supreme Court has been too supine on the subject of partisan gerrymanders. I think maybe they should have struck those Burton districts in California down. So I am not sure that, in my view of the matter, at least, racial gerrymandering stands alone as a subject of concern.

I do think that the district in *Shaw*, to pick an example, raises a couple of distinctive concerns. One, when I say extreme, what I am talking about is a district about that wide that goes for hundreds of miles across the State, pulling in people that have very little to do with each other for the purpose and solely for the purpose—well, not quite solely for the purpose—primarily for the purpose of figuring out how to elect a person——

Mr. LICHTMAN. Excuse me. How do you know that those people don't have anything to do with each other? What is your evidence? Be specific.

Mr. TAYLOR. Well, the usual reasons why people—and may I ask you to limit yourself to one interruption before I finish my point?

The reasons people are usually gathered together in districts are shape, contiguity, size, that people who live within a certain radius of each other live in the same communities, read the same newspapers, watch the same television stations, listen to the same radio stations, have the same schools, go to the same meetings, et cetera. The people in *Shaw* live a long way from each other, and those types of community interests are not applicable.

Now to turn to the other points that I think make it objectionable, in the *Shaw* case it was done almost solely for reasons of race. Actually, there were partisan reasons as well. A more contiguous, a less bizarre black district could have been drawn and wasn't drawn because Democrats in North Carolina, in order to keep themselves in office, chose to ignore that alternative.

But I think another important fact about racial gerrymandering is that unlike partisan gerrymandering, it is driven largely by debatable judicial interpretations of the Voting Rights Act. It is not a matter of democratic choice by the people of North Carolina that they wanted to have these kinds of districts. They did so in large part because the Justice Department was suing them, because other people were suing them, because there were a lot of judicial opinions around that said you have to racially gerrymander or you are going to get sued and struck down.

The last point I would like to make is, I think it is quite proper and accurate to point out that a 55 percent black district such as the one in *Shaw* is not likely to lead to the evil I fear of politicians appealing only to members of their own race, and I think that should be a factor in further consideration.

So it should be remembered, the Supreme Court didn't hold that district unconstitutional. They said, "We are troubled by its shape, we are remanding for trial, we want all the considerations that might justify it laid out." It is not inconceivable that that district might end up being upheld and that part of the rationale for upholding it would be that it is only 55 percent black and therefore the apartheid characterization doesn't really apply.

Mr. DURBIN. OK. We are going to take it back to the Chair. Then we will recognize Mr. Baer.

Mr. EDWARDS. We are pleased that the gentlewoman from Colorado, Mrs. Schroeder has arrived.

Do you have a statement, Mrs. Schroeder?

Mrs. SCHROEDER. Mr. Chairman, I just want to thank you for having this. I think this is a very important forum, and I apologize for being late. We had a markup in Post Office and Civil Service. But I am very, very glad that you are doing this.

Mr. EDWARDS. To raise the price of a stamp again?

Mrs. SCHROEDER. Mel and I did. I think we renamed every post office in America.

Mr. EDWARDS. Thank you.

Ms. WHITAKER. Mr. Arthur Baer.

Mr. BAER. Yes; I just wanted to get back to Congressman Hyde's question. The term sometimes has been used, the term "virtual representation"—that is, can someone who is white represent someone who is black, and so on and so forth. I think we are misplacing the issue. The issue isn't a question of who blacks or Latinos "or Asians" or native Americans or those protected under the Voting Rights Act can choose to represent them. The question is whether or not they have the choice who represents them. The problem is, if there is racially polarized voting, and there is voting such that those protected classes couldn't otherwise elect representatives at all, then aggregate groups so that they have a choice to be able to elect whoever they wish, and if you choose President Kennedy you choose President Kennedy.

But on a redistricting level, if your community is divided, then you can never choose anybody, because you can't vote as a group, and it is a burden that is placed particularly on protected classes. That is, in Shaw, for example, which is an extraordinary case in a number of ways, there was no allegation of vote dilution on white voters. That is, there was no harm to them. So it is an extraordinary case, because essentially it is unique in terms of creating standing for a group without injury. We had never had ideological standing before. This is essentially ideological standing.

In the area of partisan redistricting, partisan gerrymandering, the Court has spoken on some occasions. One is *Davis* v. *Bandemer.* But in an earlier case, *Gaffney* v. *Cummings,* it stated essentially courts have no constitutional warrant to validate a State plan otherwise within tolerable limits because it undertakes not to minimize or eliminate the political strength of any group but to recognize it, and, through redistricting provide a rough sort of proportional representation.

So when the Court has looked at partisan gerrymandering, such as the redistricting in the State of Connecticut, it said we are going to try to have roughly a proportionate number of seats for Republicans and Democrats. It said that was appropriate if it supported proportionality, and what *Shaw* says is that even if there is proportionality, you still can't do it perhaps because it looks bizarre. I think it is clearly a departure from Gaffney, it is clearly a departure from prior cases in terms of injury, and standing.

I mean one of the most striking things to me was the case of *Palmer* v. *Thompson* where they closed swimming pools when they sought to integrate those swimming pools through a court order. Jackson, MI, closed all those swimming pools, and the Court said there is no claim because although there may be intent, there was no harm.

Here there is no harm, and essentially you are creating a new cause of action that is wholly unique in American jurisprudence, and that is why it is an extraordinary decision.

Mr. HYDE. May I ask, Professor Baer, is it?

Mr. BAER. No, no. I am an attorney.

Mr. HYDE. Mr. Baer.

All right, Lawyer Baer. Counselor Baer.

Don't you think it is dangerous, though, for a court to start questioning the political composition of what the legislature has done? You will get a Republican judge who doesn't like a Democrat. To me, those political decisions ought to be left to the political process, and when a judge doesn't like the political balance of a State redistricting, to interject his views on that seems to me to go a long ways from our Constitution.

Mr. BAER. In the political gerrymandering cases, as far as I know, there has been no case subsequent to *Davis* v. *Bandemer* that has held unconstitutional a decision of political gerrymandering. In terms of its standard of application, what *Davis* said is that it is a long-term foreclosure in the political arena; that is, in more than one election, continuously. So I suppose if there was a self-perpetuating Democratic or Republican or X party in a State that consistently excluded one group of people so they couldn't ever elect anybody, or limited, then you have a claim or maybe to a lesser extent.

But we have something different here, I think, in race, because we have a history of exclusion, a history of nonparticipation, a history of disenfranchisement not only in terms of the franchise itself but in terms of access to other avenues of power in society.

Ms. WHITAKER. We would like to recognize Congressman Watt now, and then Mr. Nelson Lund after that.

Mr. WATT. Thank you.

I really came to this discussion for the purpose of listening and with the avowed intent of trying to stay out of the debate because the truth of the matter is, I spend so much time talking about redistricting, it is refreshing for me to get away from the issue once in a while. But a couple of the things that Mr. Taylor said I thought I probably ought not let go without some degree of correction.

His whole notion that because I live in Charlotte I have more in common with other people who live in Charlotte than I would have with people who live in Durham just has no basis for it. Mr. Lichtman did a good job and the experts did a good job of showing that statistically and based on polls at the trial of *Shaw* v. *Reno* on remand.

But just as a practical day-to-day matter, this notion that particularly at the Federal level and on issues that we deal with at the congressional level, there is something that makes me connect with people who live in suburban Charlotte because I happen to live in downtown Charlotte or inner-city Charlotte—I mean there is no basis for it. So you all need to get away from that notion.

At the Federal level, poor people, whether they live in inner-city Charlotte or inner-city Durham or inner-city New York City, have got a lot more in common with each other than they do with suburban people or rich people who live in suburbia. I mean it is more an economic commonality than even the racial commonality that exists.

I will let that go. I mean he moderated what he had to say substantially with the last point he made, and I don't want to go point for point with what he said.

What I think always interests me is something that goes back to what Barney started with when he was saying let's talk about not only the Constitution and what it allows but talk about the Constitution as maybe it should be if we were drawing it. I spend a lot of time watching what has been going on in South Africa over the last couple of years and wondering what we would do as a nation if we were starting anew and thinking about this and building a system of representation in this country as it exists now.

Would we, first of all, ignore the historical reality of what has taken place in the history of this country? If South Africa all of a sudden chose to ignore the fact that black people were black and white people were white in South Africa, and chose to be colorblind and built a system that said let's be colorblind, do we think in this room that there would be anything other than complete and utter outrage at that whole notion? If we said, "You all construct your districts there to have a representative body, but don't take into account the color of the people, don't take into account the history of the division between blacks and whites," what kind of system would we end up with in South Africa?

We would end up with a system that, because black people have had a history of being under the thumb of white people, they would vote substantially on a racially polarized basis with more justification, I would say, than white people have in this country for voting racially polarized. Yet the result would be, in all probability, a 100-percent black constituent assembly or whatever they are calling it in South Africa. The United States would express itself, the white majority in this country, would express itself with absolute and utter outrage, and there would be more justification for doing it there than there is for doing it here. At least in that country, 5 percent of the population, 99.99 percent of which is white, has all of the resources in that country. We don't have that historically in this country. So I encourage you to think about this thing less from our own kind of notion of how our friends act.

You know, one of the problems I have with news reporters is that they don't understand racially polarized voting. We talk about racially polarized voting. They don't understand that because their friends are white people who would vote for somebody black. Racially polarized voting in the South means that 80 percent of the white people will not vote for a black candidate whether he went to the University of North Carolina and graduated with summa cum laude and Yale University Law School with a law degree. They won't vote for me. That is racially polarized voting. They won't vote for me.

So this concept that we should be colorblind and let nature take its course will result in that 80 percent of the people consistently sending folks to Washington to represent North Carolina in the Congress of this country that excludes black people from being represented, and it has happened for 92 years in North Carolina. So don't talk to me about being racially colorblind. I mean this is absurd.

Mr. HYDE. Would you like juries to be racially colorblind or color conscious?

Mr. WATT. Well, that is a whole different issue.

Mr. HYDE. Oh, no.

Mr. WATT. Let me tell you the way I used to do it when I was practicing law. I never selected a jury that was on a racially colorblind basis. I always made assumptions about what people were thinking and what their background experiences were. There is no way I factored out somebody's race. The only way I could do that is put blinders over my eyes. It can't be done.

And would I like for sometime in the history of this Nation to be racially colorblind? Absolutely. I hope it occurs during the life of my children or my grandchildren. But don't talk to me about being colorblind now in this day and time in this society. It is like talking to the folks in South Africa and saying, "Hey, wake up tomorrow morning and be colorblind." It can't be done.

Ms. WHITAKER. May we please talk to Mr. Nelson Lund.

Mr. LUND. Well, it is a factual question whether this country is comparable to South Africa. I am sure we will have continuous disagreements about that. But there is a distinction, a very simple distinction, that I think hasn't gotten as much attention as it deserves today, and that is the distinction between intentional discrimination by the Government and other kinds of discrimination.

For example, polarized voting is a result sometimes of discrimination by individuals, and people of all races can engage in this kind of discrimination in choosing who to vote for. That is a fundamentally different thing than discrimination, racial discrimination, by the Government. That distinction ought to cause us to make some distinction also between the kind of intentional, racial gerrymandering that went on in the South prior to the Voting Rights Act of 1965 and on which the Voting Rights Act of 1965 I think is uncontroversial insofar as it attempts to attack that.

What the 1982 amendments do, though, is set up a results test. Once you have a results test you inevitably have the Government engaging in racial discrimination, Government-mandated racial discrimination, which is just another name for racial gerrymandering, which is what we inevitably have under the 1982 amendments.

Mr. WATT. Can I just ask a question then? Do you distinguish between discrimination and gerrymandering?

Mr. LUND. No. They are the same thing. Racial gerrymandering is a form of racial discrimination.

Mr. WATT. No, no. I don't believe so at all. Discrimination is disadvantaging somebody. Tell me how anybody got disadvantaged by the creation of congressional districts in North Carolina as they look.

Mr. LUND. No. Discrimination is treating somebody differently because of the color of their skin.

Mr. WATT. Well, I think we have got to define discrimination before we can really debate that, because I never have thought of discrimination—I mean illegal discrimination—there are discriminations that we make in all of our lives, but they are not illegal discriminations.

Mr. LUND. That is true.

Mr. WATT. And to say that gerrymandering and discrimination and illegal discrimination are one and the same is just not—I mean I don't accept that proposition.

Mr. LUND. Well, racial gerrymandering is not illegal under the decisions of the Court and the laws that this Congress has made, but it is still discrimination.

Ms. ST. CYR. Mr. Lund, let me——

Mr. DURBIN. I want to ask—one second, and we will get right back to you.

I want to ask Bernadine St. Cyr, do you have anything you want to say at this point?

Ms. ST. CYR. Yes. Discrimination is discrimination no matter whether it is intentional or unintentional, and where I am from it is a part of life.

We are just beginning to make some gains because of the Voting Rights Act, and it is only happening to us since 1992. Prior to that, in my community we made very little gain. For years we had only one black on the police jury, and after about 1980 we finally gained 2 out of 12 with a 41-percent black population. In 1992 we went to four, and that was only through litigation.

Negotiation does not work for us. Sitting around the table talking, trying to be rational, does not work for us. We did a year of that before we went to court, and it is only because of the Voting Rights Act that we were able to get some strong support from lawyers out of town—our lawyers came from Washington, DC. We are not able to use local lawyers because they don't have the resources. They will not do it because they are there to make money, and if they work on these types of cases it is unpopular for them. So it affects local attorneys just like it affects an individual like me who ran for council. And, because I participated in reapportionment, it makes it even more difficult for me to run, especially in an at-large system with a majority vote requirement. Unless we go to districts, unless we have more of them, we will continue to be underrepresented.

Mr. DURBIN. OK. I want to go to Ms. Jones, and then we will go to Mr. Markman.

Ms. JONES. Three quick points. First, as a partisan matter, not as a constitutional issue looking at the intent standard, but as a partisan matter, Mr. Lund, I would suggest to you that it is very poor public policy when you are talking about fighting the issues which involve African-Americans, Hispanics, and others being a part of this democratic process to require that Congress or anyone else point the finger for blame. Pointing out who is responsible for this problem, which is what an intent test does, sidetracks us from looking at the real issue.

The real issue is the effect of our policies, the result of our policies on people who have been disenfranchised and whom society has affirmatively acted against. I don't need, as a policy matter, for this Congress to require us as a nation to point fingers and blame one another and look for perpetrators, speaking as a policy matter.

Now, on the question that Mr. Taylor raised about the districts— and I really appreciate your thoughtfulness in grappling with this—look at this 12th District. There is a lot in common in this 12th District. It is a textile district, and they looked at this district and said, "Oh, this is the first time the State gets a textile district." It is a banking district, major banks. It is a district in which you have your historically black colleges. There are a lot of economic, business, educational reasons and interests that bring this district together.

We talk about the whole question of a district being based on race. What really happens in the system is, incumbency is first protected. Districts are first drawn to protect Democrats and Republicans in power. What the Voting Rights Act then does is come in and act as a buffer to say we will not treat our Hispanic- and African-American communities as bits of flotsam just to go fill out other districts. The Voting Rights Act said that we are going to recognize that these people also have an interest and that we will not let the political processes tear aside and break apart those interests.

Now I just want to show you, this is a district in Texas. This is Dallas. The blue is a district of Martin Frost, a Democrat. You see that district, the dark blue district? Do you see those tentacles, that huge district—the white Democrat—you see those tentacles? Those tentacles are reaching up into the light blue district. The light blue district is the district under challenge. That is Eddie Bernice Johnson's district. The dark blue tentacles are reaching up into her district, picking out black voters to fill out his district, the Democratic district. If those tentacles are not reaching up, she would have almost a complete contiguous circle. The tentacles in her district reaching up, the light blue district, are reaching up. The bizarreness comes from the inclusion of white voters. So that is why.

If you wanted to draw a district there and have a pretty, contiguous, almost a circle, you would have Eddie Bernice Johnson's district as a circle, but because other political considerations coming from incumbents above her and below her, then she gets this odd shape.

[Material has been retained in subcommittee files.]

Ms. JONES. So we have got to understand when we talk about these majority minority districts, those districts don't come first, you know, they come later.

Ms. WHITAKER. Mr. Steven Markman.

Mr. MARKMAN. I would like to make two points if I could. First of all, I do think Ms. St. Cyr makes a very important point that there is no distinction in her judgment between unintentional and intentional discrimination.

I would submit that the only way by which you can evaluate what she calls unintentional discrimination—which I think is an oxymoron, frankly—is to equate it with the absence of proportional representation. If that is not a correct definition of what she means by an absence of even unintentional discrimination, I would ask the committee to put the question to her and other supporters of the status quo. I think unintentional discrimination is absolutely equivalent to the idea of there being an absence of proportional representation.

Second, in terms of Ms. Jones' points, that is precisely the whole point here. They do have these little brackets of districts that go up into white areas, because that is the only purpose of white people in these districts, is to fill out districts that are 65 percent optimized to 100 percent population. It is 65 percent optimized districts that is the entire objective of voting rights litigators around the country.

If you have a district that is only 55 percent, more often than not, but not all of the time, that is not considered an effective district. That is not effective because blacks presumably have lower turnout and registration rates and they are not guaranteed to elect their candidate of choice.

On the other hand, if you have 75 percent blacks in a district, that wastes black voters, you don't need quite that many black votes. So the entire and the inexorable tendency of the Voting Rights Act is toward 65 percent districts.

You look at NAACP districts anywhere in the country, and their plans always contain a proportional number of districts at least that are 66.2 percent black or 63.8 percent black. They all go towards that means, and they do pull in whites. They are not segregated apartheid districts, they are districts in which whites have one function, and that is to fill out the population but not to be too influential so that they can have any influence in determining who is elected from that district.

Mr. DURBIN. Thank you, Mr. Markman.

We are going to recognize Professor Karlan, and then we want to recognize Mr. Griffith, and then we are going to Professor Lichtman, in that order. As you notice, we are trying to balance the majority, minority witnesses in that way.

Ms. KARLAN. With regard to the question of intentional versus unintentional discrimination, I think this gets back to the issue of racially polarized voting in this way. It is a series of intentional governmental racially discriminatory actions stretching back to the Constitution that has created the level of race consciousness in this country and therefore created racial bloc voting. It is not as if little black kids and little white kids woke up one day and looked at themselves in the mirror and all of a sudden became race conscious.

So to now say that although the Government intentionally acted in ways that have made people race conscious, it can somehow just snap its fingers and announce today we are colorblind makes no sense. I don't think that requires proportional representation. What it does require is that minority groups in the country be given the same opportunity that every other group has to play in the political process and get districts of their own.

It is no accident, I think, that the black community has done quite well in the administrative preclearance process under both Republican and Democratic administrations because both sets of administrations recognize that under some circumstances the interests of black groups and black politicians coalesce with the interests of white groups and white politicians.

So it seems to me that the idea that you can separate racial gerrymandering and political gerrymandering and say one is okay and the other isn't doesn't make much sense because the two are quite intertwined.

The other point is that I have noticed a number of people in their comments today make comments that if you switch the word "white" and "black," they would make no sense. For example, Mr. Markman says well, the only function of white voters put in a 65-percent black district is to be filler people who don't really have much influence. If that is true, then black voters who are in a 65-percent white district are equally just filler people who don't serve much of a function.

I have noticed several times, for example, Representative Hyde has asked well, can't a white person represent a black person? And yet there are really only two or three instances I can think of white people choosing to have black people represent them—Senator Brook, Representative Franks, and two or three other Members of Congress.

Mr. HYDE. Carole Moseley-Braun—you didn't mean to forget her?

Ms. KARLAN. No, I didn't mean to forget her.

But if we look at it, the fact is that black people have far more often voted for whites than whites have for blacks. One of the things that I find so puzzling is the notion that giving a group that in North Carolina is 22 or 23 percent of the population two out of the 12 seats is somehow proportional representation but giving a group that is 82 or 83 percent of the population 100 percent of the seat is perfectly okay. So I think we have to recognize that there has to be a sort of consistency in how we talk about black claims and white claims.

Mr. DURBIN. Mr. Griffith.

Mr. GRIFFITH. Let me inject the word "federalism." I want to address specifically the question of racial gerrymandering; is it the same as racial discrimination? No. When racial gerrymandering is predicated upon segregating voters into separate districts based upon racial classifications and it impacts upon voting rights, it may rise to the level of discrimination.

All *Shaw* v. *Reno* did was send the case back for retrial under rule 12(b)(6); that is it. The case has been retried. To my knowledge, the decision has not yet come down.

What we are dealing with, and it sounds like a replay of the 1982 and 1981 hearings—we are talking about past history of discrimination. It is very real, it did occur, it impacted upon African-American citizens in the State of Mississippi and in my county and in my congressional district. We elected in the early eighties Mike Espy who squeaked by with a 10- to 12-percent white crossover vote. He got a greater white crossover vote the next time he ran. He had not even an opponent the third time, and he is now Secretary of Agriculture in a 51.5-percent black voting age population district. There was no need to racial gerrymander.

Professor Lichtman, I think, alludes to Espy's district as being a permissible exercise in perhaps concentration of black voters. It was not. Mike Espy himself insisted that there be no racial manipulation of boundaries in that district, and it did not happen. You have now, I think, a very healthy congressional district represented very ably by Bennie Thompson, who is a friend of mine, a 10-year veteran on the county board of supervisors in our State capitol.

What I am looking at now in the federalism sense is this. We are disregarding legitimate State interests when we say that we can disregard contiguity, we can disregard compactness, we can disregard such legitimate considerations that go into the formulation of normal looking, normal appearing districts. We ask—and a court does this in response to witnesses' testimony in actual cases that are tried that perhaps you have participated in—the questions: Are there commonalities of interests that are represented in those districts? And the questions that have been asked in the most recent cases of black witnesses: Who do you most relate to, black people or the white people who represent you? And the answers inevitably are going to be, "I respond more and relate more to my black citizens in other parts of the county or the jurisdiction."

What we are doing, we are increasingly, increasingly pushing racial separation, racial polarization, through the Federal judiciary process, Steve. We are pushing it through the interpretations of section 2 that are coming down the pipe and unfortunately are going to separate us into two separate camps.

The last page of section 8 of the Wall Street Journal today has a very unfortunate editorial dealing with the drive to create a black political party in this country. That would be horrible. That would be the death of biracial coalitions, efforts to try to rebuild and repair, and I am in that second and third generation that Lani Guinier talked about to repair the bridges that had been burned or had been damaged through racism 20, 30, 40 years ago. We are not there yet; we have not arrived; we are in the process of doing it.

Racial gerrymandering sends us back light years because it allows the electorate not to be mobilized on the basis of enthusiasm for a candidate, enthusiasm over the issues, enthusiasm over the particular contest, but only on the basis of race. It completely destroys what we consider to be legitimate, traditional criteria for candidacies as well as for creation of districts.

Mr. Watt.

Mr. WATT. Are those legitimate, traditional criteria?

Mr. GRIFFITH. Contiguity——

Mr. WATT. What I mean, what is sacrosanct——

Mr. GRIFFITH. Let me give you some real clear examples, and these come from——

Mr. WATT. I don't want examples. I want to know what is sacrosanct about——

Mr. GRIFFITH. I will tell you. Respect for political subdivisions when it is embodied in State law and says don't crack a municipal boundary line, don't crack a county, don't crack an existing jurisdictional boundary line in order to reach the goal of maximizing minority voting strength in a particular district. That is a legitimate State interest or governmental interest that, on the altar of federalism——

Mr. WATT. And that should have higher priority with me than minority representation in Congress?

Mr. GRIFFITH. Absolutely not. They go into a totality of circumstances approach.

Mr. WATT. Then why are we having this discussion now? If that should not have higher priority than minority representation in Congress, why am I going to give it overriding preference over getting minority representation in Congress?

Mr. GRIFFITH. Congressman, your error is one of focus. You are looking solely at the issue of race, and I am urging that we look at the totality, at all of these factors, and they are being disregarded. In the congressional district case of *Shaw* v. *Reno* those factors were disregarded.

Mr. WATT. For 92 years in North Carolina we looked at those traditional criteria that are so time honored, and the result of that, the bottom line, the result of it was that we got no, no, no, zero, zero, zero minority representation in Congress from North Carolina.

Now should I continue? How long should I continue to give those the kind of credibility and priority without striving to get some minority representation? How long must I wait for you all to be colorblind?

Mr. GRIFFITH. The "you all" is "we all" because we are in this boat together.

Mr. WATT. How long must I wait for us to be colorblind?

Mr. GRIFFITH. When you create a positive incentive for racial bloc voting and racial polarization among both white and black voters, that is a travesty, that is an undoing of the goals of section 2 of the Voting Rights Act.

Mr. WATT. How long would you suggest I wait before I complain?

Mr. GRIFFITH. I have not waited very long in Mississippi, and I see the progress, and I have outlined it: Representative, Congressperson, individual elected party, on the basis of State, local, and Federal offices, item for item. Take a look at that. These are real areas of progress, they are realistic.

Mr. WATT. How long did they wait in Mississippi before Mike Espy?

Mr. GRIFFITH. I will admit to you there is a past history of discrimination. You have got to get beyond that, and the problem with anybody who litigates these cases is, you will hear from the plaintiff's side and from the legal foundations, that there is a past history of discrimination. I say that there are lingering effects of discrimination that become dissipated, past history becomes remote history at a point in time, and I think in many places in this country we have reached it.

Mr. WATT. How long does it take?

Mr. GRIFFITH. It depends upon the jurisdiction. In many places when you create a Zorro district that Johnny Appleseed apparently drew, such as in *Hays* v. *State of Louisiana,* or you create what is called the bug-splattered-on-the-windshield district in North Carolina, you wait a little bit longer than that, and in some cases you don't wait because you can move forward with biracial cooperation, white crossover voting that puts black candidates into office as in the State of Mississippi and as in the Second Congressional District of my State.

Mr. LICHTMAN. How many of the black members of the Mississippi Legislature come from white districts?

Mr. GRIFFITH. Bare majorities, 50, 51 percent. I could certainly give you a list before the day is out. I could fax it to you if you would like.

Ms. WHITAKER. May we please hear from Prof. Allan Lichtman, and then we will go to Mr. Richard Samp who has been very patiently waiting.

Mr. LICHTMAN. I began my opening statement with the notion that the real problem in the losses of Reconstruction was not white racism but people of good will under the misconception that Government has gone too far and that intervention is an obstacle to the colorblind society.

I think we see the same problem evidenced today, which is why I did jump in on Mr. Taylor. He clearly is a person of good will, a person who clearly has interests in mind of racial equality and racial progress. However, I think there Mr. Taylor and other people of good will are clearly operating under a series of fundamental, basic, factual misconceptions, which is why so many of the comments today by those invited on the other side have been either in terms of sheer generalities or, when they have gotten factual, have been incorrect.

That is why I asked you, Mr. Taylor, you make the statement that Mel Watt's district unites people who have nothing in common. I asked you to be specific to justify that, because there now is a record in *Shaw* v. *Reno*. As a responsible journalist you could have looked at that record and you would have seen in that record socioeconomically, politically, under things that count for representation, the communities put together in Mel Watt's district have a lot more in common than surrounding suburban areas. Yet your commentary was purely at the level of generality, that people who are separated can't be put together. Again, I am not saying there is any ill will, here, but I am saying there is a fundamental misconception.

Similarly, Mr. Markman says that these districts are 65 percent optimized minority districts and 35 percent whites are put in them merely as filler people. Again, as a basic factual matter, that is fundamentally incorrect. The specific district that Elaine Jones pointed out, Eddie Bernice Johnson's district in Dallas, is not 65 percent black, it is 50 percent black in its racial composition. Mr. Watt's district is 53 percent black in its voting age composition. The so-called bug-splattered district, District No. 1 in North Carolina, is 53 percent black in its voting age composition.

It is simply factually incorrect that the districting process has somehow produced these 65 percent optimized districts as opposed to producing the most racially diverse districts we have ever had in the history of redistricting in the United States.

Again, if you look to North Carolina, which not until 1992 had any twentieth century black representation, all those districts were, in fact, 65 percent or more optimized, except they were 65 percent or more optimized whites. That gets to my next point, that somehow racial gerrymandering, or let's call it race-conscious districting to get the pejorative out of it, is a creation of the 1982 voting rights amendments—as if the 1980 round of redistricting in North Carolina, which created the notorious hook district to avoid creating a black majority district and created all-white majority districts, was somehow purely colorblind districting and had absolutely nothing to do with race.

Let's get to the next misconception, this notion that somehow it is the enforcement of the Voting Rights Act, somehow it is the remedy, that is creating racially polarized voting and that is blocking interracial coalitions in a race-neutralized society. Nothing could be farther from the truth. You have got to prove rigorously in a court of law that racially polarized voting exists before you can even use the remedies under the Voting Rights Act.

We also have a laboratory to test this, the U.S. Congress. Look at the Senate. There are no black majority States. These white States could certainly elect blacks in proportion to the population, yet what is the black representation in the Senate? One in 100.

Look to the House, on the other hand, where you have 39 Members out of 435. With one or two exceptions, where do they come, black districts? Are the white districts or the white States electing blacks? They are not. The clear laboratory evidence again shows that this is a fundamental misconception and a fundamental misunderstanding. When these misconceptions begin to get cleared up and the reality of racially polarized voting and the reality of what these districts really represent is known, I would hope we won't make the same mistake this time that we made after the last reconstruction and we won't have to go through another hundred years of remedy.

Mr. DURBIN. Thank you.

We are going to go to Richard Samp now, and then we are going to go back to Mr. Baer, and then we are going to have the last question from Mr. Taylor.

Mr. SAMP. The fundamental misconception that Professor Lichtman referred to that somehow people don't believe that there really is racially polarized voting going on, I don't know who believes that. I think everybody here in this room agrees that racially polarized voting is a major problem in this country, and I also think most people in this room would agree that we ought to do whatever we can to try to eliminate it. What I am very concerned about—and I think I will be echoing a lot of what Mr. Griffith said—is that by the kinds of districts that we have set up as a result of the 1982 amendments, we are simply going to be increasing the extent of that racially polarized voting that everybody admits already does exist. It seems to me that is an empirical question that people can start studying in districts such as Congressman Watt's district.

But one of the problems the moment you set up a district that is not contiguous and is not compact is that people within that district are going to know the individuals, the candidates, far less well. I would venture to guess that people within the Charlotte area know of you, Representative Watt, much better based on your past experience within that area than people in the Durham area do. People who are in a compact district have an opportunity to meet the candidates. There is going to be television and newspaper articles that are going to appear about those candidates that are going to be focusing on that race. People are going to get a chance to talk to people who know that candidate well, and hopefully candidates can to a greater extent be judged based on characteristics other than their race.

But when you have people who are 150 miles away voting in the same congressional district where the focus is not going to be solely on that race, because after all we have got four or five districts that have little tentacles in that area, the one salient fact that people in Durham are going to know is who is the black candidate and who is the white candidate. That, it seems to me, is going to lead to increased racially polarized voting. That is something we need to get away from.

Mr. DURBIN. Mr. Baer.

Mr. BAER. Yes, I am going to speak briefly about juries. Congressman Hyde mentioned discrimination in juries, and I just wanted to talk about that as an analogy.

In this country at some points in our history there has been discrimination in grand juries, and in these grand jury discrimination cases people were excluded based on being of different colors and signing up on jury forms and so on. What was done was remedied essentially by ensuring that blacks and Latinos were no longer excluded from the grand jury. In the same way, section 2 and section 5 prevent exclusion of Latinos and African-Americans, Asian-Americans, and native Americans from electing representatives, and in a similar way, discrimination in the selection of the petit jury in recent cases has been held unconstitutional and now discrimination against women.

Those petit jury cases, I would say, are analogous to the *Presley* case. That is, it is one thing to say you can have a representative, it is another thing that you can actually participate in jury decisions. So by excluding powers of those who are elected, you are essentially preventing them from making decisions, and we don't want that discrimination.

Mr. DURBIN. OK.

Mr. Taylor, did you have some brief comments?

Mr. TAYLOR. Yes. I would like to respond principally to some very powerful, I think, points made by Congressman Watt, and I agree with a great deal of what he said, and in the course of that I want to confess an overstatement or perhaps an error.

Of course, people in Congressman Watt's district have things in common with each other, and to the extent that I said otherwise I retract that. The point I meant to make is that by the traditional districting criteria which are largely geographical compactness, they don't have that in common with each other.

What they clearly do have in common with each other, among other things, is significant concentrations of urban people, in particular of urban poor, and I don't deny the congressman's point that that is a fact that can properly be taken note of in redistricting, that commonality.

I think these are all matters of degree, I think I am somewhere in the middle of this panel, although we tend to polarize, to coin a phrase, what troubles me is that if carried to the limits of its logic, it seems to me that when Congressman Watt says, "I have things in common with urban people in Durham, not with suburban people nearer to where I live in Charlotte," if carried to the limits of its logic, what that seems to suggest is, we should junk geographical districting altogether. We should get rid of the system we have had since the founding of the Republic, and we should choose Members of Congress at least perhaps by electing people solely from racial groups; that would be the black candidate, the Hispanic candidate, or whatever, or perhaps social class, socio-economic—I mean split it up any way you will.

The traditional and, I think, healthy focus has been on a degree of geographical compactness, and anything that gets to too far away from that causes me concern.

And I suppose the last point is, of course we have polarized voting, we have had a long history of it. It seems to me if what we want to do is get away from it some day, I am not sure how we accomplish that by carrying racial gerrymandering to the limits of its logic.

Mr. DURBIN. Thank you.

We will turn it back to my colleague, Paige Whitaker.

Mr. WATT. May I just make one comment in response to not only what Mr. Taylor said, but we all tend to make our points by exaggerating arguments. I want to make one point to everybody is—and I can make it in response to Mr. Taylor's question—if you take an argument to its furthest extreme: Would you junk geographic considerations completely? My response to that is, I would junk geographic considerations completely if it is necessary to have representation, diverse representation, in the Congress of the United States. I wouldn't junk it and throw it out.

But I have got 90 some years of history in North Carolina that suggest to me that the use of these traditional criteria that Mr. Griffith talked about and using this geographic consideration has resulted in that which is uppermost in my value system being jeopardized and trampled on, and that is representation in the process. So let's not take all these arguments to their extremes.

We are doing this hopefully—I mean in the best of all possible worlds, as a temporary proposition. You all seem to suggest that it is going to make temporary longer, but I don't necessarily believe that. I mean I think what happened in Espy's case is a prime example. He was able to get in. Once people got familiar with him, then he became an acceptable alternative to whites who might otherwise have been elected. I think the same thing I see happening in all of these States. Once we get in and people find out that we are not terrible people, it will help to undercut and shorten the period of racial polarization, and I hope that happens. I mean I can't prove it to you with any great degree of reliability, but I can tell you that I am willing to take my chances on that happening rather than just waiting on the regular course of events to happen while I am outside the system and waiting on nature to take its course.

Mr. DURBIN. Thank you for your insights, Congressman.

Ms. WHITAKER. We are drawing to the close of this very spirited and interesting debate, and we thank you all.

In closing, we would like to ask you to make a final statement, and if you could, in the interests of times, to limit yourselves to a minute.

Mr. WATT. I have made mine already.

Ms. WHITAKER. OK.

We would like you to address yourself, generally speaking, to the future of the Voting Rights Act, where you see it going or where you think it should go into the 21st century in view of public opinion, what is going on in the courts, and what you see going on in the legislature. I would like to start with Mr. Chairman, if you have any comment, please.

Mr. EDWARDS. Let me go at the end.

Ms. WHITAKER. OK.

Ms. Elaine Jones. Oh, nice to see you.

STATEMENT OF PENDA D. HAIR, ASSISTANT COUNSEL, NAACP LEGAL DEFENSE AND EDUCATION FUND

Ms. HAIR. Thank you. I am Penda Hair.

Mr. WATT. You are the colorblind version.

Ms. HAIR. I am a staff attorney with the NAACP Legal Defense Fund, and I am sitting in for Elaine Jones.

I think in terms of where the Voting Rights Act is going, the question that this very useful session seems to ultimately point to, is, are we going to have any remedy or are we going to have no remedies? Are we going to, as Congressman Watt says, let nature take its course, or are we going to intervene in the form of the Voting Rights Act to push nature along, assuming that nature means getting to a system of color-blindness. I think my view and certainly the view of the NAACP Legal Defense Fund, is that nature—whatever that means—has not brought us to a situation where racism and race consciousness has been purged from society and that, in fact, in many situations strong remedies are needed.

So we certainly support continued enforcement, vigorous enforcement of the Voting Rights Act, and in particular the *Presley* case we think does need to be addressed by Congress in order to bring about remedies for the extreme type of exclusion that was found to exist in that case.

Mr. DURBIN. Mr. Markman.

Mr. MARKMAN. I would say again I think that the Voting Rights Act as currently understood is transforming America in very detrimental ways. Some of us on this panel apparently think that color consciousness is necessary in the short run. Others of us, including myself, think that by exacerbated color consciousness we will never get beyond it.

We are leaving for our children a legacy of a much different America than we have traditionally known, and again I would highlight the issue of cumulative voting. I am not necessarily opposed to cumulative voting myself in every context, but to suggest that the language of section 2 requires that cumulative voting be considered a practical remedy around the country is, I think, to give the courts extraordinary authority to do something very radical in our system that was never the subject of debate and that was never the subject of consideration by the Congress. I think that the courts can only consider things like cumulative voting because the language of the Voting Rights Act is so unclear and lacks any kind of internal core value.

Mr. DURBIN. Professor Karlan.

Ms. KARLAN. Well, I have litigated a number of cumulative voting cases where we used cumulative voting as a remedy, and in all of those cases we persuaded the defendants that it was a superior system because not only did it give representation for the first time to blacks in several of these places, it also gave representation to Republicans for the first time, and it seems to me that even Republicans can be a disenfranchised minority group sometimes.

Where is the Voting Rights Act going? Well, if you look at the way that administrations, both Democratic and Republican, enforce it, it is quite vigorous and quite progressive. If you look at the way State legislatures are starting to negotiate with the Justice Department, it is quite vigorous and quite progressive.

If, on the other hand, you look at what 12 years of conservative activism on the bench is producing, then you get a very different view. What frightens me about *Shaw* v. *Reno* more than anything else is that instead of interpreting the statute there, what Justice O'Connor did was to interpret the Constitution, suggesting that the Court, like the Court in the second reconstruction which struck down a number of congressional attempts to deal with problems of racial justice, will once again step in with its notion of a colorblind Constitution and stop the progress that the political system has made both on the national and State levels by enforcing the Voting Rights Act.

One last point on that is just to point out that in *Presley* v. *Etowah County,* it wasn't just the plaintiffs who argued the Voting Rights Act covered the discrimination there, it was also the U.S. Department of Justice. So this was not a case in which the political branches took the Court's side against a group of minority plaintiffs, the political branches were there with the minority plaintiffs.

Mr. DURBIN. Mr. Samp.

Mr. SAMP. Well, I am happy that Professor Karlan can agree with me that the political process ought to be permitted to run its course, and I don't think that Congress should do anything to interfere with the ability of State legislatures to make the kind of progress that has been made over the last 30 years in terms of decreases in racial polarization and in terms of increase in representation for racial minority groups. Any changes in the Voting Rights Act which have the effect of increasing racial polarization should absolutely be avoided, and certainly any attempt to overrule the *Presley* case would be one such unfortunate step.

Mr. DURBIN. Mr. Baer, do you want to go next?

Mr. BAER. Sure.

The future of the Voting Rights Act is really the future of our Nation. That is, what really the Voting Rights Act reflects is a history of exclusion, and if we change the Voting Rights Act will become obsolete, so hopefully some time soon we won't have residential segregation or racially polarized voting. Maybe that will be past history, and maybe equal employment and economic and educational opportunity will be current history and we won't have the need for the Voting Rights Act. So really what happens to the Voting Rights Act is a reflection of what will happen in all other parts of our country.

Mr. DURBIN. Mr. Griffith.

Mr. GRIFFITH. I share the concerns of Congressman Watt and I think of any minority elected official who asks how long we should wait. I don't think anybody should wait forever, and I don't think we ought to sit around twiddling our thumbs. But I do feel that if we promote racial gerrymandering and we promote race-based stereotyping of the type that has been engaged in *Hays* v. *State of Louisiana* and the *Shaw* v. *Hunt* remand trial, if we promote that, we are promoting the very worst things that can occur in our system of American democracy. It will have a corrosive effect upon race relations. It will have a corrosive effect upon coalition building among white citizens and black citizens.

I feel very strongly that, not to use the apartheid rhetoric—I think the term "apartheid" surfaced in the *Shaw* v. *Reno* decision in an unusual context, but when we start talking about such things as authenticity assumptions that Professor Guinier has advocated, saying that blacks can only represent blacks, the only representative that a black can have is one with that skin pigmentation, I think it is a travesty. I think we are presuming race-based communities of interest by doing that. We are stereotyping voters, we are doing things that the Founding Fathers never would have dreamed could be done, we are going backward. I think the fears that the subcommittee expressed in some of the minority reports that were filed in the 1982 amendments are starting to come to the surface now. One of those was that this type of tendency to promote race-based remedial action is going to be a divisive factor in local communities by emphasizing the role of racial politics. I am afraid we are retreating from some of the admirable goals of access and equal opportunity, particularly in the remedy context where cumulative voting has only been utilized not as a court-ordered, mandated solution but as an agreed solution in consent decrees. In the State of Illinois where cumulative voting was utilized, it was abandoned in 1980, and the reasons are all set out in my statement.

I don't believe Federal courts should get into the business of promoting a novel experimental system that will inevitably lead to increased racial polarization and ultimately proportional representation. I think that is where we are headed.

Mr. DURBIN. Professor Lichtman.

Mr. LICHTMAN. America is indeed a very different place than it was 30 years ago when not a single African-American from the Southern States sat in the Halls of Congress of the United States. Today American Government is more racially diverse than at any time in its history and more responsive to racial diversity than at any time in its history. Even 10 years ago, we would have not had a Congressman Mel Watt from North Carolina sitting here to explain to us what it means to have been excluded from politics for 92 years, and we all would have been very much the poorer for it.

I believe that it is the racial diversity represented by Mel Watt in our Government that is by far the best hope to transcend racially-polarized voting and to promote interracial coalitions, and that hope is clearly supported by the factual history which shows rising white support for African-American and other minority politicians once they are elected to office, like Mike Espy and like Mel Watt, regardless of the particular shape of their districts. America will remember Mel Watt long after they forget what his district looked like.

Finally, it may well ultimately be necessary, depending on how the whole *Shaw* v. *Reno* litigation comes down, for Congress to reexpress its compelling interest in remedying voting discrimination and explicitly indicate that such interest transcends geographic considerations in districting.

Mr. DURBIN. Professor Lund.

Mr. LUND. Yes, I want to take this opportunity to disagree with Mr. Markman and Mr. Griffith, both of whom indicated that they thought that the future of the Voting Rights Act was in the direction of proportional representation with that as the ultimate goal. I think that is an understatement.

As long as you have an effects test of the kind that you have in the 1982 amendments to the Voting Rights Act, proportional representation won't be enough. Those who benefit from racial gerrymandering will always have something more they can ask for and always something more that they will ask for. I will give a couple of examples, one from today.

Professor Lichtman at one point told us—and I take his word for it—that black Americans are about 11 percent of the voting age population. At another point in his remarks he said there is 1 Senator in 100, and I think he suggested that it was a shamefully low number.

The more important example, I think, is the writing of Professor Guinier. I think that is one indication of where voting rights litigation would head after you got proportional representation and I think is probably an inevitable result of the kind of test that Congress created in the 1982 amendments. Unless the Supreme Court puts a stop to it under the Constitution which they haven't shown very much inclination to do, that is probably where we are headed.

Mr. DURBIN. Ms. St. Cyr.

Ms. ST. CYR. I would just like to encourage the continuation of the Voting Rights Act and strong enforcement of it.

As I said before, we have just begun to make some gains as recently as 1992, and if we are going to continue to have hope and look forward to a better representation, look forward to a brighter future in this country, I would strongly encourage more enforcement of the Voting Rights Act.

Mr. DURBIN. Mr. Taylor.

Mr. TAYLOR. Again, I would love to see something approximating proportional representation in this country if it happened spontaneously. It won't any time soon for the reasons that have been pointed out today, although I think the elections of people like Senator Moseley-Braun and former Gov. Douglas Wilder of Virginia do indicate that blacks are not always doomed to exclusion in the absence of racial gerrymandering.

The real question, it seems to me, is how much should Congress and the courts do to push us toward proportionate representation. In my view, they need to do some, where there is strong proof of polarized voting with exclusionary effects and where remedy is possible without creating undue distortions in terms of bizarrely shaped districts or other distortions.

But I think there are strong impulses in the country and on this panel to pursue the goal of racial proportionality in a headlong fashion while throwing other considerations overboard. I understand and respect that impulse, but I fear it points toward a long-term result of freezing our electorate into a collection of rival racial factions. In the long run, I don't think that would benefit anybody, certainly not racial minorities in a country that for a long time is going to have a very lopsided white majority.

Mr. DURBIN. Thank you, Mr. Taylor.

Mr. Chairman.

Mr. EDWARDS. Well, thanks to the moderators and thanks to the panel of witnesses of different views but very sophisticated and knowledgeable views, and we are grateful for that.

What we are searching for you all addressed very intelligently. What the Subcommittee on Civil Rights will be doing for the rest of this year, and I can't plan any further than that, is to work on a remedy for what we think was a bad decision in *Presley*. We didn't have the votes or any help from the White House when we first wrote it, but it now appears that we could be on the way.

But the larger subject, after being here 32 years, is of course, that we are far, far ahead of where we were 32 years ago. We had massive support in 1964 and 1965 for the omnibus bill where actually a lot more Republicans voted for those bills than Democrats. Why? Because the solid South voted against us; 82 percent of the Republicans voted both for the Voting Rights Act and for the omnibus bill in 1964.

But I am disturbed, and you have been helpful, all of you, because of civil rights generally. For the last 12 or 13 years they have been seriously chipped away by the Supreme Court. We worked ourselves half to death in 1991 by reversing a number of them, but they are out there, and most of them were in employment areas.

But *Shaw* v. *Reno* was sort of the coup d'etat, and I could trace some of the despair of African-Americans in this country to the fact that in civil rights they were receiving so little attention. I wouldn't be surprised if that had to do with the rise or the respect that a lot of people have, not for what Louis Farrakhan has been saying and the fact that African-Americans are talking about a new political party.

It seems that the progress in civil rights has slowed down and the progress in voting rights has slowed down. At least for my six colleagues, including Mel Watt here, because of the Supreme Court decision, which I found completely unnecessary, and which is still on the books and is not anything that we anticipate is possible to reverse.

So let me invite more comments in writing. We have a record, and we would like to augment it with suggestions and comments. You have all been very helpful, and we are very grateful.

So with that, Mel, we were delighted to have you here, and you have made a major contribution. All of you made great contributions.

Thank you very much.

The subcommittee is adjourned.

[Whereupon, at 12:18 p.m., the subcommittee adjourned.]

VOTING RIGHTS

WEDNESDAY, MAY 25, 1994

HOUSE OF REPRESENTATIVES,
SUBCOMMITTEE ON CIVIL AND CONSTITUTIONAL RIGHTS,
COMMITTEE ON THE JUDICIARY,
Washington, DC.

The subcommittee met, at 9:33 a.m., in room 2237, Rayburn House Office Building, Hon. Don Edwards (chairman of the subcommittee) presiding.

Present: Representatives Don Edwards, Barney Frank, Henry J. Hyde, Howard Coble, and Charles T. Canady.

Also present: Melody Barnes, assistant counsel, and Kathryn Hazeem, minority counsel.

Mr. EDWARDS. Good morning and welcome. I'm Don Edwards of California, the chairman of the Judiciary Committee's Subcommittee on Civil and Constitutional Rights, and I have been here a long time. This is my 32d year. So I was a member of the House Judiciary Committee when the Voting Rights Act was passed in 1965 and, of course, although the voting rights bill was terribly important, the major omnibus civil rights bill in 1964. That was a great year in the history of the country. I think that we stand proud throughout the world, chiefly because we made up our minds as a nation to get rid of racial discrimination by law and not to wait until it melted away on its own.

In the early 1980's, I guess maybe 1979, Mr. Hyde and I—Mr. Hyde, who I will introduce in a minute, is the ranking minority member of the subcommittee—decided that it was time to update the Voting Rights Act and to acquaint ourselves with what was going on in the country. We traveled throughout portions of the United States to try to see what was what. Frankly, we were shocked at the discrimination in voting that still existed in the country despite the 1965 Voting Rights Act. So we came back and in 1982 we brought to the House the Voting Rights Amendments of 1982. Since then we have chiefly exercised oversight.

We are concerned these days because there is lots of action going on in voting. We think that we need some more oversight and some discussion from experts. We need education as to what the next step should be. We find that there is much discussion and a lot of uneasiness because of *Shaw* v. *Reno*, but nobody has come forth with a response to it or to tell us or suggest to us that something should be done. We are very grateful for the experts who are here today. It is very nice of you to be here.

I now yield to Mr. Hyde.

Mr. HYDE. Thank you very much, Mr. Chairman.

Parenthetically, Mr. Edwards is retiring at the end of this term. He has had 32 years in Congress. While Mr. Edwards and I never agree on anything, including what day it is, I will tell you it's a terrible loss to Congress when he leaves. It will be a diminishing of the experience and the judgment and the wisdom and the civility and the knowledge that Don has built up over those long years of service. I will miss him a great deal.

I want to thank Thomas Durbin and L. Paige Whitaker for their magnificent presiding and moderating of this very important forum. The right to vote is probably the most important of the rights. It's more important than the right of free speech. If they let you talk your head off but you can't vote, you can't implement your ideas or your views, then talking isn't all that significant. They are both very important but the right to vote is primary.

The extent to which Americans are afforded the right to vote is the subject matter of what we are discussing today. The purpose of the Voting Rights Act was to fulfill the promise of the 15th amendment to ensure that artificial distinctions based on race played no role in an individual's ability to exercise his or her right to vote.

Thirty years later, evidently we have turned this principle on its head. Race has become the preeminent factor in drawing lines for electoral districts. Racial gerrymandering is no longer a sin but a virtue. In Florida, Cuban-Americans, African-Americans, and Mexican-Americans are battling each other to draw the maximum number of race-based safe State senate seats. Some have complained, and I share their concerns, that the Voting Rights Act, which was designed to guarantee equal opportunities to participate in the electoral process, is quietly being transformed into a government-sanctioned ethnic spoils system.

In any event, we have a diverse and very experienced and knowledgeable panel to explore these interesting questions. I sure want to thank Don Edwards for calling this meeting so we can discuss these important issues. Thank you.

Mr. EDWARDS. Thank you very much, Mr. Hyde.

We welcome the gentleman from North Carolina, Mr. Coble. Do you have a statement?

Mr. COBLE. Mr. Chairman, I have no prepared statement. I presume, Henry, that you were saying good things about the distinguished gentleman from California.

Mr. HYDE. I was indeed.

Mr. COBLE. I will reiterate that, Mr. Chairman. You will indeed be missed when you invade the West again.

I think we in this country very obviously are casual about the right to vote. I read not too long ago where there was a vote somewhere in the South. Twelve percent of the eligible voters took the time to go to the polls to vote. Conversely, we pick up the paper frequently and see people who are willing to die for the right to vote. So you are right, Henry. This is indeed a very cherished privilege that we ought to exercise more zealously in this country.

Mr. Chairman, I have two meetings simultaneously going on now, so I am going to be going back and forth. I appreciate your recognizing me, Mr. Chairman.

Mr. EDWARDS. I thank you for your kind personal words and I thank you, Mr. Hyde, also.

Mr. Hyde, I wonder if you would introduce the panel.

The gentleman from Florida. I'm sorry. Do you have a statement?

Mr. CANADY. No statement, Mr. Chairman.

Mr. HYDE. He is so professorial looking that you assumed he was one of the panelists.

I will introduce the panel at your direction, Mr. Chairman.

Mr. EDWARDS. Would you be kind enough to introduce the panel and our friends from the Library of Congress who have been so helpful.

Mr. HYDE. Yes, I will

On my immediate left is Thomas Durbin, the Legislative Attorney and head of the Courts Section, American Law Division, Congressional Research Service.

On his immediate left is L. Paige Whitaker, Legislative Attorney of the American Law Division, Congressional Research Service.

Today we will have the Honorable Tyrone Brooks, who is a member of the Georgia State Legislature and president of the Georgia Association of Black Elected Officials.

Chandler Davidson, a professor of sociology at Rice University in Houston, TX. Professor Davidson is the coeditor of "Quiet Revolution in the South: The Impact of the Voting Rights Act 1965–1990."

Ira Glasser is executive director of the American Civil Liberties Union and a well-known television personality.

Brenda Wright is director of the voting rights project at the Lawyers' Committee for Civil Rights Under Law.

Anthony Chavez is director of the voting rights project at the Mexican-American Legal Defense and Education Fund.

The Rev. Jesse Jackson, who is not here yet, is president and founder of the National Rainbow Coalition, Inc.

Margaret Fung is executive director of the Asian American Legal Defense and Education Fund.

I have already introduced Tom Durbin and Paige Whitaker.

Charles Cooper is a partner with the law firm of Shaw, Pittman, Potts & Trowbridge. He formerly served as Assistant Attorney General in the Office of Legal Counsel in the Reagan administration and has been active in litigating legislative and congressional redistricting plans.

Carl Hampe is with the law firm of Paul, Weiss, Rifkind, Wharton & Garrison. He served in the Department of Justice during the Bush administration and as counsel to the Senate Judiciary Committee for Senator Alan Simpson.

Dr. Timothy O'Rourke is professor and head of the department of political science at Clemson University in South Carolina. He has served as an expert witness in voting rights litigation, including *Shaw* v. *Hunt* and *James* v. *City of Sarasota*.

Tony Snow, who is not here yet, is a nationally syndicated columnist with the Detroit News, a columnist for U.S.A. Today, a commentator on National Public Radio, and a regular contributor to "McLaughlin Group," "Crossfire," and "Inside Politics."

I understand Elizabeth McCaughey, who was scheduled to be with us, has been nominated for the Office of Lieutenant Governor on the Republican ticket in New York and probably will have to make an acceptance speech or something this afternoon. So she will not be with us.

Those are the introductions, Mr. Chairman.

STATEMENT OF THOMAS M. DURBIN, LEGISLATIVE ATTORNEY, AMERICAN LAW DIVISION, CONGRESSIONAL RESEARCH SERVICE

Mr. DURBIN. I'm Tom Durbin, as you have heard, and this is Paige Whitaker. We are election attorneys at the Congressional Research Service. We have been asked to serve as moderators and we have also been asked to give a brief presentation on some of the introductory issues on the Voting Rights Act.

In accordance with the founding principles of the Congressional Research Service, whatever we say will be neutral, objective and nonpartisan.

What I want to do first in my presentation is to go back and talk about philosophically, historically the right to vote.

Why is it today with the Voting Rights Act that we still struggle with the right to vote? Today we consider it an inalienable right. But if you go back to the 1700's and 1800's of our country, it was not a right. We based our suffrage, our right to elect officials, on English common law, and under English common law the right to vote or the right of suffrage or the privilege to vote was very limited. If you were not a white, a male, a landowner, and a taxpayer, most likely you could not vote.

When you look at the founding documents of our Constitution, the original articles of our Constitution do not mention the right to vote. The Declaration of Independence does not mention the right to vote. The first 10 amendments, the Bill of Rights, do not mention the right to vote. What you have is a situation in which the right to vote was not granted to everybody.

We are the greatest democracy, and how can we as a great democracy give this right to vote when in the past we didn't do it? Fortunately, in our articles of the Constitution we provided for article V which allowed us to change the Constitution by constitutional amendment.

From 1787, when the Constitution was enacted, until 1868 you did not see the terms "right to vote." In 1868, with the great 15th amendment, for the first time the right to vote appeared as "The right of citizens of the United States to vote shall not be denied or abridged by the United States or any State on account of race, color, or previous condition of servitude." This amendment gave black Americans, African-Americans a special privilege. They are a protected minority when it comes to the Federal and State electoral processes. It separates them from any other minority.

We see in our Constitution an evolutionary process of the right to vote. In 1920, with the 19th amendment, women were granted the right to vote. In 1960, with the 23d Amendment, you have citizens of the District of Columbia being given the right to vote for electors for President and Vice President. And in 1964, the 24th amendment abolished poll taxes and any other tax on the right to vote that the States were imposing. And in 1971, the 26th amendment granted the right to vote to citizens 18 years of age and older.

What you have basically is an evolutionary process by constitutional amendment enforcing the right to vote and guaranteeing the right to vote.

However, when you look at African-American and black Americans, for 97 years, from 1868 to 1965, there was pervasive discrimination by the States and local political subdivisions in regard to the right to vote, because in our Constitution the qualifications to vote were basically left to the States. Because of this pervasive discrimination and because our Federal judicial system could not correct that adequately and in a timely fashion, an act had to be created.

Section 2 of the 15th amendment provided that Congress has the power to enforce the right of black Americans to vote by appropriate legislation. So it took 97 years before we really began to enforce this right to vote, and that was in 1965. As the Voting Rights Act was amended in 1970, 1975, and 1982, we see that protected right of black Americans being expanded to include other protected minorities, and those were protected language minorities such as Hispanic-Americans, Asian-Americans, American Indians, and Alaskan Natives.

I want to now turn this over to Paige Whitaker, who will give you a brief presentations on the Voting Rights Act.

STATEMENT OF L. PAIGE WHITAKER, LEGISLATION ATTORNEY, AMERICAN LAW DIVISION, CONGRESSIONAL RESEARCH SERVICE

Ms. WHITAKER. Before we begin today's discussion, I will be briefly going over the specific issues relating to the Voting Rights Act that we hope will be covered in today's discussion.

First, we will be starting today with a discussion of the impact of the Voting Rights Act and the impact that it has had specifically on African-American communities, Hispanic- and Asian-American communities.

In identifying the impact that the Act has had, we would encourage you to discuss also any problems you see with the Voting Rights Act and with voting rights in general in this country and what you think the cause of these problems are.

After we have explored that area, we will be shifting the discussion over to the constitutionality and the policy rationale for voting rights remedies.

The two key sections of the Voting Rights Act, which will tend to be in the center of today's discussion, are section 2 and section 5.

Section 2, of course, applies nationwide, unlike section 5, and it created a right of action for private citizens or the Government to challenge discriminatory voting practices and procedures.

Section 5, on the other hand, applies only to certain covered jurisdictions. It sets forth the preclearance requirement. That is, certain covered areas of the country have to preclear any change in their voting practices or procedures, which, of course, includes redistricting plans, with either the Department of Justice or the U.S. district court for the District of Columbia.

Then, as we enter into a discussion of the constitutionality of voting rights remedies, there are a few court opinions that we expect to be covered today as well.

First, the landmark Supreme Court case of *Thornburgh* v. *Gingles*. This came down in 1986. The Court held that the critical question for any court in determining whether a violation of section 2 of the act has occurred is whether "as a result of the challenged practice plaintiffs do not have an equal opportunity to participate in the political processes and to elect candidates of their choice." The Court said that you have to look at the totality of the circumstances to see if there is a violation, and the Court established a new tripartite test.

First, the minority group must be able to show that it is large and geographically compact enough to constitute a majority in a single member district.

Second, that it is sufficiently politically cohesive.

Third, that the majority in that case votes as a block sufficiently to enable it to usually defeat the minority's preferred candidate.

As a result of that *Thornburgh* case, many courts have construed the Voting Rights Act in the redistricting area to mean create minority majority districts wherever possible.

Then we had all of a sudden a bit of a divergence last year with *Shaw* v. *Reno*, another case that will inevitably come up in today's discussion. That was decided in June 1993. The Court in *Shaw* held that if a redistricting scheme is so bizarre and so irrational on its face that it can be understood only to be a racial gerrymander that it will pass constitutional muster if a court finds that it is narrowly tailored to further a compelling governmental interest. For example, a community interest or geographical compactness.

The underlying principle in *Shaw* was that racially gerrymandered redistricting plans are subject to the same strict scrutiny that other State legislation that classifies citizens on the basis of race is subject to.

Finally, the last case that we expect will come up is last December's Federal court case, a three-judge court case in Louisiana in the style of *Hays* v. *Louisiana*. In that case the district was shaped like a "Z" and was commonly referred to as the Mark of Zorro District.

In that decision the court applied the holding in *Shaw* and found that the unusually shaped district was an unconstitutional racial gerrymander, because it was not narrowly tailored to further a compelling governmental interest. Therefore, the court found that the plaintiff's right to equal protection under the 14th amendment was violated by that particular redistricting plan. That was the first case we saw where a lower court applied the *Shaw* holding.

Finally, toward the end of today's discussion we would like the participants to discuss and focus on the future of the Voting Rights Act. We would like you to take into account public sentiment, legislative activity, and also judicial interpretation of the act.

Then, as a wrap-up, we will provide all the participants with 1 minute to make any closing remarks if they so choose.

Now I will turn it over to Tom, who is going to set some of the ground rules for today's discussion.

Mr. DURBIN. As moderators, we will need your cooperation in letting us know when you want to speak. Obviously, sometimes a number of hands will go up, and we are going to put your names in order. We will be alternating between a majority witness and minority witness where it is feasible so we can get both sides in.

Ms. WHITAKER. Also, at the same time we would like to encourage, as much as we can within those confines, as free an open an exchange as possible. When you are seeking recognition, feel free during your period to pose questions to one another based on a statement that you have heard or to pose questions to the group as a whole. We would encourage that as well. As Tom said, as we moderate we will be alternating as best we can between minority and majority witnesses so that there is a balanced presentation.

The first question that we would like to pose to the group and open up for discussion is, what impact do you see that the Voting Rights Act has had on the African-American, Hispanic and Asian communities? Would anyone like to start?

Professor Davidson.

Mr. DAVIDSON. I will say a few words on it.

Ms. WHITAKER. Thank you.

STATEMENT OF CHANDLER DAVIDSON, PROFESSOR OF SOCIOLOGY, RICE UNIVERSITY

Mr. DAVIDSON. I have been involved in a project that has gone on for several years now to try to get a sense of the progress which blacks and Mexican-Americans in the South have made as a result of the Voting Rights Act.

Our project has involved two sorts of things. On the one hand, we have tried to build a narrative history of the struggle for black voting rights primarily in the South since the end of the Civil War. I want to address now and probably in the course of the 2½ hours that if you lose sight of the historical context, you miss a lot of what is going on.

We were struck, first of all, by the large number of disfranchising mechanisms in the eight so-called section 5 States that we uncovered from the period of 1868, the beginning of Reconstruction, up to the present. We identified over 60 different mechanisms, some of the same mechanisms from State to State, but a large number of different laws that had been put into effect to make it more difficult, if not impossible, for blacks to vote during this period.

Most of us over the age of 50 have spent most of our lives watching the courts and civil rights activists and the Congress try to destroy these barriers to registration and voting on the part of minorities. They have just about succeeded, although not entirely.

There were four mechanisms that were clearly put into effect sometime over the last 100 years to impede blacks in their attempts to vote that are still on the books today. Some of them that have gone off the books have gone off in the last 10 to 15 years—after the Voting Rights Act had actually been passed.

A study of 11 Southern States by Prof. Jim Alt of Harvard has shown that for the most part the 1968 Voting Rights Act did what it was supposed to do, and that is, by abolishing the literacy test in the Southern States that still had them, it opened up the political process to blacks in a way that had not been opened since Reconstruction times. As a result of his research, he predicts that sometime in the 1990's the registration rates of Southern blacks and Southern whites will probably converge.

So on the question of disfranchisement, it looks to me as a result of our research that a good deal of progress has been made and that the Voting Rights Act can take a great deal of the credit for it.

The second focus of our research has been on minority vote dilution. I assume that most of the people in this room know what that is, but just for the record, it consists of laws and practices that in combination with the tendency of whites to vote one way and blacks to vote another or some other minority to vote another way, blacks or other minorities are prevented from electing candidates of their choice to office.

One of the things that we discovered in looking at the history of the eight section 5 States is that a movement got under way in the late 1940's, not long after *Smith* v. *Alright,* the Supreme Court decision outlawing the white primary in 1944, among white officials in various Southern States to put into effect laws anticipating the destruction of the Jim Crow system so far as voting was concerned. These was laws were designed to prevent blacks in the South, once they obtained the right to actually go to the polls and cast a ballot, from electing candidates of their choice to office.

I think one of the signal accomplishments of the research performed by the various people involved in this project—there are 27 people, lawyers, and scholars—is that we have shown in a systematic form the way in which laws were put on the books in most of the southern States in the 1940's, 1950's and the 1960's as a fallback to make it more difficult for blacks to have a chance to exercise their full voting rights, even at a time when they were able to actually go to the polls and vote. I don't think the widespread nature of movement to put these laws on the books in the Southern States has been fully appreciated.

I don't want to monopolize the conversation here, but let me in the next minute or two spell out a couple of the things that we looked at and some of our findings with regard to the ability of blacks in the South and Mexican-Americans in Texas to elect candidates of their choice to office.

With regard to the U.S. Congress, in 1964 there were no blacks representing the South in Congress. The first two blacks elected from the South since the late 19th century were elected in 1972, Barbara Jordan of Texas and Andrew Young of Georgia.

In 1988, before the most recent round of redistricting, we had 4 blacks elected to Congress from the 11 States in the South, and in 1993 there were 17. Virtually all of the blacks elected to Congress from the South during the period of the second Reconstruction were elected from districts that were majority black, or in a couple of cases, such as Craig Washington's district, a majority of blacks plus Hispanics. Virtually all of those districts were created as a result of the Voting Rights Act and the Justice Department exercising its oversight as a result of the act.

Much the same history is true with regard to blacks in Southern legislatures. In 1964 there were only two black legislators from the 11 Southern States. In 1993 there are 213. And virtually all of these gains were the result of the creation of new majority black districts.

I haven't looked at 1990 yet. Our project only goes up to 1990. But in the 1970's and the 1980's less than 2 percent of all majority white legislative districts in the South elected blacks to office. That, too, seems to be primarily the result of the oversight of the Justice Department as a result of section 5 and section 2.

Ms. WHITAKER. I think Professor Davidson has given us an excellent historical perspective. Does anyone have any additional comments they would like to make on the impact?

Mr. Tony Snow.

STATEMENT OF TONY SNOW, COLUMNIST

Mr. SNOW. Actually, I would just like to ask a question. When you were looking at the voting patterns in the South, were there any changes in the percentage of white voters who voted for black candidates, especially in the last series of congressional elections? Have you disaggregated white voters?

Mr. DAVIDSON. We did not look at the white voting patterns within the white districts. As I say, I haven't looked at what has happened in the 1990's, but there was no change between the 1970's and the 1980's with regard to the percentage of majority white districts who elected blacks to the State legislatures.

Mr. SNOW. I am just curious. Another thesis is, let's hope that Americans are less bigoted and that it is not simply the drawing of the districts but also the fact that people do have more open minds when they are selecting candidates. I would presume that we have broken down a few barriers and we don't simply have to solve our problems by drawing lines. That's why I was curious about the change in voting patterns.

Mr. DAVIDSON. We did look at the question of the election of blacks to office in southern cities and at-large election systems that were majority white from the early 1970's to the late 1980's. We did indeed find that there was some increase in the percentage of blacks who were elected in these at-large cities that had maintained an at-large system from the early 1970's to the late 1980's.

The other side of that is that when you compare cities that had gone from at-large to either single member districts or mixed plans, some at large, some single member seats, black representation in those cities was much higher than it was between 1974 and 1989 with regard to the cities that maintained their at-large structure.

Mr. DURBIN. Thank you. We want to recognize Congressman Barney Frank. I think he may have a statement or a response to one of the points of discussion.

Mr. FRANK. When you talked about cities which maintained at-large having an increasing number of blacks, did you account for the increasing number of blacks that lived in the cities? I guess if they are like other cities, the black population has increased.

Mr. DAVIDSON. Yes, Congressman.

Mr. FRANK. In terms of the question of whites voting for blacks, blacks have for over 100 years been voting for whites. We don't have to prove that. We know that blacks have always voted for whites. In some cases they have no choice. When we talk about whether or not there is an increase in whites voting for blacks, I would think two points. One, I assume if we were doing a comparison it would be whites voting for blacks who were running, who were nonincumbent.

The second question which I think would be useful, would do two separate things. I would also assume that African-Americans who get elected get very few white votes the first time but as they run for reelection increase their percentage of whites.

Mr. DAVIDSON. That's true.

Mr. FRANK. That is, incumbency allows them to overcome some of these things. If we were checking increases. I wish somebody would. I would be interested to see if there was that increase in whites voting for blacks when they had a choice between a white and a black as a nonincumbent, and I would also be interested in seeing what the rate of increase is once someone has been elected and people aren't dealing with stereotypes anymore, but are dealing with each other.

I say that because one of the arguments is the Voting Rights Act has been producing polarization. I believe in fact the opposite is the case. I think this statistic proves it. I think what you will find is that African-Americans running for the first time get a much smaller percentage of white votes than those African-Americans who win the election and run for reelection. The best way to diminish racial polarization is for blacks to be elected to office and to be able to deal with constituents and to get through the stereotypes. I think that would be an interesting set of statistical comparisons.

Mr. DAVIDSON. Can I just add one thing to that? In my city of Houston the pattern that we have seen when we elect some of our city council from districts and some at large, the typical pattern of a minority candidate's winning one of those at-large seats is to start out by winning a district seat and convincing the populace that indeed he or she is a good candidate and then running at large.

Mr. FRANK. The Boston City Council when I lived in Boston used to be all elected at-large and there was a big debate about how to elect them. Some of us pointed out that the question was not whether they should be elected at large but whether they should remain at large. [Laughter.]

Ms. WHITAKER. We would like to recognize Brenda Wright and then afterward Ira Glasser.

STATEMENT OF BRENDA WRIGHT, DIRECTOR, VOTING RIGHTS PROJECT, LAWYERS' COMMITTEE FOR CIVIL RIGHTS UNDER LAW

Ms. WRIGHT. I wanted to follow up for a moment on something that Congressman Frank was observing. There is some anecdotal evidence of the phenomenon that you were talking about, which is that once black or minority candidates have a chance to serve, resistance to those candidates tends to go down somewhat among whites.

I think the situation of the current Secretary of Agriculture, Mike Espy, is a good example of that. He was first elected to Congress in 1986 from a majority black congressional district created after many years of litigation in Mississippi. In his first election in that district he received only about 10 percent of the white vote and of course was able to prevail because the district was majority black in population. After he had served in Congress and proved that he could in fact represent all the people of his district his support from white voters began to go up.

I think you do see in that example and in others the fact that drawing these majority minority districts rather than fostering racial polarization, as is sometimes claimed, tends to be the mechanism by which racial polarization and stereotyped attitudes can be in fact overcome.

Mr. FRANK. I'm familiar with the phenomenon.

Ms. WHITAKER. Mr. Glasser.

STATEMENT OF IRA GLASSER, EXECUTIVE DIRECTOR, AMERICAN CIVIL LIBERTIES UNION

Mr. GLASSER. Two additional points. One is, although a legislature does not ordinarily consider questions like burden of proof in the technical, legal sense, the court does, I still think it is useful in terms of framing public policy and in deciding what kind of legislative remedies to fashion to deal with the concept of burden of proof in response to questions like, "What are whites likely to do? Are they still doing it?

Given our history and given the ample evidence of continuing discrimination and prejudicial feelings even where discrimination itself is successfully barred, I think the burden of proof on policymakers with respect to something like voting has to be that until there is a fairly clear showing that whites are no longer voting in a racially polarized way in districts where there has been a history of that, I would not want to see any relaxation of the legislative remedies that have begun to show some final results. I think that concept of burden of proof has a place here in evaluating answers in the face of inclusive evidence.

Second, I think that the fact is, which I assume everyone in this room knows but which is useful to put on the record, there has been a tremendous amount of discussion, particularly in public settings, about the *Shaw* v. *Reno* situation and about majority minority districts in general. There is a tendency when you are talking about polarization to forget that these are not apartheid districts, these are not segregated districts in the sense that we once had segregated schools by law. These are biracial districts. The subject district, Mel Watt's district in North Carolina, the subject district of *Shaw* v. *Reno* was 53 percent black after it was redrawn; Cynthia McKinney's district is 60 percent; Corrine Brown's district in Florida is 50 percent; Eva Clayton's district in North Carolina is 54 percent, and so on.

We are dealing here with biracial districts. The notion that those can be analyzed as if they were racial apartheid districts in which you didn't have to have biracial politics is just factually absurd. It is important always to remember what we are talking about. We are not talking about 90 percent districts.

Third, I think it's critical to remember a key problem here about using race as a criterion for drawing district lines or anything else that we do. That is, while it may be true in some perfect world that if we were starting on a blank slate, all racial classification should be subject to strict scrutiny and be presumptively invalid. Some of us have worked a long time to reach that day and are rather despondent that we have not yet done so. But it's important to remember that you can't have a situation where the original discrimination and the original district lines in this setting were not subject to strict scrutiny and were done for the purposes of grouping based on race and then come in and apply the strict scrutiny to the remedy.

This is a problem which occurs in all civil rights remedies, affirmative action of all kinds, but it's a vexing problem. You can't stop taking race into account at the point of remedy when you have always taken race into account at the point of discrimination. That's a problem one has to continue to keep in the forefront as this kind of a discussion goes forward.

Mr. DURBIN. Thank you.

Mr. Tony Snow.

Mr. SNOW. Three quick points. No. 1, Ms. Wright's comment about the anecdotal evidence that in fact incumbent blacks draw increasing numbers of white votes. I suspect it works both ways. It's the power of incumbency. You get in office, you do things, and people tend to support you. I suspect that would work also with whites that have significant numbers of blacks in their districts.

No. 2, the polarization thesis. Mr. Glasser, you were arguing that whites should not vote in blocks but presume that blacks do when you say that 53 percent is constitutive of an effective minority district. The assumption there is that you are going to have almost 100 percent block voting by blacks. I think that does defeat some of the purpose that at least some folks who are idealistic enough to think about breaking down racial barriers were considering in the 1960's.

We do have an imperfect world. I'm not sure that necessarily you are going to overcome that.

The other thing that is interesting to me, of course, is that the segregation problem now is worse in the Northeast. Harvard also is doing a series of studies on segregation. The South now is the least segregated part of our populace, and it may be because of some of the VRA stuff. I think the interesting factor now is that you have increasing segregation in the North and in the industrial Midwest and there are no remedies there.

Mr. DURBIN. We want to recognize the chairman.

Mr. EDWARDS. Do any of you think that *Shaw* v. *Reno* consists of a threat to the implementation of the Voting Rights Act and is contrary to the intentions of Congress in 1965? They are threatening lawsuits and some of them have already filed in five States. Is this something that is going to change the implementation of the Voting Rights Act?

Ms. WHITAKER. Mr. Glasser.

Mr. GLASSER. Yes. I think it already is in a very serious way and in a way that is probably far broader than the technical holding of *Shaw*. The *Shaw* holding really just said that a majority minority district can be challenged under the Constitution when it's extremely irregular on its face and where there is evidence that extreme irregularity was a sole function of racial gerrymandering. Even then such a district would be constitutional, *Shaw* holds, if the change were not solely done for reason of race. I think the evidence in *Shaw* will show in remand that it was not solely on race, and even if it was, it can be rebutted by a compelling State interest that it need remedy racial discrimination.

The problem that *Shaw* presents to those of us who are working to implement the Voting Rights Act is not that there are very many districts that present the same problem that the *Shaw* district presented. For that matter, we remain confident that on remand we can win *Shaw* v. *Hunt.*

The real problem is that a decision like that opens up and encourages a far broader resistance, because it's a signal to litigants to see how far the court might be willing to go. We all do that. The Supreme Court makes a decision; you read between the lines; it's not exactly clear what this might be the beginning of; and so everybody jumps into court to make claims that are far broader than the one that was upheld in the particular case to see if it gets to the Supreme Court and maybe we can get them to reverse some other things.

What is happening throughout the South now is that lawsuits are being filed. In *Shaw,* as you know, even traditional standing was relaxed. There was a real double standard created. For years we have been fighting stricter and stricter standings. People claiming discrimination in all sorts of fields—employment, housing—who had to prove personal injury. Now you had a bunch of plaintiffs who did not even claim personal injury. Some of them didn't even live in the district and they were basically asking for an advisory opinion, which the court was willing to give.

What you have all throughout now is cases that are brought testing the new districts even though the plaintiffs are aware the conditions that existed in the *Shaw* district are not there. We are having, for example, to intervene as defendants in all of those cases. By we, I mean the civil rights community in general.

While Congress cannot remedy *Shaw* directly because it involves the interpretation of the Constitution, not the Voting Rights Act, there are things around the margin that the Congress could do.

We are all being overwhelmed with these lawsuits with the strain upon our resources. The continuing existence, for example, of the inability to recover real costs and expert witness fees, which Congress could remedy and which I had hoped would have been remedied by now, is a serious problem in these cases, particularly because one is being asked to prove all sorts of factual things. Also, the use of expert witnesses in the light of *Shaw* v. *Reno* becomes even more important. Cases are not settling. Everything is going to trial. That is important.

Also, defendant intervenors fees are not recoverable at all. So the very resources of the civil rights community that have been so responsible for enforcing the Act are being strained by the consequence of *Shaw* v. *Reno* and those consequences go far beyond the relatively narrow holding of the case, if you read it that way.

Ms. WHITAKER. Thank you.

We would like to recognize Timothy O'Rourke, and then afterward Brenda Wright and Charles Cooper, in that order. Thank you.

STATEMENT OF TIMOTHY O'ROURKE, PROFESSOR, DEPARTMENT OF POLITICAL SCIENCE, CLEMSON UNIVERSITY

Mr. O'ROURKE. I wanted to make a few observations about *Shaw v. Reno.*

First, on the facts of the case, North Carolina's congressional districting plan is not a bona fide plan. The 1st and 3d Districts cross over, as do the 12th and 6th Districts. The State has advanced a theory of point contiguity under which, let's say, the red squares on a checkerboard could constitute one district because the red squares touch at a point, and the white squares could be another district because they touch at a point.

This theory of point contiguity is used where the 1st and 3d Districts literally cross over one another and where the 6th and 12th Districts also cross over one another. So it is a rather extraordinary plan, setting aside race.

Under the theory of point contiguity, if it were endorsed by the courts, geographic districting as we know it would no longer exist. States would be free to do whatever they pleased with respect to the crafting of districts.

A second point with regard to the facts of the case is that indeed it is a racial classification. While it is only a slight majority black district, it could not be a 90-percent black district because, that would violate another aspect of civil rights law. It was designed in effect to elect an African-American Congressman and it is disingenuous to suggest otherwise.

A final point I would make about the North Carolina plan and the actions of the Justice Department with respect to the enforcement of section 5 is that it is contrary to the understanding that Congress had about the results test of section 2 and the enforcement of section 5 at the time of the 1982 amendments. If Congressmen will indulge me, I would like to read a brief passage from Drew Day's testimony in the 1981 hearings on what would become the 1982 amendments. He was talking about the Justice Department's standards for enforcement of section 5 and when the Justice Department would object. He offers a hypothetical:

Take the case of redistricting plans. In a community with a 25 percent minority population, let us assume that local officials can create a compact and contiguous set of four city council districts where minorities are likely to have a sizable population advantage in one district. When the jurisdiction submits instead, however, a plan that is not compact or contiguous, or is otherwise drawn in a fashion that frustrates any prospect that minorities will gain control of one district in the plan, the Department is likely to object.

On the other hand, we might assume another set of facts in which it can be shown that no fairly drawn redistricting plan will result in minority control of one district, because of dispersed minority residential patterns, for example. The Department's response is not to demand that the jurisdiction adopt a crazy quilt, gerrymandered districting plan to ensure proportional minority representation.

And in fact, exactly what the Department demanded in the case of North Carolina was a crazy quilt, gerrymandered districting plan.

Mr. DURBIN. We would like to welcome the Reverend Jackson. Would you like to make a statement or respond to that one? Then we are going to go to Brenda Wright.

STATEMENT OF REV. JESSE JACKSON, PRESIDENT AND FOUNDER, NATIONAL RAINBOW COALITION, INC.

Mr. JACKSON. Let me express my thanks to you. I would feel awkward discussing this subject ordinarily. I would feel acutely awkward coming out of Selma. I feel embarrassed coming out of South Africa where the power structure voted a referendum to create one South Africa and knew that in its voting it would come out No. 2 in the national election. Our power structure, our white majority would never vote not to come out on top, not to mention to come out No. 2.

We say Mandela is a great Democrat because he guarantees a place for minorities. The NP boundaries are not contiguous. The KwaZulu boundaries are not contiguous. Low threshold, high participation. We are so fascinated with that Lani Guinier definition of proportional representation and shared power we sent $35 million down there to help them with voter education, voter registration, because they were determined to have one South Africa.

There are many ways that the ANC could deny white participation in South Africa. Just use numbers and overwhelm them. There are many ways that they could simply put de Klerk and Buthelezi out of business, but in their spirit of and constitutional sense of democracy they have chosen inclusion rather than exclusion and schemes.

These lines are funny looking lines. We are not fighting racial gerrymandering only; we are fighting racial overwhelming, the overwhelming use of race.

Last, what is kind of painful, frankly, is this is 29 years after Selma, and the majority has not yet made the decision to stop frustrating attempts at inclusion. Democracy is not based upon appearances; it is based upon function. The function is inclusion rather than exclusion. The function is representation for taxation.

Funny lines, as I grew up in South and North Carolina, was to pay the level of taxes we paid for the number of people we had and no representation. That was funny and vulgar and racist and wrong. These lines are drawn in reaction to a legacy of ugly, perverse, immoral racism. Here what we have done is what they did in South Africa.

Talking about reverse discrimination, which is a foolish perversion, all the white judges determined 25 years after Selma that they had found proof of race discrimination and those judges recommended to majority white State legislatures in every instance to redraw lines not for colorblind, but for color inclusion. Now they are talking about the lines look funny.

Of course the lines look funny, because the racial lining of the country looks funny. We are now having to try to offset the cultural impact of personal, biblical, and institutional racism.

I leave here today going on a 12-day tour across the South, implementing motor-voter. There are 22 States that won't implement that yet. That's the law. In Baton Rouge they expect 50,000 people to rally. The registrars will not come to register the people at the rally, using some technical excuse.

The struggle of gerrymandering, annexation, at-large, roll purging, voter intimidation is just the unrelenting will of the majority to impose tyranny upon the minority. I hope that the best gesture of our better angel will rise above the perversion of good minds talking a lot and saying nothing about how to lock people out. The best America is an inclusive one.

When I sat at that Mandela swearing-in, in Durbin I just thought suppose ANC had used its power to lock Buthelezi out and lock de Klerk out. They would have been home pouting while conspiring to undercut that Government. Instead, they have the good judgment not to get hung up on how the KwaZulu lines look or how NP lines look. They have the good judgment to look at the bigger picture of one inclusive country. They aren't but a week old and they've got that much sense.

Mr. DURBIN. Thank you, Reverend Jackson. We want to recognize Congressman Mel Watt who probably will have a statement here and who will reinforce your ideas of the problems of irregular lines and how that should not be the problem in congressional redistricting.

Congressman Watt.

Mr. WATT. I appreciate the invitation to offer a statement, but as usual I always come to these hearings for the purpose of listening unless somebody provokes me.

Mr. DURBIN. I see.

Ms. WHITAKER. We would like to recognize Ms. Brenda Wright then. Thank you.

Ms. WRIGHT. I was going to comment on a couple of points. One is a little bit of additional concrete history about minority representation in Congress and how recent that representation really is.

There are at least five Southern States which did not elect an African-American Representative to Congress during this century until 1992. North Carolina was one of those States. It was also Florida, Virginia, South Carolina, and Alabama. Each of those States, of course, with substantial African-American populations.

That is an incredibly lengthy and recent history of total exclusion, so that we are not talking about history of just a little bit of underrepresentation or a little bit of disadvantage in the political process. It's a history of total exclusion of African-American officeholding.

Those five States sent eight African-American Representatives to Congress in 1992 and it was not because they had suddenly gotten a lot of support to run in majority white districts; it was in every single case because majority minority districts were created that provided that opportunity. So I think you have to have that context in mind when you think about the decision in Shaw v. Reno, and you will not see that history anywhere in the Supreme Court's opinion.

I think that in dealing with the issue of compactness you have got to keep a couple of points in mind.

One is that the States themselves in the last decade or so have moved very far away from treating compactness as an important criterion, quite without regard to the issue of minority representation.

I want to show you the Fourth Congressional District in Tennessee as a district which extends for 300 miles. It touches the border of four States; it contains two time zones; it is a majority white district that was not remotely created in order to empower any disenfranchised majority.

In a context where States themselves are not treating compactness as always the most important criterion in their redistricting you simply cannot have a double standard that says that's all right when you are creating majority white districts but it creates a constitutionally suspect result when the district is majority minority.

I think there was an exchange at the argument of *Shaw* v. *Reno* that really summarizes the problem here. It was when Justice Stevens asked the attorney for the white plaintiffs in that case whether under his theory it would be impermissible to draw a Polish ward in Chicago. The plaintiffs' attorney said, "Well, no, of course not." Justice Stevens very gently followed up and said, "Well, what's the difference?" The plaintiffs' attorney said, "A Polish ward would not be based on stereotypes."

I think it's an exchange that just illustrates the double standard that is at work when we say, as Justice Stevens said in his dissent in *Shaw*, that it's all right to draw districts to represent union members and to represent rural interests and to represent Republicans but it's not all right to draw district lines to benefit a historically disenfranchised minority. That result is perverse, and I agree with Justice Stevens' remarks along those lines.

Mr. DURBIN. Thank you, Ms. Wright.

We are going to recognize Charles Cooper.

STATEMENT OF CHARLES COOPER, PARTNER, SHAW, PITTMAN, POTTS & TROWBRIDGE

Mr. COOPER. Thank you, Mr. Durbin.

I just wanted to provide a brief reaction to the points that Mr. Glasser made with respect to the *Shaw* v. *Reno* case. I was struck by what I considered an uncharacteristically narrow and crabbed view of the Court's holding from Mr. Glasser, uncharacteristic in that in my experience other equal protection cases applying strict scrutiny have been broadly extended and read by Mr. Glasser and those like him.

I think this same comment applies to the standing analysis. The notion that individual residents of the subject districts, whatever their race, or individual potential candidates, office seekers, would not have standing to challenge under the equal protection laws is quite striking, in light of some of the earlier positions taken by individuals like Mr. Glasser, which I think were quite correct.

I think the key point of *Shaw* v. *Reno* wasn't so much irregular lines and some kind of a constitutional test on the shape of districts or their aesthetic value. The key point there was the same point made in *Gomillion* v. *Lightfoot* when a district was cut in an "uncouth," I think was the Court's term, shape which, when matched with the demographics of the community on which it was overlaid, had only one purpose, to exclude all blacks from that Alabama district. I think it excluded all but four blacks.

There are limits to what you can do no matter how creative you are, and in today's technologically enhanced environment you can get very creative with who you can exclude and who you can include in these districts.

But I don't think the teaching of *Shaw* v. *Reno* is that a district so bizarre can't be tolerated. It is, I believe, rather that a district which has its racial purpose written on its face need not—the racial intent in the drawing of the district need not be supplemented by any other evidence. In *Gomillion* v. *Lightfoot* its purpose was on its face, and in *Shaw* v. *Reno* its racial purpose was on its face. You didn't need testimony to say why the lines were drawn the way they were. It was clear why they were drawn the way they were.

Mr. Glasser suggests there aren't many other districts like that. There are districts like that in State after State, because in every State with substantial minority populations—and I've litigated in most of them—race was the single and consistent and overriding factor that went into the drawing of the districts. Once that was satisfied, once the majority black congressional district in North Carolina was drawn, other issues could be addressed: incumbency, political issues and the rest.

The same in Louisiana where we just had a recent decision, I think mentioned by our moderators, where the second majority black district was struck down under *Shaw* v. *Reno* as a violation of the equal protection clause because it could not satisfy, at least to those judges, the compelling State interest case that the Court made clear applies to racial decisions no matter how you prove them. In that case you just proved it by looking at it. You didn't need any more.

The way I read *Shaw* v. *Reno,* it said that if you can show that a district is in an outcome determinative way based on race, you apply strict scrutiny to it just like you do any other racial classification. They remanded the case to determine whether or not it could be justified by a compelling State interest and was sufficiently narrowly drawn.

In the Louisiana case, as I read that case—Congressman Edwards, I think it does reflect on the question you have asked: Does the *Shaw* v. *Reno* case represent a threat to the Voting Rights Act or its implementation? I think it does, at least for those, as I understand the premise of your question, who believe the Voting Rights Act should be implemented in the way that it was in the Louisiana congressional redistricting and in the North Carolina redistricting. I think it does represent a threat to it. I don't think it represents, in all candor, enough of a threat to that view of the Voting Rights Act, but it does indeed represent a threat.

I think that I find some areas of agreement with Mr. O'Rourke's statements regarding the intention of section 2's amendment of the Voting Rights Act, regardless of who is right on that. In *Thornburgh* v. *Gingles,* the interpreted section was amended in a way that is very hard to understand as not essentially requiring the kind of racial line drawing that indeed we saw in one state after another.

Ms. WHITAKER. Thank you, Mr. Cooper.

We would like to recognize Anthony Chavez now, who has not had an opportunity to make a remark.

STATEMENT OF ANTHONY CHAVEZ, DIRECTOR, VOTING RIGHTS PROJECT, MEXCIAN AMERICAN LEGAL DEFENSE AND EDUCATION FUND

Mr. CHAVEZ. I would like to go back to some of the comments Mr. Glasser raised regarding the impact of *Shaw* v. *Reno* and enforcement of the Voting Rights Act. It is very much like he said. That case has begun to open up the door and now I think both plaintiffs and defendants are beginning to flounder around trying to figure out what the parameters are. One of the ways that defendants are trying to figure out the parameters is by raising *Shaw* v. *Reno* arguments against some of our proposed remedies in our section 2 lawsuits. Without enough direction right now from the Supreme Court it is difficult for courts to decide what are legal or what are valid remedies to possible section 2 violations.

As Mr. Glasser raised, it is also a problem indirectly because we are having to spend resources to defend districts that we have already drawn. Rather than moving forward actively to other forms of challenges, like the voting systems in Texas, we have to spend resources to backtrack, to go back to defend the districts that we thought were already safely in place.

In addition, I think a comment that needs to be made with regard to the shapes of districts, to apartheid districts, is that the districts are following the lines of communities, of minority cities, depending on what type of district you are looking at. It's not that the districts are creating segregation; they are merely following the residential segregation patterns that are already in place. If you were to talk to the voters that lived in those minority and majority districts, I am sure that you would find that usually they have a community of interest with the other voters that are within that district.

Mr. DURBIN. I want to recognize Congressman Barney Frank.

Mr. FRANK. I want to ask Mr. Cooper a question. If I heard you correctly, you said that with regard to Mel's district that there were a lot of districts in the country like that. Did I hear that accurately, that there were a lot of districts where race had clearly been the number one reason for drawing them?

Mr. COOPER. Yes. I believe that race was an overriding——

Mr. FRANK. In your judgment, they would all be unconstitutionally drawn?

Mr. COOPER. Not necessarily.

Mr. FRANK. You said that the lines weren't relevant for aesthetic reasons but they were evidence and they were evidence of a principle. The principle was that they were drawn on racial grounds and if they were drawn on racial grounds they were unconstitutional.

Mr. COOPER. No. I didn't say that. I said if they were drawn on racial grounds they have to be supported by a compelling State interest and narrowly tailored.

Mr. FRANK. But that would be the same for all of them. The fact that it was oddly shaped wouldn't be relevant. You said that——

Mr. COOPER. Not necessarily, Congressman.

Mr. FRANK. It's only relevant in an evidentiary sense but it's not relevant in a constitutional sense.

Mr. COOPER. It may be relevant constitutionally.

Mr. FRANK. That's not what you said.

Mr. COOPER. Then let me clarify what I said, Congressman.

Mr. FRANK. I want to make sure I understood it. I thought you said fairly clearly that the irregularity of shape was relevant only as evidence, that in fact there was no constitutional preference in terms of shape, but that the relevance of shape was that it was evidentiary. So that doesn't affect what the underlying principle is. And if you can establish the principle that racial motivation was the main factor, then every such district is under strict scrutiny and is going to have to justify itself.

Mr. COOPER. Yes.

Mr. FRANK. How many in the country would you say there are?

Mr. COOPER. That I don't know.

Mr. FRANK. You wouldn't say that they were confined only to Voting Rights Act areas. I hope you wouldn't, because that motivation has been as prevalent in the States outside the Voting Rights Act area as in.

Mr. COOPER. I would think that certain criteria call for higher levels of scrutiny under the Supreme Court's jurisprudence.

Mr. FRANK. I'm talking only about race. You said that you think there are districts all over the country where race was the primary motivation.

Mr. COOPER. Yes.

Mr. FRANK. I think you are right. I helped draw some. I helped draw one in Massachusetts in 1973. For years there was no district that represented the African-American population and we made one. We made an Irish one and a Jewish one and an Italian one and another Irish one, because we were in Massachusetts. [Laughter.]

I don't know if we had a Republican one.

There is no argument about that. Was that district unconstitutional? We were motivated by a feeling that African-Americans had too long been separated and we created a district based on putting all the African-Americans together.

Mr. COOPER. Whether it was or not, I just wouldn't be able to know.

Mr. FRANK. The statute of limitations has lapsed. This is 1973. So I'm going to admit that I made a district with other people. I didn't make it all by myself. And I had a racial motivation.

Mr. COOPER. There is no statute of limitations, Congressman, on that district if it's still there.

Mr. FRANK. It isn't still there.

Mr. COOPER. I didn't think so.

Mr. FRANK. The question is, would we have been subject under your theory to justify under strict scrutiny standards why we created such a district?

Mr. COOPER. Yes, absolutely.

Mr. FRANK. We thought African-Americans were underrepresented. So under your theory that would have been unconstitutional.

Mr. COOPER. Again——

Mr. FRANK. That was the only reason. The only reason was we thought the African-Americans——

Mr. COOPER. Do you think that's a compelling State interest? I suspect that you do, and if you do, then that would be at least——

Mr. FRANK. That would apply to Mel's district too, then. You think representing African-Americans can be a compelling State interest?

Mr. COOPER. No. I don't think that that and that alone can be, but I think there may be a compelling remedial interest.

Mr. FRANK. It's remedial if there has been a pattern of the African-Americans not having had any representation prior to that?

Mr. COOPER. Because of exclusion of African-Americans, yes.

Mr. FRANK. If they could prove that North Carolina had a history of excluding African-Americans, those districts should be OK.

Mr. COOPER. On top of that it must be narrowly tailored. Let's go to the Louisiana case again to show an example of that.

Mr. FRANK. They couldn't have narrowly tailored that any more unless they took his measurements. [Laughter.]

Mr. COOPER. You may be right. In other words, in Louisiana the Court, while it did not actually pass on whether or not the justifications were indeed compelling State interests for drawing that district the way it was drawn and for being explicitly racially conscious about it——

Mr. FRANK. What if——

Mr. COOPER. Please, let me finish.

But they did recognize that there were some interests that were advanced and they may well be compelling. They then went to the question of whether it was narrowly tailored and said it was not narrowly tailored. There were more African-American constituents within the district than were necessary for it essentially to be controlled and for individuals to elect Members of Congress of their choice and because a less bizarre district apparently could be drawn with adequate numbers. So it wasn't narrowly tailored, which is the second prong.

Mr. FRANK. So if you are agreeing to that viewpoint, you accept the legitimacy of creating a district for the purpose of electing an African-American. It's just you can't have them get too big a majority.

Mr. COOPER. You cannot segregate. You cannot racially gerrymander, according to that decision, more than is necessary to accomplish a purpose.

Mr. FRANK. So the constitutional flaw in *Shaw* v. *Reno* was too many African-Americans, but if they had drawn a district that had just enough African-Americans to win, that would have been OK?

Mr. SNOW. Let me interject a little bit. As somebody who used to live and work in North Carolina, I have a pretty good knowledge of the demographics.

Mr. FRANK. I just want to ask Mr. Cooper one more question.

Suppose they drew a district and the African-American candidate lost by 2 percent. Could they then go back the next time and change a few wards around the town so he could win? That would be OK under your theory?

Mr. COOPER. I think you need to know more about the reason for the loss. If the candidate had just been indicted for a felony, then it might well not——

Mr. FRANK. But if it was racial polarization, that might justify going back and redrawing the line?

Mr. COOPER. Potentially, under the analysis of the court in Louisiana.

Mr. DURBIN. I want to recognize Margaret Fung. Maybe she can give us an insight on how the Voting Rights Act has helped or not helped Asian-Americans.

STATEMENT OF MARGARET FUNG, EXECUTIVE DIRECTOR, ASIAN AMERICAN LEGAL DEFENSE AND EDUCATION FUND

Ms. FUNG. I hate to break up such an exciting interchange.

I think one of the reasons why there hasn't been much input among the Asian-American community on these kinds of redistricting issues is that it has only been in 1990 that Asian-American community groups have gotten involved in even commenting on plans. There are very few areas geographically in the United States where Asian-Americans can constitute a majority minority district. So when we talk about voting rights litigation for Asian-Americans, we are going to be looking more to how we are going to be able to build coalitions with other groups to create some kind of political cohesion.

The full impacts of the Voting Rights Act really have yet to be felt, in part because in this country Asian-Americans have been excluded through immigration laws such as the Chinese Exclusion Act, but more importantly, through laws that have prohibited our naturalization even up until the year 1952, which is a precondition to voting.

We still face many barriers in terms of being a predominantly immigrant community and a community that does not have high levels of English language proficiency. We especially look toward the Voting Rights Act Amendments of 1992 for language assistance, which because of the change in the coverage formula, requires bilingual assistance to be provided in jurisdictions where there are at least 10,000 language minority citizens. We have already seen the benefits in terms of how bilingual materials aid in voter registration efforts. The Justice Department actually has played a very important role in enforcing section 203 with respect to Chinese language minorities in New York City.

We think a lot of the Voting Rights Act laws that are being interpreted now perhaps in the next decade as our population increases—it's now at 7.5 million and, in the next 20 years it is estimated that the Asian-American population will be 23 million—these laws are going to be critical in order to deal with the underrepresentation of Asian-Americans in our communities.

Ms. WHITAKER. Thank you. I would like to recognize now Mr. Carl Hampe, who has been waiting patiently. Thank you.

STATEMENT OF CARL HAMPE, ESQ., PAUL, WEISS, RIFKIND, WHARTON & GARRISON

Mr. HAMPE. Thank you. I would like to address Chairman Edwards' question about the interplay between Shaw and the Voting Rights Act by beginning with a quotation from Stewart Taylor of American Lawyer magazine, who said, in effect, that he felt that the Voting Rights Act as interpreted by the *Gingles* case and the constitutional rulings in *Shaw* put race-based redistricting legal doctrine on a collision course with itself. That certainly implies that to some people in the legal community there is a tension between *Shaw* and the Voting Rights Act.

What I would like to highlight is another potential area of collision between the Voting Rights Act and *Shaw,* and that is, given recent immigration trends from 1982 to 1992, 9.5 million legal permanent immigrants have entered this country. These people might not all naturalize, but they all certainly have the opportunity to naturalize. Ninety percent of these people are from the areas of Latin America or Asia.

I don't think we have solid figures, but a very large portion of them go to live in major urban areas in California, Texas, New York, Florida and Illinois where substantial portions of this country's African-American population also exist's. I think the potential one sees, given that permanent immigration law will continue to admit approximately 850,000 legal immigrants each year—legal permanent immigrants with the opportunity for citizenship in 5 years, is that situations such as the DeGrandy litigation in Dade County become more and more likely.

It is hard to predict. One cannot say for sure that other DeGrandys will occur or won't, but if one simply looks at the numbers, looks at the Voting Rights Act and at some of the requirements that district courts will likely read out of *Shaw,* I think this sort of collision course and potential conflict within immigrant areas among African-American groups and recent immigrant groups, there is a significant potential for that.

Mr. URBIN. Mr. Tony Snow, did you have something you wanted to say?

Mr. SNOW. Oh gosh. This is so much fun. I was just going to run through a couple of points. One of the things that is obviously clear here is that if you take a look at the law, the biggest problem we have is that the *Gingles* and *Shaw* cases are inscrutable in the sense that the Court tried to have it both ways. It tried to figure out some sort of remedy for an obvious pattern of discrimination but was not quite ready to say thou shalt have x number of minority representatives.

Mr. Chairman, you asked earlier if in fact we had frustrated the intent of the original Voting Rights Act. I think Professor Davidson's testimony early on indicated that that is not the case. What we are really talking about are sections 2 and 5 of the 1982 act which remain controversial. To get to one of the questions we are going to talk about later, those are the ones I think with the most divisive political impact right now. The effects case and also having to pass Justice Department muster—those are the areas that are going to continue to be the most controversial.

I think Reverend Jackson hit it absolutely right. I may disagree with him on particulars, but the whole point is to have one United States. The question is how we in fact provide effective representation. One of the most interesting political phenomena right now is that nobody thinks they have very effective political representation, white, black or other. There is serious discussion in this country of forming a separate black political party. Forty percent of all voters say that they belong to the "none of the above" party.

I'll add another collision course here, which is increasing voter disaffection regardless of race, creed or color. That is obviously not relevant to this particular hearing, but I think it is something that one ought to be considering as well.

Brenda, I think you are right. It's wonderful that we have more representation. I have some experience with at least one of the cases you were talking about. It's not always simply the drawing of the district but again the development of black candidates who can draw constituencies.

I was an editorial page editor in Newport News, VA, in the early 1980's and a guy named Bobby Scott was running for the State senate. Bobby became the second black State senator in Virginia since Reconstruction, the first, of course, being Doug Wilder. I endorsed him as editorial page editor, spent election night with him. Bobby Scott is a member of the U.S. Congress today because he spent 10 years working effectively in the State legislature.

I think you find that around the country.

Mr. JACKSON. He's in Congress for what reason?

Mr. SNOW. Because he's a good Representative. He proved himself.

Mr. JACKSON. That isn't all.

Mr. SNOW. He's not in because he's a good Representative?

Mr. JACKSON. He's also that. He could not have won without the lines.

Mr. SNOW. Bobby has drawn in fact a significant number of white voters.

Mr. WATT. He has drawn significant white support, but he would not be in Congress but for the existence of the Voting Rights Act.

Mr. O'ROURKE. I was in Virginia at the time that was going on. There was some debate about how large the black majority would need to be in a proposed district from which everyone expected now—Representative Scott would run. At the time he was representing a majority white senate district.

Mr. WATT. But that's not the issue.

Mr. O'ROURKE. It is the issue, because part of what we are talking about is not whether we want an inclusionary system. We all do. But there is a question as to what lengths we go and whether the remedies we adopt are not themselves harmful. For example, in North Carolina. In his campaign against Senator Helms, Harvey Gant carried Mecklenburg County rather easily. Mecklenburg standing alone is almost populace enough for a single congressional district. It turns out it's split three ways in the North Carolina plan.

Mr. WATT. That's just not true.

Mr. O'ROURKE. He didn't carry Mecklenburg County?

Mr. WATT. Harvey Gant never carried a majority of the white community in Mecklenburg County.

Mr. O'ROURKE. But did he carry Mecklenburg County?

Mr. WATT. He carried Mecklenburg County but Mecklenburg County has never been big enough to be a congressional district. We have consistently not been able to elect black candidates even county-wide from Mecklenburg County. If you are going to talk about something—I said I would stay out of this unless I got provoked. I get provoked by inaccuracy, and that's just not true.

Mr. O'ROURKE. If you put Mecklenburg County together with an adjacent county, it amounts to the fact that——

Mr. WATT. Bobby Scott ran for Congress one time before. This was not the first time Bobby Scott ran for Congress. He ran for Congress and lost.

Mr. SNOW. He also ran for State senate and lost.

Mr. JACKSON. The white racism in our country is of fascist proportions.

Mr. SNOW. Wait a minute.

Mr. JACKSON. Were it not for the abolition movement to break up slavery—it wasn't voted out—if it were not for the 1954 Supreme Court—the new world order based on the 1954 Supreme Court decision, which was not a popular referendum, we would not hang our hats upon the public accommodation bill, the Voting Rights Act of 1965, as making us great. People implementing it got murdered. Were it not for those bills, we would not hang our hat on the human rights rack anywhere in the world today. That's why we can say that we are great, because it's a decision the majority never agreed with. The majority never agreed with the 1954 Supreme Court decision. You know that would have lost a popular referendum. The Voting Rights Act would not have been voted in by the white majority. So we become better kicking and screaming, led by the moral authority of the minority.

To conclude that merit would have prevailed over numbers is to conclude we have all white male Presidents because of superiority. It's because they've had preferential advantages, not because of brilliance or morality. God knows.

Mr. SNOW. I will certainly be willing to agree, but I think it's also important to note that a lot of us regard the civil rights movement, of which you are an important part, as the great shining moment of American idealism. It was probably the most stirring episode in which people really said we are going to lay our lives down for the belief in the equality of man and the importance of individual liberty, and we will lay our lives down as brothers and sisters. That is what we were talking about in the 1960's.

Mr. JACKSON. The case I'm making is there were so few. There was Thurgood Marshall. It was less than 10 people. We can says Jews and blacks were killed along with Medgar Evers. Right.

Mr. SNOW. You're talking about the victims. I'm talking about the people who were inspired by the example, including my parents who went down South to work.

Mr. JACKSON. If you personalize it. Your parents went down South to help. Mine were too afraid to go out the door to help.

Mr. SNOW. That's right.

Mr. JACKSON. That's why reducing it to personal——

Mr. SNOW. That's all you've been talking about. You've been personalizing it all along.

Mr. JACKSON. Except the bigger question is, how do we accommodate a racial reaction reality in this country? You mentioned something about the race on the face—what is that big word you used about the race?

Mr. COOPER. The racial purpose of the line drawing was on the face of the district.

Mr. JACKSON. The racial purpose is to offset the racial purpose to deny us access even when we got the right to vote: the gerrymandering; racial annexation; at large; roll purging. Just intentional schemes to delay the Voting Rights Act 25 years. A whole quarter of a century died. You've said that district looks black. It was designed to offset being overwhelmed by racism.

L was talking to a nice, respectful, white friend of mine from North Carolina who said, "But how can you deny these interests from Charlotte to Raleigh?" I said, "From our side of the track, respectfully, I see Johnson C. Smith who sent all the ANT to Charlotte." He said, "What did you say?" I see Johnson C. Smith. The stuff that we now call a public accommodations bill came right down that line. It started there. It is the community of interest that has connected Greensboro. The community of interest was defined by the oppression. That's why the connection is there.

Ms. WHITAKER. Thank you. I would like to recognize Congressman Barney Frank.

Mr. FRANK. I'm going to react very negatively to what I think is patronizing of Bobby Scott.

Mr. SNOW. It's not patronizing. He's an old friend. I'm simply talking about the district.

Mr. FRANK. But in this context it is patronizing.

Mr. SNOW. Wait a minute. You explain to me how it is patronizing, because that is interesting. I certainly don't mean to be.

Mr. FRANK. Here is what it is: He was a good one. That's the way it's coming out. That's what you are saying.

Mr. SNOW. No. All I'm saying is that—it's not that he was a good one. What I'm saying is that thankfully as a result of the civil rights movement, in part because of the Voting Rights Act, black districts developed where people do develop careers and constituencies. He's a career politician and he's effective at it.

Mr. FRANK. Are you through?

Mr. SNOW. I don't know. I may be.

Mr. FRANK. Because I really want to make a point. Again it comes across as patronizing. What you were saying was, in context, the Voting Rights Act was less important. He was a good one. The inference is that there weren't any good people before him who were African-American who ran for——

Mr. SNOW. No. I'm saying that people were shut out before.

Mr. FRANK. I am going to ask you to stop interrupting me, because I think you've said something and you don't want to hear the consequences of it, and I think this is very important. I know sometimes as a liberal you have a problem, because you are asked to go out and argue for principles which involve minimizing reality. I think you guys are on the wrong side of that one right now.

If you are trying to deny that race has been a very, very dominant factor in American politics and particularly that white southerners have often felt they would rather lose a leg than vote for an African-American, until they get to know them and then it changes, then you're on the wrong side.

You're trying to argue unrealistically. When you talked about Bobby Scott, the suggestion was that it wasn't so much the Voting Rights Act, but that finally a black arrived who was capable of doing the job and that's how Bobby Scott got elected.

The point people are making is that there have been a lot of very capable African-Americans, and, I will tell you from my years in politics, a lot of very incapable white people who get elected to office. There have been hundreds of white people less capable than Bobby Scott who got elected to all kinds of offices all over the South.

Mr. SNOW. Representative Frank——

Mr. FRANK. Yes, Bobby Scott is talented, but if it hadn't been for the Voting Rights Act as it has been interpreted, his talent would never have gotten him into Congress.

Mr. SNOW. Let me disappoint you. You're looking for a cracker to say something stupid. If I did that, I apologize. He was looking for a conservative to be saying something about race.

I agree with you. I hate to tell you this, but I do agree with you. You are absolutely right. There have been a lot of mediocre white Representatives. There have been a lot of excellent blacks with the desire to serve who have been shut out as a result of patterns of discrimination, and thank God we are breaking down the barriers.

Mr. COOPER. There is not a conservative, I'm sure, in the room who doesn't agree.

Mr. FRANK. The fact is by denigrating the Voting Rights Act, by opposing it, by trying to minimize it—you would have opposed it. People who voted against the Voting Rights Act would have prevented that from happening. Our point is that it took this Federal intervention to deal with the situation of racism. Many of us believe the racism is still there throughout America, enough so that if you substantially relax the Voting Rights Act you would have a relapse.

Mr. JACKSON. I'm a conservative. I don't understand what you guys are talking about. We chose negotiation over bloody revolution. That's conservative. We chose inclusion as opposed to exclusion. That's conservative. We chose that which is morally right, representation for taxation. That's conservative. I don't understand what we are talking about.

We are talking about using a culprit for something called racial exclusion. We ought to be fair about not even getting around the fact that we come here with the baggage of a Constitution that referred to blacks as three-fifths of a human being. Not for a season, but for 250 years, thus a congenital deformity in our culture. Another 100 years of racial apartheid made illegal by a court of nine people but not by a majority of the population. We are seeking a remedy.

As in the case of de Klerk and Mandela, we are negotiating it rather than shooting from rooftops. That's the beauty of the process. But our spirit must at least be fair and face the fact it is the racial justice deficit that creates the imperative for remedy to make all of us feel better. Don't we feel better about having these inclusive seats now than having people on the outside just protesting? Isn't that the real point?

Ms. WHITAKER. I would like to recognize Mr. Ira Glasser.

Mr. GLASSER. I think it is not real helpful to pretend that we all agree. We do not agree. Mr. Cooper mysteriously referred to "Mr. Glasser and people like him." I don't exactly know what that means. I guess it means something different from you and people

like you. I don't know what that means either. But I do know that
it has become fashionable for everyone now to say how wonderful
the Voting Rights Act of 1965 was—but where were all those people in 1965.

The test of whether we agree or not and share these principles
also has to do with history. It has to do with whether or not we
are trying to expand and maintain remedies for the continuing effects of past and current discrimination today or whether we are
invoking the principles that were used to strike down discrimination in order to block further remedial action.

That is what this is about. When you talk about the irony of my
comments on the standing question, you were not listening very
carefully to what I said. What I objected to was the double standard.

You are quite right. I and people like me have always thought
to expand standing. But I spent a lot of time in the years in which
you were in the Justice Department fighting the Justice Department about its narrow view of standing in employment discrimination cases. What I object to in the context of racial discrimination
is a double standard which says standing is expansive when whites
challenge remedies for racial discrimination against blacks but
standing is restrictive when blacks challenge the racial discrimination itself. That kind of double standard cannot be supported.

I am prepared to adopt the standing argument. You will not find
the ACLU having filed a brief in *Shaw* v. *Reno* objecting to the
standing. I will enjoy your support when we take the same position
in the context of title VII. I'm glad to hear that perhaps you agree
with that kind of standing.

The issue is that we can't have a double standard. When you talk
about *Gomillion* v. *Lightfoot* as if the principle there justifies the
way it was applied in *Shaw,* it's important to remember what
Gomillion v. *Lightfoot* was about in 1960 in Tuskegee, AL. It was
about drawing city lines in order to entirely exclude from within
those city lines black voters, excluding them entirely therefore from
the right to vote, period.

Mr. FRANK. By not putting them into another city. You're exactly
right.

Mr. GLASSER. Right. And also from all the municipal services
that the city was bound to provide to its residents.

When the Supreme Court struck that down it wasn't because the
lines were funny. It was because what was done was plain to everybody who looked at it. It was to exclude people based on race
entirely not only from voting so that they could have some say in
the decisions that affected their lives, but from the jurisdiction entirely so that whatever the votes were, they didn't get the benefit
of any services.

It is not right to invoke that principle as a justification for saying
that a 53-percent black district in a State which has never elected
a Member of Congress who was black since 1901, in a State where
you have 22 percent black and which 2 of the districts of the 12
districts were drawn to have 53 and 54 percent black cannot be
created. In the context where blacks have been systematically excluded by not-so-funny lines, by lines which were not so bizarre,
the issue isn't how the lines look; the issue isn't aesthetic. God

knows the Court has consistently said through all of its history that gerrymandering for political advantage was not going to be something it got involved in on a constitutional basis.

Margaret Fung and I come from New York where they had the 17th District which meandered, picked up a little piece of the Bronx, meandered up Manhattan's East Side, went all over the place. Talk about no contiguous interest. It crossed borough lines. Why? Because they were trying to protect an incumbent.

The Supreme Court was never going to say, "Oh, this is too bizarre, this is too funny; you can't do that." What the Court said in cases like that is gerrymandering is a political issue; we're not going to get involved in it.

When do they get involved in it? The principle which has always been accepted becomes objectionable at the point of remedy for racial discrimination. That is what the problem is. And when you are dealing with the bizarre nature of that district, with the shape, it is again important to point out that in order to have accomplished a 53-percent black majority district it was not necessary that the district be that bizarre. What made it that bizarre was the combination of that result and trying to protect incumbents.

It wasn't even by the terms of Shaw solely for the purpose of race. To say that it's OK to protect incumbents, it's OK to have political struggle between Republicans and Democrats, were you can draw lines every which crazy way, but then say it's not OK now in the context where we've failed to elect a black for 100 years, and to pretend that what we are arguing about is something about which we fundamentally agree is intellectually dishonest. We don't agree.

Mr. DURBIN. Thank you. I want to recognize Mr. Carl Hampe and then back to Mr. Charles Cooper.

Mr. HAMPE. Thank you. I would like to pick up on something that Mr. Glasser was saying. I think I agree with him that we should agree that we don't all agree on this.

I would also like to address his other point, which was, "Where was everyone, the implication being conservatives, in 1965?"

The glib answer in my case was kindergarten. What I'm trying to say sort of flows from that. I think there is an unquestioned abhorrence by everyone at this table and just about everyone in this country that specific tests and devices operated to exclude any minority from voting. They are outrageous and should be swept away with all power and swiftness possible. But when it comes down to race-based redistricting, this is another issue that is more complicated for a number of reasons. One of the reasons it is complicated are the demographic and immigration trends which I mentioned earlier. These trends will only increase the complication of race-based redistricting in the years ahead.

In order for me to state now what my position is on this, to show that we probably really don't agree—I think this issue was perhaps raised by Linda Chavez in her recent book about Mexican-Americans, but I believe her point would apply just as well to any other recent immigrant group as it would to Hispanics.

Chavez says the natural corollary to the notion that Hispanics can best represent the interests of Hispanics is that non-Hispanics can best represent the interests of non-Hispanics. This is a dangerous game for any minority to play. Historically quotas have been used as a ceiling to minority achievement, not a floor, as Jews and, more recently, Asians have discovered.

Ms. WHITAKER. Mr. Cooper.

Mr. COOPER. I did indeed use an infelicitous formulation, Mr. Glasser. I should have said "people like Mr. Glasser and those who agree with him."

It is true we don't agree on some fundamental things here and we shouldn't pretend that we do. I don't think we are pretending that we do. What we shouldn't do is magnify the things on which we disagree or be confused about the things that we truly agree on. If I did that with respect to your standing position, I stand corrected. I definitely agree we should not have a double standard in terms of who may bring lawsuits based on race or motivations for bringing the suit. I would eagerly join you in advancing that argument anywhere.

We shouldn't magnify our areas of disagreement by caricaturing them. *Gomillion.* I didn't say that the case of *Gomillion* was on all fours with *Shaw* v. *Reno.* You've made some excellent distinctions and some distinctions that in my opinion make *Gomillion* far the more evil example of racism and the use of race and a far easier case to dispose of. I simply was trying to make the point that the intent of an enterprise can indeed be disclosed on its face. That is all I was citing *Gomillion* for, an uncouth shape. When you laid that shape against the demographics of the area, it told you why it was drawn. You couldn't come in and give a different rationale for why it was drawn.

The same is true, and I think the Court saying that the same is true, for the North Carolina shape. I also think, frankly, that the post hoc effort in the Louisiana case to say that incumbency was a cofactor, an additional fact was what the Court called it, was disingenuous.

Yes; incumbency is important after the racial elements have been satisfied. That's when the incumbents gather together and they try to ameliorate damage to their interests or they advance their political goals. But, that was not what was going on in North Carolina and it wasn't what was going on in Louisiana, and the Louisiana court called it what it was.

In terms of Congressman Frank's points that some of us here are denying that race has been a dominant and overriding and savage element in our past, I'm not denying that. I agree with everything Reverend Jackson said about the immoral and vulgar use of race and I think the Voting Rights Act of 1965 was an absolutely wondrous event in this country and it has brought about wonderful results. I support it without reservation, although in 1965 I was in junior high. I'm a little senior to you but not old enough to have been particularly active.

That answers the second point which I really want to speak to that many of us denigrate the Voting Rights Act. Not hardly. To the contrary. Where I think we disagree is the same place that many of us would disagree in other areas of the so-called remedial use of race. Whether we are talking about affirmative action, contracting set-asides, or admissions to college, there are some who think that the dangers of using race and the costs of using race simply outweigh the advantages of using race even if it is for a noble and inclusive purpose. The purpose I applaud. The potential consequences I fear. That is why at the end of the day that is where I think we probably have our difference. Thank you.

Ms. WHITAKER. Congressman Barney Frank.

Mr. FRANK. A couple points.

First, I want to also stress agreement. I have no objection to saying that we can infer racial purpose from looking at the face of this thing. I'm for that, and I want to use it in other contexts. I would say not having to prove the racial motivation but being able to look at the result and say that was racist, I like that. I think that will be useful to us in other contexts. So I don't differ from your point that you should be able to infer racism from the beginning. In fact, that has been more often our problem, disparate impacts and other things. So I like that movement.

Mr. COOPER. Again, I don't think there should be a double standard.

Mr. FRANK. I agree with that. I'm saluting your intellectual honesty. I don't think others on your side or on our side have always held up to it. So I think that's important.

The other points I would want to take issue with. First, as to the Voting Rights Act. It is true that you and Mr. Hampe have the advantage of youth. I don't know what your position would have been. It may well have been you would have been for it. I will say this. Most of the critics of the Voting Rights Act today, most of those who criticize how it is now being implemented, are old enough to have had a position then were against it. Strom Thurmond was against it then and he was then older than I am now. He was almost as old then as Edwards is now. [Laughter.]

And I'm sure Jesse Helms was against it then. So I do not think I am being unfair when I suggest that people are opposed to the Voting Rights Act. I exempt you two, but the fact is that the political tendency that is now most critical is the political tendency to try to kill the bill.

Finally, and here is where we do disagree on substance, and I'm sure it's a little confused, because your last remarks were—and I appreciate the way you framed it—the disadvantages of using race may outweigh the nobility of the purpose. That's often the situation. But that is inconsistent with what you said before. I thought you were saying to me before that your objection to the use of race was not using it at all in a remedial situation but that it was overused. That the problem was not that they tried to create a district that would undo the past discrimination but that they put too many people in it.

In a situation where there is a clear history of denying African-Americans a chance to compete fairly for election to office—let me say, I think Linda Chavez' comment is just nuts. No one is suggesting that only Hispanics can represent Hispanics, but the notion that you can have a situation in which there is a very large number of any group but it's OK that none of that group ever get elected to office has not been acceptable to Hispanics, blacks, Jews, Slovaks, anybody. That's just nonsense. Nobody really believes that. It has been true of every ethnic group in America that they have looked for representation and have tried to get districts joined, not that only their own can represent them.

We are not just talking about the relationship in political science terms now of the representative to the constituency; we are talking about the relationship of the representatives to each other. What we are saying is a representative assembly in which no one has lived the life of an African-American in the South, in which no one has lived the life of a Hispanic in the United States, in which, let me add, there has been no gay person, or there haven't been any Jews, or there have been very, very few women, will not do as good a job of representing the country. That doesn't mean you automatically reproduce it, but that's the value that you are losing. To say that it's irrelevant because a non-Hispanic can represent a Hispanic is only part of the argument.

The argument also is about whether a country composed of a very diverse number of types of people be well represented when significant population groups are excluded from the decisionmaking body.

I would like to ask you, Charles—I think we are trying to find agreement—are you saying that in situations where there has been a history of discrimination you cannot use race even if you use it only enough to overcome the past discrimination and don't overuse it?

Mr. DURBIN. Thank you, Congressman Frank. We're going to go to Mr. O'Rourke and then we will go back to Mr. Glasser.

Mr. O'ROURKE. I would like to state a couple of propositions in response to Representative Frank. First of all, I was in tenth grade in Pennsylvania in 1965.

Mr. FRANK. Do you leave the old conservatives home when you come to these things? [Laughter.]

Mr. O'ROURKE. I think the 15th amendment, the 14th amendment, section 2 and section 5 of the Voting Rights Act require race-conscious redistricting. States must avoid either creating or continuing discrimination on account of race. The UJO decision suggests that States can do more than merely avoid discrimination, that States can take affirmative steps to enhance minority representation. I agree with that.

Thornburgh, however, indicates that a claim of vote dilution arises in part only when a minority group is geographically compact enough to constitute a majority in a single member district. So there is a constraint imposed by Thornburgh on the nature of a claim, and that is that a minority is entitled to a district when it is reasonably compact. That in itself is consistent with the UJO where Justice White said that the Court found it permissible for a State employing sound districting principles such as compactness and population equality to attempt to prevent racial minorities from being repeatedly outvoted by creating districts that will afford fair representation. Some of the new districts that are being created do not respond to a geographically compact minority.

Finally, I agree with Ms. Wright's point that not only are uncompact, disedifying majority black districts being created, but there are uncompact, disedifying majority white districts being created. The problem with the North Carolina plan is not really Congressman Watt's district; it's the whole plan. What is at stake is the core value of fair representation, one person, one vote, as set out by the Court in the 1960 decision.

Mr. FRANK. Let me ask you one question. You've talked about where minority districts might be constitutionally compelled and also where they might be constitutionally prohibited. I appreciate that. The question I have is—because we are a legislative body and not a court—is there a middle category?

I don't want the universe to be only situations where there are compact minorities and we have to do a district or very dispersed ones and we can't do one. Is there a range for choice? Is there a range for kind of a preference? I think that is what is important to us legislatively.

What about situations where a minority majority district is neither compelled nor forbidden? That's the important range to me. Is there such a range, or are you interpreting the courts to be saying either one or the other?

Mr. O'ROURKE. I think the short answer is yes, there is such a range. It's a judgmental question. I think the North Carolina plan exceeds the range partly because, as I said at the outset, the districts are not contiguous. Contiguity I take to be a basic feature of geographic districting.

In fact, there are more compact majority black districts that could be fashioned in North Carolina. Once you say, as Mr. Glasser has said, that more compact districts could have been drawn but for the concerns of other incumbents. Then that says to me that you have not drawn a narrowly tailored district, that in fact you have tried not only to advance the interest of racial fairness, but you have tried to do that along side of other interests such as those of white incumbents that are, in my mind, on a far lower plane constitutionally and morally.

Mr. FRANK. You are going to make me choose between my two greatest values, racial justice and incumbency? [Laughter.]

Ms. WHITAKER. Thank you, Mr. O'Rourke.

Mr. DURBIN. Mr. Ira Glasser.

Mr. GLASSER. The issue of whether race can be taken into account as part of a remedy, the fact that taking it into account is a little bit of a double-edged sword is certainly true. But the alternative cannot be to allow to remain in place—the unscrutinized discrimination that existed in the past—if there is no way to remedy it except by taking race into account.

When you have a racial violation, you have to take race into account to remedy it. You had to count people by race in order to desegregate schools; you had to count people by race in order to establish and remedy employment discrimination; you had to take race into account and count people by race in order to deal with jury discrimination. Just as no Representative had ever been elected to Congress in this century from North Carolina, it was not too long ago where you had no blacks ever on juries. You had to take race into account to do that. So you always have to do that. You can't interpose the danger of doing it or of going too far at the earlier stages of remedy, which is what is happening now in North Carolina.

Second of all, I want to point out that we are overdiscussing this question of whether majority minority districts are constitutionally permissible. They are, and *Shaw* v. *Reno* is not to the contrary. *Shaw* v. *Reno* has to be understood in the context of an earlier case, in Voinovitch, just a few months before Shaw. Justice O'Connor, writing the opinion for the majority, upheld majority minority districts and said that it did not violate the Voting Rights Act unless you could show that it was diluting or abridging the right to vote.

That allegation was not even made by anybody in the *Shaw* case, and the *Shaw* case only involves the question of assuming majority minority districts are presumptively valid under the act, which Voinovitch holds. Does it in turn violate the Constitution when on its face the district looks so bizarrely drawn, and the answer was that it is only if it is only drawn that way for race, and if a compelling interest, namely, to remedy race discrimination, is not there.

Those questions were not decided. I believe on remand they will be decided our way and that the holding in *Shaw* v. *Reno* will turn out to be a lot narrower than a lot of its proponents are now saying.

The problem we face is not what the ultimate outcome will be of that case in particular or the constitutional holding that flows from it. The danger that we face now is that it is being over broadly interpreted. People are jumping into court and we are having to defend the Voting Rights Act against constitutional challenges from a position of defendant intervenor. That leads me to suggest several things that I think Congress can do.

One, I wish you would restore the ability to recover fees for expert witnesses. That is something you can do statutorily. It should be done for the same reason that the Attorneys' Fee Act was passed in the first instance. It is part of the enforcement mechanism for civil rights laws.

Second, I understand, Mr. Chairman, that you have introduced a bill to remedy the *Presley* case which we haven't even discussed here. The *Presley* case is very similar in many ways to *Gomillion*.

Mr. EDWARDS. In the *Presley* draft that has been introduced we take care of the expert witnesses problem.

Mr. GLASSER. The *Presley* case is another example of what I call third generation discrimination which the Court has held does not come under section 5 scrutiny, and it has to, because it's a little bit like *Gomillion* v. *Lightfoot*. You remedy the discrimination. You get people elected to a body that has excluded blacks by creating single member districts instead of at large. Then, when you've got the inclusion, when you've got the participation, when you've remedied the racial exclusion, then they decide that body doesn't have any power any more. If that doesn't go to the heart of what section 5 was designed to remedy, I don't know what does.

I would urge that you move on that, because a lot of the constitutional arguments we have been having about *Shaw* cannot be remedied by Congress anyway. They are going to have to be remedied by litigation and further Supreme Court decisions.

Ms. WHITAKER. Thank you, Mr. Glasser.

Mr. COOPER. A quick question for Mr. Glasser. Just a question.

Ms. WHITAKER. Sure.

Mr. COOPER. Do you think that your view as you have just represented it of *Shaw* v. *Reno* prevailed in the *Hays* case, the Louisiana redistricting case?

Mr. GLASSER. No.

Ms. WHITAKER. In the interest of time, we are now going to turn
the discussion toward the future of the Voting Rights Act. What we
would like to do is start with the invited participants going around
the table and give everyone here an opportunity to make a closing
statement, addressing yourselves towards the future of the Voting
Rights Act and where you see the act heading in view of public sentiment, what has been going on in the legislatures, and also court
interpretation.

In the interest of time, I would like to ask you to please limit
your remarks to 1 minute, if you could.

I would like to start on my left with Margaret Fung.

Ms. FUNG. Much of the discussion about the Voting Rights Act
comes out of a biracial context of blacks and whites. I think we
need to remember that we are now in a multiracial, multicultural
society which includes many different groups.

Asian-Americans are now experiencing a very fast rate of growth,
and yet the Voting Rights Act has not yet had major impacts upon
our community. In 1992, with the passage of the Voting Rights
Language Assistance Act, I think there is a lot of potential in terms
of empowering Asian-Americans. With half of our population not
being fully proficient in English as well as up to 62 percent being
foreign born, we are looking toward the future. We have the highest naturalization rates of other groups. We are going to be comprising a greater proportion of the American population, and the
Voting Rights Act can play an important role in helping to include
Asian-Americans and encourage their participation in a democratic
society.

Ms. WHITAKER. Thank you.

Mr. Carl Hampe.

Mr. HAMPE. I would like to agree with Ms. Fung's emphasis on
the reality of the future, which is that the Voting Rights Act will
not be viewed in a biracial context but in a multiracial one.

I would like to half way return to an issue that Congressman
Frank raised, which was the concept of whether or not it makes
sense to have a Hispanic person representing a majority Hispanic
district or an Asian person representing a majority Asian district
by saying whatever the results of that individual district are in the
present. If we are looking to the future of Voting Rights Act, I
would hope we can all agree on what the best long-term interests
are of the American political system. It is something that Justice
O'Connor alluded to in *Shaw* where she says that districts obviously created solely to effectuate the perceived common interest of
one racial group is not healthy and in fact antithetical to our system of representative democracy.

What do we look toward? One hopes we look toward the situation
where a candidate who happens to be a minority is supported by
minority and majority populations either in a district or statewide,
such as the election of Gov. Bob Martinez in Florida, Gov. Doug
Wilder in Virginia, or Senator Ben Nighthorse Campbell in Colorado.

Nonetheless, I think as one looks toward the future one will see some particularly sticky questions with regard to race-based redistricting in congressional and State legislative districts. I think that is something the Congress should pay a lot of attention to and consider given the new demographic and immigration trends.

Ms. WHITAKER. Thank you.

Mr. Anthony Chavez.

Mr. CHAVEZ. I'm certainly one to agree that the future of the Voting Rights Act will be in a multiracial context, and I think in that context one has to look at what the Voting Rights Act has accomplished. It has been extremely successful in the South, but you have seen limited extension of it to other parts of the Nation. In fact, the first successful challenge to an at-large system in the ninth circuit didn't occur until the late 1980's.

I see a very busy future for the Voting Rights Act in other parts of the Nation addressing other groups in the Nation and more heavily involved in Hispanic and the Asian populations, hopefully.

Realizing that there are still problems that need to be addressed, I think we have to look at how the act is being enforced now and whether or not there are any hindrances to enforcement of the act.

I believe that you will find that one thing that has arisen in several of our cases, and I know in other cases as well, is that section 2 ends with a disclaimer regarding a right to proportional representation. What we have seen is that has been used against plaintiffs to establish a ceiling that you can't have a claim that will result in overrepresentation of a minority group. Frequently what that will end up doing is saying that the minority group has to settle for something that is somewhat less than proportional representation. So you don't even get proportional representation, and God knows you don't even have a chance of going over proportional representation. I think that is one thing that Congress needs to consider.

Following up with regard to enforcement and Mr. Glasser's comments, you have to address attorneys' fees, enhancement of attorneys' fees, and recovery of expert costs. In California, when we are dealing with issues of Hispanic representation, there is a citizenship requirement. There is an attorney that defends lawsuits out in California who always has at least four expert witnesses, requires us to always have at least four expert witnesses. If you look at the cost of experts in voting rights cases, it very frequently will exceed $100,000, $100,000 that you have no chance of recovering. When you don't have the possibility of enhancement any more under the *Burlington* decision, that doesn't allow you any opportunity to make up for the money that you lose on the expert fees.

I think the Voting Rights Act has very important work yet to do but it is very difficult to continue to work to enforce it.

Ms. WHITAKER. Thank you very much.

I would like to now turn it over to Brenda Wright.

Ms. WRIGHT. First of all, I would endorse and urge that Congress do something about the attorney fee issue. We are not greedy, but we would like to be able to recover our tremendous out-of-pocket costs, and expert testimony is absolutely indispensable, as the other witnesses have stated.

I want to say that one of the things that is most important to take away from this kind of a discussion is an understanding of where minority office-holding comes from. It can't be disputed that the use and the ability to create majority minority districts is key to minority office-holding in the United States. There are 39 Members of the House of Representatives who are African-Americans and only three of them were elected from majority white districts. That is the reality in 1994. I think we have to be prepared to deal with that reality for sometime to come.

By the way, I am referring to African-American Representatives primarily because the figures available to me are much more comprehensive on those particular statistics, but I fully endorse the necessity of looking at this on a multiracial basis.

I think that we just have to say that it is disturbing when a majority of the Supreme Court gives credence to factually unsupported myths about majority minority districts and minority office-holding while failing to discuss or even acknowledge any of the costs to democratic government of maintaining all-white elected bodies in a diverse society or any of the benefits achieved by opening Congress and other elective offices to minority representation.

I would say that when success has been so recent in so many of these instances we cannot accept the premise that the Voting Rights Act has gone too far. It is not time to cut back on and limit the act. When we have extensive regulation of the tobacco industry and it helps to cut the rate of death and disease from smoking, we don't say it's time to cut back on those regulations just when you start to achieve some success.

I would urge that Congress continue to support a strong Voting Rights Act and the creation of majority minority districts under that act as an appropriate remedy which is necessary to provide the benefits that the Voting Rights Act was intended to achieve.

Ms. WHITAKER. Thank you, Ms. Wright.

Mr. Timothy O'Rourke.

Mr. O'ROURKE. My friend Abigail Thurnstrom has made the observation that racially integrated cocktail parties may remain a rare event but racially integrated party meetings are fairly common. I think that speaks very succinctly to the progress that has been made under the Voting Rights Act.

Whatever each of us may feel individually about the wisdom or merit of majority minority districts, I think it is clear that we are approaching the limit of majority minority districts that may be fashioned under whatever definition of compact and contiguous districts. Therefore, as we look to the future, it is clear that additional minority members will be elected to Congress and to State legislatures from majority white districts, so that future progress under the Voting Rights Act depends on the creation and nurturing of biracial and multiracial coalitions.

It goes without saying, but I will say it. The next step in electoral success for racial and ethnic minorities at the gubernatorial and at the level of the U.S. Senate and the level of the Presidency will depend on the creation and sustenance of these multiracial coalitions. Those are developments that are not easily encouraged by the law except to the extent that the law can provide the moral climate which makes those developments more likely. Those are developments that will depend on individual effort within the context of the party system. To mobilize that kind of effort is not easy, and that is an immense challenge ahead.

Ms. WHITAKER. Thank you, Mr. O'Rourke.

Mr. Glasser.

Mr. GLASSER. To some extent I have already suggested that the bill the chairman has introduced which contains the *Presley* remedy and the witness fees is very, very important.

In general, it is important perhaps to end where Chandler Davidson began in any assessment of the Voting Rights Act and the continuing need for it. In 1965 there were fewer than 100 black elected officials in targeted Voting Rights Act States in the South and virtually all of those were in lower offices. There was nobody from Congress and only two in State legislatures. So they had very few, and virtually nobody in State or Federal legislative positions. Today there are nearly 5,000 in those States.

Congress perhaps needs to commission a little study, the basis on which I think it will be able to make, and should make, a factual finding that that progress was not simply because all the white voters in the South suddenly had an epiphany about merit, but that that progress was directly attributable to the Voting Rights Act and its enforcement. Its enforcement is important as well, because that goes directly to the question of expert witnesses. That change was directly attributable to the Voting Rights Act and that those kinds of numbers simply would not have occurred without it.

I think if there is any factual question in Congress' mind about that, it needs to determine whether that is so, and that it would be well worth an effort to do so.

Second, I think that it is important also to commission a study—perhaps it could be part of the same study—of remaining districts not only in the South, but remaining districts where black voters continue to be excluded and disfranchised as a result of dilution that may have occurred for racial reasons in the past and that still require application of race conscious remedies such as the Voting Rights Act today.

If there is any question that we have gone far enough, if there is any question that no further discrimination exists and no further districts require that remedy, then Congress has to determine factually whether that is so.

I think that those two factual findings will be an important element of resisting efforts, as I think you must, to in any way weaken or begin to apply the notion of sunset to the Voting Rights Act. It is far, far too early and the fact of the kind of resistance to the broad remedies of the Voting Rights Act that has arisen in the wake of *Shaw* is all the proof we should need that the problem is still with us and will remain with us.

Combined with the particular remedies in the chairman's bill, those would be the recommendations I would make.

Ms. WHITAKER. Thank you, Mr. Glasser.

Professor Davidson.

Mr. DAVIDSON. Following on Mr. Glasser's comments, let me simply say that one of our unexpected findings in the study that I reported earlier was that there are a large number of small jurisdictions in the South that are at least 10 percent black that elect at large and have no black officeholders whatsoever. Hundreds and hundreds of them. Given the fact that still today a significant portion of black people in the South inhabit small towns, I think this is a very important finding.

We are privileged to be in one of those two brief periods in American history where blacks have had anything approximating equal voting right. There was a decade or two following the Civil War, and now there has been almost three decades since the Voting Rights Act was passed.

Even during these last three decades in which admittedly progress has been made it has taken the full force of the Voting Rights Act with, by and large, aggressive Department of Justice enforcement and widespread private litigation to enable blacks in the South to elect a significant number of blacks to office. Even so, in spite of this, blacks in the 11 Southern States today are still sharply underrepresented in every one of those States.

There is still today, in my view, strong resistance by many whites, not all of them, certainly, to black office-holding. National polls have consistently shown over the last 10 years or so that as many as 25 percent of all white respondents when asked the question of whether they would vote for a capable black person for President nominated by their own party have said no.

The attitudes reflected in responses to questions of that sort and the resistance they reflect partly explains why African-Americans today are still unrepresented in office at every level of government and why single member districts with fairly drawn boundaries still increase black office-holding much more than multimember district systems do.

My reading of history and my analysis of data in our recent study lead me to conclude that it would be a serious mistake for the Supreme Court to decide, as it may have done in *Shaw* v. *Reno,* that the protections against minority vote dilution that have evolved over the past 30 years can now be dispensed with. To do so I feel would slow down or even reverse the degree of minority office-holding, a trend that could seriously delegitimize our Government.

Ms. WHITAKER. Thank you, Professor Davidson.

Mr. Charles Cooper.

Mr. COOPER. Thank you. In closing, I would first like to thank Congressman Edwards and Congressman Hyde and your colleagues for convening this gathering and for inviting me to participate.

Like Mr. Hampe, I would like to close with a single sentence from the majority opinion in *Shaw* v. *Reno:* Racial gerrymandering even for remedial purposes may balkanize us into competing racial factions. It threatens to carry us further from the goal of a political system in which race no longer matters, a goal to which the Nation continues to aspire.

As I indicated earlier, I think that there is some truth to those words and I think those words were probably fueled in large measure by the use of race. I believe the overriding use of race in congressional redistricting and in, State house and senate redistricting throughout the country, particularly throughout the South, is a phenomenon I think that was largely premised upon *Gingles* v.

Thornburgh. I think the Supreme Court witnessed this and was concerned about the sentiment that I have just shared with you. Certainly I am. I am hopeful that as Congress examines this issue that it keeps those considerations in mind and, in my hope, will reduce the incidence of that practice rather than promote it. Thank you.

Ms. WHITAKER. Thank you, Mr. Cooper.

Congressman Watt, do you have any final remark you would like to make?

Mr. WATT. Very briefly. I want to do a couple of things. No. 1, I want to make a personal comment about the importance of these series of discussions and how much we are going to miss our chairman when he leaves next year. I haven't been here long enough to get addicted to him, but it doesn't take very long. He's quite a guy. So I really think it would be remiss of me not to state the obvious, that he is a champion of those who are here in this body and the champion of the Judiciary Committee in particular.

Let me make two comments about things I value. I guess I want to make a disclaimer about what I don't value, first of all, so that it is clear that these are not personal comments.

They asked me on the witness stand in *Shaw* v. *Reno* whether in fact I didn't have something to gain from the testimony I was giving and from the outcome of that litigation. I made a disclaimer initially which reminded them that I had practiced law for 22 years and that at least for the last several years I had made substantially more money than I was making this year as a Member of Congress. So I certainly didn't have that personal financial interest at play.

What I do think I value and what we have to gain is two things. No. 1, I value living in a multiracial society. I think this is the greatest country in the world. But I also value various components of that society having some representation. I value democracy. I simply don't think that democracy has been working in this country by excluding African-Americans and other minorities from representation in elected bodies.

I don't think if we looked at South Africa and the way it has been up to a couple of weeks ago that any kind of democracy was working there, and I don't think if they had put into place a system that did not guarantee the representation of various groups in that country, participation in the future of that country, and in the future electoral process, we would have looked upon that as any kind of true democracy.

In fact, it strikes me that had we said to South Africa what the Supreme Court said in *Shaw* v. *Reno,* just be colorblind and let nature takes its course, I expect that all of us in this country would have been outraged at the result that we quite probably would have gotten.

I think it's important to continue to have a system in place, whatever it is, which gives assurance that minorities will be represented in elected bodies if democracy is going to work and if this country is going to be as great as it ought to be.

I try to stay out of these discussions because so much of the discussion is just unreal to me in a democratic society. I suppose we have got to debate these things, but some of the things I hear simply rewrite or revise history as I know it. While I aspire to this colorblind society that Justice O'Connor and Mr. Cooper just talked about, it seems to me that the larger issue is what we do in the interim between now and the time we get there, because I don't think there is anybody here who would argue with me that we have not gotten there yet.

Ms. WHITAKER. Thank you, Congressman Watt.

Chairman Edwards.

Mr. EDWARDS. I want to thank all of the participants. You have provided us with some valuable insight, and the record is going to help us a lot.

Mr. Watt, thank you for your contribution. In the very short time he has been here he has been an enormous help to all of us.

I want to thank Mr. Durbin and Ms. Whitaker. You did a very professional job and kept us all with the kind of rein that we need.

I would like to thank Melody Barnes, who is sitting behind me, and Kathryn Hazeem, the staff lawyers for the Republicans and the Democrats who thought up the idea and have managed these discussions very nicely.

Yesterday I attended the farewell ceremony at the Department of Justice for Jim Turner, who has been a professional civil service lawyer there nearly 30 years. A wonderful man. In his remarks he pointed out that it seems in civil rights as though you climb the tallest mountain and then you look and there are still taller mountains to climb. I think that is what we have here. I know that is the way I feel.

It has been difficult to do anything in the last year, of course, because we didn't have an Assistant Attorney General for Civil Rights until Mr. Patrick came aboard just 5 weeks ago. I really will move ahead as fast as possible on *Presley* and the attorney fees and expert witnesses matter.

However, I've got to warn all of you that it's a different era for civil rights. In 1964–65 the Republicans voted better than the Democrats on final passage. Eighty-one percent of the Republicans voted for the 1964 omnibus civil rights bill and for the Voting Rights Act of 1965, and only 61 percent of the Democrats, because the solid South Democrats just didn't vote for the civil rights bills.

It is different now. The Democrats aren't much better than they were then, although they will vote better than that 61 percent, because there are quite a number of Members from the South who will stick with us. For my friends, the Republicans, and that includes Henry Hyde who is a close personal friend too, it's an entirely different story now. If we can get a handful for *Presley* we will be fortunate, although we are going to try very hard.

On the racial justice vote the other day, a very simple, modest provision of the crime bill that had to do with part of the Voting Rights Act on sentencing only, I think we only got four or five votes. So it is not going to be easy. However, we will have the Department of Justice with us, I believe, although they haven't committed yet. We certainly did not have that 3 or 4 years ago when we tried to do *Presley* before. So we just couldn't bring it to the floor.

We can't have yet a colorblind society. It would be wonderful if we could. Race is a very important part of America. Until and unless we straighten out our problems with race we are going to have a difficult time. The voting rights bill has helped. All the civil rights laws have helped. We are dependent on the courts and the courts have been very conservative starting around 1982. And the Supreme Court has been very conservative insofar as the civil rights laws are concerned. *Presley* was an example, and *Shaw* v. *Reno* is a conservative opinion too, in our view. There are just quite a number, starting with *Mobile* in 1982.

I know we are going to stay in there and fight for our civil rights laws and encourage the people who care about our society and who want a peaceful society. Those who want to get a start to resolve this crime problem have to realize that a lot of it has to do with our problems with race in this country and the fact that we have nurtured an underclass of people that make it very easy for us to have a high crime rate.

All of those things fit in with a decent and fair society. That is what the civil rights laws are all about, and we had better start to get aboard, because we haven't done so well in civil rights for quite a long time.

This has been a big help today. You are all fine people for coming here and I appreciate it very much. I believe that's all. Thank you.

The subcommittee is adjourned.

[Whereupon, at 12:05 p.m., the subcommittee adjourned.]

APPENDIX

STATEMENT OF DAVID I. WELLS

My name is David I. Wells. I represent no organization, and
submit this statement in an individual capacity.

Although I am not an attorney, I have been deeply involved
in reapportionment and redistricting issues for almost forty
years. I was the successful plaintiff in *Wells v. Rockefeller,* a
case which resulted in the Supreme Court's invalidation of two
successive New York State Congressional districting statutes. I
have written numerous articles on the subject and have served as
an adviser on redistricting to many civic, political and labor
groups. Most recently, I was a member of the New York City
Districting Commission--a post to which I was appointed by former
New York City Mayor David Dinkins.

I attended the interesting "round table" discussion held by
the Committee on May 11th, and feel no need to repeat any of the
assertions made by the participants in that event. However, I do
wish to make several points not raised at that time, and to state

(381)

what I believe to be a point of view somewhat different from
those expressed by any of those who took part in the May 11th
discussion.

I was somewhat disturbed at the apparent assumption on the
part of the discussants that all liberals are monolithically
appalled by _Shaw v. Reno_ and that all conservatives are uniformly
lined up in support. I consider myself a lifelong liberal
Democrat. My initial involvement with the districting issue came
about because I believed that malapportionment unfairly
disadvantaged liberals by overrepresenting conservative
constituencies. Over the years, I have worked closely with the
labor movement and with prominent Democrats in my own state of
New York, in other states and at the federal level in Washington.
But although my initial interest in the subject was motivated by
what I perceived to be a districting system which unfairly
penalized those with whom I was in political agreement, I have
come to believe that _all_ gerrymandering is wrong--regardless of
who the perpetrators are and regardless of who the victims are--
because gerrymandering is in effect a way of _stacking the cards_:
of some people or groups attempting to arrogate to themselves the
authority to predetermine election results--to decide how
political power shall be distributed among competing groups. But
in a democracy, that power ought not to be exercised by any self-
appointed, self-anointed "experts", however benevolent they may
consider themselves. That power properly belongs to the people

as a whole.

Most of those who see nothing wrong in basing district lines on ethnicity are people of good will who quite correctly see that great injustice has been done in the past--that ethnic minorities, most notably Blacks, have been systematically excluded from meaningful participation in the political process in large parts of the country. Clearly, the "playing field" on which the "game" of politics was conducted in this country was for many years sharply tilted in one direction. But the proffered solution of those who see nothing wrong in ethnically-based districting would merely tilt a portion of that playing field in the opposite direction! I submit that *all* such tilting is wrong; that what should be sought instead is *a level playing field!*

In the course of the May 11th discussion, several of the participants (on *both* sides of the issue) appeared to take the position that there is something unique about *ethnic* gerrymandering as distinguished from partisan *political* gerrymandering. Those opposed to <u>Shaw v. Reno</u> seem to believe that racial gerrymandering is required to undo the racial injustices of the past, and that *political* gerrymandering is merely an inevitable part of the "game" (that is, that the power to create advantages through the districting process for favored political parties or incumbent officeholders is one of the

legitimate spoils of political warfare which the winners get).
And those who *favor* Shaw v. Reno seem to agree that there is
nothing wrong with *partisan* gerrymandering, but that drawing
lines to give special advantages to *racial* groups is an
abomination. I would suggest, however, that *both* kinds of
gerrymandering--ethnic *and* political--are wrong! Whether those
who hold the power to draw district boundary lines use that power
to create special advantages for one political party over another
or for some potential candidates over others or for certain
racial groups over others, and whether those advantages benefit
the same group statewide or benefit different groups in different
districts, such use of the line-drawing power flies in the face
of what is perhaps the most basic precept of democratic
government: neutral ground rules for the "game of politics".
Such use of state power inevitably places some citizens at a
disadvantage *vis-a-vis* others: Blacks in districts preordained
for Whites, Whites in districts preordained for Blacks, Democrats
in districts preordained for Republicans, Republicans in
districts preordained for Democrats, challengers in districts
preordained for incumbents and *vice-versa*.

The proper remedy for discriminatory districting is to
prohibit it--not to perpetuate it by merely reversing the tilt of
the playing field. And I submit that it is quite possible to
end *both* evils--racially-discriminatory districting as well as
districting which establishes artificial advantages for parties

5

or individuals--by adoption of simple, logical, explicitly-
worded, non-discriminatory, politically and ethnically neutral
guidelines or standards. Such standards should include:

- Reasonable population-equality;

- Geographic contiguity;

- Adherence to the greatest extent consistent with the
  above standards, to existing county and municipal
  boundaries.

- Measurable geographic compactness

I would take issue with the characterization made by one of
the participants in the May 11th discussion to the effect that
those who oppose creation of bizarrely-shaped districts are
motivated by "aesthetic" considerations. This is a "straw man"
argument. The concept of geographic compactness in the shapes of
districts has nothing whatever to do with esthetics. Requiring
that districts not be established with contorted boundary lines
is merely a way of *limiting the discretion* of the line-drawers--
not a way to mandate pleasing shapes on maps.

I stated at the outset that I was disturbed by the apparent
polarization of this issue along liberal and conservative lines.
I am even more disturbed at the apparent public perception that
African-Americans and other minority groups are uniformly lined
up on one side of this issue. In this regard, I would call the
Committee's attention to two statements.

386

One of the co-plaintiffs in the case challenging the 1992
Congressional districting in Louisiana which created a weirdly-
contorted Z-shaped district running almost completely across the
entire state was Edward Adams, a Black man who is a member of the
City Council in Grambling, Louisiana. He said he feared that
establishment of such districts would b e conducive to
politicians appealing to racial extremists and could easily lead
to the selection of "two Farrakhans and five David Dukes" in the
seven-member Louisiana delegation! *(Wall Street Journal, July
14, 1993)*.

And although I do not know his position on the specific
matter of *Shaw v. Reno*, I do note that a most distinguished
member of this House, the Hon. John Lewis of Georgia, an early
and effective leader in the battle for equal voting rights in
America, has said that "the goal of the struggle for the right to
vote was to create an interracial democracy in America..., not to
create separate enclaves or 'townships'....   The Voting Rights
Act should lead to a climate in which people of color will have
an opportunity to represent not only African Americans but...all
Americans." *(New York Times, Aug. 3, 1993)*.

The belief that the Voting Rights Act requires racial
"proportionality" in the distribution of legislative power is a
clear (and I believe dangerous) misconception--one which is
contradicted by the language of the Act itself. It is dangerous

because it would enshrine in law the notion that race is and always will be the primary consideration in American politics and government. Obviously, this has been true in the past, but in recent decades we have begun to move *away* from totally race-based politics. To reverse direction now--to move toward rather than away from a political system based permanently on ethnicity-- would be tragic.

The fruits of the kind of thinking which confirms rather than struggles against the centrality of ethnicity in public affairs can be seen all over the world today--from Bosnia to Rwanda to Azerbaijan. One would hope that the America of the 21st century will take a different path!

O.

CPSIA information can be obtained
at www.ICGtesting.com
Printed in the USA
BVHW060113061118
532208BV00018B/2061/P